DIMENSIONS OF AFRICAN AND OTHER DIASPORAS

DIMENSIONS OF AFRICAN AND OTHER DIASPORAS

EDITED BY

Franklin W. Knight

and

Ruth Iyob

THE UNIVERSITY OF THE WEST INDIES PRESS

Jamaica • Barbados • Trinidad and Tobago

The University of the West Indies Press
7A Gibraltar Hall Road, Mona
Kingston 7, Jamaica
www.uwipress.com

A catalogue record of this book is available
from the National Library of Jamaica.

ISBN: 978-976-640-459-8 (print)
978-976-640-468-0 (Kindle)
978-976-640-476-5 (ePub)

Book and cover design by Robert Harris
Set in Scala 10.25/14.5 x 27
Printed in the United States of America

CONTENTS

ACKNOWLEDGEMENTS

IT HAS ALWAYS BEEN TRUE THAT successful cooperative ventures result from the extraordinary goodwill, intellectual creativity and mental flexibility of all participants. This was especially true with this volume. It had its genesis in an exciting international conference, "Exploring Dimensions of African Diasporas", held in Baltimore, Maryland, 26–27 April 2012, under the auspices of the Center for Africana Studies of the Johns Hopkins University. The unusually collegial and highly animated open discussions helped shape the selections that form the basis of this book. The editors thank the contributing authors as well as the other participants, especially Richard Bell, Sara Berry, Leonard Brown, James Calvin, Nathan Connolly, Siba Grovogui, Frank Guridy, Michael Hanchard, Floyd Hayes III, Jared Hickman, Moira Hinderer, Kelly Baker Josephs, Tyson King-Meadows, Teresita Martínez-Vergne, Hollis Robbins, Lester Spence, James Sweet and Ben Vinson III. For two memorable days this multidisciplinary group presented stimulating intellectual ideas that continue to reverberate as the authors and editors sifted and winnowed fascinating evocations on the inexhaustible theme of African and other diasporas. We are also indebted for the insightful comments of the outside reviewers. Finally we remain enormously grateful to the University of the West Indies Press and especially to our editorial team under Shivaun Hearne, whose consummate editorial skill and graceful firmness enhanced our text while keeping us focused on our deadline.

INTRODUCTION

FRANKLIN W. KNIGHT AND RUTH IYOB

MIGRATIONS AND DIASPORAS, ALTHOUGH INTEGRAL TO the human experience, are not identical activities. Migration is the movement of individuals, families or groups from one place to another. Sometimes the move is relatively close by. At other times it is a long distance away by land or by sea or by air.[1] While modern national state legislation makes any definition of migration especially difficult, normally, people moving into uninhabited spaces or groups expanding contiguously – and in the process overwhelming the original residents – have been called settlers or colonizers. Groups adventured beyond the familiar original space of their native territories and kept on adventuring, adjusting to or dominating their physical environment. The supposition is that, in the majority of those cases, the dispersal was unidirectional and that the expatriates never returned. But it is possible that some did, beginning the sort of relationship that is encompassed in the formation of diasporas. Diasporic communities, like refugees, are difficult to define precisely. As this volume illustrates, the principal characteristics of diasporic communities change continually as they become influenced by geographical location, particular social, political and economic circumstances, and the period when they were established or came into existence. In any case, migration is a prerequisite for diaspora formation, and diasporas usually assume a life of their own once they become established.

Both migration and diaspora formation began with people from the African continent, since it is commonly accepted that mankind originated there and gradually spread all over the globe in the past two million years.[2] Indeed, just about every group of people has, at one time or the other, experienced a diaspora, or dispersal, from their original homeland. This process might have been intensified after about 10,000 BCE when *homo sapiens* acquired the necessary mechanical tools, the essential domesticated plants and animals as well as the requisite knowledge of optimal growing seasons that made possible settled agricultural communities.[3] Such settled agricultural communities permitted the development of social and political traditions along with the sense of self and of place. Emigrants from their base or sending communities could begin to make nostalgic comparisons between where they found themselves and where they had been before. Some who departed had no intention of returning; but some wished to return whether or not they could ever act on their desires. Settling in a new place made possible the formation of a diasporic community. Such diasporic communities have been around for a very long time, as people have been dispersed forcefully or voluntarily from their original homelands for millennia. Sometimes, patterns emerged from the successive dispersals; but timing, geographical location as well as the peculiar characteristics of sending and host societies played an inordinately important role in the genesis of diasporic communities.[4]

Despite their antiquity, diasporic community formation has attracted academic attention only recently.[5] And diaspora studies as a concentrated academic field has been even more recent – certainly after the 1970s. With the expansion of the field, the complexity of the theme emerges with increasing clarity and the essays in this volume present an interesting, although far from comprehensive, spectrum of approaches to the study of diasporas, especially to the complex dimensions of Africa's diasporas. This discovery of identity constitutes an essential feature of diasporas. So what exactly is a diaspora and why is the study of diasporas important?

Diaspora is a term of relatively recent inclusion in common discourse. According to the *Compact Edition of the Oxford English Dictionary* the word "diaspora" became commonly used in the English language during the later nineteenth century.[6] In the twentieth century the term almost became synonymous with the tragic history of the Jewish diaspora and the horrendous fate of its communities during the German Weimar Republic and its successor, the Third Reich.[7] But as we have stated above, diasporas have been around for a very long time, for the past three thousand years. Greeks moved from the mainland to the Aegean Isles before 1000 BCE, and even within

Africa, for various reasons but mostly for trade, people moved around the continent as well as in and out of the continent.[8] All diasporas have been fashioned by diverse forces and have responded to the exigencies of time, place and circumstances. Diasporas, therefore, constitute an interesting locale for comparative analysis, and few diasporas have been more interesting and more important than the worldwide African diaspora beginning around the eighth century.[9] Nevertheless, African diasporas represent merely one dimension of the global history of diasporic formation.

In order to make a meaningful evaluation of different diasporas it is important to state how the authors of this volume use the term. A diaspora represents an exile community that is either self-defined or defined by others, usually the host society. Normally the term does not apply to individual emigrants or some collectivity of settlers or to refugees, although these groups are not necessarily automatically excluded. Diasporas usually have some real, remembered or imagined connection to a distant homeland and so there is the interplay between a diaspora and its real or imagined homeland. It is in regard to this sense of connectivity between the two that Ruth Iyob, in chapter 1, speaks of a continuous to and fro movement, of corridors and of the construction of images. Likewise, Evelyn Hu-DeHart examines how Chinese diasporas developed over a long time not only within cities but also within open spaces along national borders and the occupants developed creative ways to forge efficacious community connections that supported their ethnic identities.

Not every migration, however, as indicated earlier, results in the formation of a permanent diasporic community. For example, the Norse expansion to Greenland, circa the tenth century, may have established settlements that endured for centuries but eventually failed.[10] The Norse may even have arrived on the North American mainland during the eleventh century, although these communities no longer persist today.[11] Other mass migrations, like those of the Moors into Iberia in the seventh century or the movements across Central Europe from the east and the west in an earlier period represented less the establishment of diasporic communities than lateral movements for purposes of territorial acquisition, permanent settlement and trade. Nevertheless, it is possible to discern diasporic movements within the larger centrifugal forces of this type of empire building, as shown by the contribution of Tamara Ganjalyan in chapter 2. The Armenian diasporic communities along the eastern frontier of an expanding Russian empire served useful commercial, political and strategic purposes from which the Russian elites benefited enormously. While such diasporas were tolerated and even overtly encouraged during the period of imperial weakness, a strong Russian empire could, and did, control its frontier eventually, reducing the strategic need for Armenian allies. Early Armenian diasporas, therefore, had significantly greater success than later ones, illustrating the importance of formative time and prevailing circumstances in the history of diasporas.

Some migratory movements represented imperial expansion.[12] For instance, imperialism was a major factor in the development of Chinese and Indian diasporas. As Evelyn Hu-DeHart illustrates, the Chinese played a commercial role similar to that of the Armenians in the Asian entrepôts established by various European empires in peripheral areas such as Macau, Hong Kong, Manila and Jakarta (formerly Dutch Batavia) before the end of the eighteenth century. By the middle of the nineteenth century, hundreds of thousands of Chinese manual labourers, along with an equal number of Indians from that Asian subcontinent, replaced or complemented African workers all across Latin America and the Caribbean, leaving a number of interesting Chinese and Indian diasporas across the hemisphere.[13] In the same way, towards the end of the nineteenth century a pronounced Japanese migration led to the formation of Japanese diaspora communities across the Americas.[14]

A diasporic community must be recognized either by the members or others who define the community as such, but it should also represent a certain critical mass of individuals. If the mass is too small to be measured or insufficient to comprise a functioning organic community, then that community may be considered to be exotic rather than diasporic. On the other hand, if the community becomes, as it has in many Caribbean societies, a majority, then it may also propel secondary dispersals of some of its own communities, especially those aligned with the pan-African movement of the twentieth century.[15] However, as in the ancient Greek example – as well as frequently in the modern era – diasporas have a way of generating organic microcosms of themselves and then launching them globally.

THE SINGULAR IMPORTANCE OF THE CARIBBEAN IN THE WORLDWIDE AFRICAN DIASPORA

In the history of the Caribbean, early European settlers were never usually identified as diasporas. That is to say, neither they nor outsiders described them as such. Nevertheless, the organic connection between European colonists in the Americas and their different metropoles constituted a pronounced feature of the early settlers.[16] In the contemporary Caribbean the term diaspora is rarely used for residents of the region – although it is a major description for Caribbean expatriates in the wider world, as Michele Johnson, Tommy Lott, Winston James and Quito Swan discuss in their contributions in this volume.

The Atlantic and especially the Caribbean created some extremely interesting models of African diasporas. Between the early sixteenth and the middle of the nineteenth century the overwhelming majority of travellers to the Americas originated in Africa. Most Africans came as enslaved workers to facilitate the European expansion into the Americas, but many also came as free companions of the early European explorers and were often culturally indistinct from their fellow conquerors.[17] These newly arrived immigrants quickly intermixed, and the miscegenated and creolized population that they created was soon considerably greater than them in number. Across the Americas creolization has quite different meanings. In this book, however, it is used to connote both demographic and cultural processes. The term originated in the early Iberian practice of animal husbandry and was originally applied to cattle born in the distant mountain pastures – literally, *criado a lo lejos*, born far away. With Iberian expansion to the Americas, the term *criollo* acquired demographic significance and was used to designate Spaniards born overseas and, eventually, anyone, regardless of race, born abroad. African slaves born in the Americas were called *criollos*, to distinguish them from the *bozales* born in Africa. In its cultural connotation, creole is used here to refer to the adoption, adaptation and eclectic amalgamation that accompanied cultural constructions in the Americas.[18] An example of such creole constructions may be found in the chapter by Yvonne Daniel on dance (chapter 6). The literature on African diasporas tends to be disproportionately Atlantic-centric.[19] This is unsurprising, since the vast majority of

Africans did arrive in this part of the world as commercial commodities and the impact of their industry dramatically changed the political, commercial and economic relationship of all the Americas with the rest of the world.

It is often not appreciated how unique are the populations of the Caribbean. Of all the experiences of demographic expansion globally only in the Caribbean was a genuinely hybrid population inadvertently created by the fusion of immigrants from Europe, Africa and Asia along with the remaining indigenous population.[20] The Caribbean colonial experiences would significantly alter the political and economic situation across Europe and, ultimately, the rest of the world. It is a very long and complicated story that may be followed in Alfred Crosby's *The Columbian Exchange* or Eric Wolf's *Sons of the Shaking Earth*, among other excellent studies.[21] But the Caribbean has been an accidental place as well as a place of accidents ever since 1492.

The Spanish originally set out to trade with Asia and accidentally discovered the Americas. They ended up settling, after 1492, in an increasing number of residential and administrative enclaves across the hemisphere. The English, French and Dutch came initially to plunder and ended up eventually settling and trading.[22] Successful settling along with successful stealing and successful trading depended on an ongoing and vital African connection.[23] This transatlantic African connection, at least through the later nineteenth century, was largely via a massive commercial transfer of enslaved emigrants. Nevertheless, African diasporas in the Americas, including the Caribbean, should not be considered solely coterminous to the transatlantic slave trade and slavery; as noted above, not all Africans who left Africa were slaves, although the majority who arrived in the Americas was indeed enslaved.[24] That experience indelibly coloured the Atlantic view, not only of Africa but of Africans. So let us briefly review the history of slavery before its advent in the Americas. What exactly was slavery and how did it come to form such an important dimension of African diasporas?

SLAVERY: ITS ORIGIN AND PRE-EUROPEAN AMERICAN FORM

Slavery constitutes the unconditional servitude of an individual, usually acquired by purchase and often legally described as chattel or a tangible form of movable property.[25] An ancient form of subordination, it has been practised by most social groups around the world. The tradition of slavery is extremely old. The word originated with the sale of Slavs to the Black Sea region in the early times. Slavery existed in European society until the nineteenth century, and quickly became the principal source of labour during the process of European colonization.[26] From ancient antiquity, slavery constituted an important dimension of social and occupational organization.[27] Likewise, forms of slavery existed among the indigenous societies in the Americas before the arrival of Christopher Columbus. Across geographical space as well as through time, conditions of slavery varied widely. In the Muslim world as well as throughout much of sub-Saharan Africa, the status of slaves was quite flexible. The condition was not always hereditary, and slaves could serve in important positions as chief administrators, confidants of political leaders, soldiers, commercial factors, or privileged guardians of holy places. In short, slaves were not always regarded as chattel.

As Ruth Iyob implies strongly in chapter 1, both enslavement and diasporic communities underwent significant changes when polytheistic entities were subordinated by monotheistic empires. Monotheism introduced rigidity and intolerance as well as mutually reinforcing social cleavages that marginalized certain members of the society. Deviation from accepted norms lost general acceptability. Societies became hierarchical with the lower orders and slaves denied most normal privileges enjoyed by the higher orders. More importantly, imperial societies began to distinguish between their own people and "others", with the "others" being inferior.[28]

Nevertheless, the variants of slavery in the American hemisphere after the sixteenth century were unusual in many respects. The general reconstruction of the American sphere after 1492 fostered systems of slavery that were quite unprecedented in human experience. Slavery in the post-Columbus Americas was a patently artificial economic, social and political construct, not a natural or organic condition, and a specific organizational response to a specific labour scarcity brought about by the decimation of the indigenous population of the Antilles. African slavery in the Americas, then, was a relatively recent development in the long course of human history. It was, additionally, quite exceptional in the universal history of slave systems, for the Americas developed both slaveholding societies (in which slaves were incidental to both the economy and society) and slave societies (in which the institution dictated the economy and profoundly affected politics, and was artificially engineered for maximum productive efficiency). While slave-holding societies adhered to some degree to ideals, creating microcosms that replicated the macrocosms of their metropolitan originators, slave societies were dominated by the narrow necessities of agro-industrial production. In the Caribbean, slave societies had concentrated enclaves of slaveholders while the reverse was true in the United States and Brazil.[29] The classical Caribbean slave society was as much an African diasporic community as it was a European commercial enterprise.

Slavery also unquestionably involved a form of power play. Slaves, by and large, did not have a voice equal to that of their enslavers' and were not allowed to articulate their views on their material conditions of life, much less directly control their territorial affairs. However, not having an equal voice should not be understood to mean that the slaves were powerless. They might have been enslaved in body, but that did not necessarily constrain their minds nor restrict their creativity. Slaves were people, and they tended to do what other people did, but within the bounds of the tolerance of their owners and the state in which they found themselves. Importantly, enslaved Africans did not arrive in the New World mysteriously bereft of their innate intelli-gence, social skills and political abilities. Africans did not undergo "social death" merely by transiting the Atlantic Ocean regardless of how desperate and dehumanizing were such crossings.[30] The concept of "social death" ren-dering Africans in bondage as *personally* dehumanized figures bereft of the capacity to construct new kinship networks or to construct new communities has been empirically proven wrong by the many diasporic communities and nations that have emerged in both the Atlantic and Indian Ocean regions. This erroneous but enduring characterization of the African as a passive and perpetual victim seriously camouflages the important contributions of the enslaved Africans during and after the period of enslavement as vital political, social and economic actors in the construction of their nations. The actions of enslaved Africans and their enslaved diasporic descendants spoke eloquently of their innermost thoughts and represented their reflections on, and reactions to, the changing world in which they found themselves. More-over, the successful development of the Americas as well as the prosperity and power of many western European states derived, as we have suggested earlier, from the unremitting industry of African slaves in the Americas.[31]

The original adventure of Christopher Columbus to the Americas did not have as its primary intention the creation of an overseas Castilian diaspora or a settlement of any sort. It began as a kind of imitation of the successful Portuguese coastal commercial activity along littoral West Africa. The desire was to make direct contact with the fabulously rich Chinese markets described by the Venetian merchant traveller Marco Polo (1254–1324). Instead of finding the Orient, however, Columbus arrived in the New World. Once there, he thought the people he encountered in the Caribbean might make good slaves, as he seemed to infer in his log of 10 October 1492, when he wrote, "They ought to make good and skilled servants, for they repeat very quickly whatever we say to them. I think that they can easily be made Christians, for they seem to have no religion. If it pleases Our Lord, I will take six of them to Your Highness when I depart, in order that they may learn our language."[32] His monarch, Isabel of Castile, thought otherwise and declared the indigenous inhabitants of the newly discovered lands to be vassals rather than slaves. Unfortunately for the indigenous Tainos, high ideals succumbed rapidly to the harsh reality of the urgent need for labour in the Americas to justify the long-distance exploration operation. The rapid decimation of the indigenous population generated an urgent and insatiable need for imported Africans to fulfil those labour needs.

NON-DIASPORIC AFRICANS

Though an extensive trade in African slaves developed, the first Africans who accompanied the early Spanish explorers were not unambiguously slaves, nor did they consider themselves apart from their fellow adventuring and conquering Iberians. Sometimes the literature on this is clear; at other times it is not.[33] Some were unquestionably free, such as Pedro Alonso Niño (1468–1505), also known as Alonso Pietro, from Palos de Moguer. He was the pilot of the *Niña* who accompanied Christopher Columbus in 1492.[34] Others were obviously servants rather than slaves in the early modern history sense. Those blacks who sailed with Columbus on his first voyage to the Americas in 1492 were clearly free men. Their descendants presumably were as free as any other Spanish adventurer in the Americas. Other blacks who accompanied the early Spanish *conquistadores* might have been servile but were probably not true slaves as the term was later understood. Nor should their experiences, regardless of the condition in which they found themselves, be equated with African diasporic construction.

Nuflo de Olano, who accompanied Vasco Nuñez de Balboa across the Isthmus of Panama, was, however, a slave. So were Juan Valiente and several others who travelled and fought with Hernán Cortés in Mexico, the Pizarro brothers in Peru, and Pánfilo de Narváez in Florida. Estebanico, described as "Andrés Dorantes' black Moorish slave", accompanied Alvar Nuñez Cabeza de Vaca in that amazing journey around the Gulf of Mexico and overland across the southwest to Mexico City in the late 1520s and early 1530s, learning several local Indian languages with consummate ease and posing, along with his companions, as holy men gifted with healing powers.[35] Reading the accounts of his extraordinary deeds, it is difficult to think of Estebanico as a slave, even if his presumed "owner" Andrés Dorantes might have thought otherwise.

Bernal Díaz del Castillo in his famous history of the conquest of Mexico describes several "blacks" who accompanied Hernán Cortés to Mexico – one of whom brought wheat; and another, a follower of Pánfilo de Narváez, introduced smallpox among the Indians with lethal results.[36] Non-Iberians were also part of the conquest of Peru. Of the 168 men who followed Francisco Pizarro to Peru in 1532 and captured the Inca at Cajamarca, at least two were black – and an additional one might have been Morisco.[37] Juan García, born in Old Castile, served the expedition as a piper and crier; Miguel Ruiz, born in Seville, was a part of the cavalry and most probably received a double portion of the spoils – as did all those who had horses. In the expanding frontier of Spanish America, the important distinction was not between slaves and freemen but rather between conquistadors and natives, or Christians and non-believers. The frequent use of the word *raza* (race) in early Spanish colonial documents represented not a biological definition but rather a conceptual distinction of cultures. The point here is not really about the social status of these black men but rather of the role of the Caribbean frontier as a sort of proscenium for the wider expansion across the hemisphere, and the eventual sites of dynamic diasporas. Indeed, the Caribbean and mainland circum-Caribbean represented not only a frontier for the pre-Hispanic cultures but also for the early Spanish intruders whose difficult reception is chronicled by Christian Cwik in chapter 3 of this volume.

The variety of real situations inherent in various frontiers led to a multiplicity of blended communities of people of African descent throughout the Americas. In some places the self-consciousness of being African or descendants of Africans – and being different from Europeans and their offspring – was stronger than in other places. For various reasons many African-descended communities across the Caribbean held strongly to links with an African homeland. In some cases those links were entirely imaginary. In the words of Winston James, they kept on "holding aloft the banner of Ethiopia".[38] Not all African diaspora communities in the New World, however, kept aloft that banner. Some, like the community in El Cobre in Eastern Cuba, skilfully combined European and African beliefs to create a lucrative niche in the Spanish overseas colonial empire.

BUILDING DIASPORAS

There was nothing ambiguous about the sense of self in the remarkable case of the enslaved and their community of El Cobre, described magnificently in two excellent books by Olga Portuondo Zúñiga and María Elena Díaz respectively.[39] In El Cobre the original copper mining company went bankrupt around 1680 and the slaves as well as the physical property – machinery, lands and buildings – reverted, as was the custom of the day, to the monarchy of Castile. The slaves of El Cobre became royal slaves with significant traditional privileges which they apparently knew better than the officials at the royal court in Spain. These elite slaves, comparable to the Habishi and Sidi of the Deccan in India, successfully exploited Spanish laws and customs to establish a viable self-sustaining and self-governing community in which their town council supervised free people. Surely this was a most anomalous situation in the American slave system, for enslaved people to have more extensive privileges than freeholders. Yet, it also illustrates the variegated ways in which diasporas originate.

When in 1780 the residents of El Cobre eventually lost their autonomy, the compromise with the inheritors of the copper company for those residents who had not purchased their freedom – or had not had it purchased for them in the intervening years – was to slot them into a peculiar new occupational category called "wage slaves". The descendants of the mining company nominally recovered their slaves and their enterprise after more than a hundred years of litigation, but they were forced to pay wages to all who remained enslaved as though they were regularly hired free labourers. What is notable about the residents of El Cobre is that, in spite of their legally recognized status as slaves and descendants of slaves, they managed to forge a new community and a new ambiguous type of socio-legal definition by their actions: the waged slave. Clearly, this diasporic community and many others in the global African diaspora did not suffer any "social death" but instead skilfully constructed new polities and operated viable economic institutions that had sustained these co-settlers of African origin and descent for generations in the Americas.

In the frontier conditions of the Caribbean this sort of ambiguity was not unusual. However, it would evaporate beneath the transforming sugar revolutions that engulfed the region later. Indeed, as Genaro Rodríguez Morel shows, between 1502 and 1518 Spain shipped out hundreds of black slaves from Iberia to the fledgling American colonies.[40] Some of these slaves, called *ladinos*, were born in Iberia, in communities of Africans found between Málaga and Huelva in southern Iberia; as such, they were Roman Catholic in religion and thoroughly Hispanic in culture. Others were imported from Portuguese trading posts along the West African coast. In the Americas they worked in the mines of Hispaniola, Mexico and Peru, dived for pearls off the Venezuelan coast, helped to build the new cities and towns, and supplemented the faltering Indian population in places where the Spanish established settlements. From this early population, a growing community of free non-white, non-indigenous people developed throughout the Americas. These descendants of various mixtures of population were unique to the colonial experience in the Americas, but until the development of the transatlantic slave trade neither slaves nor African-descended free people of colour constituted a true diasporic community.

THE TRANSATLANTIC SLAVE TRADE AND THE MAKING OF
AFRICAN DIASPORAS IN THE AMERICAS

The transatlantic slave trade formally began when King Charles I of Spain sanctioned the direct importation of Africans to his colonies in the Americas in 1518, after finally acknowledging that the potential supply of indigenous slaves was inadequate to maintain the economic viability of his fledgling overseas colonies.[41] By 1550, thousands of Africans were already being delivered to the Americas, mainly to Hispaniola. These new arrivals came directly from Africa and while some might have been converted to Roman Catholicism, the overwhelming majority was culturally African, who in their new location would continue to think atavistically about the continent from where they had been snatched and sold.[42] Given the increasing numbers and occupational concentration, these newly arrived African immigrants had no other option but to begin to build a diasporic community.

By the late sixteenth century the Portuguese started to import Africans to Brazil to create a plantation society and establish an Atlantic bulwark against other Europeans intruding along the southwestern Atlantic coast.[43] As the demand for labour grew the number of Africans imported as slaves increased, and, eventually, manual labour throughout the Americas became virtually synonymous with the enslaved Africans. Brazil alone received almost one-half of all Africans imported to the Americas between 1550 and 1870. From there it was a short erroneous intellectual leap to regard all people of African descent anywhere in the Americas as descendants of slaves. The transatlantic slave trade became a lucrative international enterprise, and by the time it ended, about 1870, more than ten million Africans were forcibly transported and distributed in the various slave systems of the Americas. Many millions more died in Africa or at sea in transit to the Americas.[44] The high volume made a difference to the construction of the transatlantic diasporas. The majority of the new arrivals were adults, and a sufficiently high proportion were females who could not only procreate but also transmit eclectic elements of African culture in their communities. Later, indentured Africans brought under service contracts merely reinforced the cultural characteristics of the extant diasporic communities.[45]

The slave trade responded to an interrelated series of factors operating across Africa, at the supply side, and also in the Americas, at the market level.[46] The trade fell into four phases, strongly influenced by the development of colonialism throughout the hemisphere. In the first phase, lasting to about 1620, the Americas were the domain of the Spanish and the Portuguese. These Iberian powers introduced about 125,000 slaves to the Americas, with some 75,000 (or 27 per cent of the total African slave exports of the period) going to the Spanish sphere and about 50,000 (18 per cent of the trade) going to Brazil. This was a relatively small flow of about 1,000 slaves per year, most of who were supplied from Portuguese forts along the West African coast. Thus, slavery in the towns, farms and mines of the Americas employed fewer African slaves (about 45 per cent of the total Atlantic trade) than those of the tropical African islands of Fernando Po and São Tomé, Europe proper, or the islands of the Madeiras, Cape Verdes and the Azores (about 55 per cent of trade). Indeed, the small island of São Tomé alone received more than 76,000 African slaves during the period, exceeding the entire Spanish-American market.

The second phase of the transatlantic slave trade lasted from 1620 to about 1700. During this time approximately 1,350,000 slaves were distributed throughout the Americas, with an additional 25,000 or so going to markets throughout Europe. During this phase the Americas became the main destination of enslaved Africans, and the trade was marked by greater geographical distribution, along with the development of a more varied supply pattern on the African side. The European component of the trade eventually dwindled to less than 2 per cent. Across the Atlantic, Brazil assumed the premier position as a slave destination, receiving nearly 42 per cent of all Africans sold on the western side of the Atlantic Ocean. Brazilian pre-eminence would be a permanent characteristic of the transatlantic slave trade. Spanish America received about 22 per cent, distributed principally in Hispaniola, Puerto Rico, Cuba, Mexico, Central America and the Andean regions of South America. The English Caribbean colonies received more than 263,000 slaves, or 20 per cent of the volume sold in the Americas. The French Caribbean imported about 156,000 slaves, or 12 per cent; and the small islands of the Dutch Caribbean bought another 40,000 slaves, or 3 per cent of slaves sold throughout the Americas.[47]

This phase before 1700 experienced a social and demographic

metamorphosis brought about by the sugar revolutions in various parts of the tropical Americas.[48] By the end of the period, the Americas were divided among a number of rival European colonies all successfully establishing plantation colonies for the production and export of tropical staple crops such as cotton, tobacco, sugar, indigo and rice. Slaves became perhaps the most important commercial commodity in transatlantic trade and the desired form of labour on the American plantations. More importantly, slavery evolved into a complex system of labour, commerce and society that was legally, socially and ethnically distinct from other forms of servitude, and almost always applied to the condition of non-free Africans. Two patterns of colonies developed throughout the Western Hemisphere: colonies designed as micro-cosms of European societies and colonies designed primarily for the efficient production of export commodities. The first group of colonies constituted the settler colonies, but also, to some degree, colonies that could be regarded as slaveholding colonies. In these colonies slaves constituted a minority of the population and did not necessarily represent the dominant labour sector. The second group formed exploitative plantation colonies marked by their overwhelming proportion of non-free members, and in which slavery formed the dominant, highly coerced labour system. These latter were the typical American slave societies.

The period between 1701 and 1810 represented the maturation of the slave system in the Americas. This third phase witnessed the apogee of both the transatlantic slave trade and the system of American slavery. During this time, entirely new societies were created throughout the tropical Americas within which African diaspora communities developed, as for example in Cuba, Jamaica, Saint-Domingue and Brazil. Altogether, nearly six million Africans – amounting to nearly 60 per cent of the entire transatlantic slave trade – arrived in American ports during the long eighteenth century. Brazil continued to be the dominant recipient country accounting for nearly two million Africans, or 31 per cent of the trade for the period.

The British Caribbean plantations (mainly on Barbados and Jamaica) received almost a million and a half, accounting for 23 per cent of the trade. The French Antilles (mainly Saint-Domingue on western Hispaniola, Mar-tinique and Guadeloupe) imported almost as many, accounting for 22 per cent of the trade. The Spanish Caribbean (mainly Cuba) imported more than

half a million, or 9.6 per cent of the trade. The nearly equal amount that
went to the Dutch Caribbean accounted for nearly 8 per cent of the trade, but
most of those slaves were re-exported to other areas of the New World. The
British North American colonies imported slightly more than three hundred
thousand, or slightly less than 6 per cent of the trade; with the small Danish
colonies of the Caribbean buying about twenty-five thousand slaves, a rather
minuscule proportion of the slaves sold in the Americas.

The eighteenth century formed the watershed in the system of American slavery. Although individuals, and even groups such as the Society of
Friends or Quakers, had always opposed slavery and the slave trade, general
disapproval of the system only gained strength from the Enlightenment and
its emphasis on rationality combined with British Evangelical Protestantism
during the later eighteenth century. Opposition to slavery became increasingly more coordinated in England and eventually had a profound impact by
helping to instigate the abolition of the English slave trade in 1807. Before
that, prodded by Granville Sharp and other abolitionists, English chief justice
Mansfield declared slavery illegal in Great Britain in 1772, giving enormous
impetus to the British Anti-slavery Society. The British legal ruling immediately freed about fifteen thousand slaves who were living in Britain with their
colonial masters; these masters estimated their immediate property loss at
approximately £700,000.[49] In 1774 the Society of Friends abolished slavery
among its members. Emancipated slaves therefore had the option of losing
themselves in the host society or building a distinct diasporic community
of their peers. They did both.

In 1776 the British philosopher and economist Adam Smith declared in
his classic study, *The Wealth of Nations*, that the system of slavery represented
an uneconomical use of land as well as resources since slaves cost more to
maintain than free workers. By the 1780s the British Parliament was considering a series of bills dealing with the legality of the slave trade. Before that,
several of the recently independent former North American colonies – then
part of the United States of America – such as Vermont, Connecticut and
Rhode Island abolished slavery within their local jurisdictions. New York
abolished slavery in the state in 1799 and New Jersey followed in 1804. After
1808 – when the British and the Americans legally abolished their component of the transatlantic slave trade – the English initiated a campaign to

end all slave trading across the Atlantic, and to replace slave trading within Africa with other forms of legal trade. Through a series of outright bribes, diplomatic pressure and naval blockades, the trade gradually came to an end around 1870.

Slavery was not only attacked from above by governments seeking to rationalize the slave market and international economies. At the same time that European governments contemplated administrative measures against slavery and the slave trade, the implacable opposition of the enslaved themselves, aided in some cases by free non-whites in the overseas colonies, increased the overall costs of maintaining the system of slavery. The African enslaved never fully accepted their enslavement and resisted it continuously in any way that they could. Everywhere, slave revolts, conspiracies and rumours of revolts engendered widespread fear among owners and administrators.[50] Small bands of runaway slaves formed stable black communities, legally recognized by their imperial powers, in difficult geographical locations such as Esmeraldas in Ecuador, the Colombian coastal areas, Palmares in Brazil, and in the impenetrable mountains of Jamaica. Because the information on these communities is so limited it is difficult to ascertain the degree to which members of such communities considered themselves members of an African diasporic community, although from their earliest conception some did.[51]

In 1791, the slaves of Saint-Domingue, taking their cue from the metropolitan French Revolution, revolted successfully under Toussaint Louverture (1743–1803) and a number of other local leaders. The radical French commissioner in the colony, Léger Félicité Sonthonax (1763–1813), saw the futility of quelling the local revolt and accepted the de facto emancipation of all slaves and their immediate admission to full French citizenship (1793). This move was ratified the following year by the revolutionary government in Paris, which also extended the emancipation to all French colonies. Napoleon Bonaparte revoked the decree of emancipation in 1802 but failed to make it stick in Saint-Domingue where the ex-slaves and their free coloured allies declared the independence of Haiti – the second independent state in the Americas – in 1804. Haiti had no option but to consider itself an African diasporic state.

The fourth and final phase of the transatlantic trade lasted from about 1810 to 1870. During that phase approximately two million Africans were sold as slaves in a greatly reduced area of the Americas. With its trade being legal until 1850, Brazil imported some 1,145,400 Africans, or about 60 per cent of all slaves sold in the Americas after 1810. The Spanish Antilles – mainly Cuba and Puerto Rico – imported more than 600,000 Africans (32 per cent), the great majority of them illegally introduced to Cuba after an Anglo-Spanish treaty to abolish the Spanish slave trade in 1817. The French Antilles imported approximately 96,000 slaves, equivalent to about 5 per cent of all slaves sold during that period, mainly for the small sugar plantations of Martinique and Guadeloupe. The southern United States also imported about 50,000 slaves, or slightly less than 3 per cent of all slaves sold, despite formally agreeing to end their international slave trade in 1807.

Altogether the consistently high importation rates for Africans before the middle of the nineteenth century left a legacy of scattered Africanized communities across the Americas.[52] The nineteenth century was also the period in which political sensibilities became pronounced in the form of national identification. With the transportation revolution of the age, all African populations anywhere became increasingly more mobile. Africans and their descendants in the various distant diasporic communities also began to articulate a growing awareness of Africa. At the same time, under various auspices, dispersed Africans began a return movement to the continent.[53]

THE ABOLITION OF THE SLAVE SYSTEMS AND THE RISE OF AFRICAN DIASPORAS

The attack on the slave trade paralleled growing attacks on the system of slavery throughout the Americas. The self-directed abolition from below that had occurred in Saint-Domingue/Haiti in 1793 was not repeated elsewhere. Instead, a combination of internal and external events eventually determined the course of abolition throughout the region. The issue of African slavery became a part of the struggle for political independence for the mainland Spanish-American colonies. Chile (1823), and Mexico along with the new Central America States (1824) abolished slavery immediately after their conflict with Spain. The British government legally abolished slavery throughout its empire in 1834, effectively ending the institution in 1838. Uruguay legally emancipated its few remaining slaves in 1842. The French government ended slavery in their Antilles in 1848. Colombia abolished slavery in 1851, with Ecuador following in 1852, Argentina in 1853, and Peru and Venezuela in 1854. The United States of America abolished slavery after its Civil War in 1865. Spain abolished slavery in Puerto Rico in 1870 and in Cuba in 1886. Finally, Brazil abolished slavery in 1888.

Emancipated people of African ancestry did not immediately receive acceptance into the free societies as had happened in French Saint-Domingue in 1793. Not surprisingly, therefore, they fashioned their reality with as much consciousness of Africa as they could find in their memories or their surroundings.54 Emancipation provided a major boost to the expansion of African diaspora communities in the Americas. It also revitalized the physical and emotional links with the African continent.

The topic of African slavery in the Americas has attracted the attention of a very large number of writers. Before the 1950s, most writers tended to view slavery as a monolithic institution. Then, as now, it was easy to lose sight of the forest for the trees – there was much discussion of slavery, and less of the slaves themselves. Standard influential studies produced in North America, like U.B. Phillips's *American Negro Slavery* (1918) and *Life and Labor in the Old South* (1929), or Kenneth M. Stampp's *The Peculiar Institution* (1956) and Stanley Elkin's *Slavery: A Problem in American Institutional Life* (1959), misleadingly described slaves as passive participants in their own cruel denigration and outrageous exploitation. In Phillips's world everyone was sublimely happy. In the world of Stampp and Elkins they were not – but they could not help themselves. Apparently neither Stampp nor Elkins read much outside their narrow field – or if they did, they discounted it. Certainly the then available scholarship of Eric Williams or C.L.R. James or Elsa V. Goveia is not evident in their works. Herbert Aptheker, in *American Negro Slave Revolts* (1943), Gunnar Myrdal in *An American Dilemma* (1944) and Frank Tannenbaum in *Slave and Citizen* (1946) tried, in those three intellectually stimulating works, to modify the overall picture, both in the public and scholarly spheres but without much success.

In 1956 Elsa Goveia published an outstanding book, *Slave Society in the British Leeward Islands at the End of the Eighteenth Century*. As Francisco Scarano notes of Goveia's work,

> Goveia's sensitive and profound study of slave society in the British Leewards . . . is doubtless one of the great works of Caribbean history in any language. The Guyanese historian revealed the ways in which, in a racialized slave society, the imperative of slave subordination permeated all contexts of social interaction, from legal system to education and from religion to leisure. Everything was predicated on the violence necessary to maintain slavocratic order.[55]

Goveia's approach inculcated the slaves with agency, a fundamental quality of which earlier writers seemed incredibly unaware. Slaves continuously acted as well as reacted to the world in which they existed, but at the heart of it, Africans were constructing and reconstructing diasporas. It became clear that Africans and their descendants were involved in every phase of the transformation of the Americas.

Some of the activities of Africans and their descendants cannot be easily categorized, described or analysed within the restrictive bipolar forms of accommodation or resistance. Indeed, a great number of people described as Africans or as African slaves in the Americas exercising occupations such as itinerant vendors, coastal sailors, ranchers, healers and property owners were not in any overt way coerced. Their lot was quite removed from that of the savagely exploited plantation field slaves, especially in the later years of the American slave systems. The condition of slavery varied too much across the Americas to be neatly categorized. Moreover, it was never a static institution. It changed enormously through time, and even in the same locality. Over time these communities transformed themselves into organic societies capable of sub-dividing further into variants of Africanized societies that were able to replicate microcosms of themselves in faraway places. The implications of this awakened collective self-consciousness, nation building and diasporic formation are examined by Jane Landers in chapter 4, Yvonne Daniel in chapter 6, Michele Johnson in chapter 7, Tommy Lott in chapter 8, Winston James in chapter 10 and Quito Swan in chapter 11.

DESCRIPTION OF THE BOOK

This volume highlights several aspects of diasporic communities around the globe and across time – not just of African diasporas. Ruth Iyob discusses in chapter 1 the alternating prominence and invisibility of African diasporas in the Mediterranean world and highlights the overwhelming impact that the introduction of monotheistic religious beliefs had on the construction of diasporic communities. Moreover as she narrates the history of the African diasporas in the Mediterranean, the Red Sea Corridor and the Indian Ocean region, what is remembered becomes reconstructed so imaginatively that facts are supplanted by fictional accounts, artistic renditions or distant memories and mythmaking. Tamara Ganjalyan in chapter 2 analyses the importance of economic markets to the Armenian diaspora communities in the early Russian empire and how they served as strategic political assets to an expanding empire. When the Russian empire was weak it relied on Armenian diasporas which were their important commercial and political allies. When the Russian empire became strong those allies became less important subjects. Armenian diasporas, however, did not constitute distinct somatic norm variations within the pluralistic Russian empire because Armenians tended to look much like other Russian citizens from that ethnically diverse empire. Christian Cwik in chapter 3 describes situations in which Africans were introduced to an area that comprised a double frontier – for the invading, colonizing Spanish as well as the indigenous populations on the peripheries of the earlier pre-Hispanic empires. Not all of Cwik's African-origin participants eventually became diaspora builders. Jane Landers in chapter 4 explores facets of institution formation among African diasporic communities within the Iberian Atlantic world and persuasively demonstrates that those essentially African-based institutions were of joint Iberian and African agency. Not only did people move about but the concepts of culture they brought with them were also subject to local variation. This represents a quintessential example of the dynamic process of institutional creolization in the Atlantic World. Somewhat like the cases described by Tamara Ganjalyan, Evelyn Hu-DeHart deals with diasporic communities formed by non-Africans throughout the Americas. Chinese overseas emigration has a long history, but it takes on special significance during the nineteenth century when the large Chinese exodus coincided with increasing anti-Chinese sentiments in the newly constituted nation states of the Americas. While the new states could demarcate fixed boundaries, they had neither the population nor adequate resources to police their newly drawn borders. Chinese migrants used these border spaces to construct transnational diasporic communities. For Yvonne Daniel, in chapter 6, the important observation is the way in which collective memory is conceived, preserved and performed in music and dance. Dance and dance music are portrayed as museums housing centuries of African identity markers, belief systems and rituals that to a large degree were reconstituted as sacred and popular music and dance styles. With the movement of peoples from one country to another, both the mind and the body "carried with them memories and histories" that were frozen in time but were constantly subject to creative recall in the ongoing process of identity creation, cultural revitalization and ritual invention. The music of revolutions, resistance and recreation are thus danced by bodies that have "housed" the lived histories that had been imprinted upon the new homelands by distinctive dance music, and the sound of drums and other musical instruments. In chapter 7, Michele Johnson examines the marginalization of the early co-settlers in Canada and the inescapable problems of secondary diasporas – especially from as complex an area as the Caribbean – in establishing their identity in an environment that varies between hostility and benign neglect. The heterogeneous and cosmopolitan Caribbean migrants to Canada are examples of a sub-diaspora. Their travels and travails illustrate the difficulties of clearly defining and tracing the contours of diasporic communities. Secondary diasporas invariably highlight problems of self-identification. In chapter 8, Tommy Lott critically examines the ongoing debates about notions of constructing diasporic group solidarity in the United States, especially when African American solidarity is predicated on "anti-black racism". Persons of African descent in the United States continually navigate an extremely complex terrain shaped by the "one-drop blood" that is unfamiliar to individuals coming from African, Caribbean and Latin American cultures where concepts of race, culture and ethnicity manifest themselves in myriad ways. Lott lucidly illustrates the distinct ways in which old and new diasporic communities adapt to the changing realties of their host society. Sometimes their actions encourage and at other times they undermine the construction of group identity and solidarity.

Diasporas often create their own rich and distinctive literary voice. In chapter 9, Jarrett Hugh Brown highlights the emblematic conflicts of diasporic societies and introduces the literature of the African Caribbean diaspora, detailing its extraordinary richness and complexity as illustrated in Claude McKay's *Banana Bottom*. Brown captures the diasporic individual's soul-felt nostalgia, anguish and predicament of transplanted minds and bodies. In many ways Claude McKay was the consummate international diasporic individual, for his lengthy sojourns in Harlem, Paris and Marseille failed to diminish his eternal love for his native Jamaica.

Diaspora is also about identity construction and the ancient process of creolization. Both Winston James in chapter 10 and Quito Swan in chapter 11 explore the relationship between the Caribbean and Bermudian variants of the African Caribbean diaspora, and the penchant for internationalism that has been an integral feature of the region throughout its history. Indeed these two chapters emphasize the fascinating role of the African diaspora of the Caribbean in promoting a pan-African movement since the later nineteenth century. Swan follows the Caribbean Black Power movement across the Americas and Africa all the way to the Pacific during the tempestuous decades between the 1950s and the 1980s.

Studies of diasporas not only inform us better of the variety and changing nature of those intrinsically interesting communities in their specific geographical locations but they also allow us to understand the wider world better. The tremendous benefits of diaspora studies are obvious. By erasing the historical invisibility of African and other diasporas we enormously enrich the historical record of the human community. History, after all, is made not just by victors or great men and women in important political and military positions, but also by common people with strong convictions going about their everyday lives and who are profoundly sensitive to what they perceive as the well-being of all people.

DIASPORA AND CREOLIZATION

As noted earlier, the Iberian expansion into the Americas introduced a new variation of the ancient connotation of the word Creole to the Castilian language. Originally a term associated with transhumance – the seasonal migration of cattle and their caretakers between high pastures and lowlands – creole came to be associated with people, especially with Iberian offspring born overseas, *el criollo*. Eventually, it referred generally to anyone born in the overseas empire regardless of their place of origin, thus, restricting the definition of creole to people of African descent greatly distorts the meaning. The inherent etymological dynamism of language gave the word a rich spectrum of meaning as it moved between and across linguistic frontiers. So the term not only has different connotations within a common language but also between different European languages. Moreover, quite often in music and cuisine – as commonly employed in Peru or Louisiana – the use of creole is merely an indication of what is local. While the word creole may mean different things to different people, it implicitly conveys an understanding of the effervescent process of sociocultural change. Creolization therefore represents an essential feature of all diaspora communities and thus may be considered timeless. Relocating people and culture to a new environment invariably infuses both with catalytic characteristics that produce novelty in manners, in customs and in thought. That, after all, has been the common experience whenever two or more different groups have come together.

NOTES

1.   Patrick Manning, *Migration in World History*, revised ed. (New York: Routledge, 2012).

2.   Patrick K. O'Brien, ed., *Philip's Atlas of World History* (London: Institute of Historical Research, University of London, 1999), 12. For global patterns of migration over time, see William H. McNeill, *The Rise of the West: A History of the Human Community* (Chicago: University of Chicago Press, 1994). For the antiquity of the African diaspora, see Joseph E. Harris, "Expanding the Scope of African Diaspora Studies: The Middle East and India, a Research Agenda", *Radical History Review* 87 (2003): 157–68.

3.   Paul Mellars, "Why Did Modern Human Populations Disperse from Africa ca. 60,000 Years Ago?" *Proceedings of the National Academy of Sciences* 103, no. 25 (2006): 9381–86.

4.   Michael A. Gomez, *Reversing Sail: A History of the African Diaspora* (New York: Cambridge University Press, 2005); Patrick Manning, *The African Diaspora: A History Through Culture* (New York: Columbia University Press, 2009).

5. For a discussion of the historiography of the term diaspora, see Patrick Manning, "Africa and the African Diaspora: New Directions of Study", *Journal of African History* 44, no. 3 (October 2003): 487–512.

6. *Compact Edition of the Oxford English Dictionary* (Oxford: Oxford University Press, 1971), 1:718. In 1876, C.M. Davies used the word to describe the expansion of Protestant churches on the continent.

7. *Webster's New Universal Unabridged Dictionary,* 2nd ed. (New York: Simon and Schuster, 1979), 504 specifically connects the word to the dispersal of Jews outside of Palestine. According to *The New Columbia Encyclopedia,* ed. William H. Harris and Judith S. Levey (New York: Columbia University Press, 1975), diaspora is the "term used today to denote Jewish communities living outside the Holy Land. It was originally used to designate the dispersal of the Jews at the time of the destruction of the Temple (586 BCE) and the forced exile to Babylonia." Studies of the Holocaust are numerous. See Doris Bergen, *The Holocaust: A Concise History* (New York: Rowman and Littlefield, 2009).

8. O'Brien, *Atlas,* 22–27.

9. See Ruth Iyob, "Memory Palaces and Prisons: Exploring the Corridors of Africa's Diasporas in the 'Then' and 'Now' " (lecture presented at the Center for Africana Studies, Johns Hopkins University, Baltimore, 18 February 2010).

10. Jared Diamond, *Collapse: How Societies Choose to Fail or Succeed* (New York: Viking, 2005).

11. O'Brien, *Atlas,* 78–79.

12. Carter Vaughn Findley, *The Turks in World History* (New York: Oxford University Press, 2005); Paul S. Ropp, *China in World History* (New York: Oxford University Press, 2010).

13. Milagros Guerrero, "The Chinese in the Philippines, 1570–1770", in *The Chinese in the Philippines,* ed. Felix Alfonso Jr (Manila: Solidaridad, 1966), 15–39; Evelyn Hu-DeHart, "Immigrants to a Developing Society: The Chinese in Northern Mexico, 1875–1932", *Journal of Arizona History* 21 (1980): 49–85; Evelyn Hu-DeHart, "Chinese Coolie Labour in Cuba in the Nineteenth Century: Free Labour or Neo-Slavery?" *Slavery and Abolition* 14, no. 1 (1992): 69–86; Walton Look Lai, *Indentured Labor, Caribbean Sugar: Chinese and Indian Migrants to the British West Indies, 1838–1918* (Baltimore: Johns Hopkins University Press, 1993); Denise Helly, *Ideologie et Ethnicité: Les Chinois Macau à Cuba, 1847–1886* (Montreal: Les Presses de l'Université de Montreal, 1979); Juan Jimenez Pastrama, *Los Chinos en la Historia de Cuba, 1847–1930* (Havana: Editorial de Ciencias Sociales, 1983); Yin Lee Tom, *The Chinese in Jamaica* (Kingston: Ching San News, 1963); Lisa Yun, *The Coolie Speaks: Chinese Indentured Laborers and*

African Slaves in Cuba (Philadelphia: Temple University Press, 2008); M.L. Bush, *Servitude in Modern Times* (Malden, MA: Blackwell, 2000).

14. Daniel M. Masterson and Sayaka Funada-Classen, *The Japanese in Latin America: The Asian American Experience* (Urbana: University of Illinois Press, 2004); Yuiko Fujita, *Cultural Migrants from Japan: Youth, Media and Migration in New York and London* (Lanham, MD: Rowman and Littlefield, 2009).

15. A brilliant examination of these recent Atlantic-wide Caribbean diasporas may be found in Laura Putnam, *Radical Moves: Caribbean Migrants and the Politics of Race in the Jazz Age* (Chapel Hill: University of North Carolina Press, 2013). See also Quito Swan, *Black Power in Bermuda: The Struggle for Decolonization* (New York: Palgrave Macmillan, 2009); Mary Chamberlain, *Family Love in the Diaspora: Migration and the Anglo-Caribbean Experience* (Kingston: Ian Randle, 2006); Mary Chamberlain, *Narratives of Exile and Return* (Kingston: Ian Randle, 2004).

16. Encarnación Lemus López, *Ausente en Indias: Un historia de la emigración a América* (Madrid: Junta de Extremadura, 1993); Ida Altman, *Transatlantic Ties in the Spanish Empire: Brihuega, Spain and Puebla, Mexico,1560–1620* (Stanford: Stanford University Press, 2000); Ida Altman and James Horn, eds., *"To Make America": European Emigration in the Early Modern Period* (Berkeley: University of California Press, 1991); Ida Altman, *Emigrants and Society: Extremadura and America in the Sixteenth Century* (Berkeley: University of California Press, 1989).

17. Franklin W. Knight, "Slavery in the Americas", in *A Companion to Latin American History*, ed. Thomas H. Holloway (New York: Blackwell, 2008), 146–61.

18. See Benjamin Nuñez, *Dictionary of Afro-Latin American Civilization* (Westport, CT: Greenwood, 1980), 147; Seymour Drescher and Stanley Engerman, eds., *A Historical Guide to World Slavery* (New York: Oxford University Press, 1998), 126.

19. See Pier M. Larson, "African Diasporas and the Atlantic", in *The Atlantic in Global History*, ed. Jorge Cañizares-Esguerra and Erik R. Seeman (Upper Saddle River, NJ: Pearson, 2007), 129–49. See also, Laurent Dubois and Julius Scott, eds., *Origins of the Black Atlantic* (New York: Routledge, 2010); Ronald Segal, *The Black Diaspora: Five Centuries of the Black Experience Outside Africa* (New York: Farrar, Straus and Giroux, 1995); Ralph Davis, *The Rise of the Atlantic Economies* (Ithaca: Cornell University Press, 1973).

20. Franklin W. Knight, *The Caribbean: The Genesis of a Fragmented Nationalism*, 3rd ed. (New York: Oxford University Press, 2012), 28–37; Alfred W. Crosby Jr, *The Columbian Exchange: Biological and Cultural Consequences of 1492* (Westport, CT: Greenwood, 1972).

21. Crosby, *Columbian Exchange*; Eric Wolf, *Sons of the Shaking Earth* (Chicago: University of Chicago Press, 1959). See also, Fray Ramón Pané, *An Account of the Antiquities of the Indians*, new ed., with an introductory study, notes and appendixes by José Arrom and translated by Susan C. Griswold (Durham: Duke University Press, 1999); Lawrence A. Clayton, *Bartolomé de las Casas and the Conquest of the Americas* (Malden, MA: Wiley-Blackwell, 2011); Daniel Castro, *Another Face of Empire: Bartolomé de Las Casas, Indigenous Rights and Ecclesiastical Imperialism* (Durham: Duke University Press, 2007); J.H. Elliott, *Empires of the Atlantic World: Britain and Spain in America, 1492–1830* (New Haven: Yale University Press, 2006); Karen Ordahl Kupperman, *The Atlantic in World History* (New York: Oxford University Press, 2012).

22. See David Abulafia, *The Discovery of Mankind: Atlantic Encounters in the Age of Columbus* (New Haven: Yale University Press, 2008), especially its excellent bibliography.

23. Genaro Rodríguez Morel, *Orígenes de la economía de plantación de La Española* (Santo Domingo, Dominican Republic: Editora Nacional, 2012).

24. David Eltis and David Richardson, *Atlas of the Transatlantic Slave Trade* (New Haven: Yale University Press, 2010).

25. According to M.L. Bush, "Modern servitude came in five basic forms: slavery, serfdom, indentured service, debt bondage and penal servitude. All shared a special state of personal unfreedom that was quite distinct from the constraints political systems normally placed on their inhabitants or societies normally expected of their members" (*Servitude in Modern Times*, 3).

26. Alberto Vieira, ed., *História do Açúcar: Rotas e Mercados* (Madeira: Centro de Estudos de História do Atlântico, 2002).

27. See Moses I. Finley, *Ancient Slavery and Modern Ideology* (Princeton: Markus Wiener, 1998); Ronald Segal, *Islam's Black Slaves: The Other Black Diaspora* (New York: Farrar, Straus and Giroux, 2001).

28. Elliott, *Empires of the Atlantic World*, 404; Charles Gibson, *The Black Legend: Anti-Spanish Attitudes in the Old World and the New* (New York: Knopf, 1971).

29. Franklin W. Knight, *The African Dimension in Latin American Societies* (New York: Macmillan, 1974); Knight, *The Caribbean*.

30. This is the position espoused in Orlando Patterson's *Slavery and Social Death: A Comparative Study* (Cambridge, MA: Harvard University Press, 1982). It is an overly generalized encryption of the process of disempowerment with a loss of personhood – a popular and elegant notion, but untenable in light of the complex dimensions of Africa's multiple diasporas.

31. See Barbara L. Solow and Stanley L. Engerman, eds., *British Capitalism and Caribbean Slavery: The Legacy of Eric Williams* (New York: Cambridge University

Press, 1987), and Barbara L. Solow, ed., *Slavery and the Rise of the Atlantic System* (Cambridge, MA: Harvard University Press, 1991).

32. Robert H. Fuson, trans., *The Log of Christopher Columbus* (Camden, ME: International Marine, 1987), 77. Servants and slaves were terms used ambiguously in the early Castilian language. Slavery was still legal in Iberia in the age of Columbus and other forms of servitude were commonplace. From his earlier experience with African slaves during his residence in Madeira, Columbus might have assumed that his new-found Antilleans could just as easily be traded.

33. Knight, "Slavery in the Americas".

34. See chapter 3 by Christian Cwik in this volume.

35. David J. Weber, *The Spanish Frontier in North America* (New Haven: Yale University Press, 1992), 44.

36. Bernal Díaz del Castillo, *The History and Conquest of Mexico*, translated by Maurice Keatinge (London, 1800; facsimile ed. La Jolla, CA, 1979), 502–4.

37. James Lockhart, *The Men of Cajamarca: A Social and Biographical Study of the First Conquerors of Peru* (Austin: University of Texas Press, 1972), 35–36.

38. Winston James, *Holding Aloft the Banner of Ethiopia: Caribbean Radicalism in Early Twentieth-Century America* (London and New York: Verso, 1998).

39. Olga Portuondo Zúñiga, *La virgen de la Caridad del Cobre: Símbolo de Cubanía* (Santiago de Cuba: Editorial Oriente, 1995); María Elena Díaz, *The Virgin, The King, and the Royal Slaves of El Cobre: Negotiating Freedom in Colonial Cuba, 1670–1780* (Stanford: Stanford University Press, 2000).

40. Genaro Rodríguez Morel, "The Sugar Economy of Española in the Sixteenth Century", in *Tropical Babylons: Sugar and the Making of the Atlantic World, 1450–1680*, ed. Stuart B. Schwartz (Chapel Hill: University of North Carolina Press, 2004), 85–114; Genaro Rodríguez Morel, "Black Slavery in the Hispanic Caribbean in the Sixteenth and Seventeenth Centuries", in *UNESCO General History of the Caribbean*, volume 3, *The Slave Societies of the Caribbean*, ed. Franklin W. Knight, revised ed. (London: UNESCO/Macmillan, forthcoming).

41. According to Rodríguez Morel, licences might have been granted for slave importation to Seville before 1518 but after issuance was formalized and taxes imposed on the imports. See Rodríguez Morel, "Black Slavery in the Hispanic Caribbean". See also Colin A. Palmer, "The Slave Trade, African Slavers, and the Demography of the Caribbean to 1750", in *UNESCO General History of the Caribbean*, volume 3, *The Slave Societies of the Caribbean*, ed. Franklin W. Knight (London: UNESCO/Macmillan, 1997), 9–44.

42. This makes it hard to accept the proposition of Louis Hartz that "when a part of a European nation is detached from the whole of it, and hurled outward into

new soil, it loses the stimulus toward change that the whole provides. It lapses into a kind of immobility." On the contrary, all immigrant societies and communities are extraordinarily resilient, adaptive and creative. See Louis Hartz, *The Founding of New Societies: Studies in the History of the United States, Latin America, South Africa, Canada and Australia* (New York: Harcourt, Brace and World, 1964), 3.

43.   Mauricio Goulart, *A escravidão Africana no Brasil (Das origins à extinção do trafico)* (São Paulo: Alfa-Omega, 1975); Katia M. De Qeirós Mattoso, *Entre esclave au Brésil: XVIe–XIXe* (Paris: Hachette, 1979).

44.   David Eltis et al., eds., *The Trans-Atlantic Slave Trade: A Database on CD-ROM* (Cambridge: Cambridge University Press, 1999). See also Eltis and Richardson, *Atlas of the Transatlantic Slave Trade.*

45.   Monica Schuler, *"Alas, Alas, Kongo": A Social History of Indentured African Immigration into Jamaica, 1841–1865* (Baltimore: Johns Hopkins University Press, 1980).

46.   Herbert S. Klein, *The Atlantic Slave Trade* (New York: Cambridge University Press, 1999).

47.   Calculations are based on Philip D. Curtin, *The Atlantic Slave Trade: A Census* (Madison: University of Wisconsin Press, 1969). Other authors have recalculated the figures provided by Curtin but their overall variations fall well within his margin of error of plus or minus 20 per cent.

48.   B.W. Higman, "The Sugar Revolution", *Economic History Review* 53, no. 1 (May 2000): 213–36.

49.   Steven M. West, *Though the Heavens May Fall: The Landmark Trial That Led to the End of Human Slavery* (Cambridge, MA: Da Capo, 2005).

50.   Michael Craton, "Forms of Resistance to Slavery", in *UNESCO General History of the Caribbean*, volume 3, *The Slave Societies of the Caribbean*, ed. Franklin W. Knight (London: UNESCO/Macmillan, 1997), 222–70.

51.   Werner Zips, *Black Rebels: African Caribbean Freedom Fighters in Jamaica* (Princeton: Markus Wiener, 1998).

52.   Jane Landers, *Black Society in Spanish Florida* (Urbana: University of Illinois Press, 1999); Philip D. Curtin, *Two Jamaicas: The Role of Ideas in a Tropical Colony, 1830–1865* (New York: Atheneum, 1970 [1955]); George Reid Andrews, *Afro-Latin America, 1800–2000* (New York: Oxford University Press, 2004); Segal, *Black Diaspora.*

53.   Rodolfo Sarracino Magriñat, *Los que volvieron a Africa* (Havana: Editorial de Ciencias Sociales, 1988).

54.   Brian L. Moore and Michele A. Johnson, *"They Do as They Please": The Jamaican Struggle for Cultural Freedom after Morant Bay* (Kingston: University of the

West Indies Press, 2001); Brian L. Moore and Michele A. Johnson, *Neither Led nor Driven: Contesting British Cultural Imperialism in Jamaica, 1865–1920* (Kingston: University of the West Indies Press, 2004); Melina Pappademos, *Black Political Activism and the Cuban Republic* (Chapel Hill: University of North Carolina Press, 2011); Rebecca J. Scott, *Degrees of Freedom: Louisiana and Cuba after Slavery* (Cambridge, MA: Harvard University Press, 2005); Kim D. Butler, *Freedoms Given, Freedom Won: Afro-Brazilians in Post-Abolition São Paulo and Salvador* (New Brunswick, NJ: Rutgers University Press, 1998).

55. Francisco A. Scarano, "Slavery and Emancipation in Caribbean History", in *General History of the Caribbean*, volume 6, *Methodology and Historiography of the Caribbean*, ed. B.W. Higman (London: UNESCO/Macmillan, 1999), 260.

CHAPTER 1

REFLECTIONS ON AFRICAN DIASPORAS IN THE MEDITERRANEAN WORLD

RUTH IYOB

THE MEDITERRANEAN REGION, A COSMOPOLITAN GEOGRAPHIC, economic and cultural region shared by the peoples of Africa and Europe and traversed by so many more peoples from distant polities constitutes an arena with few visible traces of the many African diasporas that crossed and recrossed its spaces. The inhabitants of this region who had travelled the furthest to settle there in antiquity as well as in the medieval period included those people of the Atlantic Coast of Morocco, the Red Sea, the Fertile Crescent, the Horn of Africa and the Arabian Peninsula.[1] Ancient historians and cartographers acknowledged the commercial and political interactions of the region stretching from the Iberian Atlantic to the Eastern Mediterranean and Red Sea region. They recorded the activities of both the southern and northern coastal regions as well as the hinterland routes and settlements leading to Red Sea ports such as Berenice, Adulis, Avalites and Mouza just to name a few.[2] It is, therefore, not surprising that the area was familiar to the people on both sides of the Mediterranean and countless crossings and recrossings were recorded by historians. In the postmodern period, we find that evidence of such crossings is often discredited by those who deny that Africans traversed this sea, which once had been commonly shared.[3]

Historically, the Mediterranean has been a corridor of commerce as well as a site of different cultural hubs and imperial strongholds. Place names are not necessarily the invention of folk living in the described sites. The very appellation "Ethiopia", "Africa", "Libya" and Sudan" are all terms coined mainly by ancient and medieval travellers, traders and conquerors, who were not residents of these locales. What has survived in contemporary archives and museums are the portrayals of encounters with Africans as remembered by the ancient Hellenic and Roman writers and medieval Arab geographers. In the *Iliad* and the *Odyssey*, the works of the Greek Homer (c. 800 BCE–701 BCE), the Ethiopians who hosted Olympian gods were evoked along with the hostile African auxiliaries in the Persian army of Xerxes (518 BCE–465 BCE) who fought against the Greeks. These fictive accounts reflect the relations of conflict, cooperation and exchange of goods that existed on all sides of that sea. The question arises of how the ancient Afro-Mediterranean relations which produced the earlier positive image of *Aithiopians* hosting Zeus later became overshadowed by the demonized image of the monstrous "blacks" from Africa. Pan-Hellenic political institutions which clearly demarcated outsiders and insiders differed from those of Rome whose victorious armies included African regiments from Numidia and Mauritania that fought along-side centurions against their Carthaginian rivals. Epics about Rome's Punic Wars, in which Romans sought to dominate the diasporic maritime lords of the eastern Mediterranean, demonized Hannibal without necessarily impugning his African identity or highlighting his phenotype. The surviving archives of Rome's brutal campaign of ethnic cleansing reflect the victor's narrative and leave a void in our knowledge of the narrative of the vanquished. The contemporary narratives of the Afro-Mediterranean world thus remain incomplete, and false geographic boundaries separate the southern African shores of the Mediterranean from its northern, European, shores.

The Africans of antiquity were rendered invisible although they were autonomous actors in conquests and wars in the Mediterranean. When they later re-emerged in portrayals in early modernity, they were represented as "infidels", "kaffirs" and "barbarians" to be used as chattel and their relics were kept as ornaments of wonder in cabinets of the ruling elites of Europe, Arabia and Asia. The history of Africans and their descendants who lived outside of their ancestral lands receded from reality to fictive imaginings. Egypt's Cleopatra (69 BCE–30 BCE), a symbol of the early fusion of the Afro-Hellenic world – goddess and ruler – continues to be portrayed as a "Greek" captivator of Caesar and his generals rather than as a successor to the strong queens of Africa, such as Hatshepsut (d. 1458 BCE).[4]

With the rise of Islam in the seventh century CE and the Arab conquests of North Africa, a similar portrayal of a singular identity of a composite "Arab" neglected the newest layer of identity of the Afro-Mediterranean lands from Egypt to Morocco. Again the fusion with African elements was ignored only to re-emerge eleven hundred years later in the conscious process of constructing pan-Arab and pan-African identities in the nineteenth and twentieth centuries. The much celebrated history of the emirate of *Al-Andalus* continues to be narrated as a fusion of Jewish, Christian and Islamic civilization, highlighting the feats and defeats of the *moriscos* and *marranos*.[5] The production of knowledge about this era in the humanities, in literature and the social sciences continues, today, to excise the African from the Mediterranean polities, despite the artistic reconstructions of the period which depict figures recognizable as the inhabitants of Sahelian, Saharan and sub-Saharan Africa.[6]

Much more work needs to be done and far more attention paid to the Euro-African–Arab encounters spanning the seventh and fifteenth centuries, as well as to the multiple diasporic movements that linked the Mediterranean with the Atlantic, the Red Sea and Indian Ocean regions.[7] Such inquiries need to adjust their optic scope and widen their analytical lenses to ensure that the Afro-Mediterranean region includes the histories of Africans, Arabs and Asians.[8] The history of the southern shores of modern Europe, envisioned as the Barbary Coast, has not been completely neglected, but its focus on piracy, white slavery and Christian-Islamic conflict has erased the African presence and contribution.[9]

This absence of a multifaceted and multicultural African is in glaring contradiction to the vivid, captivating and amazingly detailed portrayal of the African in the world of art and painting.[10] Whereas images of Africans are numerous and reflect the presence of Europeans as masters and colonizers, portrayals of the precolonial past when diverse communities of Africans engaged with their counterparts north of the Mediterranean in equal terms as rulers, rivals, allies, brokers and travellers remain rare. As a result, Africans in the Mediterranean remain invisible in the public memory – except as slaves, servants and ornaments of empire adorning European art collections and museums.[11] Real-life "Africans" in the Mediterranean have been rendered invisible, paradoxically, by the very production of images and texts that have portrayed them as either lachrymose figures or romanticized noblemen. Fables trumped facts and fictive imaginations inspired works of art that have survived – albeit in fragments – to the contemporary era, effectively erasing the roots of the transplanted Africans and the routes that led them to the shores of the Mediterranean.

This type of selective scholarship glosses over the historical, sociopolitical and economic context(s) within which the encounters between the polities and empires on both sides of that central sea took place and overemphasizes subjugation, thereby sculpting diverse communities into a homogeneous entity identified as African/black. I argue that the earliest construction of a homogenized African/black entity began with the erasure of the composite identity, specific histories, geographies and cultures of the diverse peoples who have come to be known in a homogenizing way as merely Africans and/or blacks. The high visibility of imaginative constructions and reconstructions of African figures in art, fiction and theatre, by its very incongruity, contributes to the invisibility of the multitudes of Africans whose experiences and memories have been subsumed into either tragic victims of enslavement and conquest or exotic personalities whose somatic difference overshadows their shared humanity.[12]

This conventional historiography that renders the plurality of the many African diasporas into a singular homogeneous identity is rooted in ancient, medieval and modern discourses and images selectively portraying Africans through a paradoxical lens. The ensuing fractured images and accompanying discourses have constructed two contradictory images and narratives of Africans and their descendants in the diaspora: as individuals in bondage, on the one hand, and as exotically ennobled, even deified, individuals, on the other.

The *first* lens is a result of the preponderance of "lachrymose" narratives which view the African continent as a conquered land, replete with decaying civilizations.[13] The lachrymose narratives have produced powerful images of the ghosts of Africans past who haunt the palazzos, piazzas, museums and texts as both servile victims and ornamental figures, adorning the history of kingdoms and empires. In paintings,[14] sculptures, novels, film[15] and even television series,[16] the representations of Africans as mere victims make it difficult to trace their voyages and the history of how they came to inhabit their new terrain. Whether displayed on canvases, etched in cameos or sculpted in marble those images achieve contrasting ends: they dehistoricize the African figures, who remain without a narrative pointing to a particular historical time of arrival or a specific geographic point of origin, while at the same time they historicize the military and political victories of Europeans and memorialize the elevated economic status of the European ruling elites.

Pietro Tacca's "Monument of the Four Moors", for example, memorializes Ferdinando I de'Medici, the Grand Duke of Tuscany's naval victory over the Ottomans in 1607. Tacca's sculpture of the African in chains, hewn in stone, gazes on the Piazza Michele in Livorno, Italy, with unseeing eyes and is devoid of any historic inscriptions except as a monument to those who deprived him of his freedom and identity. Yet beyond the artist's skill in capturing the misery of the black figure in bondage lies a known yet neglected narrative of the role of the House of Medici in the West African slave trade.[17]

Displayed in "wonder cabinets", prison pens and international museums we find a dazzling spectrum of the artefacts of many African diasporic peoples who had contributed to the building of new civilizations. Though they were deemed unequal to their Mediterranean counterparts, they were nevertheless significant contributors to the building of empires, the making of alliances and the winning or losing of battles. Our understanding of the earliest African presence in the Mediterranean and the Red Seas is informed more by the images bequeathed to us by ancient artists, craftsmen and modern painters than by verifiable historical knowledge.

Some creative reconstructions reflect positive aspects of invisible African histories, as is noticeable in the numerous depictions of the figures (conventionally recognized as Africans/blacks) of Balthazar, the gift-bearing king of Biblical lore; Bilal, Islam's first muezzin; and St Maurice, the crusader.[18] These celebratory affirmations of African personages are nevertheless outnumbered by paintings and heraldic images of those captured in servile roles and as symbols of the well-to-do.

These erasures of historical identity have even re-emerged in the twenty-first century HBO television series *Rome*, where the cameras capture the curvaceous figures of bonded African women whose presence is ornamental and symbolic of the newly acquired status of households that have successfully climbed the social ladder in Julius Caesar's Rome. Their dusky hues and bodies revealingly attired in gauzy clothes are the focus as they are ordered in and out of the narrative – one in which they have no voice. From Herodotus to Pliny to Shakespeare, the somatic difference of Africans which made them "literally spectacular" emphasized what distinguished them from other ethnic communities thereby diminishing commonly shared features as viewed by the historians, travellers and writers of the times.[19] Even Shakespeare who bequeathed to us Othello, whom we only know as the Moor, leaves us without an idea of his birthplace, his "nation" and how he came to be the heroic defender of Venice. Yet, to Shakespeare's enduring credit, Othello's dual identity as an "Afro-Mediterranean" figure is finely wrought, for he is portrayed "neither [as] an alienated nor an assimilated subject, but [as] a figure defined by two worlds".[20] The play *Othello* thus does not fit into the lachrymose lens since it depicts a complex African figure who, as a "Moor . . . of Venice", proudly identifies with his dual heritage from both sides of the Mediterranean and "elopes with a woman who he says was attracted to his escapades in an Africanesque landscape".[21] *Othello* beckons to us to readjust our lenses and to reconsider the erased narratives of his diasporic identity, representing a "lived history" of thousands of transplanted Africans in the Mediterranean.

Though the fictional figure of Othello is mused over by scholars and readers throughout the world, the history of the historical figure of al-Hassan al-Wazzan – who was born in Granada, emigrated to Fez and captured and given to the Medici pope, Leo X (Giovanni de Medici), in 1518 – remained shrouded in mystery and distorted by narrators on both sides of the Mediterranean until the publication of Natalie Zemon Davis's 2006 magisterial work.[22] Known as Leo Africanus, despite his insistence on adopting an Arabic version of his new name, Yuhanna al-Asad, this Afro-Mediterranean bequeathed to us a magnum opus, *Cosmology and Geography of Africa*, which he wrote in 1526. It was not published, however, until 1550, long after he had recrossed the Mediterranean to freedom and/or obscurity.[23] He left behind him a manuscript written in Italian which became the requisite guide to explorations of Africa. Reflecting his own personal history – as a Muslim from Granada and an asylum seeker in the sultanate of Fez – his book was retitled and circulated as a *Description of Africa* and subjected to the editing and distorting of his intellectual work.

Leo Africanus/al-Wazzan's presence in Rome and his intellectual service to Pope Leo X was widely acknowledged in European diplomatic circles, making the publication of his book in 1550 a sensational bestseller. Ironically, the study of the fate of the actual "Moor of Rome", al-Hassan-al-Wazzan, has yet to move beyond conjecture to sustained and serious scholarly attention. The distortion of his book by numerous European editors, portraying him as a zealous convert to Christianity and, at times, racist writer overshadowed his contributions to the insightful knowledge of the Afro-Mediterranean world. The literal erasure of his voice and the superimposition of a Europe seeking hegemony over the Mediterranean constructed a "voice out of the 'Orient' and the Occident at the same time".[24]

The second historical lens through which the African continent has been viewed has produced the opposite of the image of the victim; it romanticizes Africans as "noble" members of the ancient world. This type of narrative is seen in Homer's portrayal of the Ethiopians, who sent their king, Memnon, to fight for Troy, a battle portrayed as a shared event of the Afro-Mediterranean world.[25] From Greek mythology, we also have the "stellified", mythologized African queen Cassiopeia, who was banished to the skies for flaunting her beauty. Her daughter Andromeda was rescued by none other than Zeus's son Perseus. The starry narratives of a vain queen, of a valiant king fighting against the Hellenes and of a damsel in distress constitute the imaginative narrative of Herodotus's "blameless Ethiopians". Again, what these seductive narratives do not provide is a sense of the history behind these fictional representations, of what triggered the myriad African crossings to the opposite shores, of the range of activities of these earliest African diasporic communities.

MONOTHEISTIC EMPIRES AND THE PEJORATION OF THE AFRICAN

At the other end of the spectrum is the portrayal of the African as a cultural outsider in an Afro-Mediterranean world that was dominated by the ideologies of competing monotheist empires. Although the official discourse of both Christianity and Islam claimed that all adherents were equal in the eyes of the deity they venerated, the architects of the religious empires relegated the polytheist Africans to the lower rungs of Christendom and Islam. Monotheistic religions are by nature exclusionary but they also are rigidly hierarchical with a strong penchant for intolerance. The exclusion and pejoration of people of African ancestry accompanied the expansion of monotheism.

This pejoration of the black African persisted even after their conversion to these monotheist religions, mainly due to Africans' retentions of poly-theistic elements in their worship. As we examine the various dimensions of African diasporas in the Mediterranean (and beyond), it becomes clear that it is important to identify the beginning of the earliest erasures of the African *qua* African as a people with a history, a specific birthplace/nation, kinship, economic and political networks. The end of polytheism and the rise of monotheist theocracies – a Christian Rome in the fourth century and an Islamic caliphate in the eighth century – demarcate a historical time domi-nated by tales of the "converting" of local African nobles and the conquering and subjugation of the "infidel" savages. An examination of the politics, economies and "belief systems" behind the transformation from polytheism to monotheism may yield deeper insights into the roots of the homogenizing tendencies of monotheistic empires.

Whereas polytheist Rome had welcomed the many deities of its conquered peoples, the latter's refusal to submit to a single deity would later become interpreted as a sign of a dehumanized entity; this was then used as justifi-cation for turning polytheists into a servile caste on the margins of official religions. The wars of conquest and coerced conversions by monotheistic empires, beginning with Constantine's Roman Empire in the fourth cen-tury followed by the rise of Islamic empires in the eighth century, were accompanied by a gradual demonization of the characteristics which had been celebrated as valiant, beautiful and proud in the pre-Christian and pre-Islamic eras. The "noble" African of antiquity thus became gradually reconstructed as the "converted" representative assimilated into the cultural milieu of the new empires and their religious officials.

In spite of millennial efforts by modern and pre-modern official religions, African polytheism survived and provided populations with alternatives to the unforgiving and imperialistic evangelism of medieval conquerors and modern colonizers. The Iberian Inquisition and its Puritan counterpart in the United States victimized those members of the African diaspora who were deemed infidel *conversos*.²⁶ In the case of the Portuguese Empire, the curious career of Domingos Álvares illustrates the complex negotiations of a converted African who was able, in spite of the obstacles, to success-fully combine elements of his new faith with ancestral practices and thereby gain a reputation as an effective healer in his Iberian exile.²⁷ In the Afro-Mediterranean lands of Islam and the Ottoman Empire, practitioners of the *zar* and *tambour* cults were subaltern masters in the art of healing minds.²⁸ The fusion of divinities from ancestral sites with those of the new homelands has been recognized and yes, at times, vilified as ignorant superstition, but its survival and florescence, from Arabia to Anatolia to Argentina, bear tes-timony to the ways in which the ancient pluralism failed to be eradicated by the efforts of the hegemonic monotheistic empires. Those members of the African diaspora who survived various forms of inquisitional procedures submerged their African practices beneath the rituals mandated by the newer official religions, thereby safely retaining the vivacity of polytheistic plural-ism which later became legitimized as Africans' healing arts.

Almost never directly referred to as *conversos* by Christian Europeans, the majority of Africans occupied that liminal space between *familiares* and co-religionists who, during, the Crusades fought on all sides as Christians and Muslims, but in the Age of Exploration, when the European slave trade prospered, receded into the margins of their adopted societies, differentiated by the degree and shades of their blackness. The fragmented narratives of WahishI – a late convert to Islam – provide insights into individuals who fought on both sides of the religious wars in Arabia; he later became demon-ized as a lover of good wine and clothes.²⁹

The African practices that survived were deemed vestiges of barbarity, yet the European settlers in the Americas and Asia seemed unable to survive in the lands they colonized without them. Estebanico in the Spanish New Spain had many counterparts in Andalusia and Anatolia where the creativity and daring of the Africans assured not only their individual survival but attested to their unacknowledged success in the conquest and settlement of their new homelands.³⁰ Unfortunately, however, rather than being admired, they garnered the title of "trickster", which hegemonic elites in the west and east used to label such individuals as Domingos Álvares and Leo Africanus.³¹

Being aware of the ways in which African diasporas were rendered invisible and their voices muted should be viewed as a critically important first step in identifying the making of new Africanized polities from Havana to Hyderabad.[32]

The lands of the Indian Ocean, where polytheism remained the official religion and the power of Hinduism's panoply of gods endured, provided the only other region which accommodated the multiple and diverse crossings of African diasporic groups from late antiquity, the medieval period and early modernity. The African diasporic crossings of the Red Sea and the Indian Ocean demonstrate a versatile, lived history of noble as well as servile roles for Africans whose warriors and viziers came to be known as *Habshi Amarat* (African Nobles) and *Sidi* (both as an honorific title and indicator of African origin).[33] Africa's women, too, emerged as queens, *Um-al-Walid* (mothers of noble children), and as captivating consorts. Even as converts to Islam, the *Habshis* and *Sidis*, when empowered, recruited soldiers and diplomats from the African continent, thereby maintaining cultural connections to their communities of origin. In the lands of the Red Sea and the Indian Ocean, African converts to Islam continued to nurture, disseminate and embed into host communities a variety of practices and rituals from African polytheism. The African diasporas in both the East and the West left a richly textured precolonial African legacy, although this has been obscured by the homogenizing grip of Christian and Islamic empires.

This shared legacy, which we can now attribute to the dispersal of African peoples at different times and to different destinations, is manifested in the culinary and healing arts, music, dance, martial skills and the ritual preservation and rhythmic retelling of the powers of African gods practised. Although some members of the African diasporas converted to Islam, many more also conjoined their polytheistic African deities/spirits/ancestral forms of worship with the new ones they encountered in their host societies. The result was a melding of the two cultures.

MOTHERS, MEDIUMS AND MAVERICKS OF THE OLD AND NEW WORLDS: WOMEN OF THE AFRICAN DIASPORAS

Africa's women also played a role in bridging the different cultural and economic worlds. Both in antiquity and early modernity they served as economic brokers, as demonstrated by the emergence of the *signare* (women traders) in Senegambia, but their role as cultural mediums and as founts of preserved knowledge has been limited to an acknowledgement their role as healers and *griots* in the diaspora.[34] Their multidimensional roles as political and socio-economic actors were reduced to exotic symbols popularized by colonial anthropology and distorted by nineteenth century pseudoscientific theories of race.[35] Many centuries of shared history, economic activities and coexistence vanished in a world divided between the "occident" and the "orient", between "whites" and "blacks", "colonizers" and "colonized" – a world eventually demarcated by an indelible colour line that has survived into the new millennium.

There are many more narratives to unearth of these "mothers" of new polities of hyphenated/blended societies. The complex sociopolitical and economic negotiations that accompanied the process of creolization should be understood as key elements in the formation of a braided history with different strands shaping multiple new entities that – until now – have been bracketed into a melanin-based, ill-defined category of "blackness". The highlighting of a perceived essential characteristic, the darker hues of some of Africa's inhabitants, has cast shadows on the roots as well as routes undertaken by this continent's diasporas. The role of Africa's women as agents of sociopolitical and economic transformation, beyond their functions as vessels of reproduction, has yet to be examined.

The complexity of new intercommunal, interregional and interfaith relationships, moreover, has yet to be captured. The images that we have of Africa's diasporic women remain limited to their gender-based roles or to caricatures highlighting colourfully attired "dusky damsels" in poses that are taken out of cultural contexts and do not cohere with their status or the complex politics of polygamous relations.[36] For example, in the western Mediterranean, dominated by monogamy and Christianity, the discourse on Alessandro de Medici's "moorishness" and disputed parentage overshadowed any meaningful inquiry into the conditions that made such unions possible or into the existence of African diasporic communities in Urbino, Italy, in 1511.[37] Was his mother a "black African" as asserted by one author? Or was she an "eastern" woman as argued by a Fascist author in 1939 seeking to "lighten" the racial "stain" that may have been unacceptable for Mussolini and his ideologues struggling to maintain control over *Africa Orientale Italiana* two years before its collapse in 1941?[38]

In contrast, in the Mediterranean, from the eighth century until the age of exploration, we see the emergence of a nomenclature which erased the differences of ethnic and linguistic markers of the different African communities and grouped them as *o povo negro* or, literally, black people. This ill-defined category of blackness camouflages the specificity of the many different African diasporas – free and unfree – that crossed and recrossed the Mediterranean from antiquity until the abolition of slavery.

BEYOND NARRATIVES OF BONDAGE AND SURVIVAL

So how can we readjust our lenses to reconfigure our knowledge? The first step would be to reconceptualize the Mediterranean as a shared space (much like the lands of the Red Sea and the Caribbean) through which peoples of Africa moved northwards, eastwards and westwards. In short, it was a corridor leading to contiguous and more distant destinations. The second step would be to reflect on the transformation of power relations, social relations and identity formation of African polytheist societies as they encountered monotheistic empires and belief systems. A sustained inquiry into the contributions of women to the reconstitution of disparate Afro-Mediterranean communities will render numerous diasporic women visible rather than imprison them in their marginal roles as vendors of "love filters" and "sorceresses".[39]

The erasure of the shared histories of Africans – continental and diasporic – in the era of theocratic empires may appear innocuous at first glance but a sustained inquiry of their legacies indicate a deliberate fracturing of polytheist pluralism by monotheistic puritans. I argue that it is the combined power of monotheistic empires that succeeded in insidiously relegating the African to a foggy past where the "noble" *Ethiop* – savage or civilized, barbarian or cosmopolitan – could walk back to a mythic era and disappear from our memories, leaving us with only the image of a dehumanized servile and/or enslaved victim. Add to this the notion that diasporic Africans underwent "social death" and that illustrates the lachrymose narrative and blocks the multiple alternative narratives – grounded in the lived experience – of those who survived bondage, built new polities and emerged with new identities. Retracing the steps of those who crossed from the African shores of the Mediterranean, the Red Sea and the Indian Ocean requires that we go beyond transatlantic-based conventional periodization of the formation of the African diasporas and include the formation of other diasporas such as those from the Indian subcontinent present in Africa, Arabia and island communities such as the Comoros, Fiji and Mauritius.

In the Arabian lands of the Red Sea and the eastern Mediterranean, diasporic communities are linked to a specific place of origin and/or of embarkation: *Kushite* and *Habashi* (referring to the Horn of Africa), *Zanj* (East Africa) and *Nubian* (the borderlands of the Egypt and the Sudan). Although differentiated from the others equally unfortunate to lose their freedom in the many wars of late antiquity, the rise of Islam, the Crusades and territorial wars of early modernity, the failure of this system lies in its closing of the doors to further interrogation of the historical process by which different inhabitants of the continent voyaged so far from their birthplace resulting in the Africanization of various regions of the globe.

On the Indian subcontinent, it is interesting to note that the *Habshi Amarat* and *Sidi* remain anchored in the public memory as warriors, Sufi poets, kingmakers and ocean voyagers overseeing the Mughal and Janjira fleets.[40] In the Caribbean, Brazil and Argentina, African diaspora communities differentiated themselves as *Guinea, Congo, Angola* and *Mozambique,* thus linking their communities to a specific geographic space, whether real or imagined, on the African continent.[41] In Buenos Aires, the Afro-Argentines – much like the *Habshi/Sidi* elite of India – had proved themselves powerful allies to competing political elites, leading to the acknowledgement of their role as co-nationals and defenders of the rulers of the land.[42] In the Arabian Peninsula sultans, princes and presidents freely acknowledge African parentage. Although sizeable communities of people of African descent exist in these countries they are as much divided by class as by their inclusion or exclusion in the political arena.

The Caribbean is the only region which witnessed the transformation of free and enslaved persons of African heritage into majority citizens or politically significant minorities in the modern nations.[43] These island-states, inhabited by "new people" made up of indigenous communities, European settlers and African co-settlers, remain uncelebrated as icons of the resilience, creativity and rebirth of the thousands of Africans who had arrived in bondage. The Caribbean's creolized peoples epitomize new diasporic communities that reconstructed social, economic and political links with the ancestral homeland. Leading by example, the pan-Africanists of the Caribbean – from the Rastafarians to Garvey – rallied their neighbours in the United States of America with calls to the Sons of Sheba to defend Ethiopia's Emperor Haile Selassie from fascist onslaught, with some even decrying the servitude of the population to the monarchy.[44] The complexity of the cosmopolitanism of Africa's many diasporas has been ignored for too long and the time has come for all of us to look beyond the narrow twin trajectories of slavery and colonialism.

The voluntary and involuntary migrations of Africans across the Mediterrannean, the Red Sea and Indian Ocean region preceded the Middle Passage. These movements of African peoples led to the emergence of Afro-Arab and Afro-Asian communities that survived as Africanized enclaves in the far-flung outposts of the Ottoman Empire. At present, the legacies of these earlier crossings into the lands of the Red Sea and Mediterranean are reflected in the presence of communities of African descent in modern Iran, Iraq, Kuwait, Oman and Turkey, to name a few. Some found fame and notoriety, others were assimilated into royalty and many more attached to existing hierarchic local kinship networks. The rise and fall of kingdoms and dynasties shaped the contemporary status of these entities created from the blending of ethnicities, cultures and political systems. Adjusting our lenses to take on the *"longue duree"* of the history of Africa's multiple diasporas, acknowledging the horrors of slavery and the different roles of transplanted Africans in their new homelands, will enable us to understand that out of the many voluntary and involuntary voyages there have emerged new entities blending more identities than the one afforded by the prefix "African" or "Afro" to their geographic areas of settlement. The hyphenated identifiers, that is, Afro-American, Afro-Arab, Afro-Caribbean, Afro-Iberian, African-Indian, Afro-Latin, Afro-Mediterranean and the like, demonstrate the presence of cosmopolitan communities of African heritage in the twenty-first century.

Diasporic crossings created new polities which cross-fertilized human genes, cultural goods and technological knowledge to create dynamic, complex multicultural polities which until now have been defined predominantly by their survival within a political economy of bondage.[45] A major difficulty in the task of excavating the layered histories of the African diaspora is that they have, throughout the ages, been "written over" by imperial narratives. However, traces of their journeys by sea and by land can be found in oral and written stories of conquerors and the conquered as well as those unfortunate enough to be caught in-between. At times the evidence is in the cultural and biological fusion between the transplanted communities of Africans whose pathways to their new abodes were preceded by long years of residences in the Ottoman controlled areas or on the Iberian Peninsula. Bearing names such as Abderahman (Andalusia); Jalal-ud din Yakut, Malik Ambar (India); Juan Garrido (Mexico); Juan Garcia and Miguel Ruiz (Peru), these descendants of Africans – inhabiting different geographic spaces and epochs – demonstrate that not all Africans left their homelands in chains or ended their exiled lives in bondage. Some, like Garrido in the Americas represented a co-settler and a conquistador while Malik Ambar went from being a slave to a warrior and kingmaker in India. Therefore, our exploration of the multiple African diasporas should not only focus on their disempowerment but also identify how they negotiated positions of power as they established communities outside their ancestral homelands.

Under what conditions did they become integrated into their new societies? As new comers into lands where invading empires needed soldiers as well as labourers, we may find that what bound the "masters" to their "dependents" was not only ownership and bondage, but survival. Thus, conceptualizing the African diaspora as co-settlers and co-defenders of invading empires, Arabian, Iberian or Mughal, points to a more complex relationship than those imprinted in public memory in the narratives of the *Casa Senzala* or the *Arabian Nights*, for example. Even the celebratory narratives of the *quilombos* and *cimarrones* (and their counterparts in India) provide us the opportunity to further examine the reinvention of identities.[46] Clearly, the establishment of new communities of rebel outposts, whether in India, Jamaica, Brazil, Mexico or Venezuela, and their survival as discrete communities of resistance challenges the often-repeated epitaph of enslaved people as suffering a sort of "social death".[47] The people of the African diaspora were reborn in freedom and adversity; they demonstrated autonomy, leadership, valour as well as pragmatism. They successfully negotiated conditions that ensured their survival and prosperity, forged social and commercial alliances with indigenous communities and established military slave-holding elites.[48] In the process, they created hybrid societies that united different ethnic and linguistic groups as "black" diasporas from Africa – free and bonded – creating new identities and claims to territory nurtured by their blood, sweat and tears.

Much like the complex process needed for the restoration of ancient paintings, this exploration of African diasporas demonstrates a willingness to extrapolate from the faint outlines of a distant history and to trace the many routes travelled by transplanted communities originating from the African continent. The geographical proximity of the Mediterranean to the African continent and the ancient trade routes and networks that existed between them make the Mediterranean the most logical site for exploring the legacies of the earliest diasporic movements from the African continent. Using this as a starting point would allow us to trace the continuous and multiple eastward crossings of Africans into Arabia and the Indian Ocean which significantly shaped regional and international relations.

Both the Mediterranean and the Red Sea constitute transit corridors. The former enabled crossings into the Caribbean while the latter served as the bridge to the Indian Ocean region. In this exploration of westward African crossings across the Mediterranean and the Iberian-Atlantic and eastward crossings across the Red Sea and the Indian Ocean region, one finds similar trajectories across time and space. Examples of transplanted diasporic communities such as the *Habshi* of the Deccan and the phenomenal *El Cobre* community in Cuba, reflecting the emergence of royal slaves and negotiated exercises of autonomy have yet to be fully appreciated and analysed.[49] Both these new polities were co-settlers and builders of new empires in distant lands.

Deep wounds, forever distorting historical experience and the subsequent referents of identity, were inflicted on those Africans who were forced to become part of the involuntary emigrations as enslaved human beings. The abhorrent trade in human beings in modern times was an activity shared by many civilizations throughout history, and was magnified by the rise of capitalism and the insatiable demands for labour in the European colonies in the New World. Reasserting the humanity of these Africans has been a priority of scholars in the nineteenth and twentieth centuries studying the origins, development and demise of slavery as an economic and sociopolitical underpinning of the industrial era.[50] What we have yet to systematically construct is a comparative history of the many diasporas which, in the twenty-first century, have come to be known as Afro-communities or peoples of African descent. We have yet to systematically identify how the histories of creolized communities from the Mediterranean, Red Sea, Indian Ocean and Iberian Peninsula unfolded, all of which produced startling similarities and differences in such disparate places like Iraq, Istanbul, Jamaica and Trinidad.

NOTES

1.   The geography of these relations can be followed in William J. Berstein, *A Splendid Exchange: How Trade Shaped the World* (New York: Atlantic Monthly, 2008); Fernand Braudel, *The Mediterranean and the Mediterranean World in the Age of Philip II*, 2 vols. (1949; repr., Berkeley: University of California Press, 1966); Fernand Braudel, *Capitalism and Material Life, 1400–1800* (Waukegan, IL: Fontana, 1974).

2.   John Keay, *The Spice Route: A History* (Berkeley: University of California Press, 2006).

3.   For evidence of the African presence in the Mediterranean world, see Jacqueline Andall and Derek Duncan, eds., *Italian Colonialism: Legacy and Memory* (Oxford and Bern: Peter Lang, 2005).

4.   See Stacy Schiff, *Cleopatra: A Life* (New York: Little, Brown and Company, 2010), 86–87.

5.   *Moriscos* were Muslims who converted to Christianity rather than obey the various expulsion orders of the Catholic monarchs of Iberia. *Marranos* were Jews who pretended to be converts to Christianity but were suspected of secretly adhering to their religious faith.

6.   See Maria Rosa Menocal, *The Ornament of the World: How Muslims, Jews and Christians Created a Culture of Tolerance in Medieval Spain* (Boston: Little, Brown, 2002). See also Edward Kritzler, *Jewish Pirates of the Caribbean* (New York: Anchor, 2008).

7.   David Levering Lewis, *God's Crucible: Islam and the Making of Europe, 570–1215* (New York: W.W. Norton, 2008).

8.   A wonderful antidote to extant works suffering from disciplinary restrictions and myopia is the exceptional volume by T.F. Earle and K.J.P. Lowe, eds., *Black Africans in Renaissance Europe* (Cambridge: Cambridge University Press, 2005).

9.   Robert C. Davis, *Christian Slaves, Muslim Masters: White Slavery in the Mediterranean, the Barbary Coast, and Italy, 1500–1800* (New York: Palgrave Macmillan, 2003).

10.   See, for example, the book of the excellent exhibition in the Walters Art Museum, Baltimore: Joaneath Spicer, ed., *Revealing the African Presence in Renaissance Europe* (Baltimore: The Walters Art Museum, 2012).

11.   David Bindman and Henry Louis Gates Jr, eds., *The Image of the Black in Western Art*, vols. 1–5 (Cambridge, MA: Belknap Press of Harvard University Press, 2010).

12.   Geraldine Brooks, *People of the Book: A Novel* (New York: Penguin, 2008); Juan Bonilla, *The Nubian Prince: A Novel*, translated by Esther Allen (New York: Metropolitan, 2006); James McBride, *Miracle at St. Anna: A Novel of the Buffalo Soldiers of World War I* (New York: Riverhead, 2002).

13.   A narrow focus on victimhood can camouflage relations of power, conquest and survival, and can produce distorted knowledge unless historians take up the task of widening restrictive parameters. For an excellent example of scholarship that seeks to correct such "lachrymose" narratives, see Jonathan Schorsch, *Jews and Blacks in the Early Modern World* (Cambridge: Cambridge University Press, 2004), 4.

14.   Kristian Davies, *The Orientalists: Western Artists in Arabia, The Sahara, Persia and India* (New York: LAYNFAROH, 2005); Kenneth X. Robbins and John McLeod, *Habshi Amarat: African Elites in India* (Ahmedabad, India: Mapin, 2006); Cynthia Jacobs Carter, *Africana Woman: Her Story Through Time* (Washington, DC: National Geographic, 1996).

15.   *Secret Ballot: A Human Comedy* by Babak Payami, 2001. Award-winning film, best director, Venice Film Festival.

16.   BBC/HBO Series, *ROME*, Seasons 1 and 2 (2005–6).

17.   Paul H.D. Kaplan, "Italy, 1490–1700", in *The Image of the Black in Western Art. From the Age of Discovery to the Age of Abolition: Artists of the Renaissance and Baroque*, ed. David Bindman and Henry Louis Gates (Cambridge, MA: Belknap

Press of Harvard University Press, 2010), 3:183. The House of Medici flourished between the fourteenth and the eighteenth centuries.

18.   St Maurice, born about 250 CE in Thebes was martyred in Switzerland. He later became a patron saint of the North German Hanseatic League of merchant traders.

19.   Alden T. Vaughan and Virginia Mason Vaughan, "Before Othello: Elizabethan Representations of Sub-Saharan Africans", *William and Mary Quarterly* 54, no. 1 (January 1997): 29.

20.   Emily C. Bartels, "Othello and Africa: Postcolonialism Reconsidered", *William and Mary Quarterly* 54, no. 1 (January 1997): 61.

21.   Ibid., 61.

22.   Natalie Zemon Davis, *Trickster Travels: A Sixteenth Century Muslim between Worlds* (New York: Hill and Wang, 2006).

23.   Davis, *Trickster Travels*, 256–57. The only source which claims that Yuhanna al-Asad successfully eluded captivity is the acclaimed fictional account by Amin Malouf; see Amin Malouf, *Leo the African*, translated by Peter Sluglett (London: Abacus, 1994), 356–60.

24.   Christopher L. Miller, *Blank Darkness: Africanist Discourse in French Literature* (Chicago: University of Chicago Press, 1985), 13.

25.   See Homer's *Odyssey* and Ovid's (43 BCE–17 CE) *Milton Pensieroso*. Benjamin Isaac, *The Invention of Racism in Classical Antiquity* (Princeton and Oxford: Princeton University Press, 2004).

26.   J.H. Elliott, *Empires of the Atlantic World: Britain and Spain in America, 1492–1830* (New Haven: Yale University Press, 2006), 191–214; Henry Kamen, *The Spanish Inquisition: A Historical Revision* (New Haven: Yale University Press, 1998); Henry Kamen, *Empire: How Spain Became a World Power, 1492–1763* (New York: Harper Collins, 2003), 356–57.

27.   James H. Sweet, *Domingos Álvares, African Healing, and the Intellectual History of the Atlantic World* (Chapel Hill: University of North Carolina Press, 2011).

28.   Behnaz A. Mirzai, Ismael M. Montana and Paul E. Lovejoy, eds., *Slavery, Islam and Diaspora* (Trenton, NJ: Africa World Press, 2009). See also I.M. Lewis, *Ecstatic Religions: An Anthropological Study of Spirit Possession and Shamanism* (Hammondsworth: Penguin, 1971).

29.   Daniel Pipes, *Slave Soldiers and Islam: The Genesis of a Military System* (New Haven: Yale University Press, 1981). See also Bernard Lewis, *Race and Slavery in the Middle East: An Historical Enquiry* (New York: Oxford University Press, 1990).

30.   For free Hispanized Africans in the New World at the time of the Spanish conquest, see Franklin W. Knight, "Slavery in the Americas", in *A Companion*

to *Latin American History*, ed. Thomas H. Holloway (Malden, MA: Blackwell, 2008), 146–61, especially 148.

31. Davis, *Trickster Travels*.

32. Christopher Leslie Brown and Philip D. Morgan, eds., *Arming Slaves: From Classical Times to the Modern Age* (New Haven: Yale University Press, 2006). The 1560 enforcement of the Inquisition in Portuguese India (mainly Goa), Afro-Indian converts' musical performances and funerary practices were punished harshly leading to an out-migration of Afro-Indian communities to the forested hinterlands of Karnataka Africa-based practices flourish to date. For details see Pashington Obeng, *Shaping Membership, Defining Nation: The Cultural Politics of African Indians in South Asia* (Lanham, MD: Lexington, 2007), 21.

33. Mahmood Mamdani, "The Sidi: An Introduction", in *A Certain Grace: The Sidi – Indians of African Descent*, by Ketaki Sheth (New Delhi: Photolink, 2013), 8–15.

34. George E. Brooks, "The *Signares* of Saint-Louis and *Goree*: Women Entrepreneurs in Eighteenth Century Senegal", in *Women in Africa: Studies in Social and Economic Change*, ed. Nancy J. Hafkin and Edna G. Bay (Stanford: Stanford University Press, 1976), 18–44.

35. Robert J.C. Young, *Colonial Desire: Hybridity in Theory, Culture and Race* (New York: Routledge, 1995). See also, Ronald Hyam, *Empire and Sexuality: The British Experience* (Manchester: Manchester University Press, 1991).

36. Ruth Iyob, "*Madamismo* and Beyond: The Construction of Eritrean Women", in *Italian Colonialism*, ed. Mia Fuller and Ruth Ben-Ghiat (New York: Palgrave, 2005), 236–38.

37. John Brackett. "Race and Rulership: Alessandro de Medici, First Medici Duke of Florence, 1529–1537", in *Black Africans in Renaissance Europe*, ed. T.F. Earle and K.J.P. Lowe (Cambridge: Cambridge University Press, 2005), 303–4.

38. Ibid., 305–6.

39. G.P. Makris argues that women healers also have additional roles as guardians of historical knowledge and as mentors of new generations of transplanted Africans. See G.P. Makris, *Changing Masters: Spirit Possession and Identity-Construction among Slave Descendants and Other Subordinates in the Sudan* (Evanston, IL: Northwestern University Press, 2000), 259–60

40. R.R.S. Hauhan, *Africans in India: From Slavery to Royalty* (New Delhi: Asian Publication Services, 1995), 71–103.

41. George R. Andrews, *The Afro-Argentines of Buenos Aires, 1800–1900* (Madison: University of Wisconsin Press, 1980), 142–48.

42. Ibid., 149. An editor of a liberal newspaper published in 1858 went as far as to

object to the establishment of the first black newspaper, *La Raza Africana*, and rebuked its founders by asking, "Why call yourselves Africans . . . when you are really Argentines?"

43. Franklin W. Knight, The *Caribbean: The Genesis of a Fragmented Nationalism*, 3rd ed. (New York: Oxford University Press, 2012); B.W. Higman, *A Concise History of the Caribbean* (New York: Cambridge University Press, 2011); Stephan Palmié and Francisco Scarano, eds., *The Caribbean: A History of the Region and its Peoples* (Chicago: University of Chicago Press, 2011).

44. William R. Scott. *The Sons of Sheba's Race: African-Americans and the Italo-Ethiopian War, 1935–1941* (Bloomington: Indiana University Press, 1993).

45. Judith A. Carney and Richard Nicholas Rosomoff, *In the Shadow of Slavery: Africa's Botanical Legacy in the Atlantic World* (Berkeley: University of California Press, 2009), 177–86.

46. Franklin W. Knight, ed., *General History of the Caribbean*, vol. 3: *The Slave Societies of the Caribbean* (London: UNESCO/Macmillan, 1997), 169–93; Gabino la Rosa Corzo, *Runaway Slave Settlements in Cuba: Resistance and Repression*, translated by Mary Todd (Chapel Hill: University of North Carolina Press, 1988); Jane Landers, *Black Society in Spanish Florida* (Urbana: University of Illinois Press, 1999).

47. Orlando Patterson, *Slavery and Social Death: A Comparative Study* (Cambridge, MA: Harvard University Press, 1982).

48. Helene Basu, "Slave, Soldier, Trader, Fakir: Fragments of African Histories in Gujarat", in *The African Diaspora in the Indian Ocean*, ed. Shihan de Silva Jayasuriya and Richard Pankhurst (Trenton, NJ: Red Sea, 2001), 233–41. See also A. Lodhi, "African Settlements in India", *Nordic Journal of African Studies* 1, no. 1 (2008): 83–87.

49. On *El Cobre*, see Olga Portuondo Zuñiga, *La Virgen de la Caridad de El Cobre: símbolo de cubanía* (Santiago de Cuba: Editorial Oriente, 1995); María Elena Díaz, *The Virgin, the King and the Royal Slaves of El Cobre: Negotiating Freedom in Colonial Cuba, 1670–1780* (Stanford: Stanford University Press, 2000).

50. W.E.B. Du Bois, *The Souls of Black Folk* (New York: Barnes and Noble Classics, 1903).

CHAPTER 2

DIASPORA AND EMPIRE
The Case of the Armenians in Pre-Revolutionary Russia

TAMARA GANJALYAN

THE IMPACT OF THE ARMENIAN DIASPORA on the imperial policy of the
Russian empire between the late seventeenth and the nineteenth centuries
provides some very interesting insights into the role of diasporas in empire
building.[1] The theoretical literature on diasporas, especially those which refer
to diaspora communities as "middlemen minorities" or "mobile diasporas" or
"trade diasporas" all describe the changing situation of the Armenian diasporic historical experience in pre-revolutionary Russia.[2] Most studies show
that ethnic and/or religious minorities manifested characteristic features and
functions that distinguished them from the surrounding majority population
of the host country as well as from their co-nationals in their own "historic
homeland". Given the conditions of a traditional or pre-modern, feudal and
multi-ethnic society, such as the Russian empire used to be until well into
the nineteenth century, observers have made seven observations about those
middlemen minorities.

The first observation was that of a strong inner group cohesion and collective identity, often related to the belief of being a "chosen people" thus
leading to self-segregating behaviour (for example endogamy). The second
was a long history of intercultural contacts as well as acquired knowledge
and skills which, among other features, were especially advantageous in the
fields of long distance trade and diplomacy. The third was an awareness of
a real or imagined place of origin, accompanied by intentions which did not

encourage permanent settlement.[3] The fourth was a high degree of commercial success, although this did not correlate necessarily to political power. The fifth observation was the immediate roles of the diasporic communities as a link between the nobility and peasantry of the host society and between producers and consumers in urban and rural settings. The sixth observation was that such diasporic communities occupied economic niches not available to the majority population. The final observation was the acknowledgment of diasporic communities' role in the modernization process of the host country's economy and society.[4]

The ruling elite of the host society and the Armenian diasporic communities developed a kind of mutually beneficial exchange relationship. Initially the motives and interests of both sides were compatible although not necessarily congruent. As the majority population modernized and acquired the features and skills of the minority it entered into competition with the diasporic communities; more often than not, the latter, lost their privileged positions as a result.

DIASPORA IN EMPIRE

In his 1972 article, "The Alien as a Servant of Power", Lewis Coser refers to such middlemen minorities in pre-modern societies as "ideal servants of power".[5] But exactly what significance did that form of reciprocal exchange relationship have for the politics of multi-ethnic imperial societies such as the Russian empire? In the relationship between imperial centres and peripheries, middlemen minorities acted as intermediaries.[6] Several historians have described how such minorities helped to enforce and to stabilize a central political leadership's autocratic rule against feudal, bureaucratic or other competing holders of power and how they also helped to promote the imperial sovereignty of a centre over the mass of the population, especially on the peripheries of a multi-ethnic and expansive empire.

There, in the border regions of pre-national empires, where imperial rule was not yet consolidated, members of native elites as well as diasporic groups, whose well-being was dependent on the goodwill of the imperial sovereign, acted as intercultural and interethnic mediators. By connecting the central elite with the indigenous population, the middlemen minorities acted as brokers in the vertical structure of imperial relationships.[7] These cultural brokers – interpreters, missionaries, colonial administrators or commercial intermediaries – contributed to the expansion and stabilization of the imperial centre's power and thereby facilitated the colonization and/or integration of newly acquired lands.[8] In his article on the "grand strategy" of the Russian empire, John LeDonne identified as one of the basic principles of this strategy the establishment of a collection of client groups "through which imperial desires could be translated into reality without the use of force".[9] As "fifth columns" of the imperial centre, these client groups were meant "to create favorable conditions for the projection of maximum power by a highly mobile army concentrated in the Muscovite core. Baltic Germans, Lithuanians, Moldavians, Georgians, etc., facilitated the administration of empire without requiring the employment of Russians and prepared the way for Russian expansion into the frontier."[10]

The reciprocal exchange relationship between the central elite and the middlemen minorities in the case of the Russian empire led to a situation in which "the real beneficiaries of the Tsarist empire [were] peripheral groups and national minorities, who acquired positions in the imperial order, which they would otherwise never have attained".[11] Border regions of multi-ethnic empires were spaces of overlapping and competing territorial claims as well as zones of transfer and transition – of exchanging people, goods and ideas and, finally, zones of hybridization of different lifestyles.[12] Porous imperial borders facilitated the diffusion of the empire's cultural influence on neighbouring societies.[13] The imperial frontier in particular was not a static border line, but a dynamic space designed to be expanded, consolidated and integrated into the empire. In order to secure this space, empires cooperated with native elites such as the semi-nomadic Cossacks to defend the steppe borders.[14] When the empire lacked the requisite resources, foreign specialists and technologies were imported in order to help them compete in the international arena. In the time of Peter I the Great Baltic Germans were invited to modernize the empire's economy and society and impose a programme of reform from above.

Finally, middlemen minorities also played an important role in the empire's foreign relations. Their trade networks had economic significance, for example, in the field of promoting and profiting from proto-globalizing processes.[15] By importing new military technology or by frequenting strategically important trade routes, the diasporas' economic activities also gained political and military weight. The host society of these diaspora traders could use this to their advantage to improve international relations and the geostrategic, military and imperial position of the country.[16]

The international constellation shaped the relationship between the imperial elites and the diasporic minorities. This explains why the official policy of the host society towards the diasporic minorities was in part influenced by the kind, extent and importance of the latter's international contacts.[17] Pre-modern, multi-ethnic empires were, to a large extent, never insulated from external circumstances, an observation made by John A. Armstrong when he wrote "the numerous treatments which depict mobilized diasporas exclusively as victims of intra-systemic forces ignore the crucial effects of international politics upon the exchange relation between diaspora and dominant ethnic elite".[18] The international contacts of the diaspora often were eventually a major cause for the growing mistrust of the central elite in regards to the minority's loyalty.[19] This kind of mistrust may in the long run outweigh the "usefulness" of the middlemen minority as intercultural or international brokers, but it may also lead to a self-fulfilling prophecy whereby the minority reacts to that mistrust of the elite by alienating themselves from the host society. Then, the once reciprocal exchange relationship may end in an "ascending spiral of mutual hostility [which] rapidly erodes the position of the mobilized diaspora".[20] This interplay between the Armenian diaspora and pre-revolutionary Russia illustrates its role in the empire's oriental trade in the seventeenth and eighteenth centuries and in its colonization process of the eighteenth and nineteenth centuries.

ARMENIAN MERCHANTS AND RUSSIAN ORIENTAL TRADE

Armenian merchants were reported to have been active in the area of the later Russian empire since medieval times. Nevertheless, the heyday of Armenian commercial activity in Russia occurred between the late seventeenth century and the middle of the eighteenth century. Armenian merchants, the majority of whom came from the Armenian suburb of Isfahan, New Julfa (Norǰowła), dominated the transit trade in Persian raw silk and other oriental commodities along the Volga trade route to the seaports of the White and Baltic Seas, from where these goods were shipped to northern and western Europe, particularly to Amsterdam.

The monopoly of the Armenian oriental traders in Russia was secured by legal contracts between Tsar Aleksey and the merchants of New Julfa between the years 1667 and 1673. These contracts granted Armenian merchants the monopoly of the transit trade in Persian raw silk through Russia as well as a number of other privileges, which stood in direct opposition to the New Statute on Trade (*Novotorgovyj Ustav*), which was also issued in 1667 and which considerably constrained the activity of European merchants in Russia.[21] The legislative authority as well as the Armenian representatives of the Julfans stressed that the state's acquisition of taxes and customs duties, which were to be expected from that trade, was the motive behind the privileging of the Julfan merchants: "By means of the transit of the silk and other goods, Your subjects of every rank will benefit, and the foreigners [that is, Europeans], who now go by ship to Turkey in order to buy this silk and other goods [there] . . . will go to Arkhangelsk and they will bring great revenues from customs duties for the treasury . . . May this lucrative trade be in Your . . . Russian Empire and not in Turkey."[22] As a condition of their transit privilege, the Armenians were obliged to transport the entire Persian raw silk export exclusively via Russia and to abandon their old trade routes through Turkey and across the Mediterranean Sea. As a consequence, the tsarist empire would become a platform for the international silk trade. But at no time did the Armenian traders follow this treaty obligation which led to protest by the Moscow merchants, who, in their petitions, complained that not only did the Russian merchants suffer economic losses, but so also did the Russian treasury.[23]

Still, the tsars usually appeared as the defenders of the Armenian merchants and in most cases dismissed the Russian merchants' demand to confine the Armenians' trade to Russia. In order to promote, what was in the government's view, the still too low trade activity, Peter I declared to the senate in 1711 that "the Persian trade is to be increased and the Armenians are to be treated kindly if possible and they are to be provided relief so that they will feel like arriving [in Russia] more often".[24] Despite these imperial concessions the Julfans did not fulfil the contracts' provisions and continued to use their old trade routes to the Middle Eastern seaports and across the Mediterranean. What contributed to this circumstance was the lack of security for the merchants and their goods along the Volga trade route, abuses by Russian officials and insurrections in the south of the empire. Sometimes the Julfans violated the contracts, for example, by distributing goods in retail sale.[25] The topic of such continuous violations was on the agenda for discussion between the Russian envoy, Artemy Volynsky, and the Persian shah in 1717. Volynsky asked the shah to urge the Armenians to fulfil their duties, but the shah refused, explaining that "the merchants can do what they want . . . [if they are forced to not] go to other countries anymore and [only] to Russia, they will not trade anymore . . . an order of this kind is improper".[26] Finally, two years after Volynsky's negotiations and mainly at his instigation, the Julfa merchants were deprived of their privileges and equated with other foreign merchants in legal terms. In the order of 6 June 1719, it was proclaimed: "[His Tsarist Highness] granted to the Armenians a lot of advantages . . . but the merciful charity of H.Ts.H. towards them did not bear fruit in their trade from Persia. That is why H.Ts.H. now cancels all provisions of the contract. And when the Armenians want to trade in the Russian empire, they must pay the regular customs duties according to the *Novotorgovyj Ustav*, just as the foreigners of other realms."[27]

Nevertheless, in the course of the eighteenth century the Armenian merchants' oriental trade through Russia increased considerably. The annual average of transported raw silk in transit between 1676 and 1685 was 735 *pud*,[28] climbing to more than 2,000 *pud* between 1723 and 1734 and finally to 4,867 *pud* between 1743 and 1747, before falling again in the middle of the century.[29] Especially from the 1730s on, Armenians from Astrakhan mainly accounted for this increase while the Julfans' share in the Russian silk trade considerably decreased.[30] In this way, Armenians remained in a leading position in the raw silk trade with and through the Russian empire until at least the middle of the eighteenth century, albeit their general proportion of activity as silk traders in Russia gradually declined.

Although the Armenian oriental trade in Russia lagged behind the government's expectations, it nevertheless contributed to the expansion and stabilization of the economic relations of the Russian empire with the Persian and Ottoman empires. It meant revenues from customs duties for the treasury and it brought badly needed precious metals from Europe and supplied the young Russian textile industry with raw materials. In this emergent state-sponsored industry, Armenians were often active as entrepreneurs and skilled workers both in the privileged "state" as well as in privately owned manufactures.

The reasons for the remarkable economic success of Armenian merchants, especially those from New Julfa, lay not only in their efficient communication networks and trade methods[31] or in the organizational and financial weakness of the Russian merchants, but also in the specific historical and political situation which allowed the Armenians to enter into a reciprocal relationship with the government and thereby foster their advantageous position.[32]

The structural conditions that the Armenians came across in Russia enabled them to attain an early outstanding position in certain areas of commerce and industry. This inevitably led to recurrent protests from the Russian mercantile community which, however, in most cases, were hardly taken into consideration by the tsars. Thus the state's interests and those of the Russian merchants were not always congruent and sometimes even contradictory.[33] Moreover, the government, by exalting the financial interests of the treasury, often hampered the growth of domestic commerce and industry.[34]

The success of Armenian merchants and entrepreneurs in Russia, and the far-reaching concessions made to them in a time of inhibition of European commercial activity and increasing proto-national protest from the Moscow merchants, can only be understood against the background of the compatibility of the economic and political interests of the Armenians with the multifaceted motives of the tsars, which included commercial and fiscal considerations as well as foreign and strategic aims.[35] It is in this light that the exchange relationship between the elite of the Armenian merchants and the imperial government should be understood. In the course of the seventeenth and eighteenth centuries, this relationship was repeatedly renegotiated and, although its premise was to be of benefit to both sides, in its official and stipulated form of expression it made use of the concepts of "profit" (*pribyl'*) and "loss" (*ubyl'*) for the Russian state and the treasury respectively. While presenting their privileges and monopolization of the silk transit trade as being profitable for the treasury and thereby related to the tsar's self-interest, the Armenian contractual partners succeeded in preserving their special rights until 1719, despite the continuous breach of the contracts and resentment of the Russian merchants. Even after the termination of the contracts, Armenian merchants were able to defend their dominant position in Russia's oriental trade for decades to come.

ARMENIAN SETTLERS AND RUSSIAN COLONIZATION POLICY

The second important chapter in the history of the Armenian diaspora in Russia is the establishment of Armenian colonies on the southern periphery of the empire. A colony in the Russian empire meant a settlement, usually of foreign ethno-cultural origin, to which the government granted a set of economic and legal privileges along with administrative autonomy not enjoyed by other towns or communities in Russia. Typically, such colonies were set up in newly acquired lands. The distinctive feature of these eighteenth-century foreign colonies of the Russian empire was that the inhabitants of those colonies enjoyed a greater degree of freedom, civil rights and opportunities than most of the members of the ethnic Russian majority population. The manifestos of Catherine II of 1762 and 1763 brought those privileges in a legal form and granted financial aid and other benefits to the foreign colonists – land allotments, exemption from military service, relief from taxes during a certain period of time, religious freedom and their own local jurisdiction according to the laws and customs of their homelands.[36] In return, these colonies were expected to promote the demographic, economic and "civilizing" development of peripheral regions, thereby enhancing the state's material income and its position in the contemporary European imperial power competition. Moreover, the foreign colonies, by introducing new and more advanced technologies and more effective forms of production (especially in the field of agriculture), were supposed to act as a role model for the Russian peasant population, regarded by its enlightened government as "backward" compared to the western European ideals of the time.

Although some Armenian and Russian historians tended to call all historical Armenian communities or settlements in the diaspora "colonies",[37] here the term will be used only for those Armenian settlements in the Russian empire that actually were granted the legal status of a foreign colony by the tsarist government. While Armenian communities in Russia had existed since the Middle Ages, Armenian colonies were only established in the eighteenth century. This applies to a number of Armenian communities, characteristically all of which were located near or even directly on the southern borders of the empire. They received their colonial status between the 1740s and the end of the eighteenth century. Some of these colonies – Astrakhan on the Volga near the Caspian Sea, Kizljar and Mozdok in the North Caucasus, as well as Staryj Krym and Karasubazar on the Crimean peninsula – were established on the basis of older Armenian communities in the respective multi-ethnic towns while three colonies – Svjatoj Krest in the North Caucasus, New Nakhichevan (Novyj Nachičevan') and Grigoriopol in the Black Sea region – were created as entirely Armenian settlements.

Armenian merchants and artisans are reported to have lived in the area of the town of Astrakhan and in its Tartar predecessor town, Khadzhi Tarkhan (Xacitarxan), since the Middle Ages. After the Russian conquest and refounding of the town in the middle of the sixteenth century, and following the state's promotion of oriental trade and the privileging of Armenian silk traders, the Armenian community of Astrakhan continuously enlarged. Located near the Armenian marketplace, the Armenian merchants from 1630 had their own *"gostinyj dvor"* (bazaar-cum-guesthouse) in which they lived with their families and which thereby became the nucleus of the first Armenian *"sloboda"*[38] in Astrakhan. In the early eighteenth century, a second Armenian *sloboda* came into being, later separated from the older one by a canal and connected to it by two bridges.

In the years 1769–70, the German natural scientist and member of the Russian Academy of Sciences, Samuel Gottlieb Gmelin, being in attendance on Catherine II made a stop in Astrakhan during his expedition to southern Russia and Persia. In his expedition report, he described the town's Armenian population, commenting on their appearance, religious customs, their economic and political situation and their housing. Gmelin noted: "In total they count 1,281 Armenians of the male sex . . . of whom 91 are of the Catholic religion. They possess all kinds of freedoms which they could wish for and in some respects even greater [freedoms] than the Russians themselves."[39]

The Armenians as well as other oriental inhabitants of Russia did indeed enjoy a number of privileges. After the conclusion of the contracts with the Julfa merchants, other Armenian, Indian and Georgian merchants in the late seventeenth century obtained the right to settle permanently in Astrakhan. Although retail trade and trading outside of the *"dvory"* or bazaar, which had been erected for them, was prohibited for these foreign merchants, they repeatedly violated this prohibition.

Armenian and other oriental merchants were not enrolled in the merchants guilds and thus were exempted from many municipal and general obligations, such as civic and military service and the obligation to quarter soldiers in their houses (instead of which they paid a certain amount of money to support the Russian merchants and for the construction of barracks). These exemptions led to repeated protests by Russian merchants and by some governors to the central administration. The Russian merchant Fyodor Cheprakov of Astrakhan complained in 1736: "There are Armenian merchants in Astrakhan who for a long time lived in their *sloboda* with their wives and children and who do much business in whole and retail sale and who own their own shops and workshops and become rich thereof . . . they do no minor disturbance and harm to the merchants of Astrakhan who are weak and the foreign merchants possess a great fortune." He asked for the foreign merchants to support the native ones and to sell their shops because, Cheprakov reasoned, the Russian merchants of Astrakhan "are few and all that is made even worse by the many compulsory services [the natives have to do] and they [the Russian merchants] cannot expand their commerce because of the disturbance from the above-mentioned merchants".[40]

On the other hand, the petitions of Armenian merchants for the granting or preserving of their privileges were consistently successful, presumably thanks to influential advocates such as the governor of Astrakhan, Vasily Tatishchev. Based on his recommendation, the Armenians of Astrakhan in 1744 and 1746 were granted exceptional privileges. These included not only the already mentioned favours but also the right to become temporary Russian subjects, exemption from registering with the merchant guilds and the right to run their own judicial court according to their laws and customs in order to, as was explained, "stir the craving of the ones of foreign faith to come to Astrakhan".[41] A municipality (*"ratsgauz"*) which was in charge of the judicial, administrative and police matters of the Armenian, Indian, Persian, Tartar, Greek, Georgian and Bukhara merchants was established in the town. These merchant groups elected their own judges who administered the law of the respective so-called nation in case of internal disputes. Only disputes with Russians and legal appeals were judged by the Russian administration.

Despite protests from Russian merchants and from the ranks of the local authorities for the legal equalization of the Russian and the Armenian merchant, the privileges of the latter did not end. Governor Beketov in the 1760s called for a retrenchment of the oriental traders' rights but was met with a denial by Catherine II who, in her manifestos of 1762 and 1763, had promised foreign settlers in Russia not only a number of economic privileges and religious freedom but also the right to the autonomous jurisdiction of their communities. In her answer to Beketov, Catherine wrote:

> The Armenians living in Astrakhan had always had the desire to install a court according to their laws and habits, otherwise they would hardly stay here for a long time. Furthermore, their stay in Russia does not seem to be without benefit with a view to their not insignificant trade . . . So Our will is now to leave them in their former regime of jurisdiction and to only correct its disadvantages by installing new institutions, but . . . as an addition to the old ones. In order to stir their craving to live here of course it is also necessary to allow them to have a certain freedom of their kind.

The most suitable means of doing this, continued Catherine, was the establishment of the "General Court of the Asians of Astrakhan". She concluded: "We wish that these people of foreign faith are administered more with decent friendliness and benevolence than with severity and forced change of their habits."[42] But this decree also introduced a new restrictive element, namely the subordination of the "Asian Court" to the provincial administration which resulted in repeated complaints by Armenians who lamented the interference with their jurisdiction. What is more, the Armenian population had to compensate their court's Russian supervisor at the rank of a chief officer.

The judges of the Asian Court were elected on a yearly basis. The Armenian population elected three Armenians (two of them Apostolic, one Catholic) to serve as their judges. Justice in the Armenian branch of the

Asian Court was based on the "Code of Law of the Armenians of Astrakhan", written by three leaders of the Astrakhan Armenian community, Eliazar Grigoryan, Grigor Kampanyan and Hovhannes Sargisyan. The law was based on Armenian customary law, the medieval Armenian code of law of Mkhitar Gosh and Russian law. It regulated the rules of procedure of the Armenian court, civil law such as family and inheritance law, commercial and contract law and even criminal law. The penalties meted out to convicts ranged from fines to capital punishment, and also allowed for torture for the purpose of obtaining confessions.[43]

With the adoption of the "Charter on the Rights and Benefits for the Towns" in 1785 intended to unify the administration and legal status of urban dwellers throughout the empire, once again the pressure increased on Armenians to become Russian subjects and to enrol in the merchants guilds or the urban civic estate of *meščanstvo* and thereby to equalize their burden of taxes and service obligations with that of the Russian population. Consequently, the Asian Court and the Armenian self-administration practically ceased to exist. But the majority of Astrakhan's Armenians could not afford to register with the merchant guilds (which required payment) and therefore remained "non-enrolled", and thus outside the regulations of the charter. Overall the Astrakhan Armenians' economic situation began to deteriorate due to the fact that those who were enrolled in the merchants guilds were subject to all the obligations that this entailed and from which the Armenian merchants formerly had been exempt while at the same time they were denied the advantages of the merchant estate by the Russian merchants and the municipal magistrate. Armenians who did not register with the guilds were confronted with rigid restrictions of their commerce or even had to quit their trade altogether.[44] Following petitions from the Armenians, the government in 1788 permitted all those who had not enrolled in the merchants guilds or the *meščanstvo* to keep their pre-1785 legal status.[45]

In 1799, Emperor Paul I decreed a manifesto which re-established the rights and privileges not only of the Armenians in Astrakhan but of those throughout the empire. During his administration, even those Armenians already registered with the merchants guilds were finally allowed to return to the former privileged legal status established more than thirty years before:[46]

> Given the pleas which were presented to Us by the Armenians of Astrakhan,
> Kizlyar, Mozdok and all the Armenian communities of Our empire who since
> the time of their settlement distinguished themselves by industriousness,
> proper house building, virtue and exemplary behaviour . . . We are in favour
> . . . of not only supporting all former rights and advantages . . . but also of giving
> them [the Armenians] several benefits and advantages for the stimulation of
> a great zeal toward industriousness and for the continuation of their useful
> enterprises and for inspiring the appetite for imitation also by other foreign
> settlements.[47]

As a consequence, the Armenian Court was re-established the following
year.[48]

After the end of Paul's reign, the Armenians' special rights were once
again curtailed. As early as 1807, in a manifesto of Alexander I, foreign
merchants were obliged to enrol in the guilds and to become "eternal" Russian subjects or else they would be subject to restrictions of their trade. The
Armenian merchants were prompted to submit to the general municipal
regulations, which "beyond comparison excel all previous exceptional advantages".[49] The 1807 manifesto argued that previously granted exceptions for
Armenian merchants were revoked because they had been awarded on the
basis of different circumstances. Year by year the obligations of Armenians
grew and their legal situation was gradually equalized with that of the Russian population. With the incorporation of Eastern Armenia into the Russian
empire the Armenians lost a considerable part of their political importance
for the Russian government. The economic importance of Astrakhan for the
south of Russia also diminished in the nineteenth century.[50] Consequently,
from 1831 on, the privileges granted by Paul's manifesto were only applied
to those Armenians of Astrakhan, Kizlyar and Mozdok who already had
been members of the respective communities prior to 1799 but not to their
offspring or later immigrants.[51] Finally, in 1840 the Armenian courts in the
Russian empire were ultimately dissolved. This step was justified by pointing out that "the exceptional right granted to them to use their own courts
according to old and nowadays already unknown customs and habits is not
in use any more today due to the changed circumstances, and does them [the
Armenians] disadvantage".[52]

Armenian colonies were also founded in the North Caucasus which, during the eighteenth century, gained enormous geostrategic significance to Russian planning. Armenian merchants used the strategically important trade routes of the region, particularly excelling as mediators between the Caucasian mountain peoples (the so-called *gorcy*) and the Russian population on the one hand and in the trade between Russia and the South Caucasus on the other hand. However, Armenians in the North Caucasus were not only active as traders and soldiers but were also innovative in the field of agriculture. The bulk of Armenian immigration from the territories under Ottoman and Persian sovereignty into the North Caucasus headed towards the fortified towns of Kizlyar and Mozdok whose Armenian colonies, like Astrakhan before, were granted far-reaching rights and privileges.

The origins of the Armenian colony of Kizlyar date back to the 1730s when the Armenian and Georgian squadron, which had fought for the Russian army in the Caspian War against Persia the decade before, was stationed in the Kizlyar fortress.[53] During the following years, Kizlyar became a predominately Armenian town due to its strategic location on the trade routes from Astrakhan to the eastern Caucasus, to Georgia and the Caspian Sea coasts of Iran. Russia's increasing martial activity in the Caucasus boosted the strategic significance of the trade routes of the region.[54] While Kizlyar was mainly inhabited by Armenian merchants and craftsmen, diasporic Armenians pioneered several branches of agriculture, such as viticulture, sericulture, cotton and rice production, and they are said to have been the first to produce cognac in Russia.[55]

Mozdok, another town along the fortified Caucasian Line, was settled under Catherine II by so-called Persians (who in their majority were Armenians) and native *"gorcy"* willing to become Russian subjects.[56] In the first decades of the town's existence, Armenians were the majority of its inhabitants, predominately engaged in the trade between the Russian population and the *gorcy* as well as between the Russian empire and the South Caucasus.[57] Following the retreat of the Russian army from Persian territories after the campaign in 1796 Armenian archbishop Iosif Argutinsky-Dolgoruky requested the evacuation of the Armenian population from Derbent and Muškur into Russian-held lands. In 1797, after considering the potential of economic and strategic advantages of the resettlement of more than five thousand Armenian refugees to the North Caucasus, the Russian government agreed to the request for evacuations. Two years later, the town of Svjatoj Krest was founded for the settlement of artisans and merchants while Armenian peasants who were engaged in sericulture settled in a number of villages in the area.

The steppe regions north of the Black Sea were incorporated into the Russian empire as the province of New Russia in the second half of the eighteenth century. Unlike the case in the Volga region and the North Caucasus, the settlement of Armenians in the steppe regions was based on deliberate governmental action.[58] The peace treaty of Küçük Kaynarca (1774) had expanded Russian territorial holdings, bringing under its influence the nominally independent Khanate of Crimea. After installing Şahin Giray as the new khan on the Crimean throne, the Russians sought to further weaken Crimea's autonomy by removing its economically active Christian population (mainly Greeks and Armenians as well as some numbers of Georgians and Vlachs). The resettlement of these subjects of the khan on South Russian soil would also contribute to the latter's peopling and economic development.[59] A plan for the resettlement of the Crimean Christians was drafted by Field Marshal Rumyancev in 1778 and approved by Catherine II. The execution of the plan was assigned to the commander of the Caucasian Line, Aleksandr Suvorov. Suvorov established contacts with the clerical leadership of the Greek and Armenian communities and directly bargained with them for the conditions of the removal of their flock – on this occasion, the Russian side supported its words with monetary gifts.[60] Finally, in July 1778 the Crimean Christian communities, on the condition of Russia's financial support and legal privileges, agreed to their relocation.[61] Christian Crimeans' resettlement was also promoted by Archbishop Argutinsky-Dolgoruky, who had contact with Catherine's court as well as with Suvorov.[62] Financial compensation for their losses was not only promised to the resettlers, but to the Crimean khan who let his tax-paying population go after receiving one hundred thousand rubles from the Russian government together with the assurance that Russia would not interfere in the khan's internal affairs.[63] Despite these negotiations, the resettlement of approximately 18,400 Greeks, 12,500 Armenians and 380 Georgians and Vlachs (in total more than three quarters of the Crimean Christian population) turned out to be accompanied by more hardships than had been expected.[64] Russia's material support proved to be inadequate, its local officials behaved arbitrarily, and on their arrival at the negotiated place of settlement the evacuated communities discovered that their promised lands were already occupied by other settlers.[65] The hardship faced by these resettlers was great: many died on their journey as well as shortly thereafter of hunger, cold and epidemics. In late 1779, when the number of the resettled Armenians had decreased to 9,000, they were allowed to move on to the Lower Don.[66] There, the Armenian town of New Nakhichevan was founded and received the privileges of a colony being surrounded by five Armenian villages.[67] Archbishop Argutinsky was responsible for the planning of the town's construction, financed by the government.[68]

A couple of years later, a similar procedure of resettlement was followed to develop former Ottoman territory located between the rivers Bug and Dniester which had been conquered by Russia during the Russian-Turkish war of 1787–91. In 1792 the town Grigoriopol on the river Dniester was founded and settled by Armenians immigrating from the Ottoman-influenced principality of Moldova just across the river.[69] The negotiations for this second government-planned resettlement of Armenians on Russian territory began before the end of the war between the military commander and leading figure of the colonization process in Russia's southern domains, Prince Grigory Potemkin and Archbishop Argutinsky.[70] As in New Nakhichevan the Armenian resettlers were to receive material advantages and legal privileges. Again, Suvorov was one of the leading figures of the enterprise, in cooperation with Argutinsky and Stepan Davtyan, an Armenian who had negotiated with Catherine II two years before. Davtyan, who had been elevated to the rank of prime major by Potemkin and Suvorov, organized the resettlement of four thousand Armenians coming mainly from the towns of Izmail, Akkerman and Bendery to the eastern bank of the Dniester.[71] The Moldovan Armenians, too, found out that once they had left their homes for Russia, their agreed upon destination near the town of Dubossary at the Dniester river, Catherine II chose another place for their habitation, approximately ten miles to the south.[72] In 1792, Grigoriopol was founded as their new hometown and declared an Armenian colony. The erection of the town followed a general plan, confirmed by Catherine II and supervised by Governor Kakhovsky with an episcopal residence, the main church, a seminary and magistrates.[73] Grigoriopol's inhabitants' main economic trade was in animal products such as grease, which was exported via the Black Sea port of Odessa.[74]

The settlement of the region proceeded quickly thanks to the immigration of Christians from the Ottoman territories (alongside Armenians, these Christians were largely Greeks, Bulgarians and especially Moldavians). The building of forts and towns along the border further attracted additional manpower. Due to continued immigration of non-Armenians into Grigoriopol and also because of the emigration of Armenians – among them a number of merchants who moved on to Odessa – the town's Armenian population steadily decreased during the course of the nineteenth century. This decline in Armenian inhabitants can clearly be seen in the chronicles of the Armenian Apostolic Church of Grigoriopol.[75] Between 1840 and 1860 the local Armenian Church had 899 members, but by 1889 that population had decreased to 435 and seven years later to 363. Finally, in the early twentieth century the Armenian Apostolic Church of Grigoriopol counted no more than 300 members.

The two Armenian colonies of New Nakhichevan and Grigoriopol shared some common characteristics. Unlike the older Armenian communities, whose inhabitants yearly appealed to the Russian government to grant them privileges, the resettlers of New Russia from the outset bargained with the military and civil institutions of the tsarist empire to legalize the foundation of their colonies.[76]

In view of the hardships faced by Armenian resettlers from the Crimea in New Russia during the first years of their habitation, a few tried to return to their former homes on the peninsula. But it was only after the annexation of the Crimean khanate by Russia in 1783 that these returning evacuees were officially allowed to do so. Most of these returnees were soon joined by Armenian immigrants from the Ottoman empire and settled in their places of origin like the towns of Feodosija, Staryj Krym and Karasubazar. However, coming home proved difficult for some of them since after the evacuation of Karasubazar's Catholic Armenian population, their property, including the Catholic cathedral, had been conferred upon the Muslim community. Russian authorities, considering the strong outflow of Crimean Tatars to the Ottoman empire and the weak economic situation of the new Russian dominion, found themselves disinclined to offend the Tartar community and therefore did not hurry to reassign the Armenians' property to its original owners. Nevertheless, until the end of the century, the Armenian communities of both Staryj Krym and Karasubazar were granted the legal status of Armenian colonies and began to run their own municipalities.

Armenian communities in Russia need to be understood against the background of Russia's colonization and modernization policies in the eighteenth century during the reigns of Peter I and Catherine II. In accordance with the premises of an official settlement policy, which was widespread in contemporary Europe and whose primary engine was the territorial expansion of the empire, the settlement of Russian state peasants and serfs as well as of foreign so-called colonists in the underpopulated and economically underdeveloped border regions (such as the Volga und Ural regions, the Black Sea region and the North Caucasus) was meant to foster the increase of the local population as well as to promote commerce, industry and agriculture.

Colonization of Russia's own peripheral internal area was intended to develop the empire's economy and consolidate Russia's military and political sovereignty. In its relationship with foreigners, such as the Armenians, the government took into consideration alliances with co-religionists.[77] The success of the government's development plans, which rested on Armenians and other immigrants, were based on the oriental trade routes and the production of silk. Entrepreneurs who introduced new industries, such as silk production and silk processing, into Russia were granted special privileges. In addition, such entrepreneurs and long-distance traders took over the complementary functions of diplomacy, administration, military and (proto) industry.[78]

The stabilization of Russian rule in the North and South Caucasus, the integration of formerly underdeveloped border regions into the general administrative, social and economic composition of the empire, and the broadening of a native Russian commercial and industrial population could not but impinge on the members of the Armenian diaspora in their primary capacity as colonists. Consequently the Armenian communities' influence on the administration and the economy of southern Russia decreased.[79] As an outcome of this process, the Armenian colonies of the Russian empire were gradually deprived of their exceptional status in the nineteenth century. In accordance with the general evolution of contemporary Russian colonization policy, a number of decrees were issued during the 1830s and 1840s which constrained the Armenians' privileges and curtailed the colonists' exceptional legal status.[80] Finally, the Armenian courts in Astrakhan and other towns were dismantled and the Armenians of the Russian empire were integrated into the general municipal and corporative social regulations. In the late nineteenth century, the rise of Armenian as well as Russian nationalism and the radicalization of political parties led to an estrangement between Armenian and Russian elites, and only after the revolution of 1905 and the death of the minister of the interior, Pyotr Stolypin, in 1911 did they regain their traditional relationship of cooperation.

As the Russian empire modernized, the Armenian communities gradually lost their functions and privileges. This process took place over several decades until the end of the nineteenth century when the state's policy adopted an openly anti-Armenian line. The Armenian population north of the South Caucasus still displayed some of the allegedly ideal typical socio-economic characteristics of a middleman minority.

DEMOGRAPHIC FEATURES OF THE ARMENIAN DIASPORA IN LATE IMPERIAL RUSSIA

In the regions along the Volga trade route, the Armenian diaspora predominately appeared as a commercial group. Commercial activity was especially dominant in the small Armenian communities in the towns of the agrarian and rural provinces Saratov and Voronezh. Thus, in most cases, these were rather small groups of Armenian merchants who had strategically settled along the transport routes of the region (the rivers Volga, Don and Voronezh).

In Astrakhan, on the other hand, we not only find a broad commercial stratum among the Armenian inhabitants but also large groups of the intelligentsia, the nobility and the bureaucracy. Members of the Armenian diaspora, therefore, were found in commerce as well as among pensioners, in the ecclesiastic field, in the professions, the administration and among benefit recipients (this includes pupils and students who received stipends as well as orphans and the needy). Armenians in Astrakhan mainly belonged to the estates of *meščane*, merchants, honorary citizens, the clergy and the nobility. In summary, it can be stated that a considerable part of the social, cultural and political elite of the Armenian diaspora of Russia lived in Astrakhan.

Table 2.1 gives a telescoped, very general, impression of the demographic data regarding the main socio-economic characteristics of the Armenian diaspora as compared to the Russian population. Of course we have to pay attention to some regional differences which naturally appeared between the Armenian populations of the Russian empire, some of which were separated from each other by vast distances and which came into being in quite different historical epochs. In the following I therefore want to give a concise account of some of the basic features of the Armenian populations in those regions where, until the mid-nineteenth century, Armenian colonies had existed – that is, the Lower Volga region, the North Caucasus and New Russia as they were recorded in the First All-Russian Census of 1897.

Table 2.1 Armenian Diaspora Demography, 1897

	Armenian Diaspora	Russians
Number (excl. South Caucasus)	94,037	55,445,836
Urban dwellers (%)	60.78	15.70
Literate (%)	49.82	29.23
With higher than elementary education (%)	8.64	2.24
Engaged in commerce (%)	28.11	3.24
Merchants (estate) (%)	4.17	0.29
Engaged in agriculture (%)	19.82	47.50

Source: Henning Bauer, Andreas Kappeler and Brigitte Roth, eds, Die National-itäten des Russischen Reiches in der Volkszählung von 1897: A Quellenkritische Dokumentation und Datenhandbuch (Stuttgart: Franz Steiner Verlag, 1991).

As in most regions of the Russian empire the Armenian diaspora in the North Caucasus showed higher degrees of urbanization and, in most cases, also higher degrees of literacy than Russians and other non-Russians. Everywhere in the North Caucasus, Armenians were engaged primarily in trade, but also in the textile industry, hospitality industry and transportation. Most Armenians here belonged to the estate of *meščane* but they also had a relatively large presence among the merchants, the honorary citizens, the nobility and the clergy. What is striking is the high percentage of Armenians in the military and in administration in the provinces of Dagestan and Kuban. In most regions of the North Caucasus, we can observe rather typical diasporic characteristics of the Armenian minority who, in this predominantly agrarian environment, had occupied certain socio-economic niches and had taken over functions mainly in commerce but also in other fields of the economy and – in some regions – even in administration and in the military, which could not be fulfilled by the majority of the native rural and poorly mobilized population.

Similarly in New Russia (including the Crimean Peninsula), the situation was as heterogeneous as in the North Caucasus. In some regions Armenians were unusually represented among the peasant estate and active in agriculture. Although the Armenian diaspora everywhere had a more or less large presence in commerce, this field of activity predominated only in a few provinces. Otherwise, in other places agriculture, the services or even domestic occupations were paramount. Despite being less urbanized and literate than those in some other regions of the empire, Armenians in New Russia exceeded both Russians and other non-Russians in their levels of urbanization and literacy. Conspicuous is the high percentage of foreign citizens among the Armenians of New Russia. This holds true also for Odessa, where even a third of all Armenians (who in this town were mainly engaged not in trade but in the services) were foreign citizens. Thus, it can at least be suspected that those regions of New Russia and the North Caucasus lying on the shores of the Black Sea, where a great number of Armenians of foreign citizenship lived, had been the destination of Armenian refugees from the Ottoman empire, where pogroms against the Armenian population had taken place in 1895.

In certain areas of the Russian empire (such as some provinces of the North Caucasus) the imperial administrative and military apparatus included a strong presence of members of the Armenian diaspora. It seems as if the local Armenian minority had taken over functions in the military and/or civil organs of the state in support of the regional bureaucratic and military leadership respectively. At the same time, virtually everywhere, members of the Armenian diaspora were represented in commerce. Other widespread fields of activity were the food and textile industry, the hospitality industry, transportation and the personal hygiene or cosmetology industries (that is, barbers, hairdressers, operators of *banjas* and the like). In almost all regions Armenians displayed higher levels of urbanization, literacy and education than Russians and most other ethnic groups. Finally, the Armenian diaspora mainly belonged to the urban estates, in several places (such as Astrakhan) holding a large share of the secular and the clerical intelligentsia. Thus, despite some regional differences, the Armenian diaspora in pre-revolutionary Russia showed a great number of those characteristics (regarding urbanization, education, substantial activity in commercial occupations and a relatively low activity in agriculture compared to other groups of the population) that distinguish the ideal typical middlemen minorities.

CONCLUSION

Armenians were never the only diasporic minority in the Russian empire. Nor were Armenians the most important diaspora in the eyes of Russian imperial planners.[81] Nevertheless, Armenians possessed some useful characteristics that could benefit the state – in the utilitarian language of the contemporary Russian bureaucracy. Their knowledge and technical skills, some of them typical for all diasporas (language skills, trade networks based on mutual trust along lines of kin-relations, and the like), enabled Armenians to fulfil multiple functions in their host country and thereby take part in Russia's "(proto)modernization from above". Members of the Armenian diaspora in many cases occupied economic niches where they often gained a leading, or even monopoly, position as in the oriental trade via Astrakhan, in the trade with the peoples of the South and North Caucasus through Kizlyar and Mozdok, in silk production, as well as in cognac production.

On the southern frontier of the Russian empire, as in the Lower Volga region, the North Caucasus and New Russia, where imperial rule was not yet firmly established members of the allochthonous group of the Armenian diaspora whose well-being was dependent on the goodwill of the rulers became valuable mediators between the indigenous population and the empire's central elite. As cultural brokers, colonists, interpreters, merchants and diplomats, Armenians contributed to the expansion und stabilization of the centre's rule and thereby promoted the colonization and integration of recently conquered peripheral lands.

Until the middle of the nineteenth century, foreign colonists, Armenians among them, in many respects enjoyed a more privileged position in legal and economic respects than most Russian subjects of the empire. The incessant competition between Russian and Armenian merchants (who in some branches of commerce were more successful and in some respects preferred by the government) resulted in many petitions and complaints by Russian merchants as well as by some local officials.

While economic factors played an important role in the relationship between the Armenian diaspora and the representatives of the tsarist government, the nature and the development of this relationship was also influenced by the significance that the Russian leadership accorded to the Armenians in the framework of the empire's eastern policy, especially towards the Ottoman empire. This was most evident in the southern border regions of the tsars' realm which were taken from the Ottomans during the eighteenth century. The fact that the majority of Armenians who settled or who were settled in New Russia had emigrated from territories under Ottoman influence and often held ethnic or cultural-religious animosity towards the Ottomans led the Russian government to hope that they could be of use as loyal defenders of the border against an Ottoman revival.[82] In this respect, the resettlement of the Crimean Armenians to New Nakhichevan as well as the removal of Armenians from Moldova to Grigoriopol and the new inhabitants' privileges can also be seen as a continuation of a traditional Russian policy to court and win over allies or collaborators in enemy lands.[83]

The Armenian diaspora in the Russian empire, from the late seventeenth to the first half of the nineteenth century, played a role in the government's planning. They were important to the economy, politics and territorial expansion to the south and southeast. They helped in the modernization – the development of commerce, certain industries and certain branches of agriculture, or urbanization – and land reclamation along the frontier. The diaspora also helped to consolidate a centralized authority in the empire's interior as well as towards an outside world perceived in terms of competition and the struggle for international power.[84]

Members of the Armenian diaspora, especially their clerical, political and economic elites, were not mere pawns in the hand of Russian planners. At times they supported and even pioneered tsarist policies.[85] As a consequence, the elites of the Armenian diaspora often gained great wealth and prestige but some also embarked on civil and military service and ascended to the ranks of nobility.[86] Thus, what developed between the Russian and Armenian elites can be interpreted as a form of reciprocal exchange relationship based on the imperial officials' perception of the Armenians' usefulness for furthering Russian economic and geopolitical aims, but ultimately designed for the mutual advantage of both sides. Only when the cost of supporting and privileging foreigners came to be perceived by the Russian bureaucracy as outweighing the benefits to the state did the latter begin to dismiss the Armenians from their special status, and gradually unify them with the majority population, slowly turning Armenians into ordinary subjects of the tsar.

NOTES

1. The topic is being more fully developed in my doctoral dissertation at the University of Leipzig, which itself is an expansion of an earlier master's thesis at the University of Vienna; see Tamara Erkinger, "Die armenische Diaspora im vorrevolutionären Russland" (MA thesis, University of Vienna, 2010), http://othes.univie.ac.at/10042/1/2010-05-31_9947452.pdf.

2. When using the terms "diaspora" and "middleman minority" I refer to an ideal type in the Weberian sense, which of course cannot do full justice to the complexity of the social and historical situations these terms are meant to describe. In this sense, our understanding and use of these and similar terms cannot be more than analytical tools, helping us to approach and to make sense of the much more complex and faceted pictures which our empirical sources confront us with. Basic works, some of which date back to as early as the late nineteenth century, include: John A. Armstrong, "Mobilized and Proletarian Diasporas", *American Political Science Review* 70 (1976): 393–408; Edna Bonacich, "A Theory of Middleman Minorities", *American Sociological Review* 38 (1973): 583–94; Abner Cohen, "Cultural Strategies in the Organization of

Trading Diasporas", in *The Development of Indigenous Trade and Markets in West Africa. Studies Presented and Discussed at the 10th International African Seminar at Fourah Bay College, Freetown, December 1969*, ed. Claude Meillas-soux (London: Oxford University Press, 1971), 266–80; Robin Cohen, *Global Diasporas* (London: Routledge, 2008 [1997]); Lewis A. Coser, "The Alien as a Servant of Power: Court Jews and Christian Renegades", *American Sociological Review* 37 (1972): 574–81; Philip D. Curtin, *Cross-Cultural Trade in World History* (Cambridge: Cambridge University Press, 1984); Wilhelm Roscher, "Die Stellung der Juden im Mittelalter betrachtet vom Standpunkte der allgemeinen Handelspolitik", *Zeitschrift für die gesamte Staatswissenschaft* 31 (1875): 503–26; Werner Sombart, *Die Juden und das Wirtschaftsleben* (Leipzig: Duncker and Humblot, 1911); Roger Waldinger, Howard Aldrich and Robert Ward, *Ethnic Entrepreneurs* (Newbury Park: Sage, 1990); Max Weber, *Wirtschaftsgeschichte* (Leipzig: Duncker and Humblot, 1923); Max Weber, *Die protestantische Ethik und der Geist des Kapitalismus* (Tübingen: Mohr, 1920); Walter P. Zenner, *Minorities in the Middle: A Cross Cultural Analysis* (Albany: State University of New York Press, 1991).

3. Edna Bonacich, for example, speaks of the preference for "liquid" occupations which do not bind the subject to the host country for a prolonged period of time, as would be the case with agriculture or major capital investments; see Bonacich, "Middleman Minorities", 585.

4. See especially the theses of John A. Armstrong, "Mobilized Diaspora in Tsarist Russia: The Case of the Baltic Germans", in *Soviet Nationality Policies and Practices*, ed. Jeremy R. Azrael (New York: Praeger, 1978), 73–104.

5. See Coser, "Alien as a Servant of Power".

6. Although I use the terms "centre" and "periphery", I do not have in mind a linear and continuous relationship of dependency and exploitation, but rather a complex pattern of relationships characterized by a balancing act between the creation and maintenance of difference on the one hand and the incorporation and integration of a multiple heterogeneous population on the other hand; see Jane Burbank and Frederick Cooper, *Empires in World History. Power and the Politics of Difference* (New York: Oxford University Press, 2010), 11–13. In this sense, "empire" shall likewise not be understood here as a simple manifestation of imperialism, but as an expression of what has elsewhere been called the "imperial situation" and has been defined as a specific, ambivalent and uneven heterogeneity which produces its own historical dynamics; see Ilya Gerasimov et al., "New Imperial History and the Challenges of Empire", in *Empire Speaks Out: Languages of Rationalization and Self-Description in the Russian Empire*, ed. Ilya Gerasimov et al. (Leiden: Brill, 2009), 3–32, especially 24.

7.   Burbank and Cooper, *Empires in World History*, 14; Michael W. Doyle, *Empires* (Ithaca: Cornell University Press, 1986), 364; Jürgen Osterhammel, "Kulturelle Grenzen in der Expansion Europas", *Saeculum* 46 (1995): 101–38.

8.   Osterhammel, "Kulturelle Grenzen", 125.

9.   John P. LeDonne, "The Grand Strategy of the Russian Empire, 1650–1831", in *The Military and Society in Russia: 1450–1917*, ed. E. Lohr and M. Poe (Leiden: Brill, 2002), 180.

10.   LeDonne, "The Grand Strategy", 181–82

11.   Herfried Münkler, *Imperien: Die Logik der Weltherrschaft – vom Alten Rom bis zu den Vereinigten Staaten* (Berlin: Bundeszentrale für Politische Bildung, 2008), 42. See also Osterhammel, "Kulturelle Grenzen", 118; Sebouh David Aslanian, *From the Indian Ocean to the Mediterranean: The Global Trade Networks of Armenian Merchants from New Julfa* (Berkeley: University of California Press, 2011), 3–4.

12.   Alexei Miller and Alfred J. Rieber, "Introduction: Imperial Rule", in *Imperial Rule*, ed. A. Miller and A. J. Rieber (Budapest: Central European Press, 2004), 1–6, especially 5; Alfred Rieber, "Koncepcii i konstrukcii frontira: sravnitel'no-istoričeskij podchod [Concepts and Constructions of the Frontier: A Comparative-Historical Approach]", in *Novaja imperskaja istorija postsovetskogo prostranstva*, ed. Ilya Gerasimov et al. (Kazan: Centr Issledovanij Nacionalizma i Imperii], 2004), 199–222, especially 222.

13.   Alfred J. Rieber, "The Comparative Ecology of Complex Frontiers", in *Imperial Rule*, 177–207, especially 199–200; Münkler, *Imperien*, 16–18.

14.   Münkler, *Imperien*, 155–56.

15.   Aslanian, *Indian Ocean to Mediterranean*, 4.

16.   Armstrong, "Mobilized and Proletarian Diasporas", 400.

17.   Arnold Suppan, "Conclusion", in *Ethnic Groups in International Relations*, ed. Paul Smith (Dartmouth: Dartmouth University Press, 1991), 331–34, especially 336.

18.   Armstrong, "Mobilized and Proletarian Diasporas", 399.

19.   Actually, diasporas find themselves in a constant dilemma of "wanting (having to) be loyal toward the country of origin as well as toward the country of residence"; see Alois Moosmüller, "Diaspora – zwischen Reproduktion von 'Heimat': Assimilation und transnationaler Identität", in *Interkulturelle Kommunikation und Diaspora: Die kulturelle Gestaltung von Lebens- und Arbeitswelten in der Fremde*, ed. Alois Moosmüller (Münster: Waxman Verlag , 2002), 13.

20.   Armstrong, "Mobilized Diaspora in Tsarist Russia", 97.

21.   *Polnoe sobranie zakonov Rossijskoj Imperii. Pervoe sobranie (1649–1825)* [Complete Compilation of the Laws of the Russian Empire. First Compilation (1649–1825)]

(St Petersburg: Vtoroe Otdelenie Sobstvennoj Ego Imperatorskago Veličestva Kenceljarii, 1830), vol. 1, document no. 408. NB: The first compilation will hereafter be given as I.

22. V.A. Parsamjan, ed., *Armjano-russkie otnošenija v XVII veke: Sbornik dokumentov* [Armenian-Russian Relations in the Seventeenth Century. Collection of Documents] (Erevan: Izdatel'stvo Akademii Nauk Armjanskoj SSR, 1953), vol. 1, document no. 6.

23. Ibid., doc. nos. 19, 47.

24. *Polnoe sobranie zakonov*, I, vol. 4, doc. no. 2330.

25. Ašot Ioannisjan, ed., *Armjano-russkie otnošenija v pervoj treti XVIII veka. Sbornik dokumentov* [Armenian-Russian Relations in the First Third of the Eighteenth Century. Collection of Documents] (Erevan, [Izdatel'stvo Akademii Nauk Armjanskoj SSR], 1964), vol. 2, part 1, document no. 37.

26. Ibid., doc. no. 47.

27. Ibid., doc. no. 56.

28. One *pud* equals approximately 16.38 kilograms.

29. Wolfgang Sartor, "Der armenische Rohseidenhandel im 17. Jahrhundert", in *Armenier im östlichen Europa: Eine Anthologie*, ed. Bálint Kovács, Stefan Troebst and Tamara Ganjalyan (forthcoming, 2013).

30. However, a great number of Armenians residing in Astrakhan originated from New Julfa as more and more Julfa merchants settled in the southern Russian town which became the new centre of their economic and private life.

31. These have recently been studied in depth by Aslanian, *Indian Ocean to the Mediterranean*.

32. Ina Baghdiantz McCabe writes: "Political opportunity, whether negotiated or offered to a network, remains the key to their economic success. To keep these political opportunities ... these cosmopolitan networks excelled at forging congenial relations with courts and municipalities in both Asia and Europe"; see Ina Baghdiantz McCabe, "Global Trading Ambitions in Diaspora: The Armenians and their Eurasian Silk Trade, 1530–1750", in *Diaspora Entrepreneurial Networks: Four Centuries of History*, ed. Ina Baghdiantz McCabe, Gelina Harlaftis and Ioanna Pepelasis Minoglou (Oxford: Oxford University Press, 2005), 45.

33. E.S. Zevakin, "Persidskij vopros v russko-evropejskich otnošenijach XVII v" [The Persian Question in Russian-European Relations of the Seventeenth Century], *Istoričeskie zapiski* 8 (1940): 129–62, especially 162.

34. A.L. Rjabcev, "Prioritety vnešnej torgovli Rossii v XVIII veke i rol' russko-iranskich ėkonomičeskich svjazej" [Priorities of Russian Foreign Trade in the Eighteenth Century and the Role of Russian-Iranian Economic Relations], 6,

http://www.sgu.ru/files/nodes/9810/10.pdf. On the contradictory role of the
state with respect to economic development, especially that of commerce in
seventeenth- and eighteenth-century Russia, see L.K. Ermolaeva, "Krupnoe
kupečestvo Rossii" [The Major Merchants of Russia], *Istoričeskie zapiski* 114
(1986): 303–25; Wolfgang Sartor, "Die Wolga als internationaler Handelsweg
für persische Rohseide: Ein Beitrag zur Handelsgeschichte Russlands im 17.
und 18. Jahrhundert" (PhD diss., Freie Universität Berlin, 1992).

35. The tsars' pursuit of turning Russia into a platform of international silk trade
cannot be explained by economic considerations alone. This was also embedded
in the empire's eastern policy, part of which was the ambition to strengthen
Russia's influence in the Caucasus, Persia and Central Asia and ultimately
to expand the realm's borders to the south and east. The connection between
economic and imperial Russian policy became most evident in the nineteenth
century when Russia competed with Great Britain for geopolitical influence in
Persia and Central Asia.

36. *Polnoe sobranie zakonov*, I, vol. 16, doc. nos. 11720 and 11880.

37. Only after the Armenian genocide did the equivalent of the term diaspora,
"spyurk" (*sp'yowr̈k'*), came to be used in the Armenian language. Prior to that,
Armenians used to call their diaspora communities *"gaghut"* (*gałowt*) (which
derives from the Hebrew term *"galut"* for "exile"), meaning "colony".

38. A village, suburb or town district, freed from certain state obligations.

39. Samuel Gottlieb Gmelin, *Reise durch Russland zur Untersuchung der drey
Natur-Reiche. Zweyter Theil. Reise von Tscherkask nach Astrachan und dem Aufen-
thalt in dieser Stadt. Von dem Anfang des Augusts 1769 bis zum fünften Junius
1770* (St Petersburg, 1774), 146.

40. Polnoe sobranie zakonov, I, vol. 9, doc. no. 7129.

41. Ibid., vol. 12, doc. no. 8919.

42. Ibid., vol. 17, doc. no. 12307.

43. Ėvelina V. Kugryševa, *Istorija armjan v Astrachani* [History of the Armenians
in Astrachan] (Astrachan: Volga, 2007), 104–8.

44. Kugryševa, *Istorija armjan*, 109–10.

45. *Polnoe sobranie zakonov*, I, vol. 22, doc. no. 16617.

46. Ibid., vol. 24, doc. no. 17860.

47. Ibid., vol. 25, doc. no. 19169.

48. Ibid., vol. 26, doc. no. 19656.

49. Ibid., vol. 29, doc. no. 22418.

50. Ruben Osipovič Avakjan, "Sudebnik astrachanskich armjan 1765 goda, kak
pamjatnik prava i vekovoj družby meždu armjanskim i russkim narodom [The
Code of Law of the Astrakhan Armenians of 1765 as a Memorial of Law and of

the Centuries-Old Friendship Between the Armenian and Russian Peoples]",
*Materialy vserossijskoj naučno-praktičeskoj konferencii "Jurisprudencija v Sovre-
mennoj Rossi"*, 5 March 2011, http://sibac.info.

51.   *Polnoe sobranie zakonov Rossijskoj Imperii. Vtoroe Sobranie (1825–1881)* [Com-
plete Compilation of the Laws of the Russian Empire. Second Compilation
(1825–1881)] (St Petersburg, 1884), vol. 11, doc. nos. 8828 and 9196.

52.   Ibid., II, vol. 15, doc. no.13302.

53.   Though the squadron had been dismantled after the restoration of the conquered Caspian regions to Persia, its commanders had refused to go back to
Persian-held territories because they feared repressions due to their participa-
tion in the war on the Russian side, and asked for permission to stay in Russian
service. In 1736 their request was granted and the squadron was re-established
and stationed in Kizlyar. *Polnoe sobranie zakonov*, I, vol. 9, doc. no. 7026.

54.   The final dismantling of the Armenian and Georgian squadrons took place in
1764. Ibid., vol. 16, doc. no. 12152.

55.   Vartan A. Chačaturjan, "Stanovlenie armjanskich kolonij v Rossii" [The
Establishment of Armenian Colonies in Russia], *Diaspory* 1–2 (2000): 78–97,
especially 87–88.

56.   Roger P. Bartlett, *Human Capital: The Settlement of Foreigners in Russia, 1762–
1804* (Cambridge: Cambridge University Press, 1979), 41.

57.   Chačaturjan, "Stanovlenie armjanskich kolonij v Rossii", 88; Bartlett, Human
Capital, 41.

58.   Chačaturjan, "Stanovlenie armjanskich kolonij v Rossii", 89.

59.   M.G. Nersisjan, *Iz istorii russko-armjanskich otnošenii* [From the History of
Russian-Armenian Relations] (Erevan: Izdatel'stvo Akademii Nauk Armjanskoj
SSR, 1956), 14.

60.   Alan W. Fisher, *The Russian Annexation of the Crimea, 1772–1783* (Cambridge:
Cambridge University, 1970), 103.

61.   On how broad a basis the approval of Christian communities rested in reality
remains difficult to decide. A contemporary source reports that the lower strata
of the Greek and Armenian populations in particular did not want to leave their
homes. Accordingly it is to be assumed that a significant part of the Christian
"evacuees" did not leave the Crimea on strictly voluntary grounds and that
the real profiteers of the resettlement were the Greek and Armenian clerical
leaders who, after the completion of the "evacuation", again received allowances
from the Russian government. Fisher, *Russian Annexation*, 103–4. Isabel De
Madariaga, *Russia in the Age of Catherine the Great* (London: Yale University
Press, 1981), 380.

62. M.G. Nersisjan, *A.V. Suvorov i russko-armjanskie otnošenija v 1770–1780-ch godach* [A.V. Suvorov and the Russian-Armenian Relations in the 1770s and 1780s] (Erevan: Hayastan, 1981), 35–36.

63. From this amount, the khan himself received fifty thousand rubles while the other half was distributed among his brothers, the beys, mirzas (heads of the land-owning families) and officials. Ja. E. Vodarskij, O. I Eliseeva and V.M. Kabuzan, *Naselenie Kryma v konce XVIII–konce XX vekov (čislennost', razmeščenie, ètničeskij sostav)* [The Population of the Crimea from the End of the Eighteenth Century to the End of the Twentieth Century (Number, Distribution, Ethnic Composition)] (Moscow: Rossijskaja Akademija Nauk. Institut Rossijskoj Istorii, 2003), 87; Fisher, *Russian Annexation*, 104.

64. Nersisjan, Iz istorii, 27; Chačaturjan, "Stanovlenie armjanskich kolonij v Rossii", 90.

65. Chačaturjan, "Stanovlenie armjanskich kolonij v Rossii", 90.

66. Alla Ter-Sarkisjanc, "Donskie armjane: Ètnokul'turnaja charakteristika [The Don-Armenians: Ethno-cultural Characteristics]", *Sovetskaja Ètnografija* 3 (1991): 44.

67. *Polnoe sobranie zakonov*, I, vol. 20, doc. no. 14942.

68. C.P. Agajan, *Rossija v sud'bach armjan i Armenii* [Russia in the Destinies of the Armenians and Armenia] (Moscow: Meždunarodnyj gumanitarnyj fond Armenovedija im. Akademika C.P. Agajana. Armjanskij institut politologii i meždunarodnogo prava, 1994), 148.

69. Catherine II to Governor Kakhovsky, 23 February 1792, in Zapiski Odesskago Obščestva Istorii i Drevnostej [Notes of the Odessa Society for History and Antiquity], vol. 2 (Odessa, 1848), 83–84.

70. M.G. Nersisjan, ed., *Armjano-russkie otnošenija v XVIII veke, 1760–1800 gg. Sbornik dokumentov* [Armenian-Russian Relations in the Eighteenth Century, 1760–1800. Collection of Documents] (Erevan: Izdatel'stvo Akademii Nauk Armjanskoj SSR, 1990), vol. 4, doc. nos. 250, 252, 253, 255, 257.

71. Žores Ananjan, *Armjanskaja kolonija Grigoriopol* [The Armenian Colony of Grigoriopol] (Erevan: Izdatel'stvo Akademii Nauk Armjanskoj SSR, 1969), 41.

72. Ibid., 43–52.

73. A. Toramanjan, *Iz istorii stroitel'noj dejatel'nosti armjan v Moldavii* [From the History of the Building Activity of Armenians in Moldova] (Moscow: Vneštorgizdat', 1991), 45.

74. Agajan, *Rossija v sud'bach armjan i Armenii*, 165; E.I. Družinina, *Severnoe Pričernomor'e v 1775–1800 gg* [The Northern Black Sea Region from 1775 to 1800] (Moscow: Akademija Nauk SSSR, 1959), 250.

75. National Archive of the Republic of Armenia, 56/1/10044/193–94,

56/1/3221/37–39, 56/1/836/210–12, 56/1/9300/2–3, 56/1/4046/106–8, 56/1/8583/55–56, 56/1/3515/141–42, 56/16/475/92–93.

76. Chačaturjan, "Stanovlenie armjanskich kolonij v Rossii", 89; Ananjan, *Armjanskaja kolonija Grigoriopol*, 6.

77. Bartlett, *Human Capital*, 17. The religious motive of expanding Christendom and freeing Christians from the "yoke" of the infidels' rule was one of many factors driving the territorial expansion of the Russian empire in the eighteenth century; Marc Raeff, "The Style of Russia's Imperial Policy and Prince G.A. Potemkin", in *Statesmen and Statecraft of the Modern West: Essays in Honor of Dwight E. Lee and H. Donaldson Jordan*, ed. Gerald N. Grob (Barre, MA: Barre, 1967), 1–51, especially 1.

78. Andreas Kappeler, "Historische Voraussetzungen des Nationalitätenproblems im russischen Vielvölkerreich", in *Geschichte und Gesellschaft*, 8th year 1982/ issue 2: *Nationalitätenprobleme in Osteuropa*, ed. Dietrich Geyer (Göttingen: Vandenhoeck and Ruprecht, 1982), 159–83, especially 167.

79. See Chačaturjan, "Stanovlenie armjanskich kolonij v Rossii", 96.

80. L.A. Pogosjan, *Armjanskaja kolonija Armavira* [The Armenian Colony of Armavir] (Erevan: Izdatel'stvo Akademii Nauk Armjanskoj SSR, 1981), 98.

81. Here, German settlers and colonists clearly prevailed in the tsarist bureaucrats' imagination.

82. See Patricia Herlihy, *Odessa: A History, 1794–1914* (Cambridge: Cambridge University Press, 1991), 16.

83. Bartlett, *Human Capital*, 131.

84. See Chačaturjan, "Stanovlenie armjanskich kolonij v Rossii".

85. Here, there has to be mentioned the mediating function of Armenian merchants between Russians and *gorcy*, or rather between colonizers and colonized, in the North Caucasus. A similar pattern can be found in the nineteenth century in Central Asia.

86. Examples of Armenians in governmental circles include (in the eighteenth century) Ivan Karapet, adviser to Peter I on questions of Russia's eastern policy; Luki Shirvanov, Karapet's brother, and Safar Vasilev, both courtly interpreters; and (in the nineteenth century) the general governor of Kharkov and later minister of the interior, Mikhail Loris-Melikov; Andreas Kappeler, *Russland als Vielvölkerreich. Entstehung, Geschichte, Zerfall* (Munich: C.H. Beck, 2008 [1992]), 248; Sartor, "Die Wolga", 169, 178.

CHAPTER 3

THE AFRICANIZATION OF AMERINDIANS IN THE GREATER CARIBBEAN

The Wayuu and Miskito, Fifteenth to Eighteenth Centuries

CHRISTIAN CWIK

WITH MORE THAN 75 PER CENT of the Caribbean population being of African descent, the process of Africanization, or how the peoples of the Caribbean region became predominantly Africa-originated, represents an important dimension of local societies. Africanization as a process did not originate in the Americas. It already existed in the Old World before the first Atlantic transit of Christopher Columbus in 1492. This earlier precedent derived, first, from the geographical proximity of Africa and Europe and, second, from the continual invasion of African groups in southwestern Europe from the eighth century onwards. Additionally, early Europeans who came to Africa to establish trade connections were also, to some degree, Africanized. The Iberian Peninsula and the northwestern parts of Africa formed a shared transcontinental space with the Mediterranean. For Caribbean history this previous relationship means that a certain part of the so-called conquerors and first colonizers were actually Africanized Atlantic creoles who, besides other – mostly enslaved – Africans, contributed decisively to the Africanization of the population of the Caribbean.[1]

In particular, I will focus on the Africanization of Amerindians, or the indigenous peoples of the Caribbean region. Africanization of Amerindians is not a well-studied issue in Caribbean historiography. Nor is it treated comparatively across the region. Africanization of the Guajira Amerindians of South America during the seventeenth and eighteenth centuries is mentioned in several works, including by María Cristina Navarrete, Manuel Vicente Magallanes, Weildler Guerra Curvelo, Henri Candelier, Michel Perrin as well as in the edition of documents of the *Cabildo de Santa Marta* between 1529 and 1640 by Antonino Vidal Ortega and Fernando Alvaro Baquero Montoya.[2] Better studied is the history of Africanization of the Miskitos by Eugenia Ibarra Rojas, Karl Offen, Baron Pineda, Claudia García, Mary Helms, Michael Olien, Barbara Potthast and Yuri Zapata Webb.[3]

On the one hand, this chapter is the result of intensive field research on the Colombian and Venezuelan Guajira Peninsula between 2009 and 2011 as well as on the Honduran and Nicaraguan Mosquito Coast in 2003 and 2008. On the other hand, it is based on the study of historical documents located in the Public Records Office in London, Great Britain (Colonial State Papers), the Archivo Nashonal in Willemstad, Curaçao, the Archivo General de la Nación in Bogota, Colombia, and the Archivo General de Indias in Seville, Spain.

My approach to this research originated in my study of the history of Jewish and New Christian (Conversos) diasporas in the Caribbean during the sixteenth and seventeenth centuries. The documents I examined prove that Sephardic Jews and New Christians in the Dutch and English colonies traded as illicit merchants clandestinely with Spain and Portugal as well as with the "enemies" of these Iberian colonial powers: Amerindians and maroons. Most of these contacts were incorporated in broader Atlantic networks of Africanized merchants which included not only Jews and New Christians but also Catholics, Protestants and even Muslims from different European and African countries.

Below I will first describe the process of the Africanization of Europeans in the Euro-African world before 1492. Then I will give a brief overview of the arrival and early activities of Africanized people in the Caribbean and examine how this was an integral part of the expansion of the Euro-African World across the Atlantic. On the basis of two case studies – the Wayuu on the Guajira Peninsula (northern South America) and the Miskito on the Mosquito Coast (western Central America) – I will then illustrate in detail how Amerindian tribes in two different "transnational"[4] regions of the Greater Caribbean were Africanized during the seventeenth and eighteenth centuries.[5]

AFRICANIZATION IN THE EURO-AFRICAN WORLD BEFORE 1492

Since the beginning of human history, the Mediterranean was a cultural area of African, European and Asian influences. Of importance in our context was the creolization between Europeans and Africans. During the fourteenth and fifteenth centuries, the Atlantic expansion of the Europeans, mainly under Portuguese and Castilian flags, started first along the western African shores, islands and river systems. The new possibilities of seafaring intensified the contact between Europe and Africa. Creolization obtained a maritime dimension. First, Genoese sailors discovered the Canary Islands and then Castilian and Portuguese seamen followed.

But not all the so-called Europeans of that period fit into the common imagination of the "white European". Since Phoenician, Punic and Roman times, the Iberian Peninsula was a continental intersection par excellence, and some Africanization resulted from the outcome of migration and exchanges. It reached its first peak in medieval times, when the Berber Arab troops conquered the Visigoth kingdom on the Iberian Peninsula in 711. This famous African invasion crossed the Ebro River and reached the French cities of Tours and Poitiers in 741, where the Berbers lost the battle against Karl Martell. The Umayyad caliphate of Cordoba in the tenth and eleventh centuries was a transcontinental Euro-African empire but this declined in 1051 because of an invasion from the Almoravids who settled in present day Mauritania. Also the Almohads, who succeeded the Almoravids, came from a region in the south of Morocco. Between the eleventh and fifteenth centuries Almoravids, Almohads and their successors conquered and evangelized wide parts of northwestern Africa up to the Niger River. The reconquest of the southern Iberian Peninsula by the different Christian kingdoms of the north and east of the Iberian Peninsula gradually moved the frontier between the African and European spheres of influence south to Andalusia, where towns like Jerez de la Frontera, Arcos de la Frontera, Chiclano de la Frontera or Castellar de la Frontera, among others, continue to reflect this historical heritage.

The intermingling of Iberians and Africans was the logical consequence of seven hundred years of cultural and economic relations. Like the transSaharan traders, the maritime traders intensified their contacts with African merchants; both sides thus expected economic advantages. Some of them, mostly of Portuguese origin, became transcultured and changed their appearance.[6] They adopted African customs like skin scarification marks and tattoos, wore African dress and spoke at least two African languages.[7] These Luso-Africans of European and African origin were called Lançados, Tangomaos, Pombeiros, Baquianos or Imbangalas.[8] They were often Jews or New Christians (also converted Muslims), they negotiated with the most powerful African kingdoms, intermarried with local African merchant families and worked as cultural brokers on the western African coasts between Senegambia and Guinea, the Afro-Atlantic islands of São Tomé and Príncipe, Annabon, Bioko, Bissago, Cape Verde, Gorée, Saint Louis, Canarias, Madeira, Porto Santo and the Acores as well as Europe. Lançados developed important trading ports and villages on the Senegambian and Guinea river systems like Rufisque, Porto de Ale, Joala, Ziguinchor, Cacheu, Bolama, Porto da Cruz, Bissau or even the famous port of Mina.[9]

When Christopher Columbus settled on the Afro-Atlantic island of Madeira and Porto Santo during the 1470s, the islands were populated by African slaves and slave traders alike. Like others, Columbus was involved in the slave trade and knew the western African coast until the Bight of Biafra. Columbus was not African, but his agency and attitudes seemed Atlantic-creolized. Other Castilian and Portuguese conquerors who were later involved in the conquest of the Americas were also, to some degree, Atlantic creoles. There is evidence that Alonso Pietro (Prieto?), the pilot of the Niña on the 1492 voyage, was a mulatto.[10]

ARRIVAL OF AFRICANIZED PEOPLES IN THE CARIBBEAN

Without doubt the different Americas, including the Caribbean, are a world region with a long African history, or rather with a long history of African diasporas. It is an important fact that from the Amerindian perspective the so-called European invasion was an African "invasion" too. We have to realize that apart from the quantity of approximately twelve million African slaves[11] who involuntarily reached the different colonies in the Americas since the beginning of the sixteenth century, there also arrived thousands of creolized sailors (some of whom operated as buccaneers), merchants and colonists.

The involvement of Africans in Spanish and Portuguese colonial activities in the Americas is rooted in the incorporation of free and enslaved creoles and blacks into Iberian societies.[12] They were involved in conquering, trading and settling. Atlantic creoles married into Amerindian communities to intensify their contacts with Amerindian merchants and to gain influence. Both sides thus expected mutual economic advantages which, as we already know, mirrored the case from the other side of the Atlantic.

As well as Africans, creolized Africans too came to the Americas as military servants or slaves, where they participated in the Spanish campaigns that headed to the regions north of Mexico City, largely financed by the conquests of the Aztecs and the Incas. It is important to emphasize here that not all Atlantic creoles came as auxiliaries but also as conquerors, or at least merchants, agents, supervisors of mining enterprises or as personal servants. Famous creolized conquerors were Antonio Peréz, Miguel Ruíz, Juan Valiente or Juan Beltrán.[13] Creolized Africans became omnipresent in Spanish enterprises and households in the Americas.

Maybe the most famous Africanized European of the early conquest was Vasco Nuñez de Balboa. He founded in the southeastern region of the Isthmus of Panama, the port of Acla, in 1511 and used the rivers (probably the Atrato River) and paths across the Chucunaque mountains to purchase Amerindian slaves. Balboa was a skilled cultural broker who bargained with one the most powerful Native American kingdoms of the Darién governed by the Cacique Careta. These Chibcha-speaking Amerindians controlled the gold and pearl region which extended from the Atlantic region of the Río Zenu to the Pacific Gulf of San Miguel. Balboa's crossing of the isthmus in 1513 was the first European attempt to reach the rich Pearl islands right across the Gulf of San Miguel.

The Iberian crowns and the Catholic Church needed experts to explore and colonize the "wild" Caribbean shores and islands because the progress of colonization was very slow and skilled people were scarce. They found people with tropical and intercultural experience among the group of Euro-African merchants. The Atlantic creoles were of special interest because they had an exact knowledge of the difficult routes, currents and winds between Africa, Europe and the Caribbean. Many Atlantic creoles belonged to the same clan. Together with their partners in Europe, Africa and the Americas, they formed

Atlantic networks which connected Caribbean and European port cities.[14] Islands like São Tomé, Cape Verde and the Canaries as well as the long shores of Brazil and the Guianas and some Caribbean islands became illegal trading centres.[15]

To exploit silver, gold, pearls, timber and salt, the invaders needed labourers; that meant, in those days, either slaves or indentured servants. Under the flags of Castile and Portugal they enslaved Amerindians and Africans from 1494 onwards. The trade with Amerindians was a very profitable business but required stable cooperation with Native American powers. The enslavement of Amerindians by other Amerindians long before Columbus discovered the New World was commonplace. As they did in western Africa, the newcomers intermarried with the elite class of Amerindian societies.

Zambos were the result of the ethnic mixture between Africans and Amerindians, comparable with the genesis of the Mestizo throughout the hemisphere. Where Zambo cultures emerged, large numbers of runaway slaves could be found. Runaway slaves or maroons escaped from their masters or rescued themselves from slave ships after rebellions or ship wrecks. To survive in the new and inhospitable surroundings, the maroons had to join Amerindian settlements.[16] Within the settlements their roles differed from case to case and some may have been sold as slaves into a distant form of slavery. The first evidence of the existence of Zambos in maroon societies in the Americas can be found among the resistance communities of Chief Enriquillo in Santo Domingo (1519–33), King Bayamo and President Filipino in Panama (1532–54) or King Miguel in Venezuela (1551–54).[17] But there were also white and even Asian people who escaped from the colonial towns, fortresses, mines, plantations, farms and ships.

Let us now take a closer look at the Wayuu on the Caribbean coast of Colombia and Venezuela and the Zambo-Miskito on the Caribbean coast of Honduras and Nicaragua – two examples of Africanized Amerindian societies in the Greater Caribbean. Both regions were never conquered by Spanish troops and therefore could develop independently. Around 1750, two centuries after the Spanish conquest of the Aztecs and Incas, independent Amerindians still controlled over a half of Iberoamerica.[18] The development of communities of exiled or outlawed people, mainly of African origin, influenced the native societies of the two regions heavily. The Africanization of the natives throughout the centuries transformed the autochthonous societies. The new creolized societies were based mostly on African and Amerindian cultures with a small legacy of European heritage.

AFRICANIZATION OF THE WAYUU OF THE GUAJIRA PENINSULA

In 1536 the first Europeans reached the Guajira Peninsula, which is currently part of the Venezuelan state of Zulia and the Colombian department of Guajira, west of Maracaibo Bay in the location of the Ranchería River and Cabo de la Vela. By order of the German-speaking conqueror, Nicolas Federmann, the Converso, Antonio de Chávez, founded the first European settlement of Nuestra Señora de las Nieves in the delta of the Ranchería River.[19] First, pearl exploitation started across the Cabo de la Vela by the German enterprise of the Welser, who came from the present-day Bavarian town of Augsburg, in 1537. In 1538 pearl traders from the island of Cubagua founded the town of Cabo de la Vela. Two of the founders, Rodrigo de Gabraleón and Juan de la Barrera started to organize the economy and politics of the town through a decree of the 27 March 1539.[20]

The pearl (and salt) exploitation of the southern Caribbean began around 1508 in the area between the present-day Venezuelan islands of Margarita, Cubagua and Coche as well as along the Araya Peninsula. Among the merchants and craftsmen who founded Nueva Cádiz, the first Castilian town on the island of Cubagua in 1510 were New Christians like Juan de Córdoba, Francisco de Alcázar, Pedro de Jerez, García de Sevilla, Antón Bernal as well as the chronicler Andrés Bernáldez. Thanks to his records we know that these Conversos who colonized the islands across from the Peninsulas of Araya and Paria were "merchants, salesman, tax gatherers, stewards of the nobility, cloth-sellers, tailors, shoemakers, tanners, weavers, grocers, silk mercers, jewellers, moneychangers and other like traders".[21] Enrique Otte's book *Las perlas del Caribe: Nueva Cádiz de Cubagua* has detailed descriptions of the early enslavement of Amerindians and Africans as pearl divers on the island of Cubagua.[22] After permanent attacks by Caribs from the Guianas and a strong earthquake in 1539 that destroyed the centre of Nueva Cádiz, the pearl traders and their slaves moved to Cabo de la Vela on the Guajira Peninsula.

Throughout the centuries the different Amerindian groups of the South

American coast resisted the Spanish conquerors. This was one of the reasons why the conquerors, after a period of thorough explorations of the seascapes and landscapes, were only able to found a few small settlements (Turbaco in 1509; Cumaná in 1515; Santa Marta in 1525; Coro in 1526; Cartagena de Indias in 1533; and Tolú in 1534) before the foundation of Cabo de la Vela.

Similar to the experience along the western African coast, Atlantic cre-oles negotiated with the different Carib-speaking Amerindian tribes of the Guajira and bought Amerindian slaves from them. But as the Colombian historian María Cristina Navarrete describes in her article "La granjería de las perlas del Río de la Hacha: Rebelión y resistencia esclava (1570–1615)", slave acquisition could also result from hostile raids.[23] The history of the Guajira Peninsula remained, throughout the sixteenth century, a history of informal economies. The independence of the "Guajira societies" was based on different factors. The support by several Amerindian groups guaranteed the pearl elites (Señores de Canoas) of Cabo de la Vela their independence and, in reverse, the allied Amerindians preserved their own independence as well. Intermarriage strengthened the alliances between the two groups. Another factor of independence was the importation of thousands of African slaves. Smugglers and interlopers from Africa and Europe guaranteed this supply. One of these smugglers was the English captain Sir John Hawkins from Plymouth. His father, William Hawkins, already founded around 1530 a family trading enterprise mainly based on slave trading between Europe, Africa and Brazil. John Hawkins and his cousin Francis Drake continued this business. His ships piloted by Lançados and Tangomaos,[24] Hawkins sold African slaves to Cabo de la Vela and Río de la Hacha (present-day Riohacha) in the 1560s and 1570s.[25] The Señores de Canoas were a small group of about fifteen to thirty men. Among the chiefs of Cabo de la Vela we find Alonso de la Barrera as major, Bartolomé Carreño as regidor, the Converso Alonso Díaz de Gabraleón as inspector, Pedro de Ortíz as marshall and even an African-ized Baquiano (slave hunter) named Francisco de Castellanos as treasurer. Together with Amerindians and several maroon groups they controlled the illicit trade in Amerindian and African slaves. The Amerindian slaves were mostly captured in the Sierra Nevada mountains, west of the peninsula. The Guajira alliances sold the imported African slaves to the Neogranadian Highlands via Valledupar (Camino de Jerusalem) or used them as slaves for their own pearl, lumber, divi-divi and salt exploitation.

The end of the pearl exploitation in the 1580s led to a strong emigration from Cabo de la Vela to Río de la Hacha. However, the majority of the Amerindians and maroons stayed north and east of the Ranchería River where they controlled almost the entire peninsula. After 1580, craftsmen and jewellers from different regions in the Caribbean reached the town of Río de la Hacha. María Eugenio Ángeles Martínez found out that a group of approximately twenty Señores de Canoas and six hundred slaves of African ancestry were living in that town.[26] The Spanish colonial government in Maracaibo established a military post in Río de la Hacha and founded a municipal council (*cabildo*) there. The colonial influence of Maracaibo, and later Santa Marta, on Río de la Hacha remained weak. On the contrary, the Señores de las Canoas used their intercultural relations with Amerindians and maroons to dominate the town of Río de la Hacha and they extended their influence to Maracaibo, Santa Marta and even Cartagena de Indias.[27]

During the monarchical union between Spain and Portugal (1580–1640) the influence of Portuguese traders in the Americas grew fast. The establishment of an inquisition tribunal in Cartagena de Indias after 1610 was a reaction of the "old elites" against the economic activities of the Portuguese traders. From then on, all Portuguese were suspected of being "Crypto Jews". Inquisition documents of 1627 tell us the story of two Portuguese traders who dominated the pearl trade between Cartagena and Río de la Hacha: Antonio Gramaxo (or Gramajo) and Manuel Antonio de Sousa were suspected of being disguised Jews.[28] At the end of the sixteenth century the Gramaxo family established an Atlantic network of slave trading between the Cape Verdean islands, the rivers of Guinea, Brazil and Lisbon. In 1604 Antonio Gramaxo's father Francisco is recorded on the payroll of the Portuguese New Christian, Asientista Manuel de Sousa Couthino, as being an Angolan slave trader.[29] Antonio Núñez Gramaxo was one of the pioneers in the contraband in pearls, slaves, salt and Brazil wood between Río de la Hacha and the nearby island of Curaçao, where the Dutch founded a colony in 1634. After the conquest of the islands of Curaçao, Aruba and Bonaire between 1634 and 1636, the independent Guajira became an important location of commercial interest for the Dutch West India Company which established a centre of slave trading in the mid-seventeenth century on the island of Curaçao.

At the same time the Guajira Peninsula was still an area that had never

been controlled fully by the Spaniards. Different maroon groups of Africanized Amerindians dominated the area of the Central Guajira Peninsula
around Maicao and blocked the main connections between the regions of
Santa Marta, Río de la Hacha and Valledupar with Maracaibo.[30] The less Africanized Amerindian clans controlled the entire Upper Guajira Peninsula.
Dutch traders from Curaçao and English traders from Jamaica intensified
their business with the independent groups and supported their war against
the Spaniards. In the national archive in Willemstad on the island of Curaçao,
I found several documents about Jewish and New Christian merchants who
were involved in trade networks between Curaçao and the Guajira Peninsula
as well as the Mosquito Coast and the Isthmus of Darién.[31] The trading
locations on the mainland were independent territories under the control
of Amerindians and Zambos. Atlantic creoles linked these regions with São
Tome, Luanda and Cape Verde as well as with the Luso-African communities of Veracruz, Campeche, Trujillo, Portobello, Panama City, Cartagena de
Indias, Maracaibo, Tucacas, Santo Domingo, Santiago de Cuba and Havana.
Jewish Atlantic creoles founded the powerful Jewish community, Mikve
Israel, in the town of Otrabanda on Curaçao in 1659, which played an import-
ant role in the development of Caribbean trade.

The Dutch West India Company government sent its cultural brokers to
the Guajira Peninsula to trade with the Amerindian chiefs and maroon cap-
tains as well as with outlawed European merchants.[32] The close relations to
the Dutch increased the economic situation for the "outlaw societies" and the
possibilities to expand the so-called contraband commerce. The illegal trade
in firearms was the most successful business, not only from an economic
point of view but also considering the possibilities of self-defence against the
incessant attacks of Spanish troops.

After the beginning of the eighteenth century, Great Britain intensified
its colonial interest in the Americas. One part of British policy was the support of independent Amerindians and maroons in their war against Spanish
colonialism, thereby paralleling Dutch policy. This selective armament of
Amerindians and maroons on the Guajira Peninsula promoted the process of
alliances between the different Amerindians and maroons on the peninsula.
The permanent war against the troops of the viceroyalty of New Granada culminated, furthermore, in a process of Africanization among the groups and

the birth of a federated group: the Wayuu. We find mention of the Wayuu for the first time around 1750.[33] Before that time, the name "Guajiros" appeared in colonial maps and documents. In 1727 more than 2,000 Wayuu attacked the Spanish. Other attacks followed in 1741, 1757, 1761 and 1768.[34] On the 2 May 1769, the Wayuu set the Spanish town of El Rincón on fire, burning down the church and two Spaniards who had taken refuge in it. Supported by the English and Dutch, the Wayuu defended their independence and regained their territory.

The Wayuu were organized in clans following matrilineal structures. Some of the clans were more Amerindian than other clans which were more Africanized or even Europeanized. There were still distinct local and regional differences. Before slavery was abolished in the Dutch colonies in 1863, slaves escaped from Curaçao, Bonaire and Aruba to the South American coasts where they joined the Wayuu. Despite the high percentage of intermingling with Afro-Caribbean and white European people, the Wayuu described themselves as genuine Amerindians and as descendants of the Caribs. Today, the majority of Wayuu people deny any racial mixture with people of African descent.

AFRICANIZATION OF THE MISKITOS ON THE MOSQUITO COAST

Spanish colonialism failed completely on parts of the Caribbean coast of Central America. Until the end of the nineteenth century no single successful Spanish settlement could be established between Trujillo in present-day Honduras and Nombre de Dios, today's Portobello in Panama. As part of the western Caribbean, the Caribbean coast of Central America is a region of intense Jamaican-British influence and a high degree of African-Amerindian mixture. Since the second half of the seventeenth century these groups of Afro-Amerindian descent appear in different documents as "zambos", "mosquitos", "moscos", "zambo-mosquitos" and "zambos del mosquito".[35] From an ethno-historical point of view, Mary Wallace Helms already discussed the question "Negro or Indian?" in 1977.[36]

The name "Miskito" as the designation for a tribe or a special indigenous group did not exist until the beginning of the seventeenth century. Some scholars like Barbara Potthast, Germán Romero or Karl H. Offen doubt that the name Miskito refers to a river named "Moschitos", "Moscomitos" or "Mesquitos" located to the south of the Cape Gracias a Dios. The name appeared in Spanish maps in the years 1536, 1562, 1587 and 1600 as well as in Dutch maps of 1595 and 1613.[37] According to British Colonial Office sources, the term Miskito derived from the weapon, the musket, used by the Amerindians around the Cape Gracias a Dios area reflected in the descriptions, "muskeetos" or "Indiens de Moustique".[38] Missionaries like Fray Pedro de la Concepción called the Amerindians who traded in firearms and other weapons with the English, "Guaianes". In his *Diccionario Español-Sumo, Sumo-Español*, the linguist Götz von Houwald referred to the same group as "Wayah".[39]

Miskito chiefs were able to communicate in English and travelled with English buccaneers as sailors to places all over the world.[40] Almost the entire well-known "piracy literature" concerning the Mosquito Coast contains similar information like the writings of Pedro de la Concepción. The "pirate" M.W. who traded with the Miskitos around 1695–1705, mentioned in his reports "The Mosquito Indian and his Golden River" that the Miskito chief Oldman, who governed in the vicinity of the region of Cape Gracias a Dios between 1655 and 1686, was fluent in the English language and had travelled as far as Jamaica.[41] The Amerindian groups of the "Mosquitos", "Guaianes" and "Wayah" (referring to the ancestral tribes of the later Miskitos) as well as other Amerindian cultures like the Hicacas, Panamcas, Towacas, Cackeras, Ulvas, Jicaques, Payas, Sumos, Cucras, Caribes and Ramas together populated the region between Cape Cameron, San Juan River and the Segovia mountains.[42] We can conclude that the population of this region was absolutely not homogenous.

Some Dutch merchants who traded with the Amerindians of the Mosquito Coast were of Sephardic Jewish origin. One example is the famous "buccaneer" Abraham Blauvelt (alias Bluefield) who visited the Mosquito Coast several times between 1625 and 1640.[43] After the resumption of the war in 1621, the West India Company was founded in Amsterdam (Holland) in the same year to fight against Spanish commerce. Escorted by warships, the Dutch attacked Spanish military posts in northeastern Brazil, the Guiana's and the Orinoco region, the coasts and islands of northern South America

as well as the West Indies and the Central American coast. With the conquest of Curaçao in 1634, the West India Company developed the island as
a home base for all their activities in the western and southern Caribbean.
To smuggle African slaves to Trujillo, Campeche, Veracruz or even Cuba,
Dutch ships had to pass the Central American shores where they were often
shipwrecked because of the shallow waters.

Long before slaves from Dutch and English slave ships survived the well-
known shipwrecks of the seventeenth century, the Spanish had imported
hundreds of African slaves to work in the silver mining areas of Honduras as
well as along the plains of the Pacific coast of Nicaragua. African slave labour
was important in the Honduran mountains since the beginning of colonial
economy. Any form of slavery produced *marronage*, the desertion of enslaved
workers from their assigned tasks. In the mining areas of Honduras there are
references to maroon groups close to Trujillo around 1540.[44] To survive in
the relatively inhospitable areas of the Mosquito Coast, black runaways relied
on the support of local Amerindian groups. One result of this association
was of course ethnic mixture. This new Zambo-Miskito population produced
changes in the demographic, social and political structure of the Amerindian cultures and affected the economic relations between the different
Amerindian groups. Some Amerindians did not allow the runaways to settle
freely among them. They killed or enslaved some black refugees. Those
enslaved Africans who intermingled with Amerindians produced a generation of free miscegenated people because the condition of slavery was not
inheritable.

The rise of the transatlantic slave trade during the seventeenth century
influenced the African population everywhere in the Americas. Small trading companies and new groups of colonizers of Spanish and non-Spanish
origin increased the importation and use of African slaves in the western
Caribbean, in areas such as the previously uninhabited Bay and Corn islands
as well the island of Old Providence.[45] With the beginning of the seventeenth
century the Spanish colonial government in Guatemala, which dominated
the Pacific Coast of Nicaragua, encouraged the development of an intensive
plantation system. For better management of the slave importation to Nicaragua, the Spanish expanded the port of Trujillo. Maroon groups, mostly from
Dutch ships, populated the mountains of the Río Dulce and the neighbouring

islands of Guanaja, Roatan, Hog and Utila.[46] Despite a permanent process of intermingling during the first two centuries of European invasion, the Miskitos still believe in myths of shipwrecked slave ships as the source of their black ancestors.

The aforementioned English pirate and slave trader M.W. wrote in 1699 about a group of runaway slaves rescued from a slave ship from Guinea which became shipwrecked in 1639 on the coast close to the Río Coco.[47] M.W. dated a second shipwreck in 1649. Licenciado Ambrosio Tomás Santaella Melgarejo, an officer of the Audiencia of Guatemala, described a wreck of a slave ship in 1652. It is possible that the owner of this ship was the Portuguese Jewish slave trader, Lorenzo Gramajo, from Curaçao, a son of the mentioned Antonio Núñez Gramaxo (or Gramajo).[48] According to the text of Robert Hodgson, senior, at least two Dutch slave ships foundered along the southern section of the Mosquito Coast before he became superintendent between 1749 and 1759.[49] Also, Barbara Potthast mentioned a Dutch slave ship that came to grief in 1710.[50] Probably the most famous wreck of a slave ship was the one of 1641. In that year, English buccaneers took over a Portuguese slave ship and left the booty on the Mosquito Coast close to the banks of the Río San Juan.[51] The Nicaraguan bishop Garret y Arlovi described in 1711 the "famous ship wreck" of 1641 as the birth of the Zambo-Miskito culture. He refers to a black man named Juan Ramón who told him the story. Ramón reported that about one third of the slaves who survived the shipwreck escaped and founded their own "state" of *palenques* (runaway slave communities). Furthermore, he told Garret y Arlovi about the several armed conflicts between the Amerindian groups and the African maroons belonging to their "state". Bishop Garret y Arlovi described these Amerindian groups as "Caribs".[52] Finally the Africans defeated the Amerindians and they escaped to the mountains of Segovia and Chontales. The Africans kidnapped Amerindian women, reproduced by intermarriage and thus built the basis for the Zambo-Miskito culture. Also Ambrosio Tomás Santaella Melgarejo mentioned that the Africans: "bred with indigenous women and so started to establish friendly relations with the Indians who descended from the mountains to live among them".[53]

Currently, most of the Miskitos of Nicaragua consider the shipwreck of 1641 as the birth of their nation. But not all Miskitos believe that they are

Zambo-Miskitos due to the different degrees of intermingling with Africans as well as with white people. The Miskitos who almost did not mix with the African maroons of the coast were often called Tawira. Despite the physical differences, both groups shared a lot of similarities such as those the famous Olaudah Equiano recorded in 1773. Although the Miskitos practise several African traditions (often without any knowledge that those traditions originally came from Africa), the Amerindian traditions predominate. The strongest feature of their shared identity may be found until the present day in their Miskito language.[54]

The degree of intermingling depended mainly on two factors – the areas where, because of the shallow waters, most slave ships ship foundered; and, the intensity of Amerindian resistance against Africanization. We can establish that the main areas of the Zambo-Miskito population were found around Cape Gracias a Dios and Sandy Bay in the northern section and around the Pearl Lagoon in the southern section of the Mosquito Coast. According to the French buccaneer Raveneau de Lussan, who visited the Mosquito Coast in 1688, the Zambo-Miskitos settled largely in the valley of the Wanks River (modern Río Coco). Also, M.W. located their settlements along the same river.

Due to the lack of any census for the Mosquito Coast it is impossible to ascertain either the number of Miskitos at any time or the approximate size of the group of Zambo-Miskitos. It is difficult to study the number of inhabitants of the regions beyond Spanish control like the Mosquito Coast, the Darién and the Talamanca mountains, the Petén or the Guajira Peninsula.[55] Robert Hodgson, who was a superintendent in Bluefields, estimated in 1757 about ten to eleven thousand Miskitos.[56] Exact data is only available for the British colony of Black River and its vicinity where, around the year 1766, approximately 450 white men (mostly English settlers and soldiers), 4,400 African and about one hundred Amerindian slaves lived among about 10,000 Zambos and Miskitos.[57]

By the end of the seventeenth century the leader of the Zambo-Miskitos held titles like "general" and "captain". A well-known Zambo captain was Captain Kit who lived in the delta of the Coco River, where he controlled the river navigation.[58] Under the rule of the mulatto king, Jeremy I, between 1687 and about1720, the Miskitos developed Sandy Bay as their capital and held the title of "king".[59] Within the political union of all Miskitos, the Tawira held the titles of "governor" and "admiral". During the eighteenth century, the Zambo-Miskito became more and more dominant. From the first decade until the official end of the Miskito kingdom in 1896, the function of the king was held by the Zambo-Miskitos.

CONCLUSION

To claim that approximately 75 per cent of the contemporary Caribbean population is of African descent overlooks the fact that a significant part of this percentage reflects mixtures with Amerindians as well as with Europeans. This is the result of an extensive process of continual intermingling. In one case it led to the rise of powerful Zambo societies which are based on predominantly Amerindian traditions. Until the twentieth century, Africanized Amerindians like the Wayuu and the Miskitos were never conquered by any European colonial power, not by the Spanish, the British, the French or the Dutch. On the contrary, both cultures claimed successfully their independence against the Spanish invaders and thus survived not only the Spanish Conquista, but also later the national genocides of the nineteenth and twentieth centuries. Direct trading connections and military alliances with the Portuguese, British and Dutch always guaranteed their independence – economically as well as politically.

The most important agents in the process of Africanization of Amerindians were two groups: Africanized Europeans and African slaves. The European merchants who came to independent regions of the Americas were often from outlawed Africanized cultures of a Portuguese background called Lançados, Tangomaos, Pombeiros, Baquianos or Imbangalas. Controlling the illegal and legal Atlantic trade of the southern Atlantic, they incorporated (by intermarriage) most of the independent Amerindians in the Caribbean in their Atlantic networks and shared their African culture. Approximately twelve million African slaves were sold to the Americas. Thousands of them escaped and intermingled as so-called maroons with Amerindians in the inaccessible territories of the Caribbean. They played an important role in the continuation of the process of Africanization. Nevertheless, this was not the sort of African (or European) diaspora that established cohesive communities with any real or imagined connection to their ancestral cultures in Africa or Europe. Members of these diasporas went local and completely severed effective links with their ancestral origins.

Ironically, despite their physical appearance and the presence of African cultural characteristics, neither the Wayuu nor the Miskitos define themselves either as African descendants or as descendants of slaves. However, until today they still employ the skills in contraband trade and long-distance networking to maintain economic relations that derived from their foundational past. They still control their territories while cultivating their old links to other Caribbean regions far away, even to transatlantic London and Amsterdam.

NOTES

1. For the concept of the "Atlantic creole" refer to Ira Berlin, "From Kreole to African: Atlantic Creoles and the Origins of African-American Society in Mainland North America", *William and Mary Quarterly* 53, no. 2 (April 1996): 251–88; Linda M. Heywood and John K. Thornton, *Central Africans, Atlantic Creoles, and the Foundation of the Americas, 1585–1660* (Cambridge: Cambridge University Press, 2007), 13; Jane Landers, *Atlantic Creoles in the Age of Revolutions* (Harvard: Harvard University Press, 2010). By "Africanization" I mean the transformation of local societies culturally and demographically to reflect the input resulting from the inclusion of African immigrants to the local communities.

2. María Cristina Navarette, "La granjería de las perlas del Río de el hacha", *Historia Caribe* 3, no. 8 (2003): 35–50; Manuel Vicente Magallanes, *Historia política de Venezuela* (Caracas: Monte Ávila Ediciones, 1975); Weildler Guerra Curvelo, *La Guajira* (Colombia: IM Editores, 2003); Henri Candelier, *Riohacha y los indios guajiros* (Santafé de Bogotá: Ecoe Ediciones, 1994); Michel Perrin, *The Way of the Dead Indians: Guajiro Myths and Symbols*, vol. 13 (Austin, University of Texas Press, 1987); Antonino Vidal Ortega and Fernando Alvaro Baquero Montoya, *De las Indias Remotas . . . Cartas del Cabildo de Santa Marta 1529–1640* (Barranquilla, Colombia: Ediciones UniNorte, 2007).

3. Eugenia Ibarra Rojas, *Del arco y la flecha a las armas de fuego: Los indios mosquitos y la historia centroamericana 1633–1786* (San José: Editorial UCR, 2011); Eugenia Ibarra Rojas, "¿Prisoneros de guerra o esclavos? Los Zambos y los mosquitos ante la práctica de la esclavitud en los siglos XVII y XVIII", in *Haiti: Revolución y emancipación*, ed. Rina Cáceres and Paul Lovejoy (San José: Editorial UCR,

2008), 119–27; Karl Offen, "The Sambo and Tawira Miskitu: The Colonial Origins and Geography of Intra-Miskitu Differentiation in Eastern Nicaragua and Honduras", *Ethnohistory* 49, no. 2: The Caribbean Basin (Spring 2002): 319–72; Karl Offen, *The Miskitu Kingdom: Landscape and the Emergence of a Miskitu Ethnic Identity, Northeastern Nicaragua and Honduras, 1600–1800* (Austin: University of Texas Press, 1999); Baron L. Pineda, *Shipwrecked Identities: Navigating Race on Nicaragua's Mosquito Coast* (Rutgers: Rutgers University Press, 2006); Claudia García, *The Making of the Miskitu People of Nicaragua: The Social Construction of Ethnic Identity* (Uppsala: Uppsala University, 1996); Claudia García, "Hibridación, interacción social y adaptación cultural en la Costa de Mosquitos, siglos XVII y XVIII", *Anuario de Estudios Americanos* 59, no. 2 (2002): 441–62; Mary Wallace Helms, "Miskito Slaving and Culture Contact: Ethnicity and Opportunity in an Expanding Population", *Journal of Anthropological Research* 39, no. 2 (1983):179–97; Michael D. Olien, "The Miskito Kings and the Line of Succession", *Journal of Anthropological Research* 39, no. 2 (1983): 198–241; Barbara Potthast-Jutkeit, "Indians, Blacks, and Zambos on the Mosquito Coast in the 17th and 18th Centuries", *América Negra* 6 (1993): 53–65; and Yuri Hamed Zapata Webb, *Historiografía, Sociedad y Autonomía. Desde Tuluwalpa hasta las Regiones Autónomas de la Costa Caribe nicaragüense: Un pasado y un presente diferente* (Managua: Urracan, 2006).

4.   According to the paradigm of transnational history, the term "transnational" is used here although I will describe conditions in pre-national times.

5.   Greater Caribbean means the large Atlantic coast from Cape Hatteras in North Carolina to the Delta of the Amazon River in Brazil. For similar definitions, see John Robert McNeill, *Mosquito Empires: Ecology and War in the Greater Caribbean, 1620–1914* (New York: Cambridge University Press, 2010); Michael Zeuske, *Sklaven und Sklaverei in den Welten des Atlantiks, 1400–1940* (Münster: Verlag, 2006); Norman Girvan, *Cooperation in the Greater Caribbean: The Role of the Association of Caribbean States* (Kingston: Ian Randle, 2006).

6.   The term "transculturation" was introduced by the Cuban anthropologist, Fernando Ortiz; see Fernando Ortiz, *Contrapunteo cubano del tabaco y el azúcar* (Caracas: Fundación Biblioteca Ayacucho, 1987 [1963]).

7.   James Sweet, *Recreating Africa: Culture, Kinship, and Religion in the African-Portuguese World, 1441–1770* (Chapel Hill: University of North Carolina Press, 2003); Peter Mark, *"Portuguese" Style and Luso-African Identity: Pre-colonial Senegambia, Sixteenth–Nineteenth Centuries* (Bloomington: Indiana University Press, 2002); George E. Brooks, *Euroafricans in Western Africa: Commerce, Social Status, Gender and Religious Observance from the Sixteenth to the Eighteenth Century* (Athens: Ohio University Press, 2003).

8. Jonathan Scorch, *Swimming the Christian Atlantic: Judeoconversos, Afroiberians and Amerindians in the Seventeenth Century* (Leiden: Brill, 2008), 112; Katia M. de Qeuirós Mattoso, *To Be a Slave in Brazil, 1550–1888* (Rutgers: Rutgers University Press, 1982), 20; Ivana Elbl, *The Portuguese Trade with West Africa, 1440–1521* (Toronto: University of Toronto Press, 1986), 667; Zuekske, *Skalven,* 43.

9. Malyn Newitt, *A History of Portuguese Overseas Expansion, 1400–1668* (London: Routledge, 2005), 90; Richard L. Kagan and Philip D. Morgan, *Atlantic Diasporas: Jews, Conversos and Crypto-Jews in the Age of Mercantilism, 1500–1800* (Baltimore: Johns Hopkins University Press, 2009), 171.

10. Matthew Restall, "Black Conquistadors: Armed Africans in Early Spanish America", *Americas* 57, no. 2 (October 2000): 176; Rolando Mellafe, *Breve historia de la esclavitud negra en America Latina* (Mexico, DF: Secretaría de Educación Pública, 1973), 19; Juan Manuel de la Serna Herrera, *Pautas de convivencia étnica en la América latina colonial (indios, negros, mulatos pardos y esclavos)* (Mexico, DF: UNAM, 2005), 25, 27.

11. Paul E. Lovejoy, "The Impact of the Atlantic Slave Trade on Africa: A Review of the Literature", *Journal of African History* 30, no. 2 (1989): 368; Eltis et al., *Assessing the Slave Trade,* http://www.slavevoyages.org/tast/assessment/estimates.faces.

12. Jane Landers, *Black Society in Spanish Florida* (Urbana: University of Illinois Press, 1999), 7–9. On the early African diaspora in the Americas, see John Thornton, *Africa and the Africans in the Formation of the Atlantic World, 1450–1680* (Cambridge: Cambridge University Press, 1992); Vincent Bakpetu Thompson, *The Making of the African Diaspora in the Americas, 1441–1900* (London: Longman, 1987).

13. Restall, "Black Conquistadores", 183–85.

14. Jonathan I. Israel, *Diasporas within a Diaspora: Jews, Crypto-Jews and the World Maritime Empires* (Leiden: Brill, 2002).

15. João Martins da Silva Marques, *Descobrimentos documentos para a sua história, III* (Lisbon: Instituto Para a Alta Cultura, 1971).

16. Alvin O. Thompson, *Flight to Freedom: African Runaways and Maroons in the Americas* (Kingston: University of the West Indies Press, 2006).

17. Oruno Lara, *Space and History in the Caribbean* (Princeton: Markus Wiener, 2006).

18. David Weber, "Bourbons and Bárbaros: Center and Periphery in the Reshaping of Spanish Indian Policy", in *Negotiated Empires: Centers and Peripheries in the Americas, 1500–1820,* ed. Christine Daniels and Michael V. Kennedy (New York: Routledge, 2002), 79.

19. Manuel Muñoz Luengo, "Noticias sobre la fundación de la Nuestra Señora de los Remedios de Cabo de la Vela", *Revista Anuario de Estudios Americanos* 4 (1949): 58; José Polo Acuña, *Defensa de la tierra: Colonización y conflicto en la Guajira, Siglo XVIII* (La Guajira: Multiétnica y Pluricultural, 2000), 109.

20. Enrique Otte, *Las perlas del Caribe: Nueva Cádiz de Cubagua* (Caracas: Fundación John Boulton, 1977), 393–95.

21. Andrés Bernáldez, *Historia de los Reyes Católicos, Capítulo I* (Seville: Imprenta J.M. Geofrin, 1869), 341.

22. Otte, *Las perlas del Caribe*.

23. Navarette, "La granjería de las perlas".

24. About Hawkins's Lançados and Tangomaos pilots, see Harry Klesey, *Sir John Hawkins: Queen Elizabeth's Slave Trader* (New Haven: Yale University Press, 2003).

25. In 1568 Miguel de Castellanos bought 144 African slaves from John Hawkins. See Trinidad Miranda Vasquez, *La gobernación de Santa Marta (1570–1670)* (Seville: Escuela de Estudios Hispanoamericanos, 1976), 78–79.

26. María Eugenio Ángeles Martínez, *La esclavitud indígena, impulsora de las pesquerías de perlas en Nuestra Señora de los Remedios: Actas del Congreso de Historia del Descubrimiento (1492–1556)* (Madrid: Real Academia de la Historia and Confederación Española de Cajas de Ahorros, 1992), 3:615–31.

27. Navarette, "La granjería de las perlas", 40.

28. A. María da Graça Mateus Ventura, "Os Gramaxo. Un caso paradigmático de redes de influencia en Cartagena de Indias", http://www.fl.ul.pt/unidades/sefarditas/textos/textos_3.htm.

29. Enriqueta Vila Vilar, *Hispanoamérica y el comercio de esclavos* (Seville: Escuela de Estudios Hispanoamericanos, 1977), 70.

30. Vidal Ortega and Baquero Montoya, *De las Indias*.

31. The Tyrolean Jesuit father Jacob Walburger, who travelled to the Darién in 1748, described the Cuna in his letters as Jewish descendants because of their social structure, religion and their dress code. Carl Henrik Langebaek, *El diablo vestido de negro y los cunas del Darién en el siglo XVIII: Jacobo Walburger y su breve noticia de la Provincia del Darién, de la ley y costumbres de los Yndios, de la poca esperanza de plantar nuestra fe, y del número de sus naturales, 1748* (Bogotá: Edición Uniandes, 2006), 25, 88.

32. For more on Dutch West India Company activities, see Cornelis Ch. Goslinga, *The Dutch in the Caribbean and on the Wild Coast, 1580–1680* (Gainesville: University of Florida Press, 1971).

33. Christian Cwik et al., "Territorios soberanos y autónomos en el Gran Caribe, 1750–1820" (typescript, Cartagena de Indias, 2009), 5.

34. Eduardo Barrera, *La rebelión Guajira de 1769. Algunas constantes de la Cultura Wayuu y razones de supervivencia*, edición en la biblioteca virtual del Banco de la República, http://www.banrepcultural.org/blaavirtual/revistas/credencial/junio1990/junio2.htm.

35. N. Rodgers, "Caribbean Borderland: Empire, Ethnicity, and the Exotic on the Mosquito Coast", *Eighteenth-Century Life* 26, no. 3 (2002): 135.

36. Mary Wallace Helms, "Negro or Indian? The Changing Identity of a Frontier Population", in *Old Roots in New Lands: Historical and Anthropological Perspectives on Black Experiences in the Americas*, ed. Ann M. Pescatello (Westport, CT: Greenwood, 1977), 155–72. See also, Eugenia Ibarra Rojas, "La complementariedad cultural en el surgimiento de los grupos zambos del Cabo Gracias a Dios", *Revista de Estudios Sociales* 26 (2007): 105–15.

37. Barbara Potthast, *Die Mosquitoküste im Spannungsfeld Britischer und Spanischer Politik 1502–1821* (Cologne: Verlag Böhlau, 1988), 24, 52, 66, 67; Germán Romero Vargas, *Las sociedades del Atlántico de Nicaragua en los siglos XVII y XVIII* (Managua: Colección Cultural Banco Nicaragüense, 1995), 41; Karl H. Offen, "Creating Mosquitia: Mapping Amerindian Spatial Practices in Eastern Central America, 1629–1779", *Journal of Historical Geography* 33, no. 1 (2007): 254–82.

38. PRO CO 124/1, fol. 2 (1635) mentioned in Ibarra Rojas, *Del arco y la flecha a las armas de fuego*, 4; Potthast, *Die Mosquitoküste*, 66.

39. Götz Von Houwald, *Diccionario Español-Sumo, Sumo-Español* (Havana: Ministerio de Educación, 1980).

40. Around 1660 the Puritans of the island of Old Providence invited the Miskito chief Jeremy I to London, where he spent three years. Hans Sloane, *A voyage to the islands of Madera, Barbadoes, Nieves, St. Christopher and Jamaica, with a Natural History of the herbs and trees etc.*, 2 vols (London, 1707), 1:77–78.

41. M.W., "The Mosquito Indian and His Golden River", in *A Collection of Voyages and Travels*, ed. Anshaw Churchill (London: Churchills, 1732), 6:293.

42. M. Carey, "La influencia mayag na (sumo) en la historia de la costa Atlántica nicaragüense", *Revista de Historia* 14, no. 1 (2002): 73–88; and Ibarra Rojas, *Del arco y la flecha a las armas de fuego*, 5. About the concept of "buccaneering", see Franklin W. Knight, "Imperialism and Slavery", in *Caribbean Slavery in the Atlantic World*, ed. Hilary McD. Beckles and Verene Shepherd (Princeton: Markus Wiener, 2000), 157.

43. PRO CO 124/2, fol. 199 (1634).

44. Conversation with Dr Rina Caceres during her visit to Cartagena in May 2010.

45. In 1633 the Puritan settlers of Old Providence established commercial relations with the Amerindians in the surroundings of the Cape Gracias a Dios; see

Karen Ordahl Kupperman, *Providence Island (1630)–1641: The Other Puritan Colony* (Cambridge: Cambridge University Press, 1993), 166.

46. AGCA A1. 4060.31537 (1645), cited in Ibarra Rojas, *Del arco y la flecha a las armas de fuego*, 15.

47. M.W., "Mosquito Indian", 289.

48. Pedro de Rivera reported in 1742 that the ship was wrecked on the Mosquito Coast in 1652; see Christian Cwik, "Africanidad con repugnancia: los zambos y el problema de la identidad en el Caribe centroamericano", *Ariadna Tucma Revista Latinoamericana* 6, no. 1 (March 2011–February 2012), www.ariadnatucma.com.ar. About the note of Ambrosio Tomás Santaella Melgarejo, see M.M. Peralta, *Costa Rica y Costa de Mosquitos* (Paris: Imprenta General de Lahure,1898), 78; Ibarra Rojas, *Del arco y la flecha a las armas de fuego*, 16.

49. Robert Hodgson, *The Defence of Robert Hodgson, Esq.* (London, 1779).

50. Potthast, *Die Mosquitoküste*, 63–64.

51. Potthast-Jutkeit, "Indians, Blacks and Zambos", 55.

52. Peralta, *Costa Rica*, 57.

53. Ibarra Rojas, *Del arco y la flecha a las armas de fuego*, 16 (my translation).

54. About "genetic heritage" in the Miskito society of the southern Mosquito shore, see Jorge Azofeifa, Ramiro Barrantes and Edward Ruiz, "Genetic Variation and Racial Admixture in the Miskito of the Southern Mosquito Shore, Nicaragua", *Revista de la Biología Tropical* 46, no. 1 (1998): 157–65; Ibarra Rojas, *Del arco y la flecha a las armas de fuego*, 16.

55. Even though it is difficult to study the number of inhabitants due to a lack of reliable data it is not impossible; see Verena Muth, "The Tule Proto-State between Disappearance and Historical Reconstruction" (paper presented at the forty-fourth conference of the Association of Caribbean Historians, Curaçao, May 2012).

56. Ibarra Rojas, *Del arco y la flecha a las armas de fuego*, 9.

57. F.G. Dawson, "William Pitt's settlement at Black River on the Mosquito Shore: A Challenge to Spain in Central America, 1732–1787", *Hispanic American Historical Review* 63, no. 4 (1983): 677–706. About the general decline of the indigenous population in Honduras and Nicaragua under "Spanish rule", see Linda A. Newson, *The Cost of Conquest: Indian Decline in Honduras under Spanish Rule* (Boulder: Westview, 1986).

58. M.W., "The Mosquito Indian", 290. Eugenia Ibarra Rojas created a map of the Miskito settlements at the Coco River based on the information of M.W.; see Ibarra Rojas, *Del arco y la flecha a las armas de fuego*, 23.

59. The term "mulatto" was used by M.W., "Mosquito Indian".

CHAPTER 4

AFRICAN "NATIONS" AS DIASPORIC INSTITUTION-BUILDING IN THE IBERIAN ATLANTIC

JANE LANDERS

THE IBERIAN ATLANTIC PROVIDES A FERTILE space to examine the prolonged exercise in institution-building by Africans and their descendants. My scholarly career has been devoted to uncovering community networks among African diasporic populations in colonial Latin America, and also to examining the various, and sometimes multiple, identities that Africans and their descendants manifested in the colonial period. My first book was a study of the first free black town in what is today the United States, a community of escaped slaves from the British colonies who sought, and received, religious sanctuary in Spanish Florida. The town of Gracia Real de Santa Teresa de Mose, usually abbreviated as Mose, was established in 1738 on the periphery of St Augustine and is today a national historic landmark. A new visitors' centre exhibit now tells visitors about how a literate Mandinga welded a multi-ethnic community of Congos, Minas, Native Americans and other Mandingas into a robust frontier community that played a critical role in the imperial contests between Spain and England.[1]

The lessons I learned not only from Mose but also from exhaustive archival research in Spain, Cuba, Mexico and the United States, as well as from collaboration on the archaeological investigation of the original site, prepared me to study other black communities across colonial Latin America. From my work on this project and subsequent research on maroon settlements, formally established black towns and black communities within Latin American towns or cities, I have learned that Iberians paid close attention to and care-fully recorded something they designated as an African's *nación* in Spanish or *nação* in Portuguese. The concept of distinct African "identities" was superimposed on several organizations described as *cofradías* and *cabildos de nación*. This chapter highlights the significance of the institution-building processes that produced the religious *cofradías* and the political/economic *cabildos de nación* which are now recognized features of the Iberian Atlantic.[2] Their preservation in a wide variety of documentary sources was, I argue, the result of both Iberian and African agency.

By the mid-fifteenth century, Portuguese traders had established a series of slave-trading factories from which they exported enslaved Africans from Senegambia and Upper Guinea to Cabo Verde, Portugal, Madeira, the Canary Islands and Spain.[3] Slaves identified as hailing from Guinea begin to appear in the notarial registers of Seville by the 1450s but after the 1470s more spe-cific ethno-linguistic designations were given, with Jolof (Wolof) being the most common, followed by Zape and Mandinga. Muslim slaves from North Africa were variously designated as Berberisco/ca or Blanco/a and Moro/a in those notarial records.[4] Indigenous slaves also appear in smaller numbers – some identified as Guanche or Canario/a or from Tenerife, Lanzarote or La Palma, and after 1501, a few identified as Indio/a or by place of origin as Antilla or La Española.[5] Spanish attention to the ethnicity of their slaves thus began long before Spain developed American colonies and may have resulted from their concern to identify the "outsiders" in their midst.

Muslim revolts were an ongoing fear in Spain when Islamicized slaves from Cabo Verde and Senegambia led the first full-scale slave uprising on Hispaniola on Christmas Day, 1521, on Governor Diego Colón's sugar estate, La Isabela. Twenty allegedly "bellicose and perverse" Wolof-speaking slaves led the uprising, killing nine Spaniards before reaching the nearby sugar estate of Ocoa, belonging to the royal judge, Alonso Zuazo. The rebels report-edly hoped to incorporate Zuazo's 120 slaves and attack the Spanish town of Azua. Along the way they attacked the ranch of Melchor de Castro, killed his carpenter, and "stole" or incorporated more Indian and African slaves, at least twenty of whom reportedly spoke Wolof.[6]

While there is no proof the rebels from the Columbus estate were actu-ally Wolofs, Spaniards on the island certainly believed them to be, and they further believed that they rebelled because they were Muslims. Within days of the uprising (on Epiphany, in fact) Spanish officials on Hispaniola issued harsh new slave codes designed to prevent further slave rebellions.[7] In 1532 the queen specifically blamed the "prideful, disobedient, rebellious and incorrigible" Wolof slaves for the damages of the rebellions and deaths of Christians, and forbade any more to be shipped to the Indies because they corrupted more pacific Africans from other lands.[8]

Partially in fear that *bozales*, or recently arrived slaves from Africa, might introduce the dread "contamination" of Islam or other "heathen" practices, the Catholic Church had mandated the baptism of African slaves in the fifteenth century and extended this requirement across the Catholic Americas. Baptismal records thus became the longest and most uniform serial data available for the history of Africans in the Americas, and almost all recorded the baptized person's "nation" or *nação*. Once baptized, Africans and their descendants were also eligible for the sacraments of marriage and Christian burial. Through membership in the Catholic Church, they also generated a host of other religious records such as confirmations, petitions to wed, wills and even, on occasion, divorce actions. In the Iberian colonies, Africans joined church brotherhoods (*cofradías* or *irmandades*) organized along ethnic lines, through which they recorded not only ceremonial and religious aspects of their lives, but also their social, political and economic networks.[9] The Catholic evangelization effort among Africans may have appeared minimal compared to the effort expended on indigenous populations, but royal officials across the Iberian Atlantic believed that christianizing slaves might safeguard against rebellion. It is clear that free and enslaved Africans and creoles alike also saw some advantage in joining the church, and their incorporation into this institution had important cultural implications not only for those who joined it, but also for historical researchers.[10]

Not surprisingly, the earliest known black *cofradías* in the Americas were established in the first Spanish settlement of Hispaniola with the express encouragement of the Catholic Church. In 1592 a group of mulattos, quarterons and mestizos formed the *cofradía* of Nuestra Señora del Carmen y Jesús Nazareno in the Hospital del Señor San Andrés and specified that blacks and Spaniards were excluded from membership. In 1602, the Biafaran, Antón López, requested a licence to establish the *cofradía* of Nuestra Señora de la Candelaria.[11] By that date, the Biafaras had already built a chapel in the Cathedral within which they buried their dead, and so the request of López was approved. Soon after, the Sapes of Sierra Leone established the *cofradía* of Santa María Magdalena, also based in the Cathedral. The early separation of African-born and creole brothers might indicate status differentiation, although the *bozales* actually occupied the most prestigious location. Alternatively, church officials may have considered that the *bozales* required more supervision, and thus kept them literally under their roof.[12]

A report prepared at King Philip III's request in 1613 stated that more than three hundred blacks and Spaniards belonged to the Biafara-created Nuestra Señora de la Candelaria, among whom were some of the town's leading citizens. Six other brotherhoods of colour were still operating in 1613: two more within the cathedral, another in the Franciscan church, another in the Dominican church, another in the Mercedarian church, and La Pura y Limpia Concepción de Nuestra Señora, in the Hospital of San Nicolás de Bari. Audiencia officials reported that all the brotherhoods performed good works and charity and kept well-adorned chapels, and that no problems arose from the multi-ethnic memberships.[13]

As noted, many of these *cofradías* emerged unofficially and then requested church authorization. Only in 1683 did the fourth diocesan synod of Santo Domingo stipulate the requirements for establishing an officially recognized *cofradía*. These included the approval and supervision of church authorities who would conduct an annual visit to the *cofradía*, review the brotherhood's financial records and "assist" in the election of their officers. This regulation was apparently prompted by the rapid proliferation of *cofradías* across the island.

Throughout the circum-Caribbean, black communities devoted hard-earned resources to support Catholic *cofradías* that promoted social cohesion, reinforced fictive and kin networks, and recognized leadership that was generated from within the black community. As was true earlier in Iberia, public displays of religiosity and of civic organization also confirmed black claims to Christian brotherhood and membership in the larger corporate community.[14]

As important examples from Mexico illustrate, however, even *cofradías* authorized by the church could be turned against the state. Convinced that their deceased sister had been beaten to death, in 1611 more than fifteen hundred members of the brotherhood of Nuestra Señora de la Merced angrily marched her body through the streets of Mexico City to display it at the palaces of the archbishop, the inquisition and finally at the home of her owner where they threw rocks and shouted insults until dispersed. The numeric strength of this *cofradía* is impressive and reflects the dramatic rise in slave imports from Congo/Angola during the period of the joint Crowns of Spain and Portugal (1580–1640). As a result of that disturbance, worried officials deported the elderly steward of the *cofradía*, and with that the brothers began to plot in earnest, electing an Angolan king and queen to lead a Christmas-time revolt. Soon thereafter, the newly elected, but elderly King Pablo died unexpectedly and the *cofradía* staged an elaborate funeral for him. Mourners sang African songs and danced before covering Pablo's body and casket in wine and oils. The Catholic friars who were to conduct the burial at the Mercedarian monastery remonstrated to no avail and one distraught African was said to have jumped into Pablo's casket, covered himself with wine and earth, and then jumped back out with a weapon in his raised arm, crying that this was how war was launched.[15]

The following year, in 1612, Portuguese merchants reported overhearing plotters discussing that war in *"la lengua Angola"*. Arrested and tortured slaves began to give up details such as that a witch named Sebastian would cast spells and poison Mexico City's water and food supplies.[16] Officials were shocked to find that many of the implicated slaves belonged to the city's most influential residents and that some of the plotters were free. Convinced the threat was real, they reacted swiftly and harshly, publicly hanging thirty-five people (seven of whom were women). The Spaniards then nailed their heads to the gallows, quartered six of the bodies, buried the rest, and sold the surviving plotters into exile. They also forbade black gatherings; tried to enforce sumptuary laws and prohibitions against blacks carrying weapons; established new police patrols to monitor the city; and disbanded all black brotherhoods. These restrictions were all later relaxed or honoured only in the breach.[17]

Meanwhile, in Cuba, Africans were also congregating along ethnic lines, although there it is clear that black residents established at least two distinct corporate forms of organization. One was the official *cofradía* recognized and regulated by the Catholic Church, such as those in Santo Domingo and

Mexico City. In 1683 the free blacks of Havana erected a small *ermita* (shrine) devoted to the Holy Spirit (Espiritu Santo). By 1648 the devotion had become so popular and the neighbourhood around it had grown so populated that church officials declared the *ermita* an auxiliary parish. Its growth continued, and in 1661 Espirtu Santo was elevated to the status of second parish on the island, after Havana. Sometime shortly thereafter, Espiritu Santo had an auxiliary church of its own located in the Hospital of San Isidro, where during a pastoral visit in 1687, Monseñor Francisco Felix y Solans examined the only extant book of baptism of Pardos and Morenos (mulattos and blacks).[18] Thus, over the course of the seventeenth century, free blacks in Havana expanded the church on their own terms and eventually received the official recognition of the Catholic Church. Although there is no mention in church histories of a *cofradía* at Espiritu Santo, Fernando Ortiz wrote that the Ararás of Havana established a *cofradía* there in the 1690s.[19]

There has been considerable confusion in past and recent scholarship, including my own, about the nature of black corporate organization in Spanish America. The terms *cofradía* and *cabildo* have been used interchangeably, with *cabildo* the most common term used in Spanish American contexts.[20] In its common usage, *cabildo* refers to a town council or a town meeting, and no racial or ethnic meaning is assigned. In areas of heavy African importation such as Cuba, however, the added phrase *"de nación"* shifted the meaning to refer to groups organized along some form of African ethnicity. Drawing on Cuban records held in the state archives, Matt Childs has carefully tried to explicate how Africans and their descendants understood, defined and redefined ethnicities in *cabildos de nación* in the late eighteenth century; I have examined the links between *cabildo* membership and membership in free militias; and Phil Howard has examined how, under pressure, *cabildos* were transformed into associations of colour or mutual aid societies in the late nineteenth century.[21] By assuming that *cabildos* were the only corporate religious form Africans adopted, all of us ignored the black *cofradías* that persisted in Cuba and elsewhere into the nineteenth century. Their histories can be found in the rich ecclesiastical records still stored in archbishopric archives in many parts of the Americas.

As their counterparts also did in Mexico and other circum-Atlantic sites from Rio de Janeiro to Congo Square in New Orleans, blacks in Havana also developed other forms of corporate organization following ethnic or nation lines. These were referred to by various terms such as *tumbas* or *congadas* and they developed autonomously without official sanction when blacks gathered on Sundays and other feast days to make music and dance. Eventually these informal gatherings were shaped into *cabildos de nación* by worried urban officials who monitored and sought to control them.

In 1755 Bishop Augustín Pedro Morrell de Santa Cruz recorded the existence of twenty-one *cabildos de nación* in Havana. Responding to complaints about their disturbances, the bishop visited one group's *tumba* and was distressed to note that men and women drank *aguardiente* (the local rum) until senseless, danced "provocatively, in the custom of their lands" and engaged in all the excesses that thereby followed. Fernando Ortiz quoted this passage but ignored the rest of the document in which the bishop recounted a visit to one house where he prayed the rosary with the gathered Africans and presented them with an image of the Virgin.[22] Morrell de Santa Cruz reported that this outreach produced good results and he elaborated a plan to assign a catechist, adept in the particular African language, to each house "which is the same as we do with the Indians". He recommended against forbidding dances or musical instruments and believed that through peaceful suasion, the Africans would "open their eyes" and recognize the "abominations" of their former practices. "Houses of the devil" could be converted into "temples of God" or *ermitas*, thereby producing social order and saving souls at the same time.[23] While not as acclaimed as the Jesuit missionaries of Cartagena, Alonso de Sandoval and Pedro Claver, Bishop Morrell de Santa Cruz seems to have felt some calling for evangelizing Africans.

Cuban church officials never adopted Bishop Morrell de Santa Cruz's plan for reforming African *cabildos* by suasion. There is no evidence, for example, that Cuban clerics seriously studied African languages as their counterparts, Alonso de Sandoval and Pedro Claver did in Cartagena. Instead, as David Wheat's forthcoming book shows, they seem to have relied on black linguists and cultural brokers to bring "new" Africans into the church. In analysing the Cathedral records of seventeenth-century Havana, Wheat found that Angolan women almost always served as godmothers for newly imported Angolans.[24]

As their counterparts in Santo Domingo had earlier, Spanish authorities in

Havana began to regulate and reshape the disorderly African *cabildo* gatherings described by the bishop. To be legitimated, brothers had to define their devotions as well as rules of conduct in charters or constitutions. Elected officers promised to monitor their own members and expel any miscreants, and they devoted themselves to a patron saint whom they honoured on his or her feast day. In hopes that the *cabildos* would promote positive social values and good order, Spanish officials usually approved their requests to organize and granted the licences to the *cabildos*.

Matt Childs has analysed the governance of Havana's black brotherhoods or *cabildos* and finds that African-born individuals held the upper hand and the leadership of most of these nation-based corporations. Rather than outlaw African-led *cabildos* as earlier Mexican viceroys had, Cuban authorities supported this bias, hoping to pit African-born members against creoles, and thus "divide and conquer", but despite their political disabilities, Afro-creoles joined the brotherhoods, hoping to preserve some sense of African identity as Cuba's slave regime increasingly defined them by colour.[25]

Eighteenth-century *cabildo* officers in Cuba often carried military titles, such as captain, suggesting the close connection they had to militia organizations. But members still elected kings, queens and courts for carnival whom Spanish officials informally recognized as representatives of their people, much as they had the black barrio *mayorales* in sixteenth-century Seville.[26] Havana's existing *cabildo* charters usually list only male officers and members by name, but free and enslaved women also belonged. Havana's Carabalí brotherhood, Nuestra Señora de Belen, had sixty-one named male members in 1771 and 240 unnamed female members.[27]

Dues-paying members of the *cabildos* supported an array of mutual aid functions, including caring for the ill, freeing the aged and burying the dead. Despite the low economic status of most members, many of Havana's eighteenth-century *cabildos* were able through loans, bequests and savings to buy their own buildings which could not be sold without the unanimous vote of the membership. The Royal Congo *cabildo*, also known as the Cabildo Rey Mago San Melchor, from whom members claimed to be descended, owned a property on Florida Street, among others. The Mandingas owned a house on the corner of Habana and Merced, and the Ararás owned a house on Compostela Street.[28]

Although brothers and sisters were permitted to congregate at the *cabildo* houses every Sunday and on the numerous feast days to sing and dance, they were supposed to disperse by eight in the evening. But the well-attended dances and the music and crowds eventually so disturbed the "honoured" citizenry of Havana that a 1792 edict gave the *cabildos* one year to relocate outside the city walls. The same edict ordered *cabildos* to take the bodies of deceased members to the public mortuary rather than stage celebratory and "disorderly" wakes in their meeting houses. It would seem from the frequency of the pronouncements that early efforts to limit *cabildos* were no more successful than sumptuary and other sorts of restrictive legislation.[29]

The activities and observances of the black *cabildos* blended European and African cultural elements. Perhaps the most popular celebration for Africans in the circum-Caribbean was the Día de Reyes, celebrated on the sixth of January (Epiphany), and possibly chosen for the reason that one of the three magi who appeared at the birth of Christ – Melchior, Caspar and Balthazar – the last was reputedly black.[30] This was a day of licence and role-reversal on which the nations paraded through the streets of Havana, led by their newly elected kings and queens. In processions reminiscent of those of seventeenth-century *irmandades*, or black brotherhoods, in Lisbon, the participants performed African songs and dances accompanied by drums, scrapers and hollowed gourd rattles, while wearing elaborate costumes of raffia, peacock feathers, animal skins and horns, and beads. Stilt-walkers, lantern-bearers, masked figures and gymnasts added to the merriment. Throughout the day, the Africans paraded under balconies or into courtyards requesting *aguinaldos* or gratuities for the entertainment they provided onlookers.[31] Guided by an intricate vocabulary of colour, artefacts and symbols, black and white observers read the *cabildo* processions for syncretic references to their African deity of choice. For example, Cubans still recognize the patron saint of the Lucumíes, Santa Bárbara, as Shangó, the Virgin of Cobre as Ochún, and San Lázaro as Baba-lú-Ayé.[32]

The exoticism of *cabildo* processions attracted nineteenth-century artists such as Federico Miahle (1810–81) and pioneering anthropologists and ethnohistorians such as Fernando Ortiz (1881–1969) and Lydia Cabrera (1899–1991). Ever since, scholars have focused almost exclusively on the *cabildos de nación*. Because Cuba's *cabildos* had to be authorized by secular officials, their records were deposited in secular repositories such as the National Archives of Cuba in Havana and, with lesser frequency, the Archive of the Indies in Seville, Spain. Scholars have, to date, concentrated their research on these secular repositories. In contrast, not enough scholarly attention has been paid to religiously sanctioned *cofradías* and few scholars have actually examined their records.

I have been working in ecclesiastical sources since 1985, first in Spanish Florida, and subsequently in the Dominican Republic, Cuba, Brazil and Colombia. Catholic registers of baptisms, confirmations, marriages and burials yield the longest serial data available for the history of Africans in the Americas. In addition to providing critical demographic statistics on the African populations in the Americas, these records also provide detailed information on ethnicity (described in the records as *"nacões"*, *"naciones"* or *"castas"*). Entries also record, when known, parents' names and occasionally allude to birthplaces in Africa. Fictive kinship patterns are also evident in godparent and marriage sponsor choices. Such ethnic and geographic markers enable scholars to track the history of specific groups over time in the targeted areas and make comparisons across Spanish and Portuguese colonies.

In 2003, with co-directors Paul Lovejoy from York University and Mariza de Carvalho Soares of the Universidade Federal Fluminense, I launched a project entitled, "Ecclesiastical Sources and Historical Research on the African Diaspora in Brazil, Cuba, and the Spanish circum-Caribbean", that is attempting to digitally preserve these unique, and imperilled records.[33] The fragile documents are held in religious archives or local churches, at risk of the ravages of the climate, bug infestation and other natural hazards. Too often, local lay persons or parish priests are their only guardians, and most of these well-meaning individuals are unaware of the historic significance of the documents they manage, or how fragile they are. Sadly, there are few resources available to devote to preserving these treasures and if not captured quickly, some may be lost forever. The dispersed nature of the records also make them difficult for scholars to access, especially those scholars whose home countries can offer little research support. Many small churches in Cuba are no longer open and many of the records from Brazilian and Colombian churches have disappeared. For all these reasons, most of these materials we are digitizing have never been examined by scholars. The Cuban and Florida records begin in the sixteenth century, the earliest we have yet located. The Brazilian records begin in the seventeenth century and the earliest Colombian materials we have located, to date, begin in the eighteenth century.

Although the Catholic Church dictated a fairly common method for recording, we are finding interesting variations in distinct locations. In Brazil, blacks left a significant number of valuable testaments that are not generally found in the Cuban and Spanish borderland records so far examined. These Brazilian wills offer important information on the occupations, property and economy of free and enslaved Africans, as well as additional insights into fictive and kin networks and religious devotion. Brazilian and Cuban churches have also yielded a document type called *banhos* in Brazil and *expedimentos* in Cuba. All persons wishing to be married had to complete them and the betrothed had to show proof of when and where they had been baptized, state whether or not they had previously been married, give their legal status and occupation and other information pertaining to their family histories, such as their ethnicity. If they were enslaved, their owners also had to submit written permission for the slaves to wed.

I am finding that sacramental records also offer us surprising new information on important figures and events in Afro-Caribbean history. For example, José Antonio de Aponte has long been reputed to have been a *capatáz*, or elected leader or chairman, of a Lucumí *cabildo* in Havana. Matt Childs questions whether Aponte actually was a member of the *cabildo*, an assertion first made by the Cuban historian José Luciano Franco and repeated by all subsequent scholars.[34] Child's doubt seems justified since such evidence was not extracted from Aponte after his arrest, but whether or not he was a member of a *cabildo*, in the archbishopric archive in Havana, I discovered that Aponte, and various other members of the Aponte Rebellion, were members of the Catholic *cofradía* of St Joseph, founded in 1800 by the *gremio de carpinteros de lo blanco*, or guild of carpenters, and located in the Convent of San Francisco. The *cofradía* brothers called themselves the "slaves of St Joseph, Jesus, and Mary, his mother". To further complicate this issue, the brothers also referred to themselves as the *gremio*, another medieval corporate form that persisted in Havana.[35]

This *cofradía* may have been formed as a response to the growing racial paranoia in Cuba that accompanied large-scale sugar cultivation and the introduction of large populations of un-acculturated Africans or *bozales* into Cuba in the late eighteenth century. Cuban planters imported more than 70,000 African slaves into Cuba between 1763 and 1792 to work in the burgeoning sugar economy, and David Eltis has determined that approximately 325,000 slaves arrived between 1790 and 1820, over 70 per cent of whom were males. From 1827 to 1841 the black and free coloured population of Cuba grew by almost 200,000 while the white population grew by slightly more than 100,000.[36]

To assuage fears of slave revolts, in 1825 Cuba's captain general established a series of military commissions in barrios throughout the poorer and blacker extramural neighbourhoods of Havana.[37] The military interest of officials accounts for the preservation of *cabildo* records in the national archives of Cuba. They include information on members and officers, on *cabildo* properties, any legal disputes in which the *cabildos* may have been involved, and after 1825 the newly established military commissions in Havana and Matanzas also generated criminal investigations and records of *cabildo* members.

In 1835 soldiers arrested Juan Nepomuceno Prieto, sergeant second class retired of the Battalion of Loyal Blacks of Havana, and *capatáz* (elected leader) of the Lucumí (Yoruba) *cabildo* in the barrio Jesus, María y José, on suspicion of fomenting a racial conspiracy. Only eleven years earlier the captain general had granted Nepomuceno a licence authorizing him to host dances and other entertainment in his home, which also served as the brotherhood's meeting place. Since 1819 the brotherhood had celebrated the feast day of the brotherhood's patroness, Saint Barbara (patroness of the artillery and the syncretic Cuban counterpart for Shango, the Yoruba deity of war) by paying for church masses and music and processing her image from Nepomuceno's house to the auxiliary church in the neighbourhood.[38] This detail is significant because it reminds us that *cofradías* operated within the physical space of the church, while *cabildos* established connections to nearby churches, but maintained their own spaces that were not as easily or as closely monitored. Investigators seized a wide variety of documentation from Nepomuceno's house that amounts to the brotherhood's archive and these make clear the central role that Nepomuceno and the house played in the lives of the Lucumí community of the neighbourhood.

Nepomuceno's archive also shows that he was posting bonds for brothers gone astray of the law, interceding in work agreements, holding money for enslaved brothers and making *coartación*, or self-purchase, payments to their owners to ensure their steady progress towards freedom. He was planning the funerals for departed brothers, and paying for their burials and for masses for their souls. Nepomuceno served as godfather for Lucumí *bozales* recently liberated from British-intercepted slave ships such as the *Mexico* and he even arranged for the delivery, post-partum care, and proper baptism of members' children. One fascinating document provides an account of the exact costs of the midwife's services, a list of the foods provided for the mother with their costs, and the costs of the child's baptismal clothes. Someone, maybe Nepomuceno himself, was producing handwritten prayers for the brothers, some of them illustrated in water colours and featuring blond winged angels. More formally printed and illustrated prayers were dedicated to Nuestra Señora de Monserrate, Nuestra Señora de los Remedios, Nuestra Señora del Rosario and Nuestra Señora del Carmelo – all local patron saints.

Other objects of material culture seized from Nepomuceno's house were evidence that although he was a good Catholic and a loyal and distinguished official of the free black militia, Nepomuceno and his brothers simultaneously observed Christian and African religious practices that would never have been possible within the confines of the Catholic Church itself. Included in the trove of material in the possession of the brotherhood were several statues of black Africans, which the investigators termed "symbolic of their witchcraft", a container filled with eggs, and a large elephant tusk with other smaller ones arranged in a sort of display. How the brothers obtained these items is a fascinating, but unanswered, question.[39]

Much more research remains to be done before we can clearly establish the exact meaning and function of the African nation in the Iberian Atlantic. As Mariza Soares has argued for the Minas of Rio de Janeiro, the designation of nation as a very flexible concept.[40] The Africans and African descended people who enjoyed the highest respectability, prestige and trust in the Iberian Atlantic included the free *cofradías* (or *irmandades*), free militias and skilled artisan guilds. The higher status awarded these groups may have cushioned them from the crudest racism and facilitated the upward mobility of some members. Organizations like the African *cabildos* of Havana or *congadas* of Rio de Janeiro that were more African in presentation and practice clearly were regarded with more suspicion and suffered more repression.[41] Stuart Schwartz has documented the ethnic organization of Hausa stevedores in nineteenth-century Salvador da Bahia and their rebellion in the face of increasing racial and ethnic repression, while João José Reis focused on the rebellion and subsequent repression of the Muslim Malês of Bahia.[42] Paul Lovejoy's work on the same group's enslavement and deportation after the *jihads* in Africa reminds us that we must try to connect our work on Iberian American "nations" to the rich historiography on African ethnicity available to us, since it is probable that Africans adopted the American forms most similar to those they already knew and utilized these institutions to modify or ameliorate their enslavement.[43] While recognizing the tremendous changes wrought on cultural forms and ethnic identities over centuries of enslavement, dislocation and repression, we find evidence in Iberian records that Africans themselves clung to something like a *nación* or *nação* well into the nineteenth century.[44] The rich documentary evidence makes abundantly clear an astonishing creativity, versatility and innovativeness by African diasporic communities wherever they found themselves. In no sense could those Africans and their descendants be described as "socially dead". If they made such effort to preserve this "identity", however changed or changing, it behoves us as historians to continue our own efforts to explicate its meaning and significance.

NOTES

1. Jane Landers, *Black Society in Spanish Florida* (Urbana: University of Illinois Press, 1999), ch. 3.
2. For a sample of these debates see, for example, Paul Lovejoy's chapter, "Identifying Enslaved Africans in the African Diaspora", in his work *Identity in the Shadow of Slavery* (London: Continuum, 2000); Gwendolyn Midlo Hall, *Slavery and African Ethnicities in the Americas: Restoring the Links* (Chapel Hill: University of North Carolina Press, 2005); Robin Law, "Ethnicities of Enslaved

Africans in the Diaspora: On the Meanings of 'Mina' (Again)", *History in Africa* 32 (2005): 247–67; Philip D. Morgan, "The Cultural Implications of the Atlantic Slave Trade: African Regional Origins, American Destinations and New World Developments", *Slavery and Abolition* 18, no. 1 (1997): 122–45.

3. The Portuguese opened slave factories at Arguim (1448), Santiago de Cabo Verde (1458), San Jorge de Mina (1482) and São Tomé (1486). José Luis Cortes López, *Los origenes de la esclavitud negra en España* (Madrid: Mundo Negro, 1986), 80; Ivana Elbl, "The Volume of the Early Atlantic Slave Trade, 1450–1521", *Journal of African History* 38, no. 1 (1977): 31–75. Walter Rodney estimated that Portuguese slave exports rose to approximately thirty-five hundred annually by the end of the century; see Walter Rodney, "Upper Guinea and the Significance of the Origins of Africans Enslaved in the New World", *Journal of Negro History* 4 (October 1969): 327–45. A.C. de C.M. Saunders estimated that Portuguese traders sent as many as two thousand slaves annually to Lisbon in that period; see A.C. de C.M. Saunders, *A Social History of Black Slaves and Freedmen in Portugal, 1441–1555* (Cambridge: Cambridge University Press, 1982), 17–25.

4. Names and places of origin for the slaves, such as Mahoma, Hamete, Abdallah, Fatima, Suleiman, Zaima and Alí, and la Alhama, Granada, Alpujarra, Orán or Fez also help identify enslaved Muslims.

5. The fall of Málaga in 1487 sent 3,074 Muslims into slavery in Seville and the Muslim rebellion of 1500 added to that number; Alfonso Franco Silva, "La esclavitud en Andalucía al termino de la edad media", *Cuadernos de Investigación Medieval* 3 (Madrid: Marcial Pons, 1985), 26. Franco Silva's study of Seville's notarial archives also illustrates the importance of African slaves in that Spanish city. He found that of 5,271 slaves recorded in Seville in the first quarter of the sixteenth century almost 4,000 were listed as blacks or mulattoes; Alfonso Franco Silva, *Registo documental sobre la esclavitud Sevillana (1453–1513)* (Seville: Publicaciones de la Universidad de Sevilla, 1979).

6. Carlos Larrazábal Blanco, *Los negros y la esclavitud en Santo Domingo* (Santo Domingo: Julio D. Postigo e Hijos, 1967), 143–45. Also see Roberto Cassá and Genaro Rodríguez Morel, "Consideraciones alternativas acerca de las rebeliones de esclavos en Santo Domingo", *Anuario de Estudios Hispanoamericanos* 51 (1993): 101–31; Carlos Esteban Deive, *Los guerrilleros negros: esclavos fugitivos y cimarrones en Santo Domingo* (Santo Domingo: Fundación Cultural Dominicana, 1989), 31–36; and Gonzalo Fernández de Oviedo, *Historia general y natural de la Indias* (Madrid: Biblioteca de Autores Españoles, 1953), vol. 1, book 6, ch. 51.

7. While aimed primarily at enslaved Africans, these new laws also mention "blancos (meaning moriscos or Muslim slaves who converted to and then rejected

Christianity), *negros y canarios* (meaning indigenous Guanches from the Canary Islands); "Ordenanzas que dio el virrey de las Indias", 6 January 1522, Patronato 295, no. 104, Archivo General de Indias, Seville, Spain (hereafter AGI); Carlos Esteban Deive, "Las Ordenanzas Sobre Esclavos Cimarrones de 1522", *Boletín del Museo del Hombre Dominicano* 25 (1992): 133–38. These were only the first in a series of ordinances attempting to regulate the multiracial slave force in the Americas. Late into the sixteenth century, Spaniards still manned their galleys and built their Caribbean fortifications with enslaved Muslims from North Africa and the Middle East, white Christians, Jews, Canary Islanders (or Guanches), and American Indians. Landers, *Black Society*, 15–16.

8. Royal Cédula of the Queen Regent, 28 September 1532, cited in José Luis Sáez, SJ, *La iglesia y el negro esclavo: Una historia de tres siglos* (Santo Domingo, Dominican Republic: Patronato de la Ciudad Colonial de Santo Domingo, 1994), 265.

9. For examples, see the Ecclesiastical and Secular Sources for Slave Societies Digital Archive, http://www.vanderbilt.edu/esss/index.php. My primary collaborators are Mariza Carvalho de Soares of the Universidade Federal Fluminense, in Rio de Janeiro; Paul E. Lovejoy, York University, Toronto; David Wheat, Michigan State University; Pablo F. Gómez, University of Wisconsin; and Renée Soulodre-La France, King's College, University of Western Ontario.

10. Individual members of the Dominican and Jesuit orders sometimes devoted themselves to the evangelization and defence of Africans; see Frederick Bowser, *The African Slave in Colonial Peru* (Stanford: Stanford University Press, 1974), 232–57. After almost a half century working among the Africans of Cartagena (1606–52), the Jesuit, Alonso de Sandoval, wrote an important ethno-historical treatise on Africans, their capacity for conversion and the mechanics to be followed to accomplish this desired end; see Alonso de Sandoval, *Un tratado sobre la esclavitud*, trans. Enriqueta Vila Vilár (Madrid: Alianza, 1987), 363–503. His fellow Jesuit, Pedro Claver, continued Sandoval's work among the Africans of Cartagena, and the church eventually canonized him and named him apostle of the slaves; see Anna María Splendiani and Tulio Aristizábal , SJ, *Proceso de beatificación de san Pedro Claver* (Bogotá: Centro Editorial Javeriana, 2002).

11. According to Benjamin Nuñez, *Dictionary of Afro-Latin American Civilization* (Westport, CT: Greenwood, 1980), 71: "Biafara [was] an ethnic group located in Biafra (Guinea-Bissau), many of whose members were brought to the New World as slaves early in the sixteenth century."

12. Sáez, *La iglesia y el negro esclavo*, 24–32, 51–52.

13. Ibid., 327–37.

14. In 1608, during Viceroy Luis de Velasco's second term as viceroy of New Spain, he discovered a Christmas season plot allegedly conceived in the homes of free

blacks who were hosting banquets and dances for their elected king and queen and their court. This is evidence of autonomous ethnic organization akin to a *cabildo*; see Jane Landers, "Cimarrón and Citizen: The Evolution of Free Black Towns", in *Slaves, Subjects, and Subversives: Blacks in Colonial Latin America*, ed. Jane Landers and Barry M. Robinson (Albuquerque: University of New Mexico Press, 2006), 111–45. I have found similar informal (and covert) cabildos established by a network of Arará slaves owned by various religious institutions in Cartagena in the 1690s; see Jane Landers, "Conspiradores esclavizados en Cartagena en el siglo XVII", in *Afrodescendientes en las Américas. Trayectorias sociales e identitarias: 150 años de la abolición de la esclavitud en Colombia*, ed. Claudia Mosquera, Mauricio Pardo and Odile Hoffman (Bogotá: Universidad Nacional de Colombia, 2002), 181–93; Nicole Von Germeten, *Black Blood Brothers: Confraternities and Social Mobility for Afro-Mexicans* (Gainesville: University Press of Florida, 2006).

15.   On warfare in the Congo, see John K. Thornton, *Warfare in Atlantic Africa, 1500–1800* (London: UCL Press, 1999).

16.   The free black, Juan Garrido, earned a position as manager of the Chapultepec aqueduct for his service in the Spanish conquest of Mexico, and it is possible that, thereafter, this became an occupation associated with blacks, as was that of butcher. Landers, *Black Society*, ch. 1. Butchers were accused of poisoning the meat supply of Cartagena some eight years later; see, Landers, "Conspiradores esclavizados".

17.   "Relación del alzamiento que negros y mulatos, libres y cautivos de la ciudad de Méjico de la Nueva España, pretendieron hacer contra los españoles por cuaresma del año 1612 y del castigo que se hizo de las cabezas y culpados", MS 2010, fols. 236–41, no. 168, Biblioteca Nacional de Madrid, Sección de Manuscritos, transcribed by Luis Querol y Roso, "Negros y mulatos de Nueva España (Historia de su alzamiento en Méjico en 1612)", *Anales de la Universidad de Valencia* 90 (1931–32): 141–53. Nicole von Germeten discusses this incident briefly; see von Germeten, *Black Blood Brothers*, 77–78.

18.   M. Cuadrado, *Obispado de la Habana: Su historia a través de los siglos, Libro 1, Parte 1, De las parroquias* (Havana: Archbishopric Archive, n.d.), 252–53.

19.   Fernando Ortiz, *Los cabildos y la fiesta afrocubana del Día de Reyes* (Havana: Editorial Ciencias Sociales, 1992), 7–8, 14.

20.   See Nuñez, *Dictionary*, 98–99.

21.   Matt D. Childs, *The 1812 Aponte Rebellion in Cuba and the Struggle Against Atlantic Slavery* (Chapel Hill: University of North Carolina Press, 2006); Philip A. Howard, *Changing History: Cuban Cabildos and Societies of Color in the Nineteenth Century* (Baton Rouge: Louisiana State University Press, 1998).

22. Ortiz, *Los cabildos*, 7–8, 14.

23. Bishop Pedro Agustin (Morrell de Santa Cruz) to the Captain General, 6 December 1755, Santo Domingo, 515, no. 51, AGI.

24. John David Wheat, "The Afro-Portuguese Maritime World and the Foundations of Spanish Caribbean Society, 1570–1640" (PhD diss., Vanderbilt University, 2009), ch. 4 (forthcoming publication).

25. Matt D. Childs, "The Defects of Being a Black Creole: The Degrees of African Identity in the Cuban Cabildos de Nación", in *Slaves, Subjects and Subversives: Blacks in Colonial Latin America*, ed. Jane Landers and Barry Robinson (Albuquerque: University of New Mexico Press, 2006), 209–45. Mariza Carvalho de Soares also analyses the contest between African-born blacks and creoles in the religious brotherhoods of Rio de Janeiro; see Mariza Carvalho de Soares, *Devotos de Cor: Identidade étnica, religiosidade e escravidão no Rio de Janeiro, século XVIII* (Rio de Janeiro: Civilizacão Brasileira, 2000). For a detailed study on the Brotherhood of the Rosary in Minas Gerais, see Elizabeth W. Kiddy, *Blacks of the Rosary: Memory and History in Minas Gerais, Brazil* (University Park, PA: Penn State University Press, 2005). Also see Marina de Mello e Souza, *Reis negros no Brasil escravista: História da festa de coroação de Rei Congo* (Belo Horizonte: Editorial UFMG, 2002); Anderson José Machado de Oliveira, *Devoção negra: santos pretos e catequese no Brasil colonial* (Rio de Janeiro: FAPERJ, 2008).

26. Request of Joseph Antonio Carmelita and Agustín Chamiso to reauthorize the Caravalí Ungua *cabildo* of San Agustín, 22 September 1769, and Request of Antonio Ramos to authorize the fourth Caravalí *cabildo* of Nuestra Señora del Carmen, 20 February 1772, Cuba 1197, AGI.

27. Request of Juan Bautista Arensibe (*sic*) for authorization of the second Caravalí cabildo, 16 February 1771, Cuba 1197, AGI.

28. In addition to the main house at 46 Calle Florida, the Congos owned several other properties in 1796; see Ortiz, *Los cabildos*, 7–8, 14.

29. Ortiz claims the last cabildo procession was made in 1884, but cabildos existed in a modernized form of associations in Regla and other localities until driven underground by Fidel Castro. They were permitted to function openly again once Castro discovered their value for ethno-tourism. Ibid., 7–16.

30. Paul H.D. Kaplan, "Italy 1490–1700", in *The Image of the Black in Western Art: From the "Age of Discovery" to the Age of Abolition*, ed. David Bindman and Henry Louis Gates Jr (Cambridge, MA: Belknap Press of Harvard University Press, 2010), 111.

31. Ortiz, *Los cabildos*, 25–64. See also Ortiz's original article annotated and translated by Jean Stubbs, "The Afro-Cuban Festival 'Day of Kings' ", in *Cuban Festivals: An Illustrated Anthology*, ed. Judith Bettelheim (New York: Garland,

1993), 3–47; this translated article originally appeared as Fernando Ortiz, "Los cabildos Afrocubanos", in *Orbita de Fernando Ortiz*, ed. Julio Le Riverend (Havana: Unión de Escritores y Artistas de Cuba, 1973), 121–34. Ortiz compares these inversion and licence celebrations to similar winter festivities among various African groups.

32.   Lydia Cabrera, "Babalú Ayé-San Lazaro", *La enciclopedia de Cuba* 6 (1980): 268–82. Robert Farris Thompson compares nineteenth-century Cuban costuming to contemporary costumes from Nigeria and Calabar, and demonstrates the continuities of form and design; see Robert Farris Thompson, *Flash of the Spirit: African and Afro-American Art and Philosophy* (New York: Vintage, 1984), 260–67. Scholars have also found similar cultural persistence in British colonies; see John Thornton, *Africa and Africans in the Making of the Atlantic World,1400–1800* (Cambridge: Cambridge University Press, 1992); Michael Mullin, *Africa in America: Slave Acculturation and Resistance in the American South and the British Caribbean, 1736–1831* (Urbana: University of Illinois Press, 1992).

33.   Through agreement with the Catholic Church of Cuba, all the Cuban materials are now mounted on the Vanderbilt University Library Digital Collections page for public access, as is much of the Brazilian material. The Catholic churches in Angola and Colombia have not yet given permission to make additional materials preserved at Vanderbilt visible. See http://www.vanderbilt.edu/esss/index.php.

34.   José Luciano Franco, *La conspiración de Aponte* (Havana: Publicaciones del Archivo Nacional, 1963).

35.   *Archicofradías, Cofradías, y Asociaciones*, book 4, no. 9, image DSCN 0532, http://libll.library.vanderbilt,edu/diglib/esss.pl.

36.   Manuel Moreno Fraginals, *The Sugarmill: The Socioeconomic Complex of Sugar in Cuba* (New York: Monthly Review, 1976); Laird Bergad, Fe Iglesias García and María del Carmen Barcia, *The Cuban Slave Market, 1790–1880* (Cambridge: Cambridge University Press, 1995), 23–37; Allan J. Kuethe, "Havana in the Eighteenth Century", in *Atlantic Port Cities: Economy, Culture, and Society in the Atlantic World, 1650–1850*, ed. Franklin W. Knight and Peggy K. Liss (Knoxville: University of Tennessee Press, 1991), 3–39; David Eltis, *The Rise of African Slavery in the Americas* (Cambridge: Cambridge University Press, 2000). The population figures are taken from Kenneth Kiple, *Blacks in Colonial Cuba, 1774–1899* (Gainesville: University of Florida Press, 1976), 36–58.

37.   These included Guadalupe, San Lazaro and Jesús, María y José, a popular destination for urban maroons if runaway ads in the *Diario de la Habana* are to be believed. Pedro Deschamps Chapeaux, *Los cimarrones urbanos* [Ciudad

de la Habana: Editorial de Ciencias Sociales, 1983], 5–6, 8–16 Our NEH team digitized all the black sacramental records from the Church of Jesús, María y José. The investigations the military commissions launched and arrest records they generated document a shift in the types of offences for which blacks began to be arrested. Although the first year's reports focused on runaway slaves and "conspiracies" among slaves, by 1826 barrio commissioners seemed to be targeting free black militiamen, many of whom belonged to black brotherhoods.

38. All material on the Nepomuceno case is found in Comisión Militar, Legajo 11, no. 1, folios 194–334, ANC. A terrible fire destroyed much of the Jesús María neighbourhood in 1828 and the original licence for the *cabildo* was destroyed but Nepomuceno secured a replacement.

39. For more on Congo *nkisi* and European misunderstandings of African religious practices, see Wyatt MacGaffey, "Dialogues of the Deaf: Europeans on the Atlantic Coast of Africa", in *Implicit Understandings: Observing, Reporting, and Reflecting on the Encounters between Europeans and Other Peoples in the Early Modern Era*, ed. Stuart B. Schwartz (Cambridge: Cambridge University Press, 1994), 249–67; Wyatt MacGaffey, *Art and Healing of the Bakongo Commented by Themselves: Minkisis from the Laman Collection* (Stockholm: Folkens Museum, 1991). Also see John K. Thornton, *The Kongolese Saint Anthony: Dona Beatriz Kimpa Vita and the Antonian Movement, 1684–1706* (Cambridge: Cambridge University Press, 1998).

40. Mariza Carvalho de Soares, *People of Faith: Slavery and African Catholics in Eighteenth-Century Rio* (Durham, NC: Duke University Press, 2011).

41. Pedro Deschamps Chapeaux, *El negro en la economía habanera del Siglo XIX* (Havana: UNEAC, 1971).

42. Stuart B. Schwartz, "Cantos and Quilombos: A Hausa Rebellion in Bahia", in *Slaves, Subjects, and Subversives: Blacks in Colonial Latin America*, ed. Jane Landers and Barry M. Robinson (Albuquerque: University of New Mexico Press, 2006), 247–71; João José Reis, *Slave Rebellion in Brazil: The Muslim Uprising of 1835 in Bahia* (Baltimore: Johns Hopkins University Press, 1993).

43. Jane Landers, *Atlantic Creoles in the Age of Revolution* (Cambridge: Harvard University Press, 2010).

44. In that period, British mixed commissioners in Havana and Rio de Janeiro and Sierra Leone tried to record African names and ethnicities, much as Spanish and Portuguese officials had being doing since the fifteenth century. Teams led by David Eltis are now trying to ascertain naming and ethnic patterns through the Havana records while Suzanne Schwartz and Paul Lovejoy are doing the same for Sierra Leone.

CHAPTER 5

THE CHINESE ON THE US–MEXICO BORDERLANDS

Strategic Transnationalism during the Exclusion Era, 1882–1940

EVELYN HU-DEHART

LIKE OTHER ASIANS, AFRICANS AND EUROPEANS, the Chinese exported a large number of people to the Americas. Chinese migration to the United States from the mid-nineteenth to the early twentieth century evokes images of mining camps, railroad construction, settled agriculture and the many Chinatowns that dotted the North American landscape where Chinese labourers and merchants worked and lived, and where a fortunate few formed families and raised children. Less present in the common imagination were the American borderlands that constituted another kind of space that also attracted significant Asian immigrants. As was the case in the Chinatowns, these migrants to the borderlands were disproportionately workers and merchants.

The United States is defined by two extensive land borders: the better-known and controversial US–Mexico divide, and the US–Canadian frontier, which is just now emerging from the shadows of its southern counterpart in the burgeoning scholarship on American borderlands. With both international boundaries having been clearly drawn in the mid-nineteenth century – 1846 with Canada and 1848 with Mexico – the borders of the expansionist United States became more or less permanently fixed.[1] At the same time, what converged at both the northern and the southern ends of the border were frontiers.[2] These were vast, remote territories rich in natural resources;

contested lands originally belonging to the native peoples that were sparsely populated and minimally governed from the central seats of government in the United States, Canada and Mexico. These extensive frontiers were poised for economic development based on intensive extractive and global commercial enterprises once investors were alerted and markets identified: lumber, gold mining and salmon enterprises in the Pacific northwest; gold and copper mining in the southwest (Mexico's northwest); and, later, cotton, fruits and vegetables, and petroleum along the Gulf coast. Capital began pouring into these frontier areas from financiers on New York's Wall Street as well as from Europe and from Asia. Migrant labourers arrived from across the Pacific, while local peasants were rapidly displaced from communal lands and gradually proletarianized. Infrastructural improvements, notably railroads, accompanied development, along with ports, warehouses, processing and packing plants, and other modes of transportation (trans-Pacific steamships) and communication.

The history of Asian labour migration to the US West is well known, beginning with the mid-century gold rush of California, the subsequent development of agriculture in the San Joaquin delta and central valley, the construction of the transcontinental railroad, all culminating in the Chinese Exclusion Act of 1882 that eventually widened to encompass all Asians by the early twentieth century.[3] The so-called American West can be said to extend all the way north to Seattle and its border with British Colombia, Canada, out into the Hawaiian islands of the vast Pacific, and south across the border into the Pacific states of northern Mexico. When viewed through this very wide lens, the West is both a transborder and a trans-Pacific zone. Asian labourers and merchants – first Chinese (mostly from Guangdong province), then Japanese and Okinawans, Filipinos, South Asians (led by Sikhs from the Punjab) – mixed with locals and other immigrants to compete for opportunities and resources and jockey for power in a fluid environment full of raw, entrepreneurial energy and risk takers. Race and ethnicity mattered in both positive and destructive ways, often played out as co-ethnic and inter-ethnic, interracial collaborations or conflicts that may be further complicated by gender and class divisions. If Chinatowns were tight ethnic enclaves, borderlands were open multicultural spaces. Yet in both places Chinese diasporic communities flourished.

This chapter explores the construction of the northern, and southern, borderlands of the United States as dynamic and innovative transnational spaces that provided attractive diasporic opportunities for Chinese and other immigrants to North America. It also provides new perspectives on Chinese American transnationalism in North America. Furthermore, it looks at how the borderlands took on a strategic role by facilitating Chinese survival in North America and even advancing their prosperity when the United States enacted the Chinese Exclusion Act in 1882. This is especially true of the US–Mexico borderlands. Chinese on both sides of this border invented new and strengthened old ties beyond national boundaries, in effect circumventing if not entirely overcoming barriers thrown up by denied entry to the United States. Others simply created new lives and livelihoods on the Mexican side of the border that did not require physical access to the United States as long as social, commercial, business and personal ties could be maintained. In other words, the Chinese adapted to exclusion by embracing what might be described as "strategic transnationalism" on and across the US–Mexico border.

For comparative purposes, we will briefly examine the northern borderlands of the United States before proceeding to a more detailed discussion of the more important and contentious southern borderlands with Mexico. At first, the US–Canadian border presented transnational opportunities for Chinese and other Asian immigrants, although these would become sharply curtailed in the early twentieth century when Canada emulated the United States and passed its version of Asian exclusion. Towards the end of the nineteenth century, American, British and Canadian capital stimulated the growth of lumber, mining and fisheries on both sides. This resource-rich environment was also labour poor, which meant that both national economies were dependent on immigrants for work. With Europeans flocking to both countries, Chinese, Japanese and South Asians also came across the Pacific, only to confront white supremacist ideologies in both the United States and Canada that coveted their good, cheap labour but denied them political incorporation through naturalization and citizenship because of their race. James Hill, the Canadian tycoon who built the two borderlands railroad systems, the Canadian Pacific and the Great Northern, relied on a multi-ethnic labour force that was heavily Asian. During 1882, over four thousand Chinese men drifted across the border to do road grading work under the supervision of white foremen. As a contemporary journalist noted: "The financier recognizes no boundary lines, no colors or creeds or races when it comes to profitable investments."[4] Similarly, the canneries imported Japanese workers from the US side. Industries on the US side from Oregon through Alaska and Washington reversed the recruitment process. At first, industrialists and developers turned to Asian labour when white immigrant contract workers too readily jumped jobs for better wages at other seasonal sites. Asian workers soon followed suit with their own manoeuvers, facilitated by co-ethnic labour contractors acting as suppliers and brokers.

Labour contracting became a lucrative ethnic business on the border, where large firms opened offices in Seattle and Vancouver to sustain the circular networks they helped create to supply railroad construction sites, lumber mills, mines and fisheries with workers drawn from both sides of the border. When the labour pools along the border were insufficient to meet the demand, contractors imported workers directly from the Asian homelands as well as from across the Pacific in places like Hawaii. When necessary they arranged visas and supplied documents for the labour migrations they organized overseas and across land borders. They further maximized their own profits by provisioning their co-ethnic labour recruits with food and clothing out of the stores they set up, especially when sending men to remote work sites for the railroads, as well as lumber and mining companies. In addition, merchant-contractors in Vancouver deducted from the workers' paycheques (which they controlled) fees for securing jobs, transportation, accommodation and food while waiting for their work assignment.[5]

In good times, the transborder economies worked in favour of workers and their agents by allowing them to manipulate the two labour markets, and encouraging them to move back and forth to maximize wages and labour conditions. As one Vancouver mill owner explained with regard to the loss of one hundred of his Asian workers to various Washington cities: "The scarcity of workers and the wages paid in the Washington cities are responsible for the exodus."[6] Japanese fishermen creatively manipulated border space and mobility in still other ways to maximize family incomes: they worked the spring salmon season in Seattle before crossing the border for the summer season in Vancouver.

Advantages worked both ways however. First of all, employers and industrialists had access to a cheap and highly mobile labour force which they could
hire and dispatch to any site for seasonal work. They could seek workers to
hire at peak season and lay them off at low season. At the same time, they
learned to exploit the cross-border alternative labour pool to blunt the impact
of activist workers on their payroll.

With the passage of the Chinese Exclusion Act in 1882, the availability of
Chinese workers began to shrink, their ranks gradually replaced by Japanese
migrants who were not denied access to the United States until some years
later. By the century's end, Japanese labour contractors supplanted Chinese
contractors as the ethnic labour market changed over to Japanese. The largest
of them was the Seattle-based Oriental Trading Company. Whether Chinese or Japanese, these labour contractors shared common characteristics
of English-language facility, and familiarity with the Anglo-American legal
system and matters such as business contracts. Like their Chinese prede-
cessors, the Oriental Trading Company established branches in Japanese
migrant-sending cities, such as Yokohama, Wakayama, Kobe and Hiroshima.
They also actively recruited all available Asians across the US West, in states
such as Montana, Idaho, Utah and Oregon, as well as across the border in
British Columbia, and became the major supplier of railroad construction
workers for the Great Northern between Seattle and St Paul, Minnesota. The
Japanese owners of this company refined their labour contracting business
beyond what the Chinese had practised. For example, when they mobilized
work teams for the railroads, they also managed the workers by placing loyal
co-ethnic foremen among the workers, the better to maintain discipline and
communicate company orders to the work crews, such as those working on
railroads. The foreman was further responsible for protecting his work team
from being poached by other rival recruiters. But just as Chinese labourers
ran dry due to US state policies on exclusion, Japanese labour migration
came to a near standstill during the Russo-Japanese War of 1905, when the
Meiji government conscripted all able-bodied men for the war. Shortly after
that, the United States broadened the exclusion policy to include Japanese,
Koreans and South Asians, which necessitated the Oriental Company to
add to its payroll smugglers and runners who guided migrants across the
international line. At critical labour shortage moments, the Great Northern

connived with its Japanese partners to smuggle hundreds of workers from Canada. The response of both the US and Canadian governments was to install border patrol and increase vigilance, effectively bringing an end to cross-border recruiting and smuggling by 1908.[7]

According to historian Kornel Chang, whose work I have drawn from to provide this brief sketch of transborder interactions on the US–Canadian border at the turn of the last century, even under the harsh regime of the labour contractor, Asian workers continued to try to manipulate their cross-border mobility to leverage better wages and work conditions. But they also paid a high price for mobility: "The constant movement from place to place tended to hinder the development of class solidarity and consciousness, and discouraged the formation of more organized and systematic means of labor activism . . . Their perpetual movement was yet another factor, among others, explaining the lack of formal labor institutions and structures among Asian workers in the Pacific Northwest."[8]

Not surprisingly, Chinese Exclusion in the United States spurred a booming and profitable business in human smuggling across both borders, as historian Erika Lee and others have amply demonstrated.[9] On the Canadian border, a veritable "back-door route" was established in Buffalo, near Niagara Falls in the St Lawrence River Valley, for Chinese human smugglers. This lucrative business attracted white American and Canadian businessmen who formed a powerful smuggling syndicate.[10] But it was on the US–Mexico border that Chinese smuggling took on impressive proportions from 1882 through the entire duration of the exclusion period (1943). During its height, from 1882 to 1920, as many as 17,500 Chinese might have crossed the border surreptitiously, constituting the original "illegal aliens".[11] Aided by a vast network of Chinese, Mexicans and white Americans, the smugglers took advantage of this two-thousand-mile-long, poorly patrolled – despite the presence of "Chinese inspectors" – and largely permeable border. Deeply implicated was the powerful Chinese Six Companies of San Francisco, whose agents in Mexico (and Havana, Cuba) directed the trafficking, including forging documents when necessary.[12]

But not all Chinese who arrived in Mexico during the late nineteenth century found it necessary or desirable to sneak into the United States; many found reasons to remain on the Mexican side of the border. While transborder activities began to wind down on the northern border, they were gaining momentum on the southern border with Mexico, a much more violent and turbulent borderland that had experienced Indian wars, revolution, civil war and the boom and bust cycles of a neocolonial economy. The story there unfolded along different lines, because Mexicans were available to meet most of the industrial (mining and railroad construction) labour needs on both sides, leaving the door wide open for Asian immigrants (Chinese, with some Japanese, Lebanese and other Middle Easterners)[13] to fill niches in a range of small manufacturing, commercial and service activities that arose alongside the interrelated processes of industrialization, proletarianization and urbanization. Chinese exclusion in the United States accelerated the establishment and proliferation of immigrant businesses in Mexico, building on transborder characteristics by negotiating the space in between, over and above the two sovereign entities, calling upon co-ethnic networks in California and New York to comparative advantage.

Mexico was ruled by an iron-fisted, pro-development dictator named Porfirio Díaz who came to power in 1876 and immediately opened the doors of the country to foreign investment. His ascendance to power coincided with passage of the Chinese Exclusion Act in 1882, which had the effect of directing Chinese migrants to Mexico's northern border with the United States. At the same time, American and European investors poured massive capital into this region to develop mining and to build railroads after pacifying the fiercely independent indigenous Apaches on both sides of the artificial national frontiers. When Díaz was deposed by revolutionaries in 1911 an estimated thirty-five thousand Chinese had already entered Mexico.[14] Only about half had settled permanently in Mexico; the rest, having found their way illegally to the United States, returned to China or trans-shipped elsewhere in the Americas. While the Mexican Revolution (1910–20) seriously disrupted Mexican society – the uprooted millions from villages and towns either joining up with the armies of several revolutionary factions or crossing the border to the United States to work and avoid the violence – Chinese shopkeepers actually prospered during these years by remaining neutral politically while doing brisk business provisioning the towns and mobile armies. During these years, the number of Chinese grew, especially in the border state of Sonora (across from Arizona, then still a "wild West" territory characterized by mining and related processing industries), whose landscape was dotted with American-owned mining and railroad towns, along with active armed revolutionary factions. These otherwise dangerous and chaotic conditions were quite conducive to the growth of the Chinese wholesale and retail trade which had already become entrenched in the local economy.

How the Chinese made themselves into effectively the petite bourgeoisie of these frontier borderlands is a story I have documented and recounted in detail.[15] The process began even before the United States enacted its Chinese exclusion act, but accelerated with the anti-Chinese agitation becoming more frequent and violent in the US West. So it was not surprising to see California Chinese businessmen branch out, including across the border to Mexico. As early as 1873, shoe and clothing factories appeared in the port city of Guaymas and the state capital city of Hermosillo. This was soon followed by well-stocked stores that functioned wholesale and retail, in that they sold directly to customers while also setting up penniless co-ethnics with goods on credit so they could peddle or set up smaller shops in remote mining and railroad towns. One such firm was Quan, Gun, Lung y Compañía, established in 1894 with headquarters in the old mining town of Alamos. It sold a wide variety of goods, ranging from groceries and canned foods to clothing and sewing supplies, dealing in imported as well as domestic products, and had its own "well mounted factory" to manufacture shoes. In addition, the company served as the agent for Pacific Beer, *Pochutla* and *Pluma Hidalgo* coffee (products of Oaxaca in south-central Mexico), *La Violeta* cigars (from Veracruz state on the Gulf of Mexico coast), and *El Dorado* rum. The company also traded directly with New York, Chicago, San Francisco, St Louis, and Hamburg, Germany. Within Mexico, its commercial sphere extended beyond Sonora to the adjacent states of Chihuahua to the east and Sinaloa to the south, where it opened branch stores.

In a bit of aggressive self-promotion, general manager Guillermo Leytón (note how he Hispanicized his name) was described in a company advertisement in glowing terms as "an excellent Chinese who enjoys general popularity in the locality". But it is what follows that is most revealing, because the ad makes clear that "in particular he is well loved by the working people, because he willingly and readily helps them out, especially when a poor harvest or some other cause raises the prices of basic necessities; at which time Leytón – making only a little profit or perhaps none at all – sells them these articles of primary needs at prices they could afford, thereby averting the specter of hunger".[16]

By 1903 the Chinese owned at least ten more shoe factories in Sonora, producing over US$100,000 in goods each year.[17] They were not yet prominent in the wholesale trade of foodstuff and consumer goods, as Europeans (Germans, Spanish and French), Anglo North Americans and a few Mexicans dominated those large commercial activities during the Díaz period. Imperceptibly but surely, however, as new towns rapidly appeared around mining and railroad operations, the Chinese moved into peddling and itinerant retail trades. They also opened up small shops selling groceries, basic foodstuff and other consumer goods, while service businesses provided sewing, ironing, laundry, lodging and meals for Mexican workers. These peasants turned industrial workers usually left women and children behind in the villages while they sought wage labour in the foreign-owned capitalist enterprises.

By 1907, Chinese merchants had become more visible in local commerce throughout Sonora, establishing a presence in twenty-one out of the state's eighty-seven municipalities. The Chinese population in the state had increased to well over 2,000 by that year. By 1910, the year the Mexican Revolution broke out, it had increased to 4,486. As noted above, far from hurting Chinese businesses, the revolution actually stimulated the growth and spread of Chinese businesses throughout the northern Mexican border area, the region of greatest revolutionary activities.

Another factor at the time further aided Chinese commercial growth: the contemporaneous world war cut off European suppliers for the European merchants in Mexico, thus allowing more opportunities for Chinese firms to flourish, as they received more goods from the United States, especially from co-ethnic merchant houses in California's Chinatowns.[18] In this way, Chinese wholesale business increased, gradually taking over from the European trading houses in Guaymas and Hermosilla, such as García, Bringas y Cía, G. Moller y Cía. Sucesores, and D. Baston y Cía., giving them the capacity to become the major purveyor of the revolutionary armies.[19]

By the early twentieth century, it was clear that a close relationship had developed between US entrepreneurs and Chinese immigrants on several

levels. The experiences of Fong Lewis exemplified the closeness of this relationship. From 1905 to 1908, he cooked for the American Booker family of
Casa Grande, Chihuahua (the Mexican state across from Texas). Later, he
went to cook for the American-owned Madera Company. When the company mills closed down and the Americans fled to El Paso, Texas, shortly
after the Mexican Revolution broke out, Fong was thrown out of a job. In
1914, his former American employer pressed the US Immigration Service
to grant Fong temporary refuge in El Paso, so he could return to work for
this family.[20]

Other Chinese circumvented Chinese exclusion by crossing the border
as Mexicans, none more adept at leading a bi-national and transborder life
than Lee Sing. We first meet up with Lee in Tucson, Arizona, in 1879,
where he operated a successful small business dealing in beef jerky, beans
and whisky, then expanded into shoe-making in the border boom town of
Nogales, Arizona. After his engagement to a Mexican woman, he liquidated
his assets in Arizona and moved to Sonora, where he became a Mexican
citizen. Meanwhile, he continued to hold a stake in his brother's business
back in Tucson. In 1893, on a routine trip to Tucson, Lee was detained at the
border and questioned about his status as a merchant, whereupon Lee called
upon Mexican and American friends and business partners to vouch for his
Mexican citizenship, his eleven-year residency in Sonora, his Mexican wife
and three Mexican children, not to mention his considerable annual income
of eight to ten thousand pesos as the proprietor of a local general store. From
then on, Lee was able to cross the border without further difficulty. Lee Sing
was not unique, in that many other Chinese merchants owned and operated
various businesses on both sides while maintaining residence in one or the
other, or both.[21]

Another relationship between Americans and Chinese is represented by
the case of Fong Sing of Saltillo, Coahuila. He owned a restaurant within
the confines of the Mazapil Copper Company in Concepción del Oro. In
fact, Fong owned only half of the restaurant, the American company controlled the rest of the inventory, so the upstart Chinese businessman and the
wealthy American company, whose workers the restaurant served, formed
a partnership.[22]

Railroad and especially mining towns became prototypical company towns, where the foreign employers set up stores to recapture wages paid daily to workers. There they developed a modified version of the company town; instead of operating the small businesses, they allowed Chinese merchants to set up small businesses to take care of the daily minimum needs of their Mexican workers, such as canteens and boarding houses, butchers and corner grocers, laundries, tailoring and shoe repair. No Mexican town attracted disproportionately more Chinese immigrants than Cananea, Sonora (a border state with Arizona), home of the notorious American-owned Greene Consolidated Copper Mining Company. In 1903, eight hundred of the three thousand Chinese noted in the Sonora census lived in Cananea; or viewed in another way, these eight hundred Chinese were 20 per cent of the four thousand people living and working in Cananea that year. Most of them, like Fong Lewis cited above, worked as servants for American families; others, like Fong Sing, operated restaurants in partnership with the mining company. Most of them owned small fruit and vegetable stands, laundries, clothing and shoe stores (where they also manufactured these items). In a detailed 1925 census undertaken by the state government to assess precisely how much of the retail trade had been cornered by the Chinese, 410 individuals were counted in Cananea, making it the largest Chinese community in the state. Of those, 204 were grocery store owners; 22 had chicken farms; 21 were cooks; 23 had laundries; 17 were shoemakers; 11 were tailors; 7 owned factories, and only 56 were day labourers. Collectively, the Chinese business investment totalled 172,323 pesos, which was puny compared to the millions of US dollars invested, but many times the paltry 42,200 pesos of Mexican capital.[23]

If Cananea was a prototypical, one-industry company town that attracted labourers and shopkeepers, the industrial town of Torreón in the border state of Coahuila (across from Texas) attracted the attention of a special group of transnational Chinese investors. Although it was not actually situated at or near the international boundary – unlike Cananea – Torreón was located at the confluence of two railroad lines that linked Mexico's mining and agricultural products with the United States. The fast growing town lay on the Nazas River which irrigated the fertile Laguna Valley and its cotton crop. Chinese and many other foreign entrepreneurs – Germans, French, British, Italians, Spaniards – joined with forward-thinking Mexican entrepreneurs to set up modern industries and financial services. Benefiting from the generous tax abatements of the state and federal governments, they built the Banco de Londres y México, the American Bank, the Agricultural Bank, the Mercantile Bank of Monterrey, and so on. With eight big furnaces, the Fundición Metalúrgica de Torreón (foundry) was the country's most modern when it was built in 1901, fed by the mines of Coahuila and two neighbouring states. Americans built the Compañía Guayulera Continental Mexicana to refine the native guayule rubber plant for industrial use. The Germans built a new municipal market in the city. The city had potable water, electricity, a modern drainage system, a modern hospital and an electric streetcar system downtown. At the dawn of the twentieth century, its population of fourteen thousand included some five hundred Chinese, who at 3.5 per cent constituted the largest foreign colony and the most conspicuous given that their occupations and businesses were scattered all over this urban landscape.

The Chinese called Torreón *caiyuan*, vegetable garden, because they had acquired huge tracts of city land to grow fruits and vegetables for the town's daily consumption. Dubbed "Chinese gardens" by locals, and employing upwards of one hundred Chinese horticultural workers, by their sheer size and numbers they could not be missed by anyone entering the city. In addition, the Chinese established the usual types of small businesses, such as groceries and food stalls, laundries and restaurants, as well as retail shops dealing in daily consumer goods. But they did not stop here; they joined the other foreign investors to open banks and hotels. To top it off, they began laying tracks for another electric streetcar line for the town. They had a bank, originally named the Compañía Bancaria Chino y México (Hua-Mo-Yin-Hang); later, with the tramway project underway, it expanded to become the Compañía Bancaria y de Tranvías Wah Yick (Hua Yi), housed in its own building downtown by the railroad station, next to the Chinese-owned Hotel Ferrocarril (Railroad Hotel).[24]

It is not known exactly when the Chinese started arriving and investing in this flurry of activity, but given the recent development of Torreón, they must have arrived along with the other immigrants and foreign entrepreneurs eager to capitalize on the dynamic pace of development. Among the early arrivals was an English-speaking, American-trained physician from

California, Dr Walter Lim, and his wife. A prominent investor and community leader was Wong Foon-chuck, who resided in the border town of Ciudad Porfirio Díaz (today's Piedras Negras) and in the capital city of México, DF. He brought capital to invest as well as connections throughout Mexico and in Chinese communities in the United States.

Among other Chinese investors that Wong attracted to Torreón in 1906 was the intellectual and reformer K'ang Yu-wei, then travelling throughout North America raising money and political awareness for his reform movement and organization, the Baohuanghui, or, as it was better known in North America, the China Reform Association (Zhongguo Weixinhui), headquartered in Vancouver, Canada. Attached to it was the Commercial Corporation, set up to seek out promising investment opportunities in the Americas. Within a short time Kang and his disciples, who included the brothers Liang Ch'i-ch'ao and Liang Chi'-i-t'ien established branch societies in 170 cities in the United States, Canada, Hawaii, Panama, Mexico, Peru and other countries in Latin America and the Caribbean, with a claimed membership of several hundred thousand.[25] In 1903, Wong Foon-chuck and his fellow Chinese in Torreón founded the Asociación Reformista China, well in advance of the much anticipated visit by K'ang himself.[26] Accompanied by Liang Ch'i-t'ien and Lee Fook Kee, Vancouver businessman and director of the Commercial Corporation, K'ang visited Torreón twice in 1906 and 1907. Each time, he invested in property and real estate, and made handsome profits. He left the reform society and his investments in the good hands of Woo Lam Po, secretary of the reform society as well as manager of the Chinese bank.

The impressive flurry of foreign enterprises unnerved Mexican businessmen in Torreón, who formed a chamber of commerce in 1907 to consolidate their power vis-à-vis the foreigners. As they lamented in the local newspaper *El Nuevo Mundo* (the New World): "We cannot compete against the foreigners in commercial ventures. The sad and lamentable fact is that the prostration of our national commerce has created a situation in which Mexicans are replaced by foreign individuals and companies, which monopolize our commerce and behave in the manner of conquerors in a conquered land."[27] A few years later, on 15 May 1911, as revolutionary troops led by Coahuila native son Emilio Madero swooped down on the city, 303 Chinese were cut down in one bloody afternoon, including most of the *caiyuan* workers. Many of the Chinese businesses were raided and destroyed. The Chinese community in Torreón never recovered.[28]

During the course of the Mexican Revolution (1911–17), Chinese in the border region continued to feel the brunt of revolutionary fervour. If before the revolution, Mexican workers directed their hostility primarily towards American and European owners and managers of mines, railroads and other large enterprises, during the revolution they began to turn on the ubiquitous and visible Chinese shopkeepers with a vengeance, especially in company towns such as Cananea, a sort of "guilt by association" given their perceived proximity to the American owners. Anti-foreign demonstrations often degenerated into anti-Chinese mob actions.

After one particularly vicious attack in Cananea in February 1914, US consul Frederick Simpich was instructed to protect the Chinese under attack, whereupon he made plans to evacuate them in the event of a real threat to the copper company's properties and operations. Upon receiving a long list of grievances and abuses from the Chinese – such as seizure of property and excess taxes imposed by revolutionary factions – Simpich urged them to stay open for business rather than close down. He also noted that should the American company cease to operate, the situation in Cananea would become "most perilous". In his report to the State Department, Simpich offered this final observation: "The feeling against all foreigners and against Chinese in particular is very strong; the continued depreciation of money, and the subsequent rise in the cost of food . . . and the mistaken idea of the ignorant miners that American capitalists and Chinese merchants are in some way very responsible for this condition, is driving the people to increasing unrest."[29]

Consul Simpich grasped what the Chinese themselves surely must have come to understand as well: that the communities and small businesses they built on the border came with a dear price. Decades of a successful transnational strategy to transcend the limitations imposed by Chinese exclusion in the United States produced a situation increasingly viewed by common Mexicans in the throes of a social revolution as intolerable and unacceptable.

We conclude this examination of transnational practices on the US–Mexico border with one final variation on the theme, in yet another stretch of this long and porous border. Americans and Chinese on both sides of the border constructed another pattern of collaboration in the then Mexican territory of Baja California on the Pacific coast, south of California. The early development of Baja California's Mexicali Valley was closely tied to the California–Mexico Land and Cattle Company and its parent company, the Colorado River Land Company. Its owners were the southern California tycoons and *Los Angeles Times* publishers Harrison Otis and his son-in-law Harrison Chandler. Already large landowners in California's Imperial Valley, the heart of the state's burgeoning agricultural economy, acquired in 1902 the vast Andrade tract in Baja's Mexicali Valley, the natural extension of the Imperial. In both cases, agricultural development depended on harnessing the waters of the powerful Colorado River. In deciding in 1910 to put their Mexicali Valley land under extensive cotton cultivation, Otis and Chandler chose as partners not local Mexicans or fellow Americans, but Chinese entre-preneurs of California to bring Chinese contract workers across the Pacific directly to Mexico. Thus, the history of the Colorado River Land Company added another intriguing chapter to the history of the Chinese diaspora on this transpacific, transborder region.[30]

Landowners Otis and Chandler did not actually plant the cotton them-selves; rather, they leased the land to others to plant, in tracts of 50 to 1,000 acres, at rates varying from $1 to $10 per acre, depending on the condition of the land (cleared or uncleared). With taxes and other assessments added on, the cost to the lessee for a 50-acre lot ranged from $115 to $565. Signifi-cantly for our discussion, most of the lessees were Chinese, not only from California but also from China. By 1920, they were growing 80 per cent of the Mexicali cotton crop.[31] It is interesting, though not entirely surprising, that the California Chinese should have presented themselves to the Americans as partners in this enterprise, because it was well known among them that fellow immigrant entrepreneurs in Southeast Asia had established similar relationships with the British in the cultivation of rubber. To the American landowners, the Chinese partnership proved efficient, economical and, thus, profitable. First, since the land had never been cultivated before cotton, much work was required to clear and prepare the soil – arduous backbreaking tasks that the Chinese were adept at doing under the scorching sun in a semi-arid zone. Second, in this sparsely populated outpost of Mexico, the Chinese easily solved an obvious labour problem by contracting and importing co-ethnic workers directly from China, bypassing the United States and its exclusion laws.

After leasing the land, the Chinese lessee assumed all costs involved with cotton cultivation. A few rich California Chinese had their own capital to invest in this enterprise; others borrowed from Americans in southern California. They also raised some measure of capital from their own contracted workers, whom they organized into cooperatives. Each man contributed whatever he could towards the collective enterprise, working for a share of the crops rather than straight wages. During the working season, the individual received only clothing and food. This way, the workers had an actual stake in the business. They were in effect partners with the lessee who had brought them to Baja California and therefore highly motivated to make the venture a success. (These cooperatives appeared to be American adaptations of the *kongsi* system that the Chinese had perfected under the British in Southeast Asia.[32]) For the American landowner, it was a good deal indeed, for he received money at the outset for leasing out the land, then for no investment at all on his part he saw the land cleared and planted by the industrious, skilled and well-disciplined Chinese work teams. Best of all, he received 50 per cent of the harvested cotton.

In addition to landowners in Mexicali and moneylenders in California, cotton in Baja generated good business for yet another group of American businessmen, the cotton ginners, who invariably set up their operations on the US side of the border. The refined cotton would then be marketed in the United States and shipped throughout the world, with Japan a major buyer. All equipment and the bulk of supplies were also purchased in the United States. The major ginners also became leading moneylenders to Chinese planters. W.J. Hartman was a member of the ginning firm Coree and Hartman. T.J. West represented the Chinese–Mexican Ginning Company, which, despite its name, was owned by neither Chinese nor Mexican, but by an Anglo-American family in Los Angeles. W.C. Allen headed the local branch of the Globe Milling Company of Calexico, the mirror image in name and location from Mexicali, Mexico. Globe's subsidiary in Mexico was appropriately named the Compañía Algodonera de Baja California (Cotton Company of Baja California). Unlike Messrs Otis and Chandler, these Americans who invested heavily in Baja California cotton were not landowners. Instead, they bankrolled the Chinese growers and ginned their cotton. Their money did not come cheaply. According to US consul Walter Boyle of Mexicali, these ginners charged 12 per cent interest for the period from March to September, and 24 per cent for the rest of the year, "with the additional stipulation that the borrower donates a bonus of one-fourth of his cotton seed, and have the cotton ginned at the lender's gin".[33]

Not surprisingly, all sorts of Americans waxed enthusiastically about the Chinese, both as business partners and as workers. Consul Boyle described them in starkly straightforward language: "[They are] supplying an uncomplaining, hardworking, wealth-producing subject of exploitation. The favorable condition being that the Chinaman expects to be exploited and will stand for any degree of exploitation just so long as it does not exceed a fifty-fifty sharing of his profits with the exploiters." Boyle continued, the "Chinaman" was moreover regarded as "quite honest in meeting his commercial obligations".[34] This Baja California commercial cotton production enterprise came to a natural demise with the depression of the 1930s, whereupon most Chinese drifted closer to towns on the international line dividing the two countries to start restaurants and other small, mainly service-oriented businesses, or like so many co-ethnics before, they crossed the border as Mexicans to resume life and work on the other side, calling upon familiar Chinese, Mexican and Anglo American networks. Like other US consuls on the border, such as Simpich of Nogales cited above, Boyle was instructed to look after Chinese interests and to protect them when necessary.

But the Chinese were not without resources of their own to call upon. As practiced long distance travellers and sojourners, diasporic Chinese carried adaptive mechanisms for mutual aid and support, which they mobilized to defend themselves against hostile outsiders. Within China itself, when merchants, students and others left their home village, county or province to work in another part of the country, they learned to depend on others from the same clan or lineage, and from the same place and region. The restricted membership associations created on this basis are known commonly as huiguan. Later, as the need to mobilize displaced individuals who were not necessarily connected by primordial ties or mutual aid and protection, less exclusive associations were created. These sworn brotherhoods were built less on bonds of blood and place than on rituals that sealed underlying fraternal loyalty and trust. Variously termed secret societies, triads and, most ominously, tongs, these types of associations along with various kinds of huiguan made their way overseas throughout the diaspora. North America was no exception. These immigrant associations were not so much re-enacted as persisting traditional organizations as they were adaptive mechanisms for the changes that migrants encountered and had to deal with.[35]

In California's Chinatown, the first *huiguan*, which were surname associations, appeared as early as 1854. By 1877, seven such associations or "companies" had formed, with a combined membership of over 150,000. They federated to become the Consolidated Chinese Benevolent Association (CCBA), known colloquially as the Chinese Six Companies. Besides the large San Francisco Chinatown, smaller ones in North America had versions or chapters of the CCBA. They became the de facto governments for the Chinese immigrants, as local American governmental authorities were disinclined to expend time and energy to maintain order in these ethnic enclaves to which the Chinese were confined by local ordinances.[36]

The CCBA was not a commercial agency, nor a secret society, nor a labour contractor. Its main functions were to arbitrate disputes among the member associations, to keep track of the size and comings and goings of the Chinese immigrants through a close registration system; and to hire American legal counsel to fight anti-Chinese legislation and persecution by local, state and federal governments, as well as harassment by private individuals. Later, it also took on the difficult task of breaking the powerful antisocial influence of the "fighting tongs", especially when violent conflicts arose between them or there were turf wars over drugs, gambling, prostitution and other illegal but profitable activities. Funds for CCBA operations came from contributions from member associations, registration fees collected from every Chinese immigrant it registered, and other fees.[37] As noted above, the CCBA became involved with human smuggling across the US–Mexico border from exclusion's inception to its end.

Mexico's version of the CCBA was the Unión Fraternal, an open brotherhood association. As early as 1904, in the absence of any Chinese consular representation in Mexico, it began intervening with Mexican political authorities on behalf of Chinese immigrants, in particular those merchants who tried to do business in hostile environments. In one instance that year, the protest concerned merchant Arturo Fong Chong of Cananea, whose store was broken into and pillaged by a mob, causing him to lose $3,316 in cash and merchandise.[38] By 1919, the Unión Fraternal claimed a membership of five thousand with an income the prior year of $20,402 derived from admission fees, monthly dues and donations. Unlike the California CCBA which offered considerable social welfare to members (schools, hospitals, burial), the Unión's focus was almost entirely on organizing immediate, deliberate, forceful and collective responses to harassment and discrimination emanating from any governmental or political source.

During the difficult but prosperous years of the Mexican revolution, another brotherhood organization was introduced to northern Mexico from California, the often controversial Chee Kung Tong (Zhigongtang or CKT), commonly called in the Americas a Masonic lodge (*sociedad masónica*). With its name literally meaning "Justice Society", the CKT had a long history in China, Hawaii (where Sun Yat-sen was an ardent member) and California before appearing in Baja California, Sonora and other Mexican states.[39] On the Mexican border, it positioned itself as a serious rival to the Unión for the hearts, money, allegiance and trust of the Chinese community, its founders alleging that the Unión had grown too elite and removed from the base of ordinary, poor and working-class Chinese. Like other *huiguan*, CKT chapters in Mexico maintained hostels and secured employment for new arrivals, and otherwise substituted for the missing families of single male migrants in America. They solved arguments and arbitrated conflicts between members, and were also known for smuggling Chinese labourers across the Canadian and Mexican borders to the United States, a lucrative business along with prostitution, gambling and opium dens.[40]

The borderlands constituted a wide open range between and bestride two sovereign national entities. Even before exclusion, they beckoned Chinese immigrants, a largely homogenous group of young to middle-aged men from the overcrowded villages and towns of southern China, leaving home as single men, whether married or not, but usually in the company of others like themselves. They came to North America to work and to trade, with the intention to return with accumulated savings to their villages and families left behind. When exclusion foreclosed the entry of latecomers to the United

States, the Chinese amassed along the US–Mexico border, giving rise to
a phenomenon I term "strategic transnationalism". By this arrangement,
Chinese immigrants – labourers and entrepreneurs alike – expanded their
sphere of activities and economic influence on the borderlands at a time
when this border was remarkably porous and open for border crossers in both
directions. In so doing, they not only circumvented the tightest immigration
restrictions ever imposed by US law, but in fact created new opportunities
for immigrants from south China who found that passage to Mexico was
not denied as it was in the United States. But they also paid a heavy price,
for the violent attacks on Chinese persons and businesses on the Mexican
borderlands were arguably the most intense anywhere in the Chinese diaspora of the Americas. Nevertheless, the varied experiences of these Chinese
diaspora communities in those open borderlands illustrate the diverse ways
in which diasporic communities were constructed, perpetuated, marginalized or destroyed.

NOTES

1. There have been small periodical adjustments to the US–Mexican border due
to shifting changes in the Rio Grande valley as, for example, in 1964 when the
Chamizal area was returned to Mexico.

2. It is notable that in Spanish, the word for frontier and border is the same: *la
frontera*.

3. Paul M. Ong, "The Central Pacific Railroad and Exploitation of Chinese Labor",
Journal of Ethnic Studies 13, no. 2 (1985): 119–24; Susan Lan Cassel, *The Chinese
in America: A History from Gold Mountain to the New Millennium* (Lanham, MD:
Altamira, 2002); Shih-Shan Henry Tsai, *The Chinese Experience in America*
(Bloomington: Indiana University Press, 1986); Erika Lee, *At America's Gates:
Chinese Immigration during the Exclusion Era, 1882–1943* (Chapel Hill: Univer-
sity of North Carolina Press, 2005).

4. Kornel Suk Chang, "Transpacific Borderlands and Boundaries: Race, Migration
and State Formation in the North America Pacific Rim, 1882–1917" (PhD diss.,
University of Chicago, 2007), 4.

5. Ibid., 35–44.

6. Ibid., 6.

7. Ibid., 58–76.

8. Ibid., 87.

9. Lee, *At America's Gate.*

10. William H. Siener, "Through the Back Door: Evading the Chinese Exclusion Act along the Niagara Frontier, 1900–1924", *Journal of American Ethnic History* 27, no. 4 (Summer 2008): 34–70.

11. Lee, *At America's Gate*, 151.

12. Roberto Chao Romero, "Transnational Chinese Immigrant Smuggling to the United States via Mexico and Cuba, 1882–1916", *Amerasia Journal* 20, no. 3 (2004–5): 1–16.

13. Of all the immigrants to Mexico deemed at one time to be undesirable or "pernicious", Arabes or Middle Easterners are only now receiving belated attention. See Theresa Alfaro Velcamp, *So Far from Allah, So Close to Mexico: Middle Eastern Immigrants in Modern Mexico* (Austin: University of Texas Press, 2007).

14. Leo M.D. Jacques, "The Anti-Chinese Campaign in Sonora, Mexico, 1900–1931" (PhD diss., University of Arizona, 1974), 38, 51, quoting Mexican immigration figures. Charles Cumberland, "The Sonoran Chinese and the Mexican Revolution", *Hispanic American Historical Review* 40, no. 1 (1960): 191–211 estimated that as many as thirty thousand Chinese probably stayed in Mexico.

15. Evelyn Hu-DeHart, "Huagong and Huashang: The Chinese as Laborers and Merchants in Latin America and the Caribbean", *Amerasia Journal* 289, no. 2 (2002): 64–92; Evelyn Hu-DeHart, "Los Chinos de Sonora, 1875–1930: La formación de una pequeña burguesía regional", in *Los inmigrantes en el mundo de los negocios, siglos XIX y XX*, ed. Rosa María Meyer and Delia Salazar (Mexico: CONACULTA-INAH, 2003), 115–36; Evelyn Hu-DeHart, "México: inmigrantes a una frontera en desarrollo", in *Cuando Oriente Llegó a América: contribuciones de inmigrantes chinos, japoneses y coreanos* (Washington, DC: Inter-American Development Bank, 2004), 53–77.

16. Federico García y Alva, *México y sus progresos, "Album-directorio del Estado de Sonora"* (Hermosillo: Imprente Oficial, 1905–7), full page advertisement, no pagination.

17. Jacques, "Anti-Chinese Campaigns", 45.

18. Raymond B. Craib, " 'Uncovering' the Chinese in Mexico", *American Philatelist* 112, no. 4 (1998): 448–55. Quite by accident Craib acquired a cache of stamped envelopes that indicated correspondence between Chinese shopkeepers in Mexico and Central America and many Chinese wholesalers in California Chinatowns. While the addresses of senders and receivers were intact, alas, the contents have been discarded (they were obviously of no interest to the philatelist who collected these envelopes!) Nevertheless, given the names and

addresses on these envelopes, it is quite clear that these were business cor-
respondences, and one can safely surmise that they consisted of orders for
merchandise or other business-related matters.

19.   García y Alva, *Mexico y sus Progresos.*

20.   Supervisor of El Paso Station to Commissioner General of Immigration
(Department of Labor), Washington, DC, 20 May 1914, in "Records of the
Department of State Relating to the Chinese Question in Mexico, 1910–1929",
reports and dispatches sent by US consuls in northern Mexico, microfilmed
from the original deposited in the National Archives (Washington, DC) by the
University of Arizona Special Collections; hereafter cited as: NA "Chinese".
Unfortunately, the frames are not numbered.

In this collection, there are numerous requests by Chinese and Americans addressed to the US government to grant asylum in the United States
to harassed Chinese. See, for example, the State Department's response to El
Paso consul Edward's request for financial assistance to two hundred destitute
Chinese refugees gathered at Ciudad Juárez across the border from El Paso: the
State Department replied that it had no "relief fund" but in case of "real need,"
will "endeavor to obtain assistance from the Six Companies and their fellow
countrymen in the U.S.". There is no better evidence to indicate that both the
Chinese and those who observed them often saw the co-ethnics on both sides
of the international border as a transnationally connected community.

21.   Grace Peña Delgado, "At Exclusion's Southern Gate: Changing Categories of
Race and Class among Chinese fronterizos, 1882–1904", in *Continental Crossroads: Mapping U.S. Mexico Borderlands History,* ed. Samuel Truett and Elliott
Young (Durham: Duke University Press, 2004), 187–90. Delgado coined an
interesting term, fronterizos, to describe transnational Chinese, but there is no
indication that the term was used either by the Chinese or their contemporaries
during the exclusion era.

22.   Vice-consul John Silliman to Department of State, Concepción del Oro, 19
January 1914, in NA "Chinese".

23.   "Estado de Sonora. Sección de Estadística. Año de 1925. Censo chino", Archivo
Histórico del Gobierno del Estado de Sonora (AHGES), Tomo 3741; "Noticias
estadísticas comparativas de los giros comerciales e industriales con especifi-
cación de su capital invertido de nacionales y chinos establecidos en el Estado
de Sonora", 2 June 1925, AHGES Tomo 3758.

24.   Juan Puig, *Entre el Río Perla y el Nazas: la China decimonónica y sus braceros
emigrantes, la colonial china de Torreón y la matanza de 1911* (Mexico: Consejo
Nacional para la Cultura y las Artes, 1992), 147–69; Jacques, "Anti-Chinese
Campaigns", 237.

25. I have kept the traditional version of the names of K'ang and the two Liang brothers as they are so well known in history this way, rather than render their names in pinying.

26. Jung Pang Lo, *K'ang Yu-Wei: A Biography and a Symposium* (Tucson: University of Arizona Press, 1967), 170–200.

27. Raymond B. Craib, "Chinese Immigrants in Porfirian Mexico: A Preliminary Study of Settlement, Economic Activity and Anti-Chinese Sentiment", Latin American Studies Center Research Paper Series, no. 28 (University of New Mexico, 1996), 15.

28. For fuller discussions of the massacre, see Puig, *Rio Perla*; Jacques "Anti-Chinese Campaigns"; Evelyn Hu-DeHart, "Indispensable Enemy or Convenient Scapegoat? A Critical Examination of Sinophobia in Latin America and the Caribbean, 1870s to 1930s", *Journal of Chinese Overseas* 5 (2009): 55–90.

29. Consul F. Simpich to Department of State, Naco, Arizona, 26 February 1914, in NA "Chinese".

30. Evelyn Hu-DeHart, "The Chinese of Baja California Norte, 1910–1934", in *Baja California and the North Mexican Frontier: Proceedings of the Pacific Coast Council on Latin American Studies* 12 (1985–86): 9–30.

31. P.L. Bell, *Mexican West Coast and Lower California: A Commercial and Industrial Survey* (Washington, DC: Government Printing Office, 1923), 303–7; Maricela González Felix, "Los inmigrantes chinos y la hacienda pública del Distrito Norte de la Baja California, 1910–1920", in *China y las Californias*, ed. Centro Cultural Tijuana (Tijuana: CONACULTA, 2002), 71–103; Robert H. Duncan, "The Chinese and the Economic Development of Northern Baja California, 1889–1929", *Hispanic American Historical Review* 74, no. 4 (November 1994): 615–47.

32. After reading about the *kongsi* system employed by Chinese throughout Southeast Asia, I find the possibility of its adaptation in Baja California a suggestive idea. See Carl A. Trocki, *Opium and Empire: Chinese Society in Colonial Singapore, 1800–1910* (Ithaca: Cornell University Press, 1990); David Owenby and Mary Somers Heidhues, eds., "Secret Societies", *Reconsidered: Perspectives on the Social History of Early Modern South China and Southeast Asia* (New York: M.E. Sharpe, 1993).

33. US consul Walter Boyle to Department of State, Mexicali, 25 August 1920, US National Archives Record Group 59, M274, 812.00/24495.

34. Ibid.

35. William Hoy, *The Chinese Six Companies in San Francisco: Chinese Consolidated Benevolent Association* (San Francisco: Chinese Six Companies, 1942); Gary Hamilton, "Regional Associations and the Chinese City: A Comparative

Perspective", *Comparative Studies in Society and History* 21 (1979): 346–61; Him Mark Lai, "Historical Development of the Chinese Consolidated Benevolent Association/Huiguan System", *Chinese America: History and Perspectives* (San Francisco: Chinese Historical Society of America, 1987), 13–49.

36. Carl Glick and Hong Sheng-Hwa, *Swords of Silence: Chinese Secret Societies Past and Present* (New York: McGraw Hill, 1947); Eng Hing Gong and Bruce Grant, *Tong Wars!* (New York: Nicholas L. Brown, 1930).

37. Hoy, *Six Companies*, 20–23.

38. Unión Fraternal to Municipal President of Cananea, 8 October 1904, AHGES Tomo 2139.

39. Tsai, *Chinese Experience*; Fei-Ling Davis, *Primitive Revolutionaries of China: A Study of Secret Societies in the Late Nineteenth Century* (Honolulu: University Press of Hawaii, 1986).

40. Lee, *At America's Gates*.

CHAPTER 6

CARIBBEAN IDENTITIES, DANCE CONSTRUCTIONS AND "CROSSROADING"

YVONNE DANIEL

DANCE, DANCE MUSIC AND THE BODY are significant in African diaspora cultures. The primary function of dance and music alone is to provide the very necessary relaxation, relief, release and rest necessary to replenish the energy needed for other types of intellectual and physical production. However, there is a tendency to subordinate the examination of aesthetic and artistic pursuits in diaspora studies in favour of philosophical, religious, political, economic and historical analyses, which are understandably important aspects in this field. Such thinking, though, is short-sighted and perched shakily on the primary function of dance and music as recreation or entertainment, rather than more firmly on the multiple functions of artistic and aesthetic production. This limited perspective also reflects European and North American conventions that place greater significance on the mind than the body and patently fails to recognize the profoundly instructive values encountered in dance performance.

Caribbean dance and dance music offer a full range of meanings that readily display philosophical, religious, political, economic and historical connections within social, sacred and concert performances. For example, dance and dance music affirm Caribbean and other diaspora religions, and provide ample evidence of African value-systems to those who carefully analyse and compare religions, philosophies and ideologies. Caribbean dance and dance music "house" and promote pivotal Caribbean voices, often those of

the impoverished and/or beleaguered majority populations who have struggled for democratic rule and egalitarian policies. Also, dance and dance
music are important for Caribbean tourism, which is the critical resource
for most Caribbean economies and provides the guaranteed income of many
Caribbean islanders. Above all, Caribbean dancing bodies have promoted
and continuously displayed their African diaspora customs, behaviours and
values, adamantly refusing to submit to mainstream European- and North
American–derived values about the dancing body.[1]

Caribbean and other African diasporic cultures have an inherent worth,
special priorities, and a unique manner of participating in and contributing to
the global economy, politics and culture. Through dance and, especially, popular dance music, Caribbean and other diaspora bodies express sophisticated
critical thinking. Often, the ideas and opinions residing in such aesthetic
and artistic expressions are just as relevant and poignant as parliamentary
and congressional debates, or proclamations made by charismatic leaders, or
economic projections made by savvy pundits. Therefore, without including
what dance and dance music "say" and what performers communicate, an
assessment of any African diaspora site or group remains incomplete and
thereby inadequate for diaspora studies.

The following appraisal of Caribbean dance situates observations about
dance and dance music within an interdisciplinary conversation about
"danced" Caribbean identities.[2] The discussion that follows highlights the
abundant constructions of danced identities that have revealed "crossroading", that is, the intense interplay and contestation of several ethnic heritages
inside the dancing body. Crossroading may be interpreted, therefore, as one
dimension in the complex process of creolization, which inevitably accompa-
nies transfer, transplantation and sociocultural reconstitution.[3]

OVERVIEW OF DIASPORA DANCE HISTORY

Dance and music-making practices accompanied peoples of African descent
as they were transported involuntarily from the African continent to all parts
of the Americas. Both while crossing the Atlantic and in their new homelands, Africans and their descendants used their dancing and music-making

bodies to alleviate suffering, embody resistance and find respite from their horrific circumstances.[4] Scholars of African art history and diaspora dance history have long established a consensus on the general characteristics of African-based dance, and scholars of ethnomusicology and music history have done the same for African-based music. Using slightly different vocabularies, Robert Farris Thompson in 1974,[5] Kariamu Welsh-Asante in 1985,[6] and Brenda Dixon Gottschild in 1996[7] have identified the shared elements dance practitioners have transmitted in the teaching of African-based dance. These elements include: (1) the grounded and "ready-for-anything" positioning of the dancing body with (2) both torso-generated and divided torso movement; (3) body part isolation; (4) polyrhythms within the body; (5) call and response singing; (6) an emphasis on interdependent percussion; (7) allusions to ancestral and cosmic narratives; and (8) a measured, controlled or "cool" approach.[8] Distinctions between West and Central African dance in the Americas seem to be found in a predominance of either style or form.[9]

Two major dance styles that originated in West and Central Africa are salient in the Caribbean diaspora. These are both predicated on the standard "qualities of movement" used in dance analysis: sustained, percussive, restrained, vibratory and swing movements, which jointly yield numerous stylistic differences. For example, sustained, often undulating, movement is emphasized in the Fon-derived Haitian *yenvalou*; percussive kicking movement is emblematic of the Cuban Yoruba divinity Chango and percussive movement can also be seen in the shoulder pulses of the Haitian *mayi*; restrained movement is characteristic within the very tense stretches of the Cuban Yoruba dance for Babaluaye; vibratory movement is found in the Haitian *petwo* and in Cuban Carabalí (Abakuá) traditions; and swinging movement is found in the side-to-side swaying of the Cuban *yemaya* and in the semi-circling legs of the Haitian *Ibo*. These Caribbean examples of qualities of movement also suggest the multiple styles and stylistic variations derived from West African dance heritage.

On the other hand, central African derived dances in the diaspora exhibit form over style. A circle with solo and duet competitions and/or chases is the most prevalent form in the Caribbean, as in the Cuban *rumba* or Haitian *Congo*. Central African derived dances also display characteristic movement: there is hip isolation galore in bumping, circling, shifting, lifting and releasing movements. A clear example of Central African heritage is seen in the circular form and alternating hip movements of the Haitian *Congo dance*. Thus, throughout the diaspora, West African dance styles are profuse while Central African dance forms are pronounced; that is, West African dance styles are found frequently, but such profusion of styles is not found for Central Africa in African diaspora dance. Most often, the circular form and prominent hip movements described above are what are most evident and characteristic of Central African-derived dances in the diaspora.

African musical legacies have been described and analysed by many scholars including J.H.K. Nketia in 1965,[10] Olly Wilson in 1981 and 2001,[11] and Sam Floyd in 1999.[12] The most characteristic elements are as follows: (1) an emphasis on rhythm in general and polyrhythm in particular, (2) drum and percussion batteries in which the lowest-voiced instrument leads, (3) use of wind, brass and string instruments, (4) call-and-response vocal and instrumental form, (5) *melissma* or extreme elaboration of melody, (6) the pentatonic scale, (7) variable scale degree emphases, and (8) distinctive use of repetition, all within a multitude of musical forms. An ensemble or community of dancers, musicians and ritual or social participants perform Caribbean and other diaspora styles and forms, often within an open expanse in front of a drum and percussion battery. Caribbean dance and dance music involve an abundance of improvisation,[13] rhythmic intricacy and focused repetition. These elements are present in both sacred and social dance movements and dance music, in combat and parading forms, in tourist and concert performances, and in colonial as well as contemporary forms throughout the diaspora. Almost all dance and dance music forms have had "identity" as a basic meaning within performance, that is, most dances bodily state "who I am" or "who we are".[14]

Although elite colonists, administrators and colonial writers denigrated African identities, African admixtures and almost all "things African", multiple aspects of continental African heritage were preserved in emergent Caribbean territorial cultures. These are found in maroon and creole societies, African-based religions, drum dances, and chants and songs in African-derived languages. The existence of localized folklore and proverbs spanning the sixteenth to the twenty-first century also attests to the preservation of African-based communal memories and the construction of new rituals to commemorate new transatlantic kinships and identities. What was apparently forgotten or lost in transit between the African continent and the Americas was recaptured, fortified, repaired or reconstituted by means of intermittent contacts with *bosales* (enslaved Africans brought from the continent of Africa) or, later, with "returnees", that is, Africans who travelled between the New World (the Caribbean and Brazil) and countries in Africa (Sierra Leone, Liberia, Ghana, Togo, Benin and Nigeria), both during and after the human trade terminated around the end of the nineteenth century.[15] Just as music and dance could indicate and often confirm which African ethnic groups were present in any given locale of the Americas, so too can dance and music herald the specific heritage and history of the Atlantic African diaspora in the Caribbean islands, Latin America, the United States and Canada.

DANCED IDENTITIES FROM THE SIXTEENTH TO THE EIGHTEENTH CENTURIES

In the earliest Atlantic crossings and subsequent settlements, uprooted Africans and their diasporic descendants danced "remembered" drum dances in secret quarters of the plantation and in maroon fortresses. Dance researchers surmise that most were sacred performances that called upon African ancestors and cosmic spirits to protect and sustain the enslaved and those cut off from their African heritage in the perilous circumstances of colonialism, alienation and later of coloniality.[16] At the very least, drum dances bodily projected differing African identities. For example, within Haitian Vodou, Jamaican Cumina, Cuban Santería, Carriacouan and Trinidadian Big Drum and other African-derived religions in the Caribbean, Africans and their descendants invoked remembered divinities through particular drum, gestural and chant patterns. Each ethnic group projected its "African nation" or heritage identity in specific movements danced to specific drum rhythms.[17] In related circum-Caribbean and Afro-Latin sites, drum dances were used similarly, for example, in Surinamese Winti and Brazilian Candomblé religions. Performance was spiritual and religious but also political, in that, by dancing, drumming and singing, African descendants confronted colonial domination with African-based, remembered and inspired dance and music practices. Vibrant dances and rigorous rhythms have continued and developed for five centuries, despite repression, ridicule and marginalization.[18]

All drum dances were not sacred performances; both those referred to above and others were used on social occasions as well. Drum dances like *yucca* and *makuta* that linger today in Cuba or like evolved forms of the *djuba*, *bamboula* and *calenda* in the US Virgin Islands provided intermittent recreation during the colonial period.[19] Similar social dances are still found in cultural and tourist performances; all signal African and European ancestry as well as specific Caribbean identities.

More prevalent today and across the entire Caribbean are "Caribbean quadrilles" which are ensemble couple, line and square dances that were derived from many seventeenth and eighteenth-century court dances on the European side of the Atlantic. In this chapter – in a bold and broad sweep, I refer to the many European heritage dances as *"contredanses"* and the related American line, square, and couple dances as Caribbean quadrilles. On this side of the Atlantic, Caribbean quadrilles were also plentiful and seemingly

Figure 6.1 Quadrilles: Cuban *tumba francesa* in rehearsal, with erect backs, 1999. Courtesy of Patricia Gonzalez

unrelated, for example, the Haitian *affranchi*, the Martinican *bele* and *haut taille*, the Guadeloupian *kadril*, the Cuban *tumba francesa*, the Dominican *sarandunga/jacana*, the Jamaican and Virgin Islands *quadrille*, the Curaçaoan *kuadría*, and so on. Each named dance displays the performers' distinct island identity.

In public, away from their residential areas and so-called private domains, Africans were coerced to replace African movements and forms with European movements and forms. African descendants performed imitations of colonial imitations of European *contredanses*.[20] Historically, colonial and postcolonial elites, both black and white, practised the exceedingly erect postures and codified dance movements of the *contredanses* in an effort to raise the standards (so they believed) above those practised by the usually poor and uneducated performers of drum dances. A succinct example of what many Caribbean islanders have thought of *contredanse*-derived performances versus drum dance performances is found in a rare study of Barbadian dance by Susan Harewood and John Hunte:

> Discussions of social dance practices with older Barbadians suggest that, for some communities, dance was caught up in the demarcation of what was deemed decent and indecent and how that demarcation affected any hope that the poor might have for social advancement . . . "Decency" was defined in rather narrow ways that gave Europeans and European-derived cultural practices privilege over African and African-derived cultural practices . . . It [decency] was presented as a major qualification for social advancement.[21]

Importantly, not all African descendants in the Caribbean thought this way. Some held on to African values and camouflaged their disdain for European preferences. They seemed to absent themselves from African ancestral ways by maintaining seventeenth- and eighteenth-century *contredanse*-derived quadrille forms even as they developed and practised individual couple dances in the late eighteenth and nineteenth centuries. As time went on, Caribbean quadrille dancers came from many sectors, including church groups, dance schools, working-class groups, and upper-class parlour, salon and ballroom entertainment groups.[22]

The popularity and widespread practice of Caribbean quadrilles from the eighteenth century to the present have been scrutinized through detailed

156

Figure 6.2 Quadrilles: Martinican *bele* 1, with tilted backs, 2002.
Courtesy of Philippe Bourgade.

Figure 6.3 Quadrilles: Martinican *bele* 2, with tilted backs, 2013.
Courtesy of Camee Maddox.

music, dance and cultural analyses by musicologists, ethnomusicologists, dance anthropologists, and Latin American and Caribbean historians. Several results point to the imitation of European practices and the maintenance of European values; many rely on the cultural processes of creolization, while others include African agency, such as camouflaged confrontation, finessed resistance, and the maintenance of African practices and values.[23]

Caribbean people developed their own attachments to *contredanse*-derived dances after the coercive performances during the period of enslavement. Over time, they remembered their New World ancestors dancing quadrilles and they relished the immediate fun and delight of group dancing to "calls" from a leader that announced a new round of dance steps and sequences. They also performed then, as well as now, in a calm and deliberate (hence "cool") manner. They were following African cultural values about respect for the ancestors and adopting a polite and honorific performance demeanour when they treasured New World *contredanses*. African descendants consciously honoured what their New World African ancestors danced, how they danced and how they resisted the oppression of their social circumstances through dance; they have done so continuously to the present. In some ways, the *contredanse*-derived Caribbean quadrilles remain early, perhaps archaic, versions of the electric slide, the *cha cha* slide, country line dancing, *casino de la rueda* or Cuban group *salsa*, and related ensemble couple dances.

Additionally, in colonial times, descendants of Africans in the Caribbean performed quadrilles as a means of either attaining higher social status or judging the social status of others. As Dominique Cyrille's music history research has emphasized, Africans and their descendants performed the same dances that Europeans used to judge a person's social status in revolutionary France at the end of the eighteenth century.[24] Africans appropriated line and square, set and figure dances, relying on the same values and understandings as Europeans of what constituted proper dancing and thus eligibility for higher social ranking. As dance movement analysis and anthropological research have revealed also, the value European's placed on dance itself from the sixteenth century through to the eighteenth century was similar to the high esteem that most traditional African societies held (and still hold) for dance.[25]

In dance performance then, and centuries thereafter, African performance of the European *contredanse* form may have been attempts to gain European approval and Caribbean prestige, decency or social advancement, but it also continued to generate a deep sense of individual and communal awareness, enabling performers to assert their individual identities, group identities and sometimes a comparative sense of their societal ranking. The non-verbal language of dance movement in the colonial era allowed for the emphasis of a preferred human identity over a presumed enslaved chattel identity. *Contredanse*-derived performance thus camouflaged challenges to enslaved and subjugated social standing made by African descendants and trans-formed the dance into a finessed form of resistance.

Behaviours in dance performance match values in society to whatever extent possible, and are resignified, if necessary, as time goes by. Today, African descendants perform *contredanse* variations to mark their Caribbean identities and, simultaneously, to underscore the change from European dom-ination to Caribbean sovereignty; that is, most Caribbean quadrilles highlight contemporary Caribbean identities over previous colonial identities.[26] In a few cases, performance reiterates continuing colonial attachments. In 2006, for example, I witnessed a performance in St Thomas, Virgin Islands, that symbolically re-enacted the transfer of ownership and power from Denmark to the United States after 262 years. Virgin Islanders still marked their (cur-rent) American, colonial status with an eighteenth-century inspired court dance, *lancers*,[27] and then, with various other quadrilles and oratory perfor-mances. In this case, they used bodily displays to underscore the long-lasting ties to colonial enterprises that still exist.

Besides drum dances and quadrilles, another dance genre yields multiple danced identities in colonial and contemporary accounts throughout the Caribbean. Parading and carnival dances, while of ancient practice, currently promote Caribbean identity in the modern world. Since the first celebratory processions for saints' days on church grounds and, later, within and around island cathedrals, Caribbean and other diaspora peoples have been display-ing their historically Catholic and Protestant commitments through dance and performance. Masking, role reversals, costuming as devils, undertak-ing mock battles, providing poetic social commentary in oratory and dance dramas, and parading dances – like the *conga/comparsa* in Cuba, the *rara* in Haiti and the *gagá* in the Dominican Republic – promoted social abandon,

Figure 6.4 Children's Parade, Tom Thumb Wedding, Fort de France, Martinique. © Chester Higgins Jr/chesterhiggins.com.

gluttony and excess in advance of the forty days of fasting and sacrifice during Lent.[28] Stock characters echoing historical Jonkannu traditions in Jamaica, mud-soaked naked bodies parading in Trinidadian carnival, red devils in Martinique, and gargantuan headdresses on scantily clad, young women in circum-Caribbean Brazil, all testify to the many identities that are displayed and promoted during carnival. Carnival masquerading, where identity is illusive and multiplied, does not obscure basic Caribbean, Latin, Afro-Latin or other identities. In a variety of costumes, gestures, speeches, songs and dances, carnival performers assume and assert preferred identities other than those ascribed to them in routine, daily life.

Examples of all dance genres that are noted generally for the colonial period are still performed today – both sacred and social drum dances, *contredanse*-derived variations, and parading and carnival dances. These dances indicate African, European and creole heritages as well as island, if not regional, identities. By their very continuity, these dance types display a physical communication that insists on an African-derived, Caribbean identity.

DANCED IDENTITIES IN THE NINETEENTH CENTURY

As nations developed across the American continents, African-derived rhythms and dance vocabularies impacted the formation and selection of national identities through dance – like the Argentine *tango*, the Brazilian *samba*, the Cuban *danzón* and *rumba*, the Dominican *merengue*, the Guadeloupian *gwoka*, the Haitian *mereng*, the Martinican *bele*, the Puerto Rican *danza* and *bomba*, and the Trinidadian *calypso*.[29] These dances and their dance music were influenced tremendously by African-descended musicians who played variously for military marching bands, colonial salons, ballroom festivities, sacred African rituals and secular African celebrations. The diasporic and creole artisan class dominated this particular occupation since the role of musician was not highly esteemed among members of the Caribbean ruling classes before the late eighteenth and early nineteenth century. Diasporic and multi-ethnic musicians drew upon their diverse musical knowledge bases and injected intriguing combinations, resulting in new rhythms and fresh approaches to the dance music of the day.[30]

The new rhythms promoted new dance movements that connected deeply with a sense of local Caribbean identity. The enthusiastic dancing public reinforced the call for a separation from European colonial centres. Each country and its diverse population claimed and promoted a common identity through new, creative "national" dances. The excitement and emotion bound up with local identity inside the dancing body ultimately fed into the strong political currents of nationalism (and vice versa) that permeated the nineteenth and twentieth centuries.

In some cases, political activities stimulated or generated particular dance forms. For example, salon or ballroom creations called *danzas* (or pan-Caribbean *danzas*) signalled and symbolized the independence that nationalists in Puerto Rico, the Dominican Republic and Cuba were seeking in the nineteenth century. Dancing *danza* couples "acted out" independence from Spain on Caribbean ballroom floors. Couples danced in any direction across the floor, turned whenever they felt like it, embraced as they danced face-to-face (which was then a risqué thing to do), and shifted the metre of the European waltz's 3/4 tempo to mainly, although not exclusively, a Caribbean 4/4 tempo. Caribbean *danzas* conveyed the idea that colonial imitations of court dances to a set series of music with set dance figures or patterns in lines and squares were irrelevant by the early nineteenth century, mirroring the lack of Caribbean submission and adherence to European control in the broader society. Thus, the Puerto Rican *danza* and the Cuban *danzón*, the two most important dances of the era, heralded a national spirit non-verbally and influenced local power dynamics. The dancing couples were no longer simply enslaved, subjugated or occupied colonials, but active resisters and new representatives of emerging sovereign island nations expressing agency.[31]

In other cases, the practice of dancing and music-making supported or reflected the history of the era. For example, the Dominican *merengue* and the Haitian *mereng* have remained the choice of the people of Hispaniola for two centuries. *Merengue/mereng* dancing continues as the national dance on the two-nation island, as well as a symbol of national resistance and effective popular defiance against authoritarian rule in Haiti.[32] Additionally, within an historical and diasporic perspective, the *merengue/mereng* and its music almost inevitably recall the history of Santo Domingo/Saint Domingue/Hispaniola – the first black republic, the first slaveless society of the Americas, or a liberated African-derived Haitian, Dominican and Caribbean identity. While dancing the *merengue/mereng*, dancers have no tentativeness or reticence. The body alternates from right to left evenly and gracefully; feet are planted securely as they alternate also; hips thrust to the right and left, often with the pelvis pushing forward; and partners sense one another as they dance either boldly across the space or intimately grinding and swaying from side to side. Over centuries, dancers have been proud and confident as they demonstrate their *mereng/merengue* and, equally, their Haitian, Dominican or Caribbean identities.

In sum, dances of the nineteenth century reflected and sustained the nationalist mood of the era. Identifying with a European identity was temporarily passé; local Caribbean identity was the rage. National dance performance expressed the people's comfort and pride with the new nation-state identities that permeated elite and emerging elite classes across the Americas. However, while all social classes performed versions of the Puerto Rican *danza* and the Cuban *danzón*, for example, their national acclaim and popular performance did not provide an answer to the national dance challenges performed by the Caribbean lower-classes.

At the same time, creative drum dances, like the Puerto Rican *bomba* and the Cuban *rumba*, were percolating in popularity and might have challenged *danzas* across the Caribbean if African descendants had had a voice in such determinations. *Bomba* and *rumba* performances took place in marinas, *solares* (open-air courtyards in crowded urban tenement housing) or in poor rural areas where challenges to the national dance question were performed mostly by dark-skinned rather than light-skinned dancers. There had been no contest over which dance would represent the nation during the eighteenth century: the Caribbean quadrilles dominated the drum dances that existed, just as elite colonists dominated the enslaved. National representation in dance during the nineteenth century was another thing, however, as segmented parts of society danced differing dances: danzas dominated drum dances officially, but national dance identity began to be openly contested, and that contest continues even today. In fact, the Cuban government has only recently (February 2012) accorded national patrimony to the *rumba*, and, to my knowledge, the bomba continues as an historic creole creation, but not one that officially represents Puerto Rico and its people.

The contestation of dance has to do with which social sector selects and establishes national norms. "Decent dancing" and "indecent dancing" within the Caribbean from the nineteenth century to the present are codes for the ambivalence that still surrounds African heritage in the Caribbean and for the embarrassment of both Caribbean "blacks" and "whites" concerning institutionalized slavery and its residue. Aspersions of indecency are attached to the drum dances performed by the predominantly dark-skinned lower classes while the ballroom dances of the predominantly light-skinned upper classes are credited as decent performances.

"CROSSROADING": THE CREOLIZING MARROW OF CARIBBEAN DANCE

I turn now to a review of the specific structural form characterizing European and African dances. Europeans preferred or had a tendency to dance with their spines elongated and torsos stabilized, leaving the arms and legs free for expressive, balanced, codified movement. West and Central Africans,

Figure 6.5 Cuban casino with Caribbean positioning for maximum potential of hips, leg, and arm movement, 2013. Courtesy of Ruxandra Ana.

in contrast, preferred or had a tendency to dance with their backs bent deeply forward, feet grounded and knees fully flexed so that any body part (including the torso) was free for the elaborate, irregular and visually accented action of specific body parts, or in dance parlance, isolations.[33] These two extreme body positions merged over time into a new creole body position for social dancing, a preferred "Caribbean" posture that included a straight, but slightly tilted spine and gently flexed knees. This specific positioning of the dancing body facilitated hip movements and hip accents in all directions and in all qualities of movement also.

Regardless of the forms that diaspora dancing and dance music took, the content of the dance was always the product of a mélange, a creolization, a hybridity, or what I prefer to call "crossroading". This coined term references the intermingling of indigenous, European, African, Middle Eastern and Asian cultures within the diaspora dancing body and its physical expressions to produce a new, inventive and/or diverse dance vocabulary.[34] In other words, several cultural paths came together *within* the performers who were dancing and making music, resulting in the appearance of unique diaspora dance creations over time (as exemplified by the drum dances, quadrilles and national dances previously discussed).

The dances and music arising from crossroading in the Caribbean are unique and popular, and have spiralled throughout the music and dance worlds in an utterly contagious fashion.[35] Crossroading has also had an indelible influence on the concert dances and concert music of the diaspora.[36] Crossroading requires interaction among various traditions and new currents. It requires an interpenetration of ideas and concepts, and root positions so that the understanding of each tradition, old or new, is grounded as innovative performance develops. In spiritual terms, it is at the crossroad that the material and spiritual worlds open into a new dimension, which, for dance, signifies the exquisite crossing and blending of all legacy roads inside the body. In performance, crossroading does not depend on hints, simple motifs or "sampling"[37]), which are superficial glimpses of heritage and historical remembrances made visible in the dance; it relies on unquestionable and detailed familiarity with multiple dance traditions. Crossroading permits and encourages a never-ending depth, and always aims to achieve the highest levels of understanding, sensitivity and creativity in the dance.

CROSSROADING AND CONSTRUCTIONS OF IDENTITY IN MODERN TIMES

Crossroading within the dancing body has led to several constructions of dance, and these have projected the various Caribbean identities I have previously discussed, as well as other diaspora identities in the Americas. The first crossroading generation of dances and dance music in the Caribbean was a multicultural construction, pointing to two or more specific historical legacies and to the originality and creativity that flourished among ethnic groups living together on Caribbean islands and related mainland shores – mainly during the mid-nineteenth and early twentieth centuries. Examples of such first generation multicultural dances are the *son, danza, danzón, rumba, bomba, samba, mereng, merengue, calypso* and *bele linó* to name a few (that is, both drum dances and ballroom dances). These social dances and their music were derived from European and African "parent sources" and became genuine creole creations that expressed specific Caribbean island identities.

First-generation constructions of danced diaspora identity can be found in concert dance as well. For example, world-renowned choreographer Katherine Dunham used local Haitian dance, European ballet and American modern concert dance of the 1930s to create concert and movie choreographies.[38] Within Dunham's performances, a Caribbean identity accompanied the identity of the "exotic other" that was popular during the early Hollywood cinema era. Dunham's much publicized identity as the first African American choreographer to penetrate Hollywood and an international audience advertised her Caribbean research and adopted life in Haiti. Her works were quickly presumed to have Caribbean, as well as other "exotic" roots. While using ample references to Middle Eastern, African and imaginary spaces in sets, costumes and movement, many of Dunham's choreographies were based in Haitian, balletic and modern dance vocabularies and often retained a Caribbean and/or diaspora identity.

Another example of crossroading in concert dance surfaced during the late 1950s and early 1960s with a group of revolutionary Cuban dance artists. Led by Ramiro Guerra, Cuban dancers used Martha Graham and other modern concert dance techniques from the United States and Europe as well as Yoruba and other African dance traditions in Cuba to formulate *danza cubana* or Cuban modern dance. Cuban identity was chiselled from such first generation, multicultural dance constructions.[39] Interestingly, concert stage venues have also promoted Caribbean drum dances like *bomba* and *rumba*, as these have declined as popular social dances, but have remained of particular interest both within and outside their own communities. They are often presented as staged history or living traditions and are first generation constructions of danced identities.

Intra-Caribbean innovation and creativity among several island cultures marked a second generation of Caribbean dance constructions. The "parent sources" for social and popular dances in the twentieth century were already mélanges, creoles, or hybrids. Intra-Caribbean constructions of danced identity were instigated by hybrid popular music and mainly took their names from the dance music, for example: Jamaican *reggae* and *dancehall*, Martinican and Guadeloupian *zouk*, Trinidadian *soca*, Cuban *batarumba* (or *rumbabatason*), *timba* and *reggetón*, and Afro-Brazilian *sambareggae* (all of which are ballroom and public dancehall forms of social and popular dance and music). The dances thickly combined and meshed Caribbean, African American, and Afro-Latin dance movements that at one level signalled particular island identities (that is, Cuban, Haitian, French Caribbean, Afro-Brazilian) and at another level simply signalled a Caribbean regional identity.

Concert venues rarely include second generation, intra-Caribbean constructions, since these are mainly social and popular dances that do not demand specifically trained performers or include modern dance or ballet. By omitting intra-Caribbean dance from their repertoires, concert gatekeepers have demonstrated their preferences. When intra-Caribbean constructions do appear on stage, they are framed as "folk" or erroneously as "ethnic" dance,⁴⁰ and are interspersed in musical theatre acts, perhaps occasionally in operas, but mainly in community performance, tourist settings and in "ethnic dance festivals" that take place in parks, plazas, halls and only rarely on the concert stage. In these latter spaces, they still illuminate specific Caribbean and other identities.

The latest generation of Caribbean dance constructions displays complex inter-diaspora constructions of identity within both popular and concert performance. In the twenty-first century, Caribbean, Latin American and African dance elements are interwoven within American concert dance or European ballet elements, as well as within African, Caribbean, North American, European, Middle Eastern and/or Asian forms so that clear boundaries for dance vocabularies, styles, and forms are *not set*. What is remarkable is the depth of familiarity that exists among differing dance traditions *within* the dancing body. The choreographies of the seasoned members of this generation are gripping, impressive and powerful communicative agents marking true twenty-first-century diaspora identities. Perhaps clear examples can best be gleaned from short dance descriptions and snippets of the following concert artists' biographies (in alphabetical order): Gabri Crista, Nia Love, Augusto Soledade and Merián Soto.

Guggenheim fellow awardee Gabri Christa uses her background in dance performance with film. She draws inspiration from her youth in Curaçao and family in Suriname, as well as from her years of experience dancing with the national modern dance company of Cuba, teaching dance in Puerto

Rico, and as a member of the Bill T. Jones Company in the United States. Her work has many themes and is atmospheric, but her dance vocabulary is unmistakably inter-diasporic, with noticeable legacies from Curaçao, Suriname, Cuba, Puerto Rico, the United States and the Netherlands. In one of her dance films, "Savoneta: Another Building #2", she dances in a touching duet to Curaçaoan popular music inside a bona fide, but empty plantation villa in Curaçao. She emphasizes the feelings of being inside such an historic space with the ghosts of misery, the scars of torture and pain, and the love and joys of her companion. She explores the hollow rooms, wallows in mud outside, thrashes in the Caribbean Sea and affirms love and love relationships in a gorgeous, but historically hostile environment. She investigates who she or her character is, given the plurality of identities that roam historic plantation spaces today.[41]

Nia Love, Fulbright fellow and artistic director of Blacksmith's Daughter, employs Ghanaian court gestures, Akan ritual sequences, Japanese Butoh expression, Indian yoga, modern US dance techniques and the "black experience" to plot an initiation scene in "Remembrances of the Castle I". Cool, clear lighting and striking, spotted costumes identify her character as an initiator, chief, healer, or spiritual leader who delineates the powerful circle, drawing wisdom and responsibility in and pushing fear and the unknown out. She waves her horsehair wand and twirls her head in incredulous circles as she monitors a neophyte's actions, and instigates specific gestures and behaviours. She acknowledges the neophyte's power and access to knowledge as she also keeps her contained within the circle and simultaneously within the squared cardinal direction points. Dancers, who stand on their heads in strong yoga positions throughout that section of the piece, mark the cardinal points and anchor the power of the two dancers inside and just outside of the circle. The scene reverberates with Love's profound sensibilities, drawn from lived experiences in Cuba dancing with Alicia Alonso, in Japan with Min Tanaka, in Ghana with Nana Akuoko Sarpong, and in the States with Senegal's Marie Basse-Wiles. Her multiple identities as a New York City denizen; an African American, a West African and Caribbean dance performer; an American, African and Japanese-derived choreographer; and an American dance researcher yield an inter-diasporic dance vocabulary.[42]

Guggenheim awardee Augusto Soledade's choreography is influenced by the rich and distinctive culture of his native Brazil and by his training with American Brazilianist dance artist Clyde Morgan and Jamaican choreographer Garth Fagan. One of his latest compositions, "Cordel", is based on a nineteenth-century Brazilian tradition where poems and stories that were published in books were hung on string (*cordel*) to be sold by street vendors. The stories retell fairy tales, medieval legends and contemporary soap opera dilemmas among other things. Soledade's "Cordel" encompasses profuse body part isolation, unique rhythms, dazzling designs, stunning performers and new music collaborations galore as he juxtaposes the *tango* and *hip hop* for an examination of dance, human history and emotions. His choreography comes most often from modern concert dance, but his themes and movements come from Brazilian folk traditions, Latin American traditions, African rituals and American popular dance materials. His inter-diasporic offerings alternate Brazilian, Central and West African and American legacies, but they always promote his Afro-Brazilian/American identity.[43]

"Bessie" dance award winner and National Endowment for the Arts awardee, Merián Soto, tells the tale of her grounding in improvisation by means of popular, traditional dance.[44] She cites her early formal dance training as inadequate for her most meaningful choreographic output. When she finally experienced the cultural dance of her roots, the Puerto Rican *bomba*, she found an entry into her most serious and satisfying work. In a solo to popular salsa music by the Cuban ensemble, Irakere, titled "Sacude" or "In a Shaking Mode", she displays salsa movements, steps, sequences and poses within a dense, improvisational concert piece. There, she integrates popular and concert dance styles, traditional and modern forms, American modern dance and improvisation, Puerto Rican popular dance, and Cuban or African-derived traditional dance and music materials. Her work dwells in the spontaneous and the cultural, articulating transnational and inter-diasporic identities.[45]

There are many other diaspora dance artists who project their identities through dance. Isaura Oliveira combines her Brazilian dance heritage with her American experiences and advanced yoga training. Awilda Sterling Duprey blends her Puerto Rican heritage and Jamaican experiences. Neri Torres mixes her Cuban heritage and her Chinese Cuban history. Intra-island and inter-diaspora creations have been developed in the Caribbean but also in

Caribbean diaspora sites across the globe – in London, Paris, Miami, Oakland and the Bronx as well as Cartagena, Caracas, Montevideo, Melbourne, Tokyo and Helsinki. The flow of dances and dance music has been in both directions: for example, *reggae* and *dancehall* came from the Caribbean and spread worldwide, while *salsa* and *zouk* came from Caribbean diaspora enclaves and then spread to the Caribbean and the world. Dances are crossing national, international and aesthetic borders, drawing on indelible cultural connections and making identity complex and situational.

CROSSROADING, CREOLIZATION AND THE DIASPORA DANCING BODY

Crossroading not only involves the diasporic body dancing new materials, nor does it simply involve a cultural process or impetus by which new dances are constructed. It is also a body experience of danced exquisiteness – especially noticeable in diaspora concert dance artists, but also in diaspora specialists of drum dances, quadrilles, or parading dances and in public performers of popular social dances as well. For many dancers and musicians in many diaspora dance sites, the body itself is a crossroad of history, culture and body knowledge. Despite hegemonic European and North American influences, the African connection to nature, spirit energy and the physical body has persisted within dance practices throughout the Caribbean and other diaspora sites. These three important elements mark a nexus of intense interest that surfaces from within the body while it is dancing and making music and makes diaspora dancing and music-making particularly satisfying. Moreover, crossroading has been an integral aspect of the creolization process, demonstrating the creativity that lives on within all human beings, and people of African descent in particular, regardless of their physical conditions and social circumstances.

The connection of nature, spirit energy and the body is readily manifested in diaspora sacred performance, as I have analysed fully elsewhere.[46] For the present discussion, I restate that religious and spiritual adherents to African-based religions learn and are regularly encouraged to be aware of and trust their instincts and their bodies. While dancing in African-based religions, the brain continues to be in charge of the body, but the body remains an indispensable, relevant and constant information resource. During dance and music ceremonies and also within non-dance rites and non-musical procedures, bodies are summarily scanned and surveyed for minute and whole-scale changes.

Dancing bodies are "read" in terms of differing qualities and quantities of spirit energy and, importantly, in terms of direct representations in nature. In sacred sites and performances, adherents first view and assess the type of energy they witness in a performance and then attach the spirit or divinity who has and represents that sort of energy to the viewed performer. For example, soft undulations in the upper body and/or gentle swinging movements of the arms and hands would signal Yemaya energy in a Cuban performance and the viewer could then "read the body" of the performer as having or manifesting Yemaya energy. Each divinity has a direct relationship with something in nature; for this brief example, Yemaya is associated with ocean water, making the reading of the body include the recognition of water as well.

Outside of sacred performance, the diaspora dancing body has been critical throughout the history of the Americas (beyond the European male gaze upon the African-descended female body). At a theoretical level, African heritage was looked upon unfavourably and most often rejected by colonists as well as modern postcolonialists; at the practical level, however, there was simultaneous acceptance and rejection of African-derived bodies, and separation as well as interchange between African and European descendants. In the moments of the dance, however, diaspora dancing bodies – individuals, couples, groups of dancing African and European descendants – often transcended those boundaries that were promoted by a hegemonic culture. Engagement with fresh rhythms, new sounds and satisfying movements produced innovative steps and sequences, and, with repetition, intensification, condensation or augmentation, became social and popular dances that were associated with specific types of dance music. Familiarity and satisfaction with new dances and their music facilitated strong and consistent group identification with the dances. The identities that were thereby produced were promoted (and continue to be featured) as African-based, creole or diaspora identities.[47]

What is lost in the dance process of crossroading and perhaps in moments of other forms of creolization are the force of cultural hegemony, a domineering material worldview and an objective approach. Deepening into dance performance and music-making pushes the spirit forward (sometimes understood as higher consciousness or the subjective or real you). Dwelling inside the dancing and/or music-making body challenges ordinary identities and the relevance of their accompanying values. Most often, these singular, everyday identities dissipate in the movement and are passed over in the music. Hegemony is suspended; only genuine, profoundly felt, subjective, and perhaps alternating, identities are revealed.

The result is the evaporation of hierarchy within knowledge systems: the emphasis on the mind over the body is not commonly found in dancing cultures of the Americas. Within the Caribbean and other diaspora sites, the body does not hold an inferior position in dance or dance music; rather, the body is integral to the mind, the dance and the dance music. Diaspora movement qualities, preferences and tendencies reveal that diaspora dancing and diaspora dance music are fundamental to New World cultural development, as well as to genuinely comprehensive American history. Both from the dance and the dance music perspectives, the dancing body is critical. For the Caribbean especially, the history of crossroading within the body reveals an African diaspora identity that is being recognized more regularly and completely as time and research increase. That identity is multiple, complex, irregular and situational, but is also connective and shared among diasporic communities of the Americas.

CONCLUSION

The original encounter among indigenous Americans, Europeans and Africans resulted in an internal mixing or "crossroading" that became the essential marrow of Caribbean dance. Crossroading fostered and generated a luscious "dancescape" of particularly fluid identities – dense hybridity, incredibly intertwined diversity and layer upon layer of history within performance. Within social and popular dances in particular, multiple heritages existed and emerged as "crossroad" ethnicities, along with the values and concerns of the dancing public in a specific era or moment in time. Caribbean and other diaspora performers often asserted their local or regional identities, and sometimes, they confronted a presumed identity while asserting a preferred identity. Extreme crossroading surfaced in concert dance, since concert dance usually sums up the rich and diverse lived experiences of dance artists. Contemporary Caribbean and other diaspora dance artists fathom many cherished and simultaneously different identities within concert performance. Their crossroading, as well as that of current social and popular diaspora performers, also suggests an abiding identity – one that acknowledges history, tradition and continuity while also relishing diversity, innovation and change. As one African story goes: "Tradition continues like the river. The river changes somewhat as it takes in unique and different things that fall or from time to time are thrown from both sides of its banks. Still, the river remains the same at its centre and continues with core principles and values anchored in its deepest and longest on-going currents."[48] In the case of Caribbean dance, the core of that river is African and yields its abiding African diaspora identity among related others.

Caribbean and other diaspora dance artists and ordinary dancers as well popular dance performers reach back in history to draw on traditional movements, forward to draw on innovations of their own time, and laterally to draw on material from their old and new neighbours. They literally and physically incorporate the details of multiple dance traditions and creatively convey immediate interests, ongoing concerns, riveting desires, and/or insatiable longings. Africa – imagined or felt – is rarely absent, although occasionally marginalized. Most often today, African heritage is vibrant and meaningful in diaspora dance and dance music. Multicultural, intra-Caribbean and inter-diaspora dance constructions are exemplary of the crossroading that occurs within the dancing body. Such dance constructions are at the very heart of Caribbean dance, illuminating and projecting Caribbean and other diaspora identities from within the marrow of performance. Rooted in geographic and bodily movements and centuries of creolization, crossroading produces and reflects dynamic and inalienable features of Caribbean and other diasporic identities.

NOTES

1. For African religion and philosophy, and their relationship to dance, see Margaret Thompson Drewal, *Yoruba Ritual and Thought: Play, Performance, Agency* (Bloomington: Indiana University Press, 1991). See also Roger Bastide, *African Religions of Brazil* (Baltimore: Johns Hopkins University Press, 1978); William Bascom, *Sixteen Cowries: Yoruba Divination from Africa to the New World* (Bloomington: Indiana University Press, 1980); William Bascom, *Ifa Divination: Communication between Gods and Men in West Africa* (Bloomington: Indiana University Press, 1969); Marcel Griaule, *Conversations with Ogotemmêli: an Introduction to Dogon Religious Ideas* (Oxford: Oxford University Press, 1965). For an interesting plunge into African American views and versions of African religions, see Nzinga Metzger, "Life in the Banyan Branches: African Americans and the Órísá Tradition in Philadelphia" (PhD diss., Florida State University, 2010). For a global view of dance and politics, see Susan A. Reed's overview of the field in "The Politics and Poetics of Dance", Annual *Review of Anthropology* 27 (1998): 503–32 and Yvonne Daniel's Cuban study, *Rumba: Dance and Social Change in Contemporary Cuba* (Bloomington: Indiana University Press, 1995). For dance music and politics, see Gage Averill's Haitian study, *A Day for the Hunter; A Day for the Prey: Popular Music and Power in Haiti* (Chicago: University of Chicago Press, 1997). For studies on dance and political economy, see Deborah Thomas's Jamaican study, *Modern Blackness: Nationalism, Globalization, and the Politics of Culture in Jamaica* (Durham, NC: Duke University Press, 2004), and Marta Savigliono's Argentine study, *Tango and the Political Economy of Passion* (Boulder: Westview, 1995). For dance and tourism, see Adrienne Kaeppler, "Polynesian Dance as 'Airplane Art'", *Dance Research Journal* 8 (1973): 71–85; Jill Sweet, "Burlesquing the 'Other'", *Annals of Tourism Research* 6 (1989): 62–75; Anita Gonzales, "Mambo and the Maya", *Dance Research Journal* 35, no. 2, and 36, no. 1 (2003–4): 131–45; Yvonne Daniel, "Caribbean Performance and Cultural and Economic Globalization", in *Dance Transcending Borders*, ed. D. Urmimala Sarkar Munsi (New Delhi: Tulika, 2008), 155–81; Yvonne Daniel, "Dance Performance in Tourist Settings: Authenticity and Creativity", in *Annals of Tourism Research*, ed. D. Evans-Prichard, 23, no. 4 (1996): 780–97; and Yvonne Daniel, "Economic Vitamins of Cuba: Sacred and Other Dance Performance", in *Rhythms of the Afro-Atlantic World*, ed. M. Diouf and I. Nwankwo (Madison: University of Michigan Press, 2010), 19–40.

2. Much of this chapter extends ideas found in Yvonne Daniel *Caribbean and Atlantic Diaspora Dance: Igniting Citizenship* (Urbana: University of Illinois Press, 2011) and in Yvonne Daniel, *Dancing Wisdom: Embodied Knowledge in*

Haitian Vodou, Cuban Yoruba, and Bahian Candomblé (Urbana: University of Illinois Press, 2005), both of which heavily rely on Brenda Gottschild's *Digging the Africanist Presence in American Performance* (Westport, CT: Greenwood, 1996). I am grateful for permission from the University of Illinois Press to make further use of these works. Additionally, I am especially thankful for Leonard Brown's invitation to collaborate on the original presentation during the Diaspora Symposium at Johns Hopkins University in Baltimore, Maryland, and I am indebted to Franklin W. Knight and the Johns Hopkins Center for Africana Studies for allowing me the satisfying experience of engaging in dialogue with interdisciplinary diaspora colleagues.

3.   I further explain my use of "crossroading" later, but here I note that I was inspired to rethink terms and coin this one after listening to a CD entitled *Crossroads* by Lucie Antones, Yudh Elyes and my cousin Longineu Parsons (see www.tribaldisorder.com), and I thank them respectfully for their impetus.

4.   For a detailed history, see other chapters in this volume and also, Franklin W. Knight, The *Caribbean: The Genesis of a Fragmented Nationalism*, 3rd ed. (New York: Oxford University Press, 2012); Eric Williams, *From Columbus to Castro: The History of the Caribbean 1492–1969* (New York: Vintage, 1984), and, for a pie chart in percentages regarding varied European (and United States) trafficking, see Eltis et al., *The Trans-Atlantic Slave Trade*, http://www.slavevoyages.org/tast/database/search.faces.

5.   See Robert Farris Thompson, *African Art in Motion* (Berkeley: University of California Press, 1974), 1–45.

6.   See Kariamu Welsh-Asante, "Commonalities in African Dance: An Aesthetic Foundation", in *African Culture: Rhythms of Unity*, ed. Molefi Asante and Kariamu Welsh Asante (Westport, CT: Greenwood), 71–82.

7.   See Gottschild, *Digging the Africanist Presence*, 11–19.

8.   In the line of Thompson's (*African Art in Motion*) and Gottschild's (*Digging the Africanist Presence*) "aesthetic of the cool", here "cool" means "slick", "composed", "calm", "prepared", "deliberate" in countenance and deportment.

9.   Since there is not a fully developed literature on the vast number of dances in continental Africa, conclusions about West and Central African contrasts in the diaspora are made guardedly; however, the evidence thus far for the circum-Caribbean region shows signs of distinctions between West and Central African legacies, as I report here and in Daniel, *Caribbean and Atlantic Diaspora Dance*, 69–76.

10.   J.H.K. Nketia, "The Interrelations of African Music and Dance", *Studia Musicologica* 7 (1965): 91–101.

11.   Olly Wilson, "Association of Movement and Music as a Manifestation of a Black

Conceptual Approach to Music Making", in *Essays on Afro-American Music and Musicians*, ed. Irene V. Jackson (Westport, CT: Greenwood, 1981), 1–23, and Olly Wilson, " 'It Don't Mean a Thing, if it Ain't Got That Swing': The Relationship Between African and African American Music", in *African Roots/American Cultures: Africa in the Creation of the Americas*, ed. S. Walker (Lanham, MD: Rowman and Littlefield, 2001), 153–68.

12.   Sam Floyd, "Black Music in the Circum-Caribbean", *American Music* 17, no. 1 (Spring 1999): 1–37.

13.   The exception occurs where drums are used as tonal language and improvisation is not generally accepted since adherence to language tones and pitches is critical; see for example, Abakuá drumming in Cuba or Ghanaian traditional drumming on the continent.

14.   Among many other examples, see Molly Ahye, *Golden Heritage: The Dances of Trinidad and Tobago* (Petit Valley, Trinidad: Heritage Cultures, 1978); Barbara Browning, *Samba: Resistance in Motion* (Bloomington: Indiana University Press, 1995); Dominique Cyrille, "Sa Ka Ta Nou (This Belongs to Us): Creole Dances of the French Caribbean", in *Caribbean Dance from Abakuá to Zouk*, ed. S. Sloat (Gainesville: University of Florida Press, 2002), 221–46; Julian Gerstin, "Musical Revivals and Social Movements in Contemporary Martinique: Ideology, Identity, and Ambiguity", in *The African Diaspora: A Musical Perspective*, ed. Ingrid Monson (New York: Garland, 2000), 295–328; Anita Gonzalez, *Jarocho's Soul: Cultural Identity and Afro-Mexican Dance* (Lanham, MD: University Press of America, 2004); Brenda Dixon Gottschild, *The Black Dancing Body: A Geography from Coon to Cool* (New York: Palgrave Macmillan, 2003); Alma Guillermoprieto, *Samba* (New York: Knopf, 1990); Beryl McBurnie, *Dance Trinidad Dance* (Port of Spain: Little Carib Theatre/Beryl McBurnie, 1953); Rex Nettleford, *Dance Jamaica: Cultural Definition and Artistic Discovery* (New York: Grove, 1985); Cynthia Novack, *Sharing the Dance: Contact Improvisation and American Culture* (Madison: University of Wisconsin Press, 1990); authors in Susanna Sloat, ed., *Caribbean Dance from Abakuá to Zouk: How Movement Shapes Identity* (Gainesville: University Press of Florida, 2002); authors in Patrick Taylor, ed., *Nation Dance: Religion, Identity, and Cultural Difference in the Caribbean* (Bloomington: Indiana University Press, 2001); Lavinia Williams Yarborough, *Haiti: Dance* (Frankfurt am Main, Germany: Bronners Druckeri, c.1958), and so on. See Susan Foster, *Reading Dancing: Bodies and Subjects in Contemporary American Dance* (Berkeley: University of California Press, 1986) for more information on interpreting dance and dance writing in general.

15.   J. Lorand Matory, *Black Atlantic Religion* (Cambridge: Cambridge University Press, 2005), 46–50, 53, 65, 66, 94, 95.

16.   See Anibal Quijano, "Coloniality of Power, Eurocentrism, and Latin America", *Nepantla* 1, no. 3 (2000): 139–55.

17.   The term "nation" became one way that displaced and colonized Africans were able to remain connected to a sense of heritage and ancestry; it did not infer "state" or "nation state".

18.   See also, Daniel, *Dancing Wisdom*, 94–147; cf. Matory, *Black Atlantic Religion* for significant differences regarding continuity and change in African-based religions. Also, see cultural story quoted near conclusions in this chapter.

19.   For comparative analyses of early drum dances, see Julian Gerstin, "Tangled Roots: Kalenda and Other Neo-African Dances in the Circum-Caribbean", *New West Indies Guide* 78, nos. 1–2 (2004): 5–41; also slightly updated reprint in Sloat, *Making Caribbean Dance*, 11–34.

20.   For Caribbean quadrille studies on the English Caribbean, see Kenneth Bilby and Daniel T. Neeley, "English-Speaking Caribbean: Re-embodying the Colonial Ballroom", in *Creolizing Contradance in the Caribbean*, ed. P. Manuel (Philadelphia: Temple University Press, 2009), 231–70, and Cheryl Ryman, "When Jamaica Dances: Context and Content", in *Making Caribbean Dances*, ed. S. Sloat (Gainesville: University of Florida Press, 2001): 97–131; for the French Caribbean, see Gerstin, "Musical Revivals", 295–328, and Dominique Cyrille, "The Politics of Quadrille Performance in Nineteenth-Century Martinique", *Dance Research Journal* 38, nos. 1–2 (2006): 43–60; for the Spanish Caribbean, see Edgardo Diaz Diaz and Peter Manuel, "Puerto Rico: The Rise and Fall of Danza as National Music", in *Creolizing Contradance*, ed. P. Manuel (Philadelphia: Temple University Press, 2009), 51–112 and 113–54. For the Caribbean as a whole, including the Dutch and former Danish islands, see Daniel, *Caribbean and Atlantic Diaspora Dance*, 41–76.

21.   Susan Harewood and John Hunt, "Dance in Barbados: Reclaiming, Preserving, and Creating National Identities", in *Making Caribbean Dance*, ed. S. Sloat (Gainesville: University of Florida Press, 2002), 268–69.

22.   Ibid., 277–78.

23.   For Caribbean analyses, see Cyrille, "Politics of Quadrille", 43–60; Yvonne Daniel, "An Ethnographic Comparison of Caribbean Quadrilles", *Black Music Research Journal* 30, no. 1 (2010): 1–31; and all authors in Manuel, ed., *Creolizing Contradance*. For historical analyses of Latin American forms of quadrille and couple dances, see John C. Chasteen, *National Rhythms, African Roots* (Albuquerque: University of New Mexico Press, 2004).

24.   Cyrille, "Politics of Quadrille", 47, 49–54, 56.

25.   Daniel, *Caribbean and Atlantic Diaspora Dance*, 45–47, 74–75.

26. See Yvonne Daniel, "A Critical Analysis of Caribbean *Contredanse*", *Transforming Anthropology* 17, no. 2 (October 2009): 146–53.

27. From a comparative dance perspective and in terms of body movement, attitude, expression and structural form, nineteenth-century lancers was part of a huge contredanse repertoire, which really began in the early courts of Louis XIII (1610–43) and Louis XIV (1638–1715). For a view of the particular performance described here, see Daniel Research Videos at the Center for Black Music Research in Columbia College, Chicago.

28. See Catherine Evleshin and Yvonne Daniel, "Parading the Carnivalesque: Masking Circum-Caribbean Demands", Daniel, Caribbean and Atlantic Diaspora Dance, 108–28; also Donald R. Hill, Calypso Calaloo: Early Carnival Music in Trinidad (Gainesville: University Press of Florida, 1993), 211–20; Richard D.E. Burton, Afro-Creole: Power, Opposition, and Play in the Caribbean (Ithaca: Cornell University Press, 1997), 156–220.

29. For different approaches to dance and nationalism, see historians Chasteen, *National Rhythms* (Argentina, Brazil and Cuba); Louis A. Perez, *Cuba: Between Reform and Revolution* (New York: Oxford University Press, 1988), and *On Becoming Cuban: Identity, Nationality, and Culture* (Chapel Hill: University of North Carolina Press, 1999); see ethnomusicologists Edgardo Diaz Diaz, "Merengue dominicana: una prehistoria musical en diez pasos", in *Merengue en la cultura dominicana y del caribe*, ed. Darío Tejeda and Rafael Emilio Yunén (Santo Domingo: Centro León/Instituto de estudios caribeños, 2006): 179–210; Diaz Diaz and Manuel, "Puerto Rico", 113–54; Paul Austerlitz, *Merengue: Dominican Music and Dominican Identity* (Philadelphia: Temple University, 1997), and Deborah Pacini, *Bachata: A Social History of a Dominican Popular Music* (Philadelphia: Temple University Press, 1995); see music historian Jean Fouchard, *La méringue: danse nationale d'haïti* (Ottawa, ON: Editions Leméac, 1973); see sociologist Ángel Quintero Rivera, "Ponce, the Danza and the National Question: Notes Toward a Sociology of Puerto Rican Music", *Cimarrón: New Perspectives on the Caribbean* 1, no. 2 (1986): 49–65 and *Cuerpo y cultura: Las músicas "mulatas" y la subversión del baile* (Madrid: Iberoamerican, 2009) (the Americas); see performance studies specialist Marta Savigliono, *Tango and the Political Economy of Passion* (Boulder: Westview, 1995); and see anthropologist Daniel, *Caribbean and Atlantic Diaspora Dance*, 77–92.

30. See Quintero Rivera, *Cuerpo y cultura*, 105–8; Manuel, *Creolizing Contradance*, 101; Diaz Diaz and Manuel, "Puerto Rico", 117; Michel Largey, "Haiti: Tracing the Steps of *Méringue* and *Contredanse*", in *Creolizing Contradance in the Caribbean*, ed. P. Manuel (Phildelphia: Temple University Press, 2009), 212–13, 216.

31. See the Puerto Rican case in Quintero Rivera, "Ponce", 49–65. See the case

of the Americas and/or Latin America in Quintero Rivera, *Cuerpo y cultura*,
104–8, 205–74 *Revista ciencias sociales: Nueva Epoca, Música popular e identidad
cultural en América latina y el Caribe*, no. 4 (1998): 11–26, and in Edgardo Diaz
Diaz, "Introducción".

32. See Averill, *Day for the Hunter*.

33. See Gottschild, *Digging the Africanist Presence*, 12–14, 17–19, 59–79.

34. I found dance historian Susan Manning's use of a similar term, "cross-viewing",
intriguing; see "Watching Dunham's Dances", in *Kaiso!! Writings by and about
Katherine Dunham*, ed. Veve Clark and Sara Johnson (Madison: University of
Wisconsin Press, 2005), 256–66. Her term is defined as "the possibility for
spectators to catch glimpses of perspectives conditioned by subjectivities and
social identities that differed from their own" (257). My term, while focusing on
the body and movements coming from intimate acquaintance with varied historical backgrounds, coincides with Manning's two-way cross-viewing, where
blacks and whites in her case, and performers, participants, audiences, and
certainly critics and dance investigators in my case, can perceive the legacies
of identity that are projected within dance performance.

35. See Susan Cashion and Ron Porter, "Latin American Dance", *Encyclopedia
Britannica Online*: http://www.search.eb.com.offcampus.lib.washington.edu/
eb/article-9439495 (2008); see also Yvonne Daniel and Nia Love, "Dance in the
African Diaspora", in *Encyclopedia of the African Diaspora*, ed. C. Boyce Davies
(New York: ABC/CLIO, 2008), 2:356–66.

36. Quintero Rivera traces American popular music within the European classical tradition in *Cuerpo y cultura*, 205–74; see also 59, 70, 93, 112–16, 242–49.
Manuel similarly reviews Caribbean music history through the nineteenth
century, including the interchange between popular and European/North
American classical traditions in *Creolizing Contradance*, 1–50.

37. "Sampling" is the injection of bits and fragments of something popular and
well-known into something else.

38. See Joyce Aschenbrenner, "Katherine Dunham: Reflections on the Social and
Political Contexts of Afro-American Dance", special edition of *Dance Research
Annual* 12 (1980): 41–47; cf. Manning, "Watching", 236–66, and K. Dunham,
"Plan for an Academy of West African Cultural Arts", in *Kaiso!! Writings by and
about Katherine Dunham*, ed. Veve Clark and Sara Johnson (Madison: University
of Wisconsin Press, 2005), 407–11.

39. See Ramiro Guerra, "My Experience and Experiments in Caribbean Dance", in
Making Caribbean Dance, ed. S. Sloat (Gainesville: University of Florida Press,
2010), 51–57; also Suki John, "The Ténica Cubana", in *Caribbean Dance from
Abaduá to Zouk*, ed. S. Sloat (Gainesville: University of Florida, 2002), 73–78.

40. See Joann Kealiinohomoku's classic article, "An Anthropologist Looks at Ballet as an Ethnic Dance", *Impulse* (1969–70): 24–33.

41. See video, http://www.youtube.com/watch?v=Ra62Prd6Vng.

42. See video, http://www.youtube.com/watch?v=FkZzM8a1W5A.

43. See video, http://vimeo.com/40957410.

44. Merián Soto, presentation at Rutgers University, 14 October 2011.

45. See video, http://vimeo.com/31624004.

46. Daniel, *Dancing Wisdom*.

47. Consider the mounting evidence of African-based and African-influenced culture throughout the Americas, for example, Sheila Walker, ed., *Conocimiento Desde Adentro: Los afrosudamericanos hablan de su historia y sus pueblos* (La Paz, Bolivia: Programa de Investigación Estratégica en Bolivia, 2010), and Sheila Walker, ed., *African Roots/American Cultures: Africa in the Creation of the Americas* (Lanham, MD: Rowman and Littlefield, 2001); George Reid Andrews, *Afro-Latin America, 1800–2000* (New York: Oxford University Press, 2004); Chasteen, *National Rhythms*. See also studies of dance and dance music in the Caribbean and Latin America, for example, Noel Allende-Goitía, "The Mulatta, the Bishop, and Dances in the Cathedral: Race, Music, and Power Relations in Seventeenth Century Puerto Rico", *Black Music Research Journal* 26, no. 2 (2006): 137–64; Quintero Rivera, *Cuerpo y cultura*; Yvonne Daniel's review of Quintero Rivera, *Journal of Caribbean Studies* 40, no. 1 (2012): 197–204; Deborah Pacini, "Amalgamating Musics: Popular Music and Cultural Hybridity in the Americas", in *Musical Migrations*, ed. F. Aparicio and C. Jáquez (New York: Palgrave Macmillan, 2003), 13–32.

48. Original source unknown. Story told on differing occasions in varied ways by mentoring community scholars in Suriname, Cuba, and the United States.

CHAPTER 7

"THE *SPEAR* IS BLACK WITH A PURE GOLD POINT"
Articulations of "Blackness" in Toronto during the 1970s

MICHELE A. JOHNSON

THE PRESENCE OF PERSONS OF AFRICAN descent in Canada has usually
been perceived as fairly recent and certainly problematic. Assumed by many
to be constituted almost entirely of Caribbean migrants, who despite their
complexity have come to represent a synecdoche for "blackness", along with
some more recent "continental" African communities, the long history of
"blacks" in Canada has been largely sidelined or erased from the national
narrative. While there have been some overtures made to acknowledge other
marginalized groups, such as aboriginal "First Nations" (though they remain
legally and socially demarcated, largely separated and relegated), as strands in
the "founding narrative" of Canada, there have been few gestures to include
"black" Canadians. This is entirely in keeping with Canada's tendency to
link its identity to the idea of the "Great White North", replete with symbolic
images of snow, wilderness, emptiness and innocence. While some scholars
have actively challenged and deconstructed that idea of fundamental "whiteness",[1] the project to excavate blacks' contributions and insert their presence
into the Canadian metanarrative has far fewer proponents.

The scholarship addressing blacks' presence in Canada faces a number of
hurdles, some of which turn on the questions of who is assumed to "belong"
to the nation and, conversely, who are assumed to be outsiders and therefore
treated with varying levels of suspicion/scepticism and subjected to scrutiny/
surveillance. As David Austin argues persuasively, the construction of the

Canadian "nation" was facilitated by the creation of conjoined discourses of inclusion (descendants of British and French colonists) and exclusion (almost everyone else) along with a strategic acknowledgement of the presence of aboriginal peoples.[2] For those second or twelfth generation "African Canadians" or those whose more recent arrival has earned them the appellation of "new Canadians", the posing of the loaded question of "origins" – "Where are you *really* from?"[3] (which is repeated with *insistence* should the answer indicate anything other than "foreignness") – begins the dance of exclusion or a grudging, conditional and marginalized inclusion.

For marked groups like blacks in Canada, negotiating this dance was/is a challenge especially because they remain outside of the imagery of what constitutes "real" Canadians. This is so because, as Andrea Davis argues, "For blacks bringing with them historical linkages to slavery and more recent connections to 'third world' and formerly colonized spaces, that right to belong is always tenuous."[4] Further, how could blacks simultaneously embrace identities which tied them to specific historical experiences, widely varying agendas, a multiplicity of "homelands", significant regional differences, competing political visions and common experiences of marginalization? For the wider society almost automatically homogenized *the* black experience in Canada and situated that experience outside of the national narrative of foundation and evolution. The insertion of black tiles into the Canadian mosaic was thus as disruptive and threatening to the master narrative as it was restorative and simultaneously potentially destabilizing to many in various black communities. This chapter examines one instance of the struggles to define, articulate, negotiate and promote visions of "blackness" in "the True North, strong and free", and to investigate the difficulties that persons of African descent in Canada experienced in joining "real" Canadians in the resounding promise: "O Canada, we stand on guard for thee!"[5]

By the 1970s, the articulations of "blackness" by persons of African descent within the parameters of the Canadian nation state included a complex series of negotiations. While many "black" individuals and groups in Canada strove to find a place within a country that utilized their labour (although frequently not to the full extent of their qualifications) and enjoyed aspects of their culture (but preferred not to deal with their "issues"), some created large and small cultural institutions through which "black" voices could be heard. However, the questions of what those "black" voices should sound like and what they should say were neither clear nor settled. Some of the voices emanated from social heritage-based organizations which claimed to speak for certain groups on particular issues (such as systemic poverty and police harassment) while others were to be heard through the institutional "black" alternatives to the "mainstream" organizations, from which blacks were excluded, and which cared not to speak on their behalves.[6] While engaging with the long shadow of racism cast by histories of enslavement and segregation as well as with multiple origins, regional and urban/rural differences, consistent exclusion from educational opportunities, decent jobs and housing, disproportionate experiences of poverty, crime and negative portrayals, the black communities in the 1970s struggled to understand their place in Canada.

One site of these multiple negotiations was to be found in the local newspapers and magazines which emerged within the black communities across Canada. These often both served those communities and offered critiques of the circumstances of containment which many persons experienced. This was the mandate of *Spear: Truth and Soul Magazine of Canada*, which spoke to the constantly shifting identities that persons of African descent in Toronto had to negotiate during the first half of the 1970s.[7] When *Spear* was launched in August 1971, its editor, J. Ashton Brathwaite, wrote about the vision of the magazine:

> We at *Spear* publication are extremely proud to bring you this new magazine . . . You might think to yourself that there are [sic] an adequate circulation of magazines of this nature, therefore, the publication of *Spear* is unnecessary. While we at *Spear* fully agree that such magazines as *Ebony, Jet, Tan,* and *Essence* provide you with many enjoyable moments of reading, we are of the firm opinion that you would feel much prouder of your very own thing. This is, and emphatically so, not an insinuation that *Spear* is discriminating against Blackness on petty geographic grounds. On the contrary, *Spear* believes in promoting the beauty of Blackness irrespective of geographic location . . . Last, but not least, *Spear* is owned, controlled and published by Black people, about Black people, for everyone.[8]

However, this determination to promote the beauty of blackness would be no simple task since, from the outset, the magazine was "scoffed at by the white big shots and the small white shots alike as 'Black Power' literature". For Brathwaite, it was especially ironic that "many 'Black big shots' behave in similar manner, for the same reason". Consequently, he and other members of the staff were "constantly confronted and promptly ridiculed by 'intelligent' 'Blacks' wanting to know, 'Why all those Black faces?' " He lamented that these critics "subscribe[d] to and ['beautified'] their living rooms with white publications in which the only sign[s] of blackness [were] the printed words".[9] According to Sheldon Taylor, "It was disgusting to see Blacks trying their hardest to relate to Canadian magazines – and newspapers – that were and still are white, white through and through." He continued:

> As a Black youth in Toronto, prior to *Spear*'s arrival, I found no magazines that were relevant to me. The closest ones were *Ebony* and other Johnson publications because they were Black. But they were strictly American, and it so happened that I was living in Canada. Sure, many people refer to it as the 51st state, which I am in no great hurry to deny, but I found that there was still a need for the Blacks in Canada to have a magazine that was published right here by Blacks, for Blacks.[10]

An advertisement for *Spear* advised readers that if they wanted to "be in on BLACK . . . then [they should] read *Spear*" as this magazine "brings you face to face with personalities in the Canadian Black community who are worth knowing . . . We publish everything you want to know about Black."[11] The magazine's early logo, which included a spear placed diagonally across its name and Mr. Peabody's declaration in a letter to the editor that "The *Spear* is Black with a pure gold point",[12] may have said a great deal about how images of blackness could be used in defence of persons of African descent in Canada.

There is no doubt that the "pure gold point" that *Spear* hoped to make would be about the experiences of blackness within the Canadian context. However, which articulation/s of blackness would be encouraged to percolate in the magazine's pages was as much about the publication's internal vision as it was about its expected audiences. The larger society tended to produce simplistic representations of blackness, distilling it into a monolithic zone of inscrutable and dangerous foreignness, so it is interesting to witness the complicated expressions of blackness with which *Spear* and its readers engaged during the 1970s. In a process that was not homogenous, linear, tidy or consistent, *Spear* sought to penetrate the cold fog of Canada's racialized relegation of black people with its "pure gold point". However, as members of the black communities would continue to testify, the issues of race relations and racism in a nation state that trumpeted a multicultural agenda were both difficult to address and to rectify.

Among the various means by which persons of African descent in Canada could reinsert themselves into the nation's narrative was to tell of the long history of the black presence in the country; these stories had largely been erased. This would enable, for example, the re/inscription of persons like Mathieu da Coste, "a negroe" who had lived in the country from as early as 1606,[13] into the nation's "founding narratives", and the recuperation of the excised experiences of enslaved Africans like Oliver Le Jeune who was sold in New France in 1628,[14] and hundreds of others who laboured primarily as domestic servants in Montreal.[15] The restorative historical project would also speak to the spread and intensification of the enslavement of Africans across the provinces due to the British conquest of New France in 1763[16] and the arrival of the United Empire Loyalists during and after the American Revolution.[17] A critical historical examination would unravel the myth of Canadian tolerance that is suggested by the experiences of the "Black Loyalists", African Americans who were offered guarantees of freedom and land by the British in exchange for their support during the American Revolution, half of whom left Nova Scotia for Sierra Leone in 1792 in the wake of unfulfilled promises.[18] Many of those who remained behind only managed to eke out a living from rocky soils and low-wage jobs amid the cold Canadian backdrop of poverty, segregation and racism.[19] Similarly, there is little information about the 550 Jamaican Maroons who were exiled to Nova Scotia in 1796 after their second war against the British, and whose intense dissatisfaction led to another mass migration to Sierra Leone in 1800.[20] And few are aware that after the War of 1812, when the British (once again) offered freedom and protection to African Americans who joined them in their fight, thousands migrated to the Maritime Provinces where they and other groups of blacks, enslaved and free, continued to suffer the prejudice that resulted from association with a race-based system of slavery.[21]

While these histories of enslavement of and settlement by Africans remain unknown and/or unacknowledged by many Canadians, there *is* celebration of the 1793 Abolition Act in Upper Canada (Ontario) which prevented the further importation of enslaved persons, but little focus on its gradualist provisions which would have resulted in the emancipation of the grandchildren of the enslaved.[22] If Canada's own history as a slave society before the British Emancipation Act (1833)[23] remains mysteriously silenced, there is a great deal of commemoration of its role in the fabled Underground Railroad which facilitated the movement into Canada of an estimated fifty thousand enslaved African Americans between 1815 and 1860;[24] that many then returned to fight in the American Civil War, to find their families and to seek opportunities they said were not available in "Canaan" is not usually part of the narrative.[25] While there was no wholesale legal segregation in the provinces, during the nineteenth and into the twentieth centuries, in some places theatres, hotels and cemeteries were separated and blacks were not allowed to run for public office, sit on juries or have business licences, while school segregation remained legally possible in Canada West (Ontario) and Nova Scotia into the 1960s.[26] Blacks in those provinces and their counterparts in British Columbia and the Canadian Prairies were also negatively affected by ugly local prejudices as well as the government's Immigration Act of 1910 which promoted a restricted and exclusive selection of immigrants, curtailing further general black immigration.[27]

In the first half of the twentieth century, the small numbers of blacks who were allowed into Canada arrived primarily as labourers, whether they were Caribbean men recruited to work on ships and in the steel mills in Nova Scotia,[28] or as temporary farm workers,[29] or female domestic servants. By 1965 the latter constituted the largest group of African-descended migrants in Canada.[30] All these groups were also joined by black students, primarily from the Caribbean, who were largely blamed for the eruption of student "radicalism" in the mid-1960s and of espousing Black Power sentiments in their confrontation with the authorities at the Sir George Williams University in 1969.[31] During the 1970s and beyond, increasing numbers of "continental" Africans came to Canada, whether as students, skilled workers, entrepreneurs or refugees, and they added a multiplicity of ethnicities, languages, experiences and definitions of "blackness" to the Canadian context.[32] These were the many sorts of "historical blackness" which could be invoked as a claim for inclusion in the nation, and recognition of black Canadians, Canadian blacks, blacks in Canada or persons of African descent living in Canada.

For its part, *Spear* presented its readers with historical "truths", and delivered an analysis which centred on experiences of blackness. This was evident in an article in *Spear* by Mary Kelly. She interviewed Leo Bertley, a Trinidadian-born professor at Vanier College who had migrated to Canada in the 1950s and who was a chronicler of the history of blacks in Canada. She reported the following argument by Bertley:

> Black history has always been present in Canada . . . We participated in the discoveries and explorations, we were fur traders, trappers, interpreters and negotiators . . . Look at Matthew DaCosta [Mathieu da Coste], who served as Samuel de Champlain's interpreter. He was prized because he could speak the languages spoken by the Indians in the Maritimes. He didn't take any correspondence courses, so he must have been here earlier to know the languages.[33]

In another article, also referring to the early presence of DaCosta, "a teacher and interpreter of the Mic Mac language", educator Dorothy Wills pointed out the historical truth that blacks were never really embraced by Canada:

> The Black man's contribution to the development and growth of Canada has never been acknowledged. Check out the work of the slaves in New France, and the ones who accompanied the United Empire Loyalists. Because of the lack of acknowledgement of our contributions, and because of either overt or covert racism, our people have, of necessity, cultivated a way of life which is really a legacy of slavery and racism.[34]

Sheldon Taylor carried the narrative of the black historical presence further by informing *Spear*'s readers that slavery used to exist in Canada although the educational books were silent on the matter:

> Most modern day school text books mention the migration of the United Empire Loyalists to Ontario during the eighteenth century. However, no mention is made of the Blacks who migrated to Ontario and, in particular, Toronto at precisely the same time . . . [They came] as slaves of the United Empire Loyalists. Their origin in Toronto and Ontario can be directly linked to slavery that was very much an institution during the eighteenth century in the Canadas.[35]

Addressing further discrepancies between the official historical record and the factual record, Taylor broached the topic of abolitionism in Canada. He informed readers that "Dr. Daniel Hill has documented the fact that the first Parliament of Upper Canada passed legislation to inhibit further importation of slaves in 1793. However, it was not until 1834 that slavery was officially abolished in Canada."[36] He also noted that "During the war of 1812, Black soldiers fought side by side with the White counterparts. One famous Black soldier was Richard Pierpoint, alias 'Captain Dick.' He organized a Corps of Black Militia during that war and fought on the side of the British". Further, said Taylor, "Black soldiers took part during the rebellion of 1837."[37] Even the celebrated and mythologized Underground Railroad which brought black migrants into towns where they established black settlements, businesses and institutions came under scrutiny.[38] As Taylor asked:

> If Canada represented such a haven, why did the majority of Blacks stampede back to the United States during the period of Reconstruction? This suggests that many Blacks preferred the overt racist actions in the United States . . . Canadians told Black fugitives that they were welcome, only to react with hostility when the welcome had been braved. Many fugitives saw the "Lion's Paw" not as a protector, but as more of a subtle suppressor.[39]

If any were in doubt about the lessons of history, *Spear* had a "Did You Know?" section to set the record straight. Some of the factual responses to the question posed were: "many of the slaves who ran to Canada in search of Freedom found that Black 'freedom' in Canada was so scarce that they headed back over the border immediately after the civil war in large numbers", and "there was a Windsor, Ontario, by-law which stipulated that 'all Negroes be off the street by 6:00 pm' ".[40]

Danny Gooding, the publisher of the magazine, spoke of the long history of black people in Canada in reference to their contributions to the nation: "People of African descent are very much a part of Canada, having first arrived in this country in the 18th century as slaves. Since then, we have contributed as fully as any other ethnic group in building Canada and we have helped the country meet its population requirements by increasing our numbers through procreation and through immigration."[41] With the growth of the black population to a quarter of a million people by the mid-1970s,

Gooding believed there was a need for a black voice, such as that offered by
Spear, since "[l]ike many progressive-thinking people in the community, we
were particularly concerned by the tendency among the establishment media
to deliberately ignore the Black segment of the society [or link the community
to] crime, immigration problems, welfare cases, rising unemployment or
something demeaning".[42] In order to address the issues in the community,
he wrote:

> we are going to have to speak for ourselves . . . We will also have to showcase
> our unique culture and history, present our triumphs and failings from our
> own objective viewpoint and provide a medium of communication between
> the Black person in Canada, and others across the world . . . We must also
> continue to function as a vital part of the Black community's contributions to
> the multicultural and multiracial mosaic that is Canada.[43]

The Canadian historical narrative may have erased persons of African descent
from the national story, but Bertley, Wills, Taylor, Gooding and others sought
to correct this, to claim the place of blacks in the nation and to challenge the
Canadian narrative of racial tolerance and liberalism.

However important that historical presence was for claims to the nation,
by the 1970s the majority of blacks, including all but one of the entire staff
of *Spear*,[44] were recent migrants of African descent for whom problems
associated with immigration and belonging were among those with which
many newcomers grappled and which, according to Gooding, the magazine
intended to address. Both inside the nation, due to the long historical presence
of blacks in the country, and outside, due to their "new immigrant" status,
some persons of African descent in Canada moved back and forth across lines
of "legitimacy" that the wider nation state might have been anxious to erect.
These unstable categorizations were particularly useful in escaping attempts
to determine who belonged, those who "fit" into the nation, even as Canada
was itself trying to understand the material and discursive agenda of "the
multicultural and multiracial mosaic that is Canada".

Therefore, whereas one construction of blackness in Canada focused on
the reclamation and insertion of persons of African descent into the national
historical narrative and as legitimate Canadians in their own right, another
seemed to articulate "new" separate/d identities. In this latter scenario,

members of the community, from their actual, symbolic and self-articulated positions outside of the nation, voiced strident criticism of the anti-black racism with which they engaged in the Great White North. For many persons of African descent in Canada, there was no moment in the modern history of the nation which captured the need for this critique, advocacy and activism better than the "Sir George Affair".

On 11 October 1969, when those who remained of the anti-racism protestors in the Sir George Williams University computing centre prepared to leave the building after what seemed to be fairly benign encounters with the Montreal police, and what they hoped was an imminent positive resolution of their concerns, the police stormed the building. In the ensuing melee, a fire erupted and the equipment was destroyed. Dubbed the "computer centre party" by some, the "occupiers" were part of the student movement that had percolated within Sir George for more than a year, and which had as its catalyst an accusation of racism made by a group of Caribbean students against one of the university's professors. As the smoke billowed from the building and concern grew for the people inside, many of whom were black, the veneer of Canadian tolerance and liberalism was peeled back, as some white Canadians began to chant, "Let the niggers burn!"[45]

In the aftermath, ninety-seven persons were arrested: some were released, others went to trial and threats of deportation hung over the Caribbean students whose plights galvanized responses across the Caribbean region, especially in Trinidad and Tobago.[46] As the consequences of that "moment of blackness" (in which so many whites had participated) carried over into the 1970s, *Spear* kept members of the black community aware of developments. In May 1973, for example, Betty Ann Jordan reported that Rosie Douglas and Ann Cools, who had been arrested "on a charge of illegal occupation of the computer centre of the Sir George William University in Montreal" were still involved with the legal battles in the cases against them. According to Jordan, when Douglas and Cools entered the Montreal courtroom, they were "accompanied by dozens of sympathetic Black supporters who all understood the fight and plight of these two courageous Black soldiers. Among the supporters were Mrs. Dorothy Wills of Montreal, Chairman of the National Black Coalition in Canada . . . which had previously refused to give any support to the original campaign for bail in 1969." This change in position drew a positive response from Douglas who said he was "pleased to see the NBC stand up to the responsibility to fight racial oppression in Canada".[47]

By June 1974, *Spear* reported that Douglas's circumstances had changed. Sister Obiageli (the Canadian chairperson of the African Liberation Support Committee and the secretary of the International African Liberation Support Committee) reported:

> Eleven months have elapsed since Black community worker and political activist Rosie Douglas began serving a 30-month prison sentence in Quebec. Douglas was convicted by an all-White jury on a charge of "unlawful occupation" in connection with the 1969 Sir George Williams University incident ... [I]n May, 1973, Douglas was issued a special certificate ... [which] branded [him] a "risk to national security" ... Douglas will be deported back to the "Associate State" of Dominica upon the completion of this sentence.[48]

Reflecting on his incarceration and imminent deportation, Douglas declared to Obiageli, "The fact that I am in the process of spending 30 grueling months in jail and facing deportation from a conviction on the same charges that people were acquitted on tells me that the oppressor is determined to set an example using his usual device as was earlier in the century against the Honourable Marcus Garvey (1930) – that is, political victimization."[49] Taking the larger view of the black liberation struggle, and analysing, among other things, the contributions and assassination of Amilcar Cabral, Douglas ended the interview by declaring: "Through the experience acquired during the course of the las[t] decade of struggle the colonial submissiveness of our people have [*sic*] been qualitatively transformed: hope has replaced hopelessness, rebellion has replaced rancor and resignation, determination has replaced apathy and total liberation is about to replace centuries of humiliation, frustration and docility."[50] For many persons of African descent in Canada, the actions of the "computer party" were symbolic of the frustration felt at the unwillingness of the wider white Canadian community to recognize its racist systems of control and silencing. Although the incident started out with at least half of the arrested persons being white, the association among the crisis at Sir George, articulations of blackness and student/political radicalism were not lost on blacks in the society. As Rosie Douglas awaited deportation, his insistence on a black vision of his experiences would go a far way to confirm him, and others, as "courageous Black soldiers" in the fight against Canadian racism.[51]

By adopting a mantle of blackness which tied them to other blacks and placed them at the margins of and in some cases, outside of the nation, it was possible for many of the contributors to *Spear* to level criticism at Canada. Well aware of the tendency among white Canadians to assume their moral and cultural superiority over their American neighbours due to their "open, tolerant society" and their lack of slavery, segregation or racism (all of which were, of course, present), Brathwaite compared the conditions of blacks in Toronto in the 1970s to those of African Americans in Philadelphia, "the city of brotherly love" and concluded that there were important similarities in their conditions.[52]

The magazine also included special reports on a number of issues affecting many blacks in Canada who were treated as intrinsically illegitimate. One of those was an analysis of the increasingly hostile relationship between the black residents of Toronto and the city's police force. According to H.A. Dalton Clarke, in February 1973 the National Black Coalition Committee sent a letter to the Task Force on Policing in Ontario requesting an enquiry into "the relationship between the police and Blacks in Ontario . . . as Blacks, Negroes, Creoles, Mulatoes [*sic*], Coloured persons . . . want to be accorded the same quality of policing, as might be expected by the members of this sitting Task Force". The committee's other point of concern was "that there be no limitations as to the number of Blacks employed in the police forces, either as civilians, employees, or regular staff throughout all levels".[53] The committee, said Clarke, wanted to ensure that "from our community there can be drawn people to provide and take part in the decision-making process of policy administration, and last but not least, they also are concerned about the effectiveness of the present system of investigating all allegations of malfeasance, especially in areas of police brutality, intimidating, belittling, and general insensitivity towards minority groups".[54] Further, the committee argued that as the population of Toronto grew and as the "visibility factor increase[d], so [did] the suspectability [*sic*] of individuals who are Black". Since there was a concern that "[i]n the minds of some law enforcement officers there is almost a prediction in relating, or associating certain breaches of the law to the Black community", there was a desire that there be oversight of the representatives of the state. "[P]olice facilities should become more accessible to the public service associations to improve understanding of the police force, and to assist in the furthering of community social work, . . . youth leagues, and sharing of facilities would help." In addition, the committee tabled "a request for an effort to attract and enable forces to obtain police for our multi-cultural society".[55]

According to Clarke, in a previously circulated brief, Mr Massiah of the National Black Coalition Committee pointed to the authorities' intolerance of the black youth culture:

> [M]ost of the Blacks that come into conflict with the police are under the age of twenty-five, they are youthful Blacks, and it has become fashionable among our youths to wear Afro style garb and in some instances Afro style hair. This trend has been equated with Black militancy, and in general if the police are informed concerning contemporary Black attitudes, they would realize that our youths are simply optioning for a culture which [is] regarded [by] them as being more relevant to their origins.[56]

The possibility that the authorities might conflate popular "cultural black-ness" with political militancy was certainly a concern. When persons of African descent in Toronto chose to envelop themselves in the symbols of rad-icalized "blackness", by choosing to wear their blackness upon their bodies, they both built bridges across the boundaries which might have separated the black communities due to their widely differing histories and transgressed the bounds of Canadianness. These manoeuvres required more of a flexi-bility of definitions, identities and agendas than any simple or monolithic articulation of blackness would suggest.

Another focus for the magazine was the severe economic hurdles which many members of the black communities faced, and which seemed to link them together in "experiences of blackness". That concern was addressed by Charles Roach in 1973, who in a wide-ranging discussion, urged *Spear*'s readers to consider the application of "ethnocentrics". He asked, "Did you know that in Toronto, a city with about 65,000 blacks, there are less than six black business enterprises which employ more than six persons? The largest employer, 'The Underground Railroad Restaurants,' has fewer than 20 full time employees. And did you know that Toronto is supposed to where

Canada's most economically progressive blacks are found?"[57] He pointed out that black businesses, where they existed, were comprised of "people who could not find jobs and were fed up enough to try to make it on their own. A man and wife team running a pattie [sic] shop; a black woman and her step-daughter sewing dresses; a self-employed tradesman-carpenter or plumber – trying to make ends meet – this is black business in Canada."[58] In order to break the cycles of poverty and dependence, he believed a new strategy was needed:

> An Ethnocentric Economy is a short-term strategy for economic advancement of impoverished minority groups in a free-enterprise society. The plan calls for the spending of all money within the impoverished community so far as that is humanly possible. Black people in applying Ethnocentrics will have to develop their own private and co-operative businesses with which they will do all their dealings insofar as this is possible. This kind of plan could only be carried out where black people live in large enough numbers in a tight geographic area.[59]

Lest anyone characterize the practice negatively, Roach pointed to other "minority groups" in Toronto – Italians, Jews, Portuguese and Greeks – who had practised ethnocentrics to build financially strong communities. "They live together, buy from each other, they control their neighbourhoods and own property that they occupy, they also employ each other and are faithful to their cultural roots."[60] In like manner, he said,

> Blacks must learn to love their own culture to the point of exclusion of incompatible cultural values. As far as possible, they must eat their own special foods; enjoy their own special music; wear their own special clothing; have their own special religions; enjoy their own special art and literature; idolize their own special heroes, and educate their children in their own special way. In this way they would learn to respect each other and live together.[61]

Whether they were members of the historical black communities, or were more recent migrants from the Caribbean or various African nations, Roach urged actions based on an "ethnocentric" alliance. "Ethnocentrics" may well have been a solution to the ills of the communities but it also potentially marked and separated persons by their "blackness" in a society that was all too eager to participate in that essentializing demarcation, separation and marginalization. Furthermore, any assumption that the construction of a "black community" supportive of its own would be easy was challenged by some of the critiques levelled in the magazine. In 1972, Taylor reported that "it was hoped that African Liberation Day would involve more black people in community affairs. Unfortunately this did not occur and instead division and mistrust of each other distroyed [sic] any accomplishments." Taylor continued that since that time, "positive action in the Black Community has digressed tremendously. Those of us who for years have been a part of [the] community effort, cannot help but feel a sense of remorse after so many of our Youth Organizations and projects have folded due to the lack of will power and individual involvement."[62] In the following year, Clyde Carter similarly lamented the lacklustre support for African Liberation Day, which he said was "vitally important to their political and social welfare".[63] He wrote:

> As the few conscious minded Blacks marched from Moss Park to the Mathew Henson Garvey Park some other Blacks spent their time standing in their doorways of homes and stores pointing and laughing at the proud people who were courageously walking [in the rain] and chanting "Africa for Africans," "Africa for Africans" . . . As I walked with the few, some of which saw the importance of Pan African Liberation, it became quite clear to me that there is a lack of education among Blacks in Canada concerning The Black Liberation Struggle.[64]

To hold the expectation that being of the same race would result in a shared vision of political action across the many groups of blacks in Canada was to engage in multiple and potentially contradictory manoeuvres. On the one hand, that sort of vision applied a pan-Africanist lens to the communities while the trajectories of their varying histories did not result in an *automatically* melded community; on the other, it may well have assisted in the homogenization of the communities, an action in which the larger Canadian society was implicated. The "division and distrust" as well as the apparent apathy or even disaffection with "black moments" like African Liberation Day needed to be addressed, and strategies of cooperation and alliances created rather than assumed. For those who watched but did not join, who mocked but did not support the march, there was not only one way to be "black". And for Afro-Caribbean migrants, who constituted the largest of the many communities of blacks and who were assumed by many to constitute *the* black community in Toronto, this was certainly the case.

Until the 1960s, except for relatively small, tightly controlled labour schemes and some students, black Caribbean migrants were largely excluded from the Canadian space. The reasons for this, according to Joseph Mensah, were directly connected to race-based prejudice and exclusion. "Historically, Canadian immigration policy has been racist . . . The conventional wisdom in pre-1960s Canada was that Blacks, in particular, were physically, mentally and morally inferior to Whites, that the influx of Blacks would inevitably create racial problems in this country."[65] From the prohibitive Immigration Act of 1906 through Robert Borden's declaration in 1908 that the Conservative Party (which would become the government in 1911) "stands for a white Canada"[66] to the Immigration Act of 1910 tabled and passed by the Wilfred Laurier government, the sentiments were clear. The latter prohibited the entry of immigrants who belonged to "any race deemed unsuitable to the climate or requirements of Canada, or of immigrants of any specified class, occupation or character", and was used as a means to restrict black immigration.[67] These general sentiments were repeated by Canadian prime minister, Mackenzie King, in 1947 when he declared that "the people of Canada do not wish, as a result of mass immigration, to make a fundamental alteration in the character of our population".[68]

Not surprisingly, the 1952 Immigration Act which grew out of ideas such as these excluded certain persons "for reasons [of] nationality, citizenship, ethnic group and geographical area of origin".[69] Vague enough to escape direct charges of racial discrimination, the act was nonetheless the tool of the nation's selective, exclusive and racist immigration policies.

However, in the wake of the World War II and an expanding economy, by the mid- to late 1950s, the need for a larger labour force resulted in a reappraisal of the policies and the formal end to the preferential treatment of prospective white immigrants in 1962. With an emphasis, instead, on educational achievement and professional skills as a basis for (selective) immigration, there was a significant increase in the migration of Afro-Caribbean people. This was even more marked after 1967 when the "points system" was used to calculate the eligibility of potential immigrants: those who were of optimal working age, who had higher educational achievements and were in high-priority occupational groups were ranked more highly than others. It was under these conditions that, according to some scholars,

Afro-Caribbean migrants came to be recognized as among the most educated and highly skilled of any immigrant group.[70]

In spite of this, according to W.W. Anderson, "along with Native Canadians, Blacks and Caribbeans share the lowest levels in Canadian society". Caribbean migrants, the vast majority of whom are black, were disproportionately relegated to low status jobs (despite their relatively high education) and their children were consistently streamed into vocational pursuits.[71] As a result, says Frances Henry, Caribbean migrants in Canada experienced "differential incorporation" due partly to shortcomings on the migrants' part, but for her, "discrimination and racism in mainstream society and its resistance to change to meet the needs of new citizens [were] at the core of the 'problem' ", that is, the societal racism that Afro-Caribbean migrants faced affected all aspects of their lives in Canada.[72] Cecil Foster's declaration about the black experience in Canada, "that can be so full of hope and promise but at the same time can also be darkened by what Blacks have come to recognize as benign racism – racism with a smile on its face",[73] would have resonated with members of the Afro-Caribbean community in Toronto in the 1970s.

In the face of these difficulties, according to Henry, Afro-Caribbean migrants coped through networking, reliance on religion, new identity formation, celebration of the "roots" subculture among the youth and the politics of race. They also managed through entrepreneurism and the creation of support groups and associations.[74] But instead of finding a place within the mosaic of an apparently inclusive nation state, Afro-Caribbean persons in Canada regularly reported a certain sense of "home-less-ness" and experienced what Henry labelled the "sojourner mentality",[75] where the desire to return to a mythical, idyllic Caribbean home made it difficult to embrace Canada as home. After all, said Henry, many Afro-Caribbean migrants would agree with the statement that "Canada is where you live, 'home' is where you come from".[76]

Although the *Spear* promoted itself as a "black" magazine, and its focus was certainly on matters which could be construed to be of concern to persons of African descent in Canada, it spent a significant amount of time focused on the Caribbean itself. Readers were reminded or informed about the "tree frogs, crickets, distant music, rain on the roof and a cock crowing at dawn; the relaxation of being in a culture where noise is not regarded as pollution . . . and the taste sensations of Stabroek market, papayas, soursop and fishcakes from a stall with 'a little bit of sour' " that Joan Latchford experienced in Guyana.[77] Patricia Jordan urged those who intended to go to Jamaica to try the "good cuisine, peas and rice, salt fish and ackee or dip and fall back. Night life on the Island is out of sight, you will have no problem finding the action. Reggae is synonymous with Jamaica and that sound will sweep you of [sic] your feet. VISIT JAMAICA AND YOU WILL NEVER FORGET THE EXPERIENCE."[78] Qwesi Clarke painted a picture of Barbados which included "a wide variety of scenic beauty which ranges from the flat dry plains of St. Philip in the south, to the steep hilly ridge and narrow valleys from the Scotland district towards the Eastern Atlantic shore, with its towering white-capped surfs, and . . . the west leeward south-western coasts, where there are miles of enchanting, white coral sand beaches".[79] The positive portrayals of distant homelands where blacks (and other non-whites) dominated the landscape, politics and culture painted idyllic pictures that may well have helped those in Toronto to step outside of the unwelcoming Canadian nation and to claim another, a "black space", a "black home", from which they came and to which they might return. Even where the idea of "return" remained a sustaining fantasy, it provided those who were in but not of Canada a space from which to construct an outsider perspective from within.

In addition to the descriptions of these "black" Caribbean places (which actually contained some of the most diverse populations in the world), *Spear* featured discussions about the region's fate. In June 1975, readers were updated on the meeting of the Commonwealth which had taken place in Kingston, Jamaica, and resulted in a "10-nation committee to produce a plan that will work towards closing the gap between rich and poor nations – a plan which Jamaican Prime Minister Michael Manley called a 'significant breakthrough' ". In addition, the final communiqué from the conference "strongly warned the present Rhodesian authorities and their lackeys to hand over the reign[s] of power to its Black majority or risk armed struggle".[80] That the economic gap-closing committee was clearly unsuccessful and black Rhodesians would, indeed, have to resort to armed struggle to gain their independence would later make the conference's declarations seem ineffective. Similarly, the disillusionment that would attend later analyses of Caribbean regional integration was not yet visible in the early stages.

In 1973, Glyne Murray reported to *Spear*'s readers about the "Birth of the Caribbean Community and Common Market" (CARICOM) which, it was hoped, would "alter the face of the region possibly for ever". According to the report, replacing the Caribbean Free Trade Area [Association] (CARIFTA), which had been launched in 1968 [1965], the expectation was that CAR-ICOM would be a means of "speeding up and co-ordinating the economic and social development of the Caribbean". However, while the countries sought a common ground, as had the countries in the European Economic Community, "there would be no freedom of movement of people, labour, skills and capital in the Caribbean".[81] Despite these severe limitations, in the 1970s, hope continued to attend the activities of the group. As Harold Hoyte informed *Spear*'s readers in 1976, "The hand of fate has started to write in very bold letters, the destiny of the Caribbean. It is the destiny of integration . . . the prime ministers of Jamaica, Barbados, Trinidad and Tobago, and Guyana met and resolved more matters in their bid for economic integration than has been achieved at many a conference before."[82] The inability of the region's leaders to convert these aspirations into much more than confer-ences and reports would remain a source of disillusionment well into the twenty-first century.

In the areas of cultural production, the "black" Caribbean was also fea-tured in articles about the nostalgia that came with listening to "the simple sweetness of the voice of Alton Ellis, singing one of the songs that ushered in . . . [the rock steady] era",[83] and in-depth interviews with internationally renowned musicians such as Jimmy Cliff who discussed his musical career and encouraged aspirants to seek strength and inspiration in their histories:

> Check yourself and your history, then the history of your people, and you learn . . . So if you take history and go back and find that our people were real and did positive things, the knowledge will give you strength, and you will be able to make it. When you have nothing to hold on to, it makes you weak. We made civilizations and we can do it again. Don't give up.[84]

Cliff's invocation of the universal "we" may have been a specific call to the Jamaican and wider Caribbean communities which dominated "blackness" in Toronto in the period, or to a wider pan-Africanness or even to both since, despite all the differences that could become the foci of the various communities, their experiences of blackness often served as a source of comparison and possible alliance.

This possibility was at the heart of Samory Moumie's question, "Could Reggae lead to Pan-Afrikan [*sic*] Unity?"[85] According to Moumie whereas Caribbean residents were all familiar with "Al Green, The Stylistics, or Aretha Franklin, . . . if you ask any African living in the United States about Dennis Brown, Byron Lee and the Dragonaires, The Mighty Sparrow, or even Bob [Marley] and the Wailers . . . he wouldn't know who or what you were talking about." This, Moumie said, was because "Just as the oppressor has kept the curtain of silence on Africa, he has done the same to the Caribbean." It was hoped that, following on the success of Johnny Nash as well as the decision by Eddie Kendricks to record reggae-inspired music in Jamaica, and to promote the sound in the United States, reggae would help to bring the communities together, "and who knows; it may turn out to be a concrete expression of PAN-AFRICAN UNITY".[86] But, as with every articulation of blackness this was not as simple as it seemed.

The article was placed opposite a promotion of "Extravaganza '73: The Byron Lee Show and Dance" at the Four Seasons Sheraton featuring the "Dynamic Men of the Caribbean" with guest artist Roberta Sweed; the advertisement included a picture of Byron Lee holding a guitar.[87] There were other references to "Jamaica's magical musician Byron Lee [who] brought his Dragonaires to Toronto . . . and captivated the hearts of Soul folks wherever he appeared, which is not an unusual thing for him".[88] That Moumie would include Lee as one of the possible sources of the reggae music that might lead to "Afrikan Unity" reminds us that Caribbean culture as well as articulations of blackness were quite complex since one of the most popular exponents of cultural "Afro-Caribbeanness" was Chinese-Jamaican Byron Lee (and his Dragonaires).

Further complicating expressions of cultural blackness was the "Jamaican-born Willowdale, Ontario, resident" Jackie Mittoo, crowned the "keyboard king" who graced the cover of *Spear* in November 1975. Mittoo explained in an interview with Patti Vipond that "he was there when the reggae beat was being developed and he was one of those who helped in its birth". Criticized by some for not using black musicians in his "sweetened" reggae versions (which included strings, horns or orchestral accompaniment) which seemed to do better in Canada than the "rhythm roots" versions popular in Jamaica, Mittoo responded:

> I have no control over that section. The Canadian Talent Library selects for you top Toronto performers they feel are qualified. In fact, they go from studio to studio to do records and t.v. and radio spots. Personally . . . I am not prepared to sacrifice my years of hard-earned music experience to project political aspects into focus. Everyone has the choice of ambition and progress in life, and I, being one individual, cannot decide every definite procedure.[89]

Any automatic designation of reggae and its artists as part of the "black revolution" ought to be made with caution. Not only was Mittoo an Afro-Jamaican, but as a resident of Ontario he knew well the racist political context within which many blacks/Afro-Caribbean migrants lived, and yet he divorced himself from the responsibility of hiring black musicians, and invoked the validity of his individual ambitions. The enunciation of individual blackness could be at loggerheads with expectations of politically defined and activist blackness; Mittoo's statements in a magazine such as *Spear* may well have indicated a resistance among some blacks/Afro-Caribbean migrants to being corralled into a preordained declaration of what was an accepted "black" position.

If reggae music and the cultural life that it engendered were the foci of the contributors to *Spear*, so too was the annual black/Afro-Caribbean carnival, Caribana. According to Winston Ali (chairman of the Carnival Development Association of Toronto), Caribana was originally developed as "a contribution of Caribbean peoples to Canada's Centennial celebration in 1967" and by 1975, it had become "the most popular and most colourful summer attraction in the city [Toronto]".[90] In anticipation of the parade of ten bands (each with between fifty and five hundred members), calypso music, steel bands and revellers, Ali sought to remind the public "that discipline is also an essential ingredient" and thanked the Metro Toronto Police Force for their "patience, co-operation and understanding in the past". He concluded: "While a few critics might share a different view, this new culture to Toronto ha[d] managed to overcome many obstacles, achieving a basic unity, in which West Indians and the rest of the city's Black population are fused in a most admirable fashion at least once a year. Perhaps it is the best example of balance and coexistence."[91]

If Ali presented a positive vision of the festival, including its role as a unifier of West Indian *and* "the rest of the city's Black population", Junior Anthony had another view. For him, "The annual Caribana festivity, as it is currently conceived, is nothing but a grossly incriminating affront to the intelligence and dignity of Black people in Toronto. Caribana is irrelevant, escapist, exploitative and racist." He felt the festival could be made relevant if it addressed the social problems facing the West Indian community in Toronto by:

> (1) [getting] West Indians to realize that they are a Black people, their history is that of Black people, and their future is that of a Black people; (2) [building] strong ethnic organizations to mobilize our people into an effective bargaining position with the civil and political authorities so that our rights and privileges can be guaranteed; and (3) [establishing] an amicable and working liaison with the Black Canadian and other Black communities in the city with a view to co-operating in seeking solutions to common problems and in attaining common objectives.[92]

According to Anthony, the festival masked the reality of Caribbean migrants who were "a displaced and home-sick people", was exploitative since it was "organized by West Indian negroes, about West Indian creoles, and for a white-folks audience", and was racist "to the extent that [it] has the effect of perpetuating an image of African descendants as being wild, crazy, stupid and purposeless people". In order to correct the direction of the festival, he proposed that the festival should be organized by black associations in the city, that there should be a "definite, articulated theme . . . relevant to the preserving and sharing of our Black African heritage". He further wrote:

> The ultimate aim of the entire enterprise is to seek to activate as wide a base of participation as possible by all Black people in Toronto in a single cultural event and identification. With this approach, Caribana will be serving as a medium to celebrate our Blackness and to preserve and share our Black heritage. A Black Caribana can definitely help to bring about a greater . . . understanding and unity among Toronto's Black population. We do need an annual Caribana festivity, but it must be relevant and purposive. Right on for a liberated and Black Caribana![93]

Since the annual festival was perceived by its organizers as a moment of "black" culture and a contribution to the Canadian landscape, and by critics as a confirmation of racist stereotypes of blackness, there was some contestation of what represented the best, most authentic and acceptable articulations of blackness. Further, since Caribbean carnivals were primarily to be found in the southern and eastern Caribbean, it could not be assumed to be a "pan-Afro-Caribbean" festival. And in any event, since the discussions excluded the non-black Caribbean, such as the significant Indo-Caribbean population and influential musicians like Byron Lee who participated in the festivities, the representation of Caribana as an articulation of Afro-Caribbean and "black" culture was unstable at best.

Within the context of 1970s Toronto the tendency by some to assume that "blackness" meant Afro/Caribbeanness was also reflected in the discussion of a number of issues, including the experiences of Caribbean migrant children in the Canadian educational system. By 1973, according to Clyde Carter, members of the community felt a need to establish "the Black Library, the Black Heritage Association and the Black Education Project . . . the three foremost organizations whose activities [would be] geared to the re-education of Black people" and which could "proudly claim to be successfully assisting to build the kind of community spirit which prevails at present". However, those institutions depended on "contributions obtained from the community for their operation".[94] Their efforts were deemed necessary because of the apparent educational crisis among young black people which had also inspired "remedial" action: "The alienation of Black youth in the school system, the culture shock suffered by West Indian immigrants and the insensitive attitudes of some school authorities to the problems of these children created an enthusiasm amongst students at universities and community colleges who were involved on a part-time basis in the various organizations, to consolidate their efforts into a full-time summer activity."[95] Sponsored by the federal government under the "Opportunities for Youth" programme, students at the University of Toronto and Ryerson Polytechnic Institute began the programme called "Headstart for New Canadians" in 1972, which continued in 1973 under the auspices of the Ryerson Afro-Caribbean Association.[96]

According to Carter, this sort of intervention was necessary because "many of the teachers and guidance counsellors in the school system are unaware of the existing educational facilities in the West Indies, or have no concept of

West Indian culture. Their ignorance results in these children being incorrectly assessed . . . branded as hostile or unmanageable . . . stigmatized and the process of alienation begins." Further, since within the Canadian educational system "the child is given little or no opportunity to gain any knowledge of the historic development of his people" and the "school libraries although well stocked with Canadian and European literature, have very little information related to Africa and West Indian cultures", the community had to step in. But, for Carter, black/West Indian parents were not without blame. He wrote:

> [many of them are] engrossed in the accumulation of money and property, hence they cannot afford [the] time to properly attend to the needs of their children. Their attitude is that the Canadian school system is obviously better than the ones at home, and if the child is not getting a proper education, something must be wrong with him. In many cases without justification, the child is coerced into submission to the school system by authoritarian parents. The traumatic experience which confronts the child is not realized and a push-pull cycle develops in which the child finds himself as a lost soul between two forces of repression.[97]

Carter's analysis of these different circumstances was interesting as was his conflation of "black youth" and "West Indian immigrants" which was a pattern that some contributors and analysts avoided, but which was quite common. This was the case with Dorothy Wills who asked readers to "imagine the place of a Black Canadian child in the school system which has middle-class teachers and which expects the child to conform to the norms of a White North American society" but who had grown up "black":[98]

> In the Black community, our way of life is different in the way we speak to each other, raise our children, our attitudes to each other and surroundings, our aspirations and many other factors. But Black folks are expected to know two cultures and live them simultaneously. Black adults learn to cope, but it is traumatic when a Black child is expected to live and act [according to] White [society's] norms, values, and habits which he has not yet learned or internalized, if he is coming from a Black home, as he begins his first days at school.[99]

Wills expressed concerns about the challenges to "West Indian/Caribbean blackness":

Teachers have been known to ridicule young children from the West Indies because Canadians in their age group have long since become self-sufficient in the area of dress. Teachers have also been known to make fun of Black children's hair to the point where these children have kept their wool hats on during school hours to avoid ridicule. When the teacher adopts any of these attitudes, what is the example being set for the other children in the school to follow?[100]

Wills's implication of teachers in the pressures placed on Black children is poignant. For our purposes, the almost seamless transition from "black" to "West Indian" suggests an articulation of "blackness" within the Torontonian society that was not limited to the flattening impulses of the master-narrative. However, not only was this inaccurate, it was strongly resisted by some members of the "black" community. According to Helen Laws in a letter to the editor, "You talk real big and bad about promoting Blackness within the Canadian environment, yet you mention not a word about Black Canadians. As a Black Canadian, I should inform you that West Indians are not the only Blacks in Canada."[101]

Given the variety of trajectories of black histories in Canada, it should not be surprising that the visions of blackness and the agendas that emanated from them were neither monolithic nor fixed. The tendency to flatten "blackness" into Caribbeanness which was evident in the wider society, and even among some of those who spoke out to promote blackness, was resented by some black Canadians who believed their struggles and histories were engulfed by the waves of West Indians who arrived in the second half of the twentieth century. And when they were acknowledged at all, the black Canadians (who might themselves be splintered into many groups) were invoked only in a historical sense, as a means of claiming historical legitimacy but with no contemporary presence, or relevance. As Taylor reminded readers:

Many have classified the Canadian Black as being stereotyped and non-aggressive. Comparisons have been made to demonstrate the Canadian Blacks' docility. This is an injustice, since in a semi-hostile society, one develops hopes that if things aren't too bad today, tomorrow could be better. In such a society, it is necessary to employ social improvisations. This is what Canadian Blacks have learned to do. Like the American Black, they too have fought the Klu [sic] Klux Klan, they've had to combat job and housing discrimination.[102]

No wonder people like Helen Laws felt a need to register their dissatisfaction with the omission of Canadian Blacks from most, if not all, of the versions of (non-historical) blackness in Canada.

The many articulations of blackness pointed to multiple and porous identities among persons of African descent, who could deploy apparently contradictory strategies of claiming to belong and asserting rights of inclusion by virtue of their history in Canada while simultaneously championing *foreign* blackness and distancing themselves from the often hostile "whiteness" of Canada. The concurrent existence of and strategic movements between claims to inclusion and acknowledgement of exclusion presented the separate or joint potentials to violate attempts to construct boundaries of legitimacy.

As Taylor argued, "The Black man has been here in Canada almost as long as the White man. The epithet, Canadian Black, does exist. It simply means a Black individual who was born in Canada or who obtained citizenship in Canada."[103] Not only was it possible to envision a historical/legitimate and a contemporary migrant/militant blackness, but in Taylor's vision, the multiple and unified articulations presented real possibilities. As he said,

> now a new Black Canadian is born. Not only is he Canadian, but he readily recognises his Blackness . . . He has been influenced by the American, African and West Indian, and a new bond has materialized. His so called dormancy is being replaced by a more contemporary attitude; that of a new necessary militancy. Canadians are now realizing that their demands for a decent job wage and equal opportunity will have to be met. No longer will the Canadian Black remain the sleeping constrictor. Canada is partly his; he fought for it time and again. He has emerged, and is rightfully demanding his slice of the Canadian apple pie.[104]

While Canadian blacks might have rejected Taylor's ascription of militancy to the influence of the "foreign" blacks, according to this line of reasoning, Canadian blacks, black Canadians, blacks in Canada, Africans in Canada, Afro/Caribbeans, African Canadians and every sort of person of African descent in Canada had claim to the nation, despite its questioning of their legitimacy. And as Taylor urged the readers of *Spear* to "Black On!"[105] it is possible that they could choose any or all of those identifications of blackness.

NOTES

1. Andrew Baldwin, Laura Cameron and Audrey Kobayashi, eds., *Rethinking the Great White North: Race, Nature, and the Historical Geographies of Whiteness in Canada* (Vancouver: University of British Columbia Press, 2011).

2. David Austin, "Narratives of Power: Historical Mythologies in Contemporary Québec and Canada", *Race and Class* 52, no. 1 (July 2010): 19–32.

3. The constant and insistent repetition of this question, directed at non-whites in Canada, is the starting point for Melanie Ash's discussion of Will Kymlicka's theories of "multicultural citizenship". According to Ash, Kymlicka's definition of two types of immigrant/"foreign" communities in Canada – the 'national minorities' (First Nations and French Canadians) and mere 'ethnic groups' – is "an extraordinarily naïve treatment of the Canadian immigration debacle". See Melanie C.T. Ash, "But Where Are You REALLY From? Reflections on Immigration, Multiculturalism, and Canadian Identity", in *Racism, Eh? A Critical Inter-Disciplinary Anthology of Race and Racism in Canada*, ed. Camille A. Nelson and Charmaine A. Nelson (Concord, ON: Captus, 2004), 398–409. See also Joseph Mensah, who mentions the question "No, I mean where are you originally from?" as one of those irritating enquiries which blacks and other visible minorities have to answer. Mensah, *Black Canadians: History, Experiences, Social Conditions* (Halifax, NS: Fernwood, 2002), 219.

4. Andrea Davis, "Black Canadian Literature as Diaspora Transgression: The Second Life of Samuel Tyne", *Topia: Canadian Journal of Cultural Studies* 17 (Spring 2007): 32.

5. For an explanation of the history and meaning of the Canadian national anthem, from which the quotes in the text were taken, please see the Canadian government's website, "Canadian Heritage", http://www.pch.gc.ca/pgm/ceem-cced/symbl/anthem-eng.cfm#a0.

6. See Daniel G. Hill, "Negroes in Toronto, 1793–1865", *Ontario History* 55, no. 2 (1963): 73–91; Linda Brown-Kubisch, *The Queen's Bush Settlement: Black Pioneers, 1839–1865* (Toronto: Natural History, 2004); Judith Fingard, "Race and Respectability in Victorian Halifax", *Journal of Imperial and Commonwealth History* 20, no. 2 (1992): 169–95; Judith Fingard, "From Sea to Rail: Black Transportation Workers and their Families in Halifax, c.1870–1916", *Acadiensis* 24, no. 2 (1995): 49–64; Donald H. Clairmont and Dennis William Magill, *Africville: The Life and Death of a Canadian Black Community* (Toronto: Canadian Scholars' Press, 1999).

7. Between 1971 and 1976, the magazine *Spear* had a number of subtitles. In addition to *Truth and Soul Magazine of Canada*, there was *Truth and Soul, Truth*

and Soul Magazine, and *Canadian Magazine of Truth and Soul.* Throughout this chapter, the magazine will simply be referred to as *Spear.*

8. J. Ashton Brathwaite, editorial, *Spear,* August 1971. An "exact reproduction of the first editorial" was published in *Spear,* August 1976, 30.

9. J. Ashton Brathwaite, "From the Editor", *Spear,* August 1972, 4.

10. Sheldon Taylor, "In My Opinion", *Spear,* August 1972, 26–27.

11. Subscription advertisement, *Spear,* November 1975, 5. The annual subscription cost was $5.00 in Canada, $6.00 in the United States and $7.00 elsewhere.

12. Mr. Peabody, letter to the editor, *Spear,* August 1972, 5.

13. Mathieu da Coste (there are multiple spellings, including Matthieu Da Costa) was a "Negro servant" who worked as an interpreter between the French and the Mi'kmaq during trading expeditions to Acadia. See Robin W. Winks, *The Blacks in Canada: A History,* 2nd ed., Carlton Library Series 192 (Montreal: McGill–Queen's University Press, 2000), 1.

14. Ibid., 1–2.

15. Winks relies on the research of Marcel Trudel of l'Université d'Ottawa who argues that the local records indicate that there were about 3,604 enslaved persons in New France in 1759; the majority were aboriginal and 1,132 were "Negroes". See ibid., 9; Marcel Trudel, *L'esclavage au Canada français: Historie et conditions de l'esclavage* (Quebec: Presses universitaires Laval, 1960). See also Kenneth Donovan, "Slaves and their Owners in Ile Royale, 1713–1760", *Acadiensis* 25 (Autumn 1995): 3–32; William Riddell, "The Slave in Canada: Before the Conquest", *Journal of Negro History* 5, no. 3 (1920): 263–72; William Riddell "Notes on the Slave in Nouvelle-France", *Journal of Negro History* 8, no. 3, (1923): 316–30.

16. Historians estimated that by 1776, there were about two thousand enslaved persons of African descent in Nova Scotia alone. Enslaved Africans were also to be found in Cape Breton, Prince Edward Island, Newfoundland (where they were used in the fisheries), in Lower Canada (Quebec) and Upper Canada (Ontario). See Winks, *Blacks in Canada,* 24–60; Roy F. Fleming, "Negro Slaves with the United Empire Loyalists in Upper Canada", *Ontario History* 45, no. 1 (1953): 27–30; Frank Mackey, *Black Then: Blacks and Montreal 1780s–1880s* (Montreal: McGill-Queen's University Press, 2004); William Riddell, "The Slave in Upper Canada", *Journal of Negro History* 4, no. 4 (1919): 372–95; William Riddell, "Slavery in the Maritime Provinces", Journal of Negro History 5, no. 3 (1920): 359–75; William Riddell, "The Early British Period", *Journal of Negro History* 5, no. 3 (1920): 273–92.

17. See Riddell, "Slavery in the Maritime Provinces", and Riddell, "Early British Period".

18. According to James Walker, the governor of Virginia, John Murray (Lord Dun-
     more), offered guarantees of "freedom" to enslaved persons owned by "rebels" if
     they would join the Loyalist cause. Historians estimate that between three and
     eight hundred enslaved African Americans immediately joined the British and
     were labelled the "Ethiopian Regiment". The British offer was reissued by Sir
     Henry Clinton and again by Sir Guy Carleton. "The Book of Negroes" included
     the names of 1,336 men, 914 women and 750 children who were taken to Nova
     Scotia. However, those who had left before the formal evacuation were not
     included in these numbers so the total is actually larger, although historians
     have no way of knowing exactly how large. See James W. St G. Walker, *The
     Black Loyalists: The Search for a Promised Land in Nova Scotia and Sierra Leone,
     1783–1870* (Toronto: University of Toronto Press, 1992); Barry Cahill, "The
     Black Loyalist Myth in Atlantic Canada", *Acadiensis* 29, no. 1 (1999): 76–87;
     James Walker, "Myth, History and Revisionism: The Black Loyalists Revisited",
     Acadiensis 29, no. 1 (1999): 88–105; Simon Schama, *Rough Crossings: Britain,
     the Slaves and the American Revolution* (Toronto: Canada Penguin, 2008).

19. As Walker argues, while white Loyalists received land and had a choice of loca-
     tion, 60 per cent of the black Loyalists received no land and those who did got
     land that rarely exceeded one-acre lots located on the edge of white townships.
     See Walker, *Black Loyalists*.

20. See Winks, *Blacks in Canada*, 78–95; Mavis Campbell, *Nova Scotia and the
     Fighting Maroons: A Documentary History* (Williamsburg, VA: Dept. of Anthro-
     pology, College of William and Mary, 1990); Allister Hinds, " 'Deportees in
     Nova Scotia': The Jamaican Maroons, 1796–1800", in *Working Slavery, Pricing
     Freedom: Perspectives from the Caribbean, Africa and the African Diaspora*, ed.
     Verene A. Shepherd (Kingston: Ian Randle, 2002), 206–22; Lennox O'Riley
     Picart, "The Trelawny Maroons and Sir John Wentworth: The Struggle to Main-
     tain Their Culture, 1796–1800", *Royal Nova Scotia Historical Society Journal*
     44 (1996): 165–87.

21. According to historians, at least three thousand persons migrated to the Mari-
     times under these conditions. The American government claimed that the
     British authorities had removed their "property" illegally and demanded that
     they either return the (formerly) enslaved Americans or pay for their freedom.
     After a great deal of negotiation, in 1827 the British government paid £250,000
     for "slaves and other property" confiscated during the war. Once more, Nova
     Scotia received the bulk of the so-called refugees of the War of 1812, while some
     went to New Brunswick. See Winks, *Blacks in Canada*, 114–41; Peter Meyler and
     David Meyler, *A Stolen Life: Searching for Richard Pierpoint* (Toronto: Natural
     Heritage, 1999); W.A. Spray, "The Settlement of the Black Refugees in New

Brunswick, 1815–1836", *Acadiensis* 6, no. 2 (Spring 1977): 64–79; Harvey Amani Whitfield, " 'We Can Do as We Like Here': An Analysis of Self Assertion and Agency Among Black Refugees in Halifax, Nova Scotia, 1813–1821", *Acadiensis* 32, no. 1 (Autumn 2002): 29–49.

22. See Winks, *Blacks in Canada*, 96–113; Allen Stouffer, *The Light of Nature and the Law of God: Antislavery in Ontario, 1833–1877* (Baton Rouge: Louisiana State University Press, 1992); Ged Martin, "British Officials and their Attitudes to the Negro Community in Canada, 1833–1861", *Ontario History* 66, no. 2 (June 1974): 79–88.

23. Emancipation Act (1833) was passed in the House of Commons on 7 August 1833 and was signed into law by royal assent on 28 August 1833. By that act about eight hundred thousand slaves across the British Empire (most of them in the Caribbean) were emancipated and slave owners received £20,000,000 in compensation for the loss of their "property". Unlike the Caribbean, there is no evidence of the period of apprenticeship (which ended in 1838) in Canada. See Winks, *Blacks in Canada*, 111.

24. The African Americans who crossed into Canada tended to congregate on the border with the United States, mostly in southwestern Ontario (St Catharines, Windsor, Amhertsburg, London, Chatham, Dresden, Toronto, Oro), where they established such black communities as Dawn, Wilberforce and Elgin/Buxton. See ibid., 114–41; Adrienne Shadd, " 'The Lord Seemed to Say "Go" ': Women and the Underground Railroad", in *"We're Rooted Here and They Can't Pull Us Up": Essays in African Canadian Women's History*, ed. Peggy Bristow et al. (Toronto: University of Toronto Press, 1994), 41–63; Jason Silverman, " 'We Shall be Heard!' The Development of the Fugitive Slave Press in Canada", *Canadian Historical Review* 65, no. 1 (1984): 54–69; Peter Meyler, ed., *Broken Shackles: Old Man Henson from Slavery to Freedom* (Toronto: Natural Heritage, 2001); Jacqueline L. Tobin and Hettie Jones, *From Midnight to Dawn: The Last Tracks of the Underground Railroad* (New York: Doubleday, 2007); Victor Ullman, *Look to the North Star: A Life of William King* (Toronto: Umbrella, 1969); Karolyn Smardz Frost, *I've Got a Home in Glory Land: A Lost Tale of the Underground Railroad* (Toronto: Thomas Allen, 2008); Bryan Prince, *One More River to Cross* (Toronto: Dundurn/Natural Heritage, 2012).

25. See the testimonies which appear in Benjamin Drew, A *North-side View of Slavery: The refugee, or, The narratives of fugitive slaves in Canada related by themselves; with an account of the history and condition of the colored population of Upper Canada* (Boston: J.P. Jewett, 1856).

26. Kristin McLaren, " 'We Had No Desire to Be Set Apart': Forced Segrega-tion of Black Students in Canada West Public Schools and Myths of British

Egalitarianism", in *The History of Immigration and Racism in Canada: Essential Readings*, ed. Barrington Walker (Toronto: Canadian Scholars' Press, 2008), 69–81; Winks, *Blacks in Canada*, 288–336.

27. See F.W. Howay, "The Negro Immigration into Vancouver Island in 1858", *British Columbia Historical Quarterly* 3, no. 2 (1939): 101–13; Crawford Kilian, *Go Do Some Great Thing: The Black Pioneers of British Columbia* (Vancouver: Douglas and McIntyre, 1978); Winks, *Blacks in Canada*, 309, 311; R. Bruce Shepard, *Deemed Unsuitable: Blacks from Oklahoma Move to the Canadian Prairies in Search of Equality in the Early 20th Century Only to Find Racism in their New Home* (Toronto: Umbrella, 1997); Harold Troper, "The Creek-Negroes of Oklahoma and Canadian Immigration, 1909–1922", *Canadian Historical Review* 53, no. 3 (1972): 272–88; Stewart Grow, "The Blacks of Amber Valley: Negro Pioneering in Northern Alberta",*Canadian Ethnic Studies/Etudes Ethniques du Canada* 6, nos. 1–2 (1974): 17–35 ; R. Bruce Shepard, "Plain Racism: The Reaction Against Oklahoma Black Immigration to the Canadian Plains", in *Racism in Canada*, ed. Ormond McKague (Saskatoon, Fifth House, 1991), 15–31.

28. According to Agnes Calliste, "[d]espite their skills, most of them were restricted to jobs in the Sydney mines and the steel plant's coke ovens because of the segregated workforce and the myth that blacks could withstand the heat better than whites". Agnes Calliste, "Race, Gender and Canadian Immigration Policy: Blacks from the Caribbean, 1900–1932", *Journal of Canadian Studies* 28, no. 4 (Winter 1993/1994): 135.

29. These farm workers labour/ed on farms in Alberta, Quebec, Manitoba, Saskatchewan, Nova Scotia, New Brunswick, Prince Edward Island and Ontario (where 90 per cent of the recruited are placed), but they were not (and are not) legally allowed to stay in the country beyond their annual contracts.

30. Between 1910 and 1911, one hundred women from Guadeloupe were recruited to work in Quebec as domestic servants, and in 1955 the Canadian authorities and some British Caribbean governments launched the West Indian Domestic Scheme. By 1965, the scheme had permitted the migration of 2,690 Caribbean women, more than all the Caribbean immigrants who had come to Canada before 1945. Since it was one of the few means by which Caribbean people could migrate to Canada during the 1960s and 1970s many nurses, teachers, secretaries, clerks and trained service workers used this avenue for the prospect of personal and familial improvement. See Calliste, "Race, Gender and Canadian Immigration Policy", 140–41; Audrey Macklin, "On the Inside Looking In: Foreign Domestic Workers in Canada", in *Maid in the Market: Women's Paid Domestic Labour*, ed. Wenona Giles and Sedef Arat-Koç (Halifax: Fernwood, 1994), 13–39; Abigail B. Bakan and Daiva Stasiulis, eds., *Not One of the Family:*

Foreign Domestic Workers in Canada (Toronto: University of Toronto Press, 1997); Makeda Silvera, *Silenced: Talks with Working Class Caribbean Women about their Lives and Struggles as Domestic Workers in Canada* (Toronto: Sister Vision, 1989); James Walker, *The West Indians in Canada* (Ottawa: Canadian Historical Association, 1984), 1; Agnes Calliste, "Canadian Immigration Policy and Domestics from the Caribbean: The Second Domestic Scheme", in *Race, Class and Gender: Bonds and Barriers*, ed. Jesse Vorste (Toronto: Garamond, 1991, 136–69.

31.   See Dennis Forsythe, ed., *Let the Niggers Burn! The Sir George Williams University Affair and its Caribbean Aftermath* (Montreal: Our Generation, 1971); Dorothy Eber, *The Computer Centre Party: Canada Meets Black Power* (Montreal: Tundra, 1969); David Austin, "All Roads Led to Montreal: Black Power, the Caribbean, and the Black Radical Tradition in Canada", *Journal of African American History* 92, no. 4 (Autumn 2007): 516–39.

32.   Between 1946 and 1960, Africans made up 0.3 per cent of the immigrants to Canada. Between 1960 and 1980, due to changes in the immigration law, that proportion rose to between 1 and 2 per cent of the country's immigrants. The majority of continental African immigrants are from South Africa, Tanzania, Ethiopia, Kenya, Ghana, Uganda and Nigeria. They have been joined fairly recently by refugees from Ethiopia, Biafra/Nigeria, Sudan, Somalia and Rwanda. *Statistics Canada*, 1996.

33.   Mary Kelly, "Chronicler of Black Canadian History", *Spear*, May/June 1976, 20–23.

34.   Dorothy Wills, "The Black Child in the Canadian School System", *Spear*, August 1976, 49.

35.   Sheldon Taylor, "Black Settlement in Toronto: Slaves Were Pioneer Immigrants", *Spear*, September 1974, 24, 26–27.

36.   Sheldon Taylor, "Canadian Black Historical Portrait in Perspective", *Spear*, October–November 1974, 24–30. Daniel Grafton Hill III (1923–2003) was born in Missouri and moved to Canada in 1950. He earned a PhD from the University of Toronto for his dissertation, "Negroes in Canada: A Sociological Study of a Minority Group" (1960) and would go to become a noted sociologist, civil servant, human rights activist and the first full-time director of the Ontario Human Rights Commission (1962–73) and later Ontario ombudsman (1984–89). He was also a co-founder of the Ontario Black History Society (1978). See the website dedicated the "The Life and Times of Daniel G. Hill," Archives of Ontario http://www.archives.gov.on.ca/en/explore/online/dan_hill/introduc tion.aspx

37.   Taylor, "Canadian Black Historical Portrait".

38. See Taylor, "Black Settlement in Toronto", 24, 26–27. See also Esther Lucas, "Historic Sketch of Canada's First Black Baptist Church", *Spear*, August 1976, 63; Betty Riley, "The 'Coloured Church' of Montreal: An Intimate Thumbnail Historical Account", *Spear*, June 1974, 24–26.
39. Taylor, "Canadian Black Historical Portrait in Perspective".
40. "Did You Know?" *Spear*, August 1972, 54.
41. Danny Gooding, "Our Strength is Need: A Statement from *Spear*'s Publisher, Danny Gooding", *Spear*, August 1976, 8–9.
42. Ibid., 8.
43. Ibid., 8–9
44. The main persons behind the magazine (according to a 1972 article) were Danny Gooding, publisher, who was born in Barbados and "came to Canada 6 years ago after spending 11 years in England"; J. Ashton Brathwaite, editor and layout artist, who was also Barbadian and, like Gooding, had migrated to Canada "6 years ago after spending 6½ years in England"; Jeff Browne, responsible for circulation and photography, was another Barbadian who had moved to Canada three years previously; H.A. Dalton Clarke, who handled photography and advertising, was also born in Barbados and had migrated to Canada six years previously; Betty Ann Jordan, who produced the Black History segment, was born in Trinidad; Sheila Kennedy ("Our Girl in Soulville"), who wrote on music, was born in Washington, DC; Sheldon Taylor, who was the Youth Section editor, was born in St Kitts; Dionne Brand, who was born in Trinidad, contributed poetry to magazine. See "The People at *Spear*", *Spear*, August 1972, 55.
45. For a full account and analysis of this moment in African-Canadian history see Forsythe, *Let the Niggers Burn*.
46. See Austin, "Narratives of Power".
47. Betty Ann Jordan, "Another Chapter in the Sir George William Incident: Petition for Bail Extention [sic]", *Spear*, May 1973, 46.
48. Rosie Douglas, "Guidelines for Institution Building and Problem Solving: A Prison Interview with Rosie Douglas", by Sister Obiageli, *Spear*, June 1974, 10–12.
49. Rosie Douglas, "A Look into the Future: Concluding Rosie Douglas' Interview in Leclerc Prison, Montreal", by Sister Obiageli, *Spear*, September 1974, 32–35.
50. Ibid., 35.
51. After his deportation, Roosevelt (Rosie) Bertrand Douglas returned to Dominica, became involved in politics, and led the Dominica Labour Party to victory in a coalition government; he died on 1 October 2000, only eight months after taking office as prime minister. See Polly Pattullo, "Rosie Douglas", *Guardian*,

5 October 2000, http://www.guardian.co.uk/news/2000/oct/05/guardianobit-uaries.pollypattullo.

52. J. Ashton Brathwaite, "J. Ashton Brathwaite Speaks Out!!" *Spear*, October 1972, 34–35.

53. The National Black Coalition Committee was comprised of T.F. Massiah (chairman), Arthur Downes (secretary) and Sheldon Taylor. See H.A. Dalton Clarke, "Report on Police and Blacks in Canada: A Review", *Spear*, June 1973, 15–17.

54. Ibid., 15.

55. Ibid., 15.

56. Ibid., 16.

57. Charles Roach, "Ethnocentrics: A Plan for Black Advancement", *Spear*, June 1973, 42–43.

58. Ibid., 42.

59. Ibid., 43.

60. Ibid., 43.

61. Ibid., 43.

62. Sheldon Taylor, "To the Point", *Spear*, February 1973, 34. African Liberation Day was celebrated on 27 May 1972.

63. Clyde Carter, "African Liberation", *Spear*, July 1973, 17, 20. African Liberation Day was celebrated on 26 May 1973.

64. Ibid., 17.

65. Mensah, *Black Canadians*, 69.

66. Walker, *West Indians in Canada*, 9.

67. Calliste, "Race, Gender and Canadian Immigration Policy", 133; See Shepard, *Deemed Unsuitable*.

68. Winks, *Blacks in Canada*, 435. Winks points to *Canada, House of Commons Debates*, 1947, 1 May 1947, 352, 365 as his source.

69. Walker, *West Indians in Canada*, 10.

70. According to Joseph Mensah, by 1996, persons of African descent in Canada numbered 573,860 (and constituted 17.95 per cent of the racial/visible minorities); by 2006, that number had risen to 783,795 (15.46 per cent of the racial/visible minorities); 60.44 per cent of them lived in Ontario while another 23.99 per cent lived in Quebec. The rest of the black population is currently scattered across Alberta, British Columbia, Nova Scotia and Manitoba, with small numbers in New Brunswick, Saskatchewan, Prince Edward Island, the Yukon, Newfoundland, Labrador, Nunavut and the Northwest Territory. Mensah's figures rely on the data from Statistics Canada, *Census of Canada* which would not include the (unknown) numbers of persons who, for one reason or another, were not captured by the census. See Mensah, *Black Canadians*, 80–81, 152;

see also J.J. Macionis and L.M. Gerber, *Sociology* (Scarborough, ON: Prentice, Allyn, 1999), 492.

71. Wolseley W. Anderson, *Caribbean Immigrants: A Socio-Demographic Profile* (Toronto: Canadian Scholars' Press, 1993), 16–18.

72. Frances Henry, *The Caribbean Diaspora in Toronto: Learning to Live with Racism* (Toronto: University of Toronto Press, 1994, 1999), 11, 16.

73. Cecil Foster, *A Place Called Heaven: The Meaning of Being Black in Canada* (Toronto: Harper Perennial Canada, 1996), 14.

74. Henry, *Caribbean Diaspora*, 17.

75. Ibid., 43.

76. Ibid.

77. Joan Latchford, "Impressions of Guyana", *Spear*, May/June 1976, 32–35. The article was accompanied by seven photographs, all except one were of Afro-Guyanese people.

78. Patricia Jordan, "Travel: Jamaica", *Spear*, February 1973, 46.

79. Qwesi Clarke, "Travel: Barbados", *Spear*, March 1973, 46–48. The article includes three pictures: one of Bridgetown, one of tourists watching two limbo dancers and one of a harbour policeman in uniform.

80. Eugene Agu-Onwumere, "Kingston Conference Overview: The Commonwealth is Still Viable in the '70s", *Spear*, June 1975, 36–39. The article included four pictures, each of which featured Manley and one of which included Canadian prime minister, Pierre Trudeau, and Margaret Trudeau as well as Beverly Manley.

81. Glyne Murray, "Birth of the Caribbean Community and Common Market", *Spear*, October 1973, 8–9. Although Murray referred to the Caribbean Free Trade Area, CARIFTA meant the Caribbean Free Trade Association; the association had been launched in 1965, not 1968 as was reported in *Spear*.

82. Comment by Harold Hoyte, "Caribbean Destiny in the Making", *Spear*, August 1976, 20–21. The conference took place on 9 June 1976. The article was twinned with a full-page picture of Jamaican prime minister, Michael Manley.

83. Noel, "Jamaica Reggae Sound", *Spear*, November 1972, 36–39, 49. The article included two pictures, one of Bob Marley, the other of Derrick Harriot.

84. Patti Vipond, "Inside Jimmy Cliff", *Spear*, March 1976, 16–21. The article includes five pictures, including a full-page photograph of Jimmy Cliff and another adorns the cover of the issue.

85. Samory Moumie, "Could Reggae Lead to Pan-Afrikan Unity?" *Spear*, October 1973, 6.

86. Ibid., 6.

87. "Extravaganza '73: The Byron Lee Show and Dance", *Spear*, October 1973, 7.

88. *Spear*, September 1972, 45. There are two pictures accompanying the caption, one of the crowd dancing, and other of Byron Lee, guitar in hand.

89. Patti Vipond, "Keyboard King Jackie Mittoo", *Spear*, November 1975, 20–28. The article includes seven pictures of Mittoo, five of them had him playing the keyboard.

90. Winston Ali, "Carnival in Toronto: A Riot of Colours and Pageantry", *Spear*, July/August 1975, 56–58.

91. Ibid., 58.

92. Junior Anthony, "Caribana Follies: Is Festival a Cop Out?" *Spear*, July 1974, 38–39.

93. Ibid., 39.

94. Clyde Carter, "Headstart for New Canadians", *Spear*, July 1973, 44.

95. Ibid., 44.

96. The programme operated from 3 July to 23 August 1973 from 8:50 a.m. to 5:00 p.m., Monday to Friday, at Ryerson Polytechnic Institute, Jorgenson Hall, 380 Victoria Street. Carter, "Headstart for New Canadians", 44.

97. Ibid., 44.

98. Wills, "Black Child".

99. Ibid., 49.

100. Ibid., 49. The article is accompanied by six photographs, one of Wills and five which featured black children in a school context.

101. Helen Laws, letter to the editor, *Spear*, August 1976, 31.

102. Sheldon Taylor, "Canadian Black Historical Portrait in Perspective", *Spear*, October–November 1974, 30.

103. Ibid., 26.

104. Ibid., 30.

105. Sheldon Taylor, "In My Opinion" *Spear*, August 1972, 27.

CHAPTER 8

WHEN DIASPORAS MEET

Black Solidarity and Inter-Ethnic Intersections
in the United States of America

TOMMY L. LOTT

AFRICA'S MULTI-ETHNIC DIASPORAS, LIKE ALL OTHER diasporas, engage
in identity formation and construction which are shaped by varying contexts
of time, place and circumstance. In the United States, old and new diasporas inhabit differentiated social, economic and political habitats which have
produced varying levels of solidarity at different times in the history of the
nation. This chapter, based on my personal experiences, identifies several
complex factors reflecting the fluid relationship between multi-ethnic diasporas and a collective, that is, a black identity grouping that has until now
been presumed to embrace and to be embraced by all members of African
diasporas equally. While teaching at the University of Massachusetts, Boston, in the 1980s, I was recruited by some of my Caribbean students to be
the faculty advisor for a new Caribbean students' organization. Once the
Caribbean students' organization was officially established, I was approached
again by some of my Cape Verdean students who also wanted to start up their
own student organization. Since the Black Students Union already existed,
I suggested housing all three organizations under a more general rubric
of "Pan African Students' Association". Several vocal members of both the
Caribbean and Cape Verdean student groups expressed opposition to being
lumped in with other black ethnic groups.

I will use this case of black student resistance to being included under a single black umbrella organization to illustrate several dimensions of an important question regarding the limitations of diasporic notions of black solidarity. A good starting point is Tommie Shelby's recent proposal to treat culture as inessential to black solidarity in the American context.[1] He wants to view culture as a detachable feature of pan-ethnic black solidarity; and notwithstanding the many different black cultures and the wide disparities in the degree of cultural "thickness", he also denies any need for an underlying collective culture.[2] Instead, Shelby believes all that is required for black solidarity in the American context is a commonly shared experience of anti-black racism. He concedes with reluctance that this shared experience is tantamount to having a collective identity – as "victims of anti-black racism".[3] This allows for a black identity without a commitment to a black culture.

As a strategy to accommodate black cultural diversity, Shelby's proposal to disallow culture a role to play, so as to prevent any hindrance it may pose (these will be explained below), is understandable. However, when culture is employed by some black ethnic groups to evade or minimize anti-black racism, such practices do not square with Shelby's presupposition that the experience of anti-black racism is commonly shared among all black people. Indeed, I want to consider certain strategies, involving racial classifications, which suggest that anti-black racism is an insufficient basis for pan-ethnic black solidarity. I consider several cases in which *exiting* the black identity collective, rather than seeking it, has been a preferred option.

When there are multiple black ethnic groups in a multiracial society such as the United States where group solidarity is required to deal effectively with anti-black racism, there are two important and interrelated questions. First, there is a question of what counts as group solidarity. Should only those who self-identify as black people be included, or should those the government classifies as black also be included – even when they do not identify themselves as black? Secondly, given that each black ethnic group has its own specific agendas, are they in keeping with the shared agendas of a more encompassing pan-ethnic group? In the case of the three black student organizations, to the extent that the focus of each is ethnically exclusive, shared goals across ethnic lines seem unlikely. The question remains, however, as to whether, in the wake of pan-ethnic splintering, the ends of a specific ethnic group are compatible with those of a pan-ethnic group. Given the reluctance by many black ethnic groups to embrace a broader pan-ethnic identity, it is important to consider more closely the question of whether African Americans, West Indians and Cape Verdeans all share the same experiences – and, hence, aspirations – here in the United States. I will indicate why, despite some of the difficulties posed by black cultural diversity, a strong commitment to the affirmation of specific black cultural identities, along with opposition to anti-black racism, must be included among the ends of pan-ethnic black solidarity.

The case of the Caribbean Students' Association, with its multi-ethnic mix of West Indian students, represents a version of pan-ethnic group solidarity – albeit one restricted to West Indians. Despite its divisive undercurrent, this phenomenon suggests a reason to suppose that an umbrella organization, such as the pan-African students' association I had proposed, can function in a similar manner, as a more broad-based pan-ethnic group in which ethnic diversity is fostered without sacrificing group solidarity. The parallel between these cases breaks down when we consider that it is not the differences in the ends of group solidarity at the level of each ethnically specific group that impedes the formation of an all-inclusive black diaspora group. Rather, the impediment is a strong desire not to be lumped in with other black ethnic groups. This predicament seems to have a parallel at the international level, where we face the same question regarding the possibility of constituting a pan-African group with shared ends. The negotiation, by black ethnic populations, of their, often transnational, social identities in the American multiracial context seems to be producing racial and ethnic hierarchies, rather than the formation of pan-ethnic group solidarity.

BLACK ETHNIC DIVERSITY AND THE SHADOW OF THE COLOUR LINE

Some of the structural influences that shape ethnic identities in the United States are important to consider when we attempt to understand why black people are splintered into ethnic groups. While the US Census Bureau uses a racial category that identifies a diverse black pan-ethnic group, mass media stirs up trouble by employing the term "African American" as a generic reference to black people. When an ethnically specific group name is used to refer to a plurality of culturally different black ethnic groups, such as, Jamaicans, Haitians or Nigerians, it is no surprise that many members of these diverse groups are not too pleased to be lumped into the African American category. By allowing both a specific ethnic group name, such as African American, and a generic group name, such as black or Negro, the Census Bureau accomplished by fiat what I aimed to do with a generic name for the three black student organizations at the University of Massachusetts. By creating a category that includes African Americans as a specific ethnic group and non-African Americans as members of a black race, they have figured out a way to institutionalize an all-inclusive group category in which to place all black people in America. Of course, the aim of their group construction is to count black people that live in the United States for policy purposes. Unlike the aim of the appellation I proposed for an umbrella group for the three black student organizations, group solidarity is not an end that the Census Bureau aims to promote.

Race is the common denominator for the creation of a pan-ethnic group in the case of the university students' organizations as well as the US Census Bureau.[4] In both cases, the target populations that will be included within these multi-ethnic categories are assumed to be black people. In Massachusetts, however, Cape Verdeans – many of whom have parents born in, and have relatives living in, Africa – are not classified as black people. At the federal level, dissatisfaction with the racial categories used by the Census Bureau is accommodated by allowing self-reporting. This feature of the census-taking instrument, however, admits data regarding race and ethnicity based on criteria that sometimes conflicts with other norms for group identification and inclusion that have been well-established, either by the group or by American society at large – as in the case of the one-drop rule.[5]

This problematic aspect of the use of self-reporting by the Census Bureau is especially true for the Latino-Hispanic category. Although the term "Hispanic" is used in the census as an ethnic category – to refer to members of a linguistic group – it is also pan-ethnic, encompassing a diversity of nationalities and cultural groups. Unlike other census categories that are pan-ethnic *racial* groups, in the Hispanic/Latino case, any can be chosen. What has been a source of confusion for Hispanic/Latino respondents to the census survey is the designation of the "Hispanic/Latino" pan-ethnic category as ethnic only. Even though this category is grounded in Latinos sharing a common language, it is nonetheless constructed on the same logic of race, according to which each ethnic group is located within a larger biological racial category. The result of having a generic category that is racially ambiguous for Latino/ Hispanic respondents is that, in Spanish Caribbean and Latin American nationalities that are known to have a high percentage of Afro-Latinos, the predominant choice has, until recently, been the white category.[6]

This outcome is complicated by the fact that, not only do some Latinos physically appear to be white, black or mixed-race, but also that, unlike the US Census Bureau, they are from countries that are not governed by the American one-drop rule. Haney-Lopez points out that since the 1980 census, more Latinos respondents are choosing to self-identify as "Other", or as a member of the Latino race rather than white. This shift from choosing the white category can be understood as their rejection of the bifurcation of race into black and white. They see themselves as members of a "Latino" race, which is neither white nor black.[7]

In a recent documentary, *Black in Latin America*, Henry Louis Gates Jr contrasts several Dominican spokespersons' on Dominican racial identity with several Haitian spokespersons' on Haitian identity, to explain to his American audience how Dominicans can shed their African background and consider themselves a mixed-race group of "Indios" who, because of their mixture, are no longer black people. They soon discover, upon their arrival in America, that language and music are, for the most part, the only means Americans, including other Latinos, have of distinguishing Domin- icans from African Americans. The need to maintain a distinct identity and garner institutional recognition as a distinct ethnic group, often inclines Afro-Latinos, such as Dominicans, to opt to *escape* anti-black racism by occu- pying a de-racinated "Latino" status. Haney-Lopez reports that fewer than 3 per cent of Latinos self-identify as black and that nearly a third of them are living below the poverty level, which exceeds the rate for African Americans. In the case of Dominicans the rate is 36 per cent. This low socio-economic status of Afro-Latinos has led some researchers, including Haney-Lopez, to suggest that their interests would be better served if they were classified as black rather than Hispanic.[8]

Black ethnic diversity in the United States is beginning to reflect what Du Bois referred to in *Dark Princess* as "a shadow of the color line".9 Du Bois was primarily concerned with the anti-black racism maintained by other people of colour, from Asia and the Middle East, that was a hindrance to the inclusion of black people in a movement to resist global imperialism. His characterization of this situation, where other people of colour maintain a version of anti-black racism, can be applied to the situation in which black people in America splinter into their respective ethnic groups. In place of a pan-ethnic social formation that fosters pan-ethnic group solidarity, there has instead developed a practice of what I shall call "ethnic positioning" within a socio-economically structured racial hierarchy.

It would be misguided to account for the massive opting out of black identity by Afro-Latinos in the United States without acknowledging their strong cultural tie with other Latinos, sometimes involving kinship, and in which language is paramount. Despite their lower socio-economic status, when the incentive of escaping anti-black racism is added, opting out of the black diaspora in the United States seems to override all else, including economic self-interest. This phenomenon of a group of black people opting out of their black identities on cultural grounds and, by doing so, changing their racial status exemplifies a method of dealing with anti-black racism that is antithetical to the idea of black solidarity.

AFRO-LATINOS AND THE VANISHING BLACK BASEBALL PLAYERS

The influence of mass media on our understanding of race and ethnicity cannot be overstated. How do we account for the frequently made racial distinction between African American and Afro-Latino baseball players? The ESPN documentary, "The Vanishing Black Baseball Players", dealt with the decline of African American players from nearly 20 per cent to less than 10 per cent over the past two decades.[10] The *increase* in Afro-Latino baseball players went unremarked, however, because they are no longer counted as black people. This newly accorded racial status stands in stark contrast to the situation Afro-Latinos faced prior to Jackie Robinson breaking the colour line.

Latinos from Cuba and elsewhere have played major league baseball since 1910, although only those who looked white were allowed in with less pay. By contrast, darker-skinned Latinos who played in the Negro Baseball League flourished and, in fact, several owned Negro League teams.[11]

Now that the colour line in major league baseball has been crossed, Afro-Latinos who earlier would not have been allowed to play, because they were black, are no longer considered black people – due to their ethnic difference. This shift in racial categories, at the level of institutional practice and media representation facilitates the exploitation of less expensive Afro-Latino players by white owners of major league teams. As I have indicated above, a strong cultural and, sometimes, even kinship tie with other Latinos, as well as a desire to escape anti-black racism, provide incentives for Afro-Latinos to opt for a deracinated status. The fact that Afro-Latinos have been granted a non-black status in major league baseball is an indication that not all black ethnic groups have a shared experience of anti-black racism, when some are granted a socially privileged status.

When a deracinated, "honorary", status is bestowed on a black ethnic group in a racially charged context, this practice contributes another dynamic to the manner in which anti-black racism is practised. Angelo Falcon's analysis of the 1990 Latino National Political Survey that looked at Latino pan-ethnicity and the Latino view of the Census Bureau's racial categories has several interesting findings. Focusing specifically on data collected from New York Puerto Ricans by interviewers who rated the respondents' skin colour as "very light", "light", "medium", "dark" and "very dark", over 60 per cent of respondents identified themselves as white, 38 per cent identified themselves using "Latino referent" terminology, while only 4 per cent identified themselves racially as black – compared to the 16 per cent that the interviewers identified as dark-skinned.[12] The interviewers rated 70 per cent of the respondents as equally divided between light- and medium-skinned, with only 14 per cent very light.

Haney-Lopez has urged that, given the racial differences among Hispanics, the census should employ enumerators to take colour into account as a measure of discrimination and socio-economic disadvantage. He distinguishes between white, black and Latino Hispanics and points out their relative socio-economic positions within America's racial hierarchy – "with white and black marking the extremes, and Latino Hispanics consistently in between".[13] The fact that 36 per cent of Dominicans and nearly a third of all black Hispanics are living below the poverty level – exceeding the rate for African Americans – leads Haney-Lopez to maintain that the socio-economic status of black Hispanics provides a better reason to classify them as black rather than as Hispanic.

The main difficulty with Haney-Lopez's proposal to reclassify Afro-Latinos is that it would discount their right to self-identify as members of a "Latino" race, due to their darker colour. This new racial identity, imposed by the government, would be a change in policy that many Afro-Latinos would most likely not support. For policy purposes, Haney-Lopez believes the racial status of Afro-Latinos ought to be acknowledged in government data. In the 1990 Latino National Political Survey, Falcon notes that a high percentage of New York Puerto Ricans of all shades believed they were less discriminated against as a group than were African Americans.[14] Even though Puerto Ricans suffer a higher poverty rate than African Americans in New York City, in the survey they were less supportive of increased welfare spending than were African Americans. Given their self-identification as Puerto Rican, it is not clear that they would support policies that aim to help black people. A concern with the preservation of their non-black racial status seems to override self-interest in this case.

ANTI-RACISM AND THE ENDS OF GROUP SOLIDARITY

In his account of Asian American pan-ethnicity, Yen Le Espiritu employs a protest model involving a plurality of Asian-American ethnic groups, based on the idea of eradicating anti-Asian racism.[15] Although Asian American pan-ethnicity began in the 1960s, Espiritu cites the racially motivated killing of Vincent Chin in 1982 by two laid-off auto workers, who sought revenge against Japan for the decline of the US auto industry, as the spark that ignited a pan-ethnic protest movement. The growth of pan-ethnic organizations, however, was fostered by the inclusion of Asian Americans under anti-discrimination law – most importantly, the federal government's Statistical Policy Directive 15.[16]

Espiritu's account of Asian American pan-ethnicity provides a useful means of assessing Shelby's proposal regarding pan-ethnic black solidarity. According to Espiritu, Asian American pan-ethnicity was motivated by a specific political purpose of resisting anti-Asian racism. Shelby argues that the eradication of anti-black racism and racial equality are values that all black people share, and that this is adequate grounds for pan-ethnic black solidarity. Some of Espiritu's observations regarding the limitations of the Asian American pan-ethnic movement grounded on anti-Asian racism are instructive for understanding why the black solidarity Shelby champions is more likely to suffer a similar fate.

Espiritu uses a dual framework of *primordialism* and *instrumentalism* to account for certain aspects of Asian American pan-ethnicity. The primordialist emphasizes sentimental cultural ties, whereas the instrumentalist leans more towards self-interest. Due mainly to language differences, and the lack of a collective culture, Espiritu points out that primordialism eventually gave way to a more viable instrumentalist grounding of Asian American pan-ethnicity. Following Orlando Patterson's observation regarding "ethnic switching", he maintains that membership in the Asian pan-ethnic group is only for the sake of obtaining comparative advantage vis-à-vis membership in a specific Asian ethnic group.[17] In addition to noting self-interest as a factor influencing this practice of switching from a specific ethnic identity to a pan-ethnic identity, we must not overlook the extent to which the practice itself speaks to a role that cultural identity plays in group allegiance and cultural affirmation. Unless circumstances absolutely require a switched identity to be permanent, the practice of switching can be understood as a means of retaining one's native culture, while claiming a social identity that is more advantageous.

Shelby's account of black solidarity employs a model of pan-ethnicity that is similar to Espiritu's. I have already indicated why the force of his argument – that the shared end of seeking the eradication of anti-black racism is sufficient for pan-ethnic black solidarity – is diminished by his presupposition that all black people have a shared experience of anti-black racism. One important lesson to be derived from Espiritu's study of Asian American pan-ethnicity is that their group solidarity could not be sustained, in the long run, solely on the basis of all members valuing the eradication of anti-Asian racism.

Espiritu discusses several developments, each involving switching categories, that influenced the eventual splintering of Asian Americans into specific ethnic groups. In addition to the switching from a specific ethnic group to a pan-ethnic group, there were also cases of switching motivated by self-interest, which involved moving from one racial category to another. Espiritu uses, for example, the Association of Indians in America, representing Indian businessmen from South Asia who succeeded in changing their racial status from white to Asian in order to qualify for government programmes. More importantly, however, is the case of Filipinos, as a group, opting out of the Asian American category, for this set a precedent that other Asian ethnic groups would follow. Espiritu reports the irony of the ends being sought by Asian American pan-ethnic organizations. They were engaged in a protracted struggle to eliminate the Census Bureau's pan-ethnic Asian American *racial* category. They advocated a change from the generic pan-ethnic classification as Asian Pacific Americans to the use of appellations for each ethnic category. On the 2010 census form, this change appears as a list of nine specific ethnic groups and two separate groups titled "Other Asian" and "Other Pacific Islander". There is no generic category – as in the case of black people – or reference to race. This outcome seems to suggest that Asian American pan-ethnicity has come to an end.

Espiritu presents a more favourable view of this outcome. He points out that the pan-ethnic movement to end pan-ethnicity has resulted in the establishment of networks across ethnic lines that can be utilized in future pan-ethnic endeavours. The splintering is motivated by a desire to maximize the self-interest of each specific ethnic group with regard to federal and state policies based on Directive 15. Filipinos had opted out earlier to increase their share of government benefits that would, otherwise, have had to be divided among all the Asian American ethnic groups. Although each group's economic interests were a key factor, this concerted effort to "de-lump" the category of Asian Americans also indicates the importance of national and cultural identities in pan-ethnic formations. What seems to be a destabilizing factor is actually a requirement for an Asian American pan-ethnicity that is more viable in the long-run. With a diversity of Asian American ethnic groups retaining their specific cultural identities, and with the construction of pan-ethnic networks devoted to the struggle against anti-Asian racism,

Asian Americans can switch from their specific ethnic identities to pan-ethnic identities when moral emergencies, such as the Vincent Chin murder, require this.

The distinction Shelby adopts between thick and thin culture is sometimes used by sociologists as a means to discuss different levels, or degrees, of cultural identification. With regard to immigrant populations, this would refer, perhaps, to the level of retention, or loss, of a native language by second and third generation offspring. Shelby employs this distinction to argue that, while not all black people identify with a black culture, they all experience anti-black racism and have a desire to eradicate this. He insists that a shared commitment to this political end only requires a black identity in this thin sense. To deal with cultural diversity as a factor inhibiting black solidarity, he rejects the idea of grounding pan-ethnic group solidarity on a shared culture. He insists upon a notion of thin black identity that only requires a shared experience of anti-black racism. Cultural diversity is a hindrance to black solidarity only when cultural identity is given a role to play.

Shelby's thin conception of black identity is meant to be co-extensive with the US Census category, which distinguishes black people by reference to their having certain visible, inherited physical characteristics, or their having a particular biological ancestry. He claims that "there is little room for choice about one's 'racial' identity. One cannot simply refuse to be thinly black."[18] While his point, that this is an imposed identity that is inescapable, seems undeniable, he overextends it to apply even in cases where a black person does not "look" black and conceals her genealogy to pass for white. He maintains that she "would still *be* black, in the thin sense, even if never found out". He does not explain how she would still be vulnerable to anti-black racism.

Although Shelby's concept of thin black identity is fashioned to achieve a pan-ethnic end, in his discussion of "nonblack modes of self-preservation" he does not consider the practice of strategic passing by very light-skinned black people for white.[19] He wants his concept of thin black identity to accommodate the "assimilated black" who, for a variety of reasons, chooses not to identify culturally. However, the clash of (class) assimilation with cultural identification should not overshadow the even thinner non-black mode of passing, which rejects race as well as culture. The point of this particular "nonblack mode of self-presentation" is to evade anti-black racism by not being considered a black person. In such extreme cases of thin black identity, there are black people who are not victims of anti-black racism.

When Shelby's concept of thin black identity is applied to mixed-race black people, it appears to be imposing a racial category. The point of the mixed-race movement was to challenge the one-drop rule. This objective suggests that these persons would prefer a mixed-race category rather than be required to self-identify as black.[20] For them, an imposed racial classification is not, as Shelby maintains, "inescapable". Shelby wants thin black identity as an official racial classification because he thinks this is "all that would be needed for the administration of civil rights laws and the enforcement of antidiscrimination statues".[21] Given this line of reasoning, his use of thin black identity serves no purpose in this case, because mixed-race black people are equally protected under antidiscrimination statues as members of a mixed-race category.

CONSTRUCTING A BLACK MODEL MINORITY

In his book *West Indian in the West*, Percy Hintzen discusses the formation of a group of Caribbean people in Northern California who have deliberately represented themselves as a black model minority.[22] He cites, as the key ingredient for this construction, the highlighting of a foreign-born status. This is done for a twofold reason: to set them apart from African Americans; and also to allow them to claim an international status – a feature of their social identity that likens them to Asian Americans in Northern California, the majority of whom are now also foreign-born. There are other ingredients, such as their emphasis on the exoticness of their island heritage. Most important, according to Hintzen, is their exclusionary practices with regard to African Americans. He points out that practices such as operating restaurants where African Americans are not welcomed, sponsoring cricket rather than soccer matches and criticizing affirmative action policies are motivated by a desire to generate public self-representations that distinguish them from African Americans.

There are several issues raised by Hintzen's case of a West Indian pan-ethnic formation in Northern California. First of all, it illustrates how a version of Shelby's proposal can prove to be a hindrance to the outcome he seeks. Unlike the category shifts made by Afro-Latino baseball players and the Dominican and Cape Verdean populations in Boston, the Northern Californian West Indian pan-ethnic formation did not seek to opt out of being racially classified as black. Instead, along with a desire for socio-economic advancement, they were motivated by a group-specific political end of evading anti-black racism by invoking their ethnicity as a mark of distinction. The issue I want to consider is whether white Americans perceive all foreign-born black people – not just West Indians – as significantly different from African Americans. If this is true, it further erodes Shelby's presupposition that all black people in the United States are equally subjected to anti-black racism.

Stigmatization is a particular form of anti-black racism that, according to Shelby, cuts across ethnic and even class differences. Glen Loury employed this term to explain a special kind of racism directed mainly towards black high achievers. Shelby, however, takes it to apply generally to all black people.[23] According to Loury, this phenomenon occurs when black professionals who display competence fail to live up to a black stereotype of incompetence that fulfils white expectations. It is strictly an empirical question whether foreign-born black people are equally subjected to this kind of stigmatization, or whether it is reserved by whites strictly for African Americans. To the extent that these expectations do not apply to them, having a foreign-born status is a distinction that matters in this regard. The Northern Californian West Indians that Hintzen studied aimed to exploit this rather nuanced shift in white expectations. This practice of deliberately constructing a black model minority reveals a political difficulty for Shelby's notion of black solidarity. Rather than expressing solidarity with other black people, Hintzen notes that, in this case, the end being sought by claiming a model minority status is a cross-racial *class* identity with whites.

THE ENDS OF PAN-ETHNIC BLACK SOLIDARITY

The splintering of black people into their respective ethnic groups suggests that, as a shared value, anti-black racism does not always foster black solidarity. Many Afro-Latinos and mixed-race black people have avoided being victims of anti-black racism by opting out of the census classification, while some West Indians have sought a "model minority" status that distinguishes them within that classification. How might this tendency towards ethnic splintering be employed to foster pan-ethnic ends that benefit all black people? There are several important lessons to be drawn from Espiritu's study of Asian American pan-ethnicity that also seem to apply in the case of black pan-ethnicity.

Shelby's equation of his concept of a thin black identity with the census classification reflects his concern with government enforcement of anti-discrimination policy. His focus on anti-black racism as a value shared cross-culturally is borne out by recent, highly publicized police brutality cases – in which moral outrage among black people has been fairly universal. The problem is that this outrage also often has been short-lived and dominated specifically by the concrete issue of police malpractice.[24] Shelby is more concerned with issues pertaining to class than to black ethnic diversity, and, because of this, he rightly takes socio-economic disparity and cultural assimilation by upwardly mobile black people to be major hindrances to black solidarity.[25] His emphasis on anti-black racism as sufficient ground for black solidarity was meant to cure what he acknowledges to be a cross-cultural "malady". I have identified several alternative ways of dealing with anti-black racism that have been adopted by various black ethnic groups to indicate the limitations of his focus on class. He wrongly presupposes, however, that racial bonding as a result of anti-black racism will override cultural bonding. The splintering of black people in the United States into specific ethnic groups indicates that, for many ethnic blacks, especially those that are transnational, maintaining a bond with their native cultures is indispensable.

I want to consider ways to accommodate the threats that ethnic splintering – engendered by the desire many black immigrant populations have for culturally specific bonding – poses for Shelby's view.[26] Unlike the claiming of a model minority status by West Indians who are motivated by a desire for social mobility, the claiming of a non-black/deracinated/mixed-race status by Afro-Latinos is not always consistent with their ethnic group's self-interest – as in the case of Dominicans.[27] In such cases, opting for a non-black social identity is taken to be more beneficial than joining ranks with other black ethnic groups to end anti-black racism.

Despite these differences, Afro-Latinos as well as West Indians are known to engage in the practice of ethnic switching. As a means of gaining privilege in a racial hierarchy, for some Afro-Latinos, switching is sometimes a viable option dictated by prudence. Haney-Lopez's proposal to classify Afro-Latinos as black is well-intended as a means of addressing poverty. However, there is no need for Afro-Latinos who self-report as non-black Hispanic to be switched by census takers to a black racial category; rather, they should be permitted to self-identify under a deracinated Latino category. The census already permits Afro-Latinos to claim a black racial identity *and* their Hispanic ethnic identity. While many Afro-Latinos may, against their best interests, elect not to identify as black, what should not go unnoticed here is that the option for Afro-Latinos to engage in switching already has been officially institutionalized by the US Census Bureau.[28]

In keeping with lessons learned from Espiritu's study of Asian American pan-ethnicity, the best response to the practice of switching is not to police it. Many Afro-Latinos identify with Latinos *and* with black people. Their practice of ethnic switching is so routine that, from a pan-ethnic standpoint, it might be wise to view it as merely a cosmopolitan by-product of intersecting black diasporas in the United States, and not as a barrier to pan-ethnic black solidarity.[29] When the objective of ethnic switching is to seek a higher positioning in a racial hierarchy managed by whites, there arises an ethical worry regarding this practice. It is unwise to suppose, as Shelby does, that it is always in the interests of each black ethnic group to join ranks to seek to end anti-black racism; switching gains a footing in circumstances where an advantage can be gained by not joining ranks. A moral constraint on the practice of switching would be whether, in a particular case, it is incompatible with pan-ethnic ends. For good reasons, ethnic switching need not always aim to promote pan-ethnic ends in order to be justified. However, ethnic switching that involves hypocrisy which supports anti-black racism exceeds a moral limit. For example, if a model minority, whose achievement is based on merit, were to take a public stand against affirmative action policy while accepting the benefits of this policy as a victim of anti-black discrimination, this would count as unethical.

Hintzen notes that there is an interesting interplay between West Indians and African Americans in the Northern Californian case. On the one hand, West Indians exploit the black middle-class professional networks and resources in Silicon Valley to promote the West Indian model minority myth. On the other hand, African American professional classes use their relationship with West Indian professional classes to refute the African American stereotypes. It is unclear whether this kind of cross-cultural exchange fosters pan-ethnic black solidarity. Nonetheless, an ethnic group that aspires to be a black model minority can represent itself as morally superior to other black people with regard to religious and family values, work ethic and the like, as in the case of Elijah Muhammad's Nation of Islam, without the tendencies towards elitism and social separation that they display publicly posing a threat to pan-ethnic solidarity.[30]

Pan-ethnic ends have a role to play in certain cases involving conflict between black ethnic groups. The application of social policies that were established to remedy the long-term effects of anti-black discrimination, for instance, involve questions regarding the extension of affirmative action policies to black immigrant populations. In an episode of *Tony Brown's Journal* (2004), Bobby Austin, an African American administrator at the University of the District of Columbia, and Abdulaziz Kamus, an Ethiopian refugee who immigrated to New York in 1984 and now a merchant living in Washington, DC, engaged in dialogue involving a wide range of issues pertaining to pan-ethnic black identities.[31] The discussion began with the question of whether specific programmes should be reserved for African Americans who suffered through a period of legal segregation that recent immigrants have not experienced – although anti-black discrimination still exists. There was also an interesting exchange involving issues regarding ethnic identities that led all the participants to acknowledge that cultural identity was more important than racial identity for many black ethnic groups. With regard to entitlements slated for African Americans, there was a question regarding the social status of the children of black immigrants who have "mixed ethnicities". Cross-cultural dialogue of this sort is a starting point for the establishment of pan-ethnic networks that go beyond the question of whether set-asides are reserved for African Americans. A parenthetic end would be to seek ways to promote black business and economic interests mutually across ethnic lines.

The creation of a cross-cultural forum for black students was the pan-ethnic objective I initially sought as a faculty advisor for the three student organizations. What I learned from their resistance to being placed into a single umbrella group was that the multitude of black student organizations they established, in fact, enhanced pan-ethnic ends by requiring the university to recognize a diversity of well-organized black students who represent their respective ethnic groups. Indeed, I soon realized that all black students at the university benefited from each ethnic group having its own agenda. More importantly, I think, was the manner in which the creation of these organizations brought about more open cross-cultural dialogue between all the black ethnic groups on campus. This cross-cultural dialogue is an essential starting point for understanding the intersection of old and new diasporic groups, and the interaction of pan-ethnic networks in their collective pursuit of achieving their desired ends.

NOTES

1. Tommie Shelby, *We Who Are Dark: Philosophical Foundations of Black Solidarity* (Cambridge, MA: Harvard University Press, 2006), ch. 4.
2. Shelby uses the terms "thick" and "thin" to gauge an individual's racial identity. All black people have a thin racial identity, but some do not have a thick cultural identity. A black person with only a thin black identity, either by choice or upbringing, does not identify with a black culture. While Shelby does not deny that culture can foster cross-ethnic cohesion and unity, he does very strongly deny that it is a necessary condition for black solidarity.
3. Shelby, *We Who Are Dark*, ch. 4.
4. I use the term "pan-ethnic" to refer to the race-ethnic categories employed by the US Census Bureau. There are five generic categories – white, black, Hispanic, Asian American andNative American – under which multiple ethnic groups are listed. For example, African American, Jamaican, Haitian, etc. are listed as "Black", while Cubans, Mexicans, Puerto Ricans, etc. are listed as "Hispanic". Hence, the term "black" refers to a racial group comprised of multiple ethnic groups and the term "Hispanic" refers to a linguistic group comprised of multiple ethnic groups.
5. A. Hollinger, "The One Drop Rule and the One Hate Rule", *Daedalus* 134, no. 1 (Winter 2005): 18–28. For an interesting discussion of the social meaning of race, and what it means to be considered a black person, see Lionel McPherson

and Tommie Shelby, "Blackness and Blood: Interpreting African American Identity", *Philosophy and Public Affairs* 32 (2004): 171–92.

6. See William A. Darity Jr, Jason Dietrich and Darrick Hamilton, "Bleach in the Rainbow: Latino Ethnicity and Preference for Whiteness", in *The Afro-Latin@ Reader: History and Culture in the United States*, ed. Miriam Jimenez Roman and Juan Flores (Durham: Duke University Press, 2010), 485–98; "Afro–Puerto Rican Testimonies: An Oral History Project in Western Puerto Rico – Against the Myth of Racial Harmony in Puerto Rico", also in *The Afro-Latin@ Reader*, 508–11.

7. Ian Haney-Lopez, "Race on the 2010 Census: Hispanics and the Shrinking White Majority", *Daedalus* 134, no. 1 (Winter 2005): 45–48.

8. Ibid., 48.

9. W.E.B. Du Bois, *Dark Princess* (New York: Harcourt Brace, 1928; repr., Jackson, MS: Banner, 1995).

10. The ESPN broadcast was based on an article by Tom Verducci, "The African-American Baseball Player Is Vanishing: Does He Have a Future?", *Sports Illustrated*, 7 July 2003. The conflation of black and African American runs rampant throughout Verducci's discussion. For example, he claims that "the Boston Red Sox do not have a black starting pitcher, or everyday player for the first time since 1961". In 2003, Pedro Martinez, a dark-skinned Dominican with celebrity status, was a starting pitcher for Boston. This conflation was repeated in an article posted on the ESPN website on 21 April 2011. There is a chronological list of statistics showing the decline of black players, with no acknowledgment of the growing percentage of black Hispanic players.

11. Adrian Burgos Jr, "An Uneven Playing Field: Afro-Latinos in Major League Baseball", in *The Afro-Latin@ Reader: History and Culture in the United States*, ed. Miriam Jimenez Roman and Juan Flores (Durham: Duke University Press, 2010), 127–41.

12. Angelo Falcon, "Puerto Ricans and the Politics of Racial Identity", in *Racial and Ethnic Identity: Psychological Development and Creative Expression*, ed. Herbert W. Harris, Howard C. Blue and E.H. Griffith (New York: Routledge, 1995), 193–208.

13. Haney-Lopez, "Race", 46.

14. Falcon, "Puerto Ricans and Politics", 201.

15. Yen Le Espiritu, *Asian American Pan-ethnicity: Bridging Institutions and Identities* (Philadelphia: Temple University Press, 1992).

16. Victoria Hattam, "Ethnicity and the Boundaries of Race: Rereading Directive 15", *Daedalus* 134, no. 1 (Winter 2005): 61–69.

234 Tommy L. Lott

17. Orlando Patterson, "Context and Choice in Ethnic Allegiance", in *Ethnicity: Theory and Experience*, ed. N. Glazer and P. Moynihan (Cambridge, MA: Harvard University Press, 1974), 168–86; Orlando Patterson, "Ethnicity and the Pluralist Fallacy", *Change* (March 1975): 348.

18. Shelby, *We Who Are Dark*, 208.

19. Shelby acknowledges that the struggle against anti-black racism includes whites who support racial equality. He also acknowledges that black solidarity may not be the only way to end anti-black racism. Ibid., ch. 4.

20. Naomi Zack, "Mixed Black and White Race and Public Policy", *Hypatia* 10, no. 1 (Winter 1995): 120–32.

21. Shelby, *We Who Are Dark*, 209.

22. Percy Hintzen, *West Indian in the West* (New York: New York University Press, 2001).

23. Glen Loury, *The Anatomy of Racial Inequality* (Cambridge, MA: Harvard University Press, 2002), ch. 3.

24. In George Zimmerman's murder trial in 2013, the ruling that his killing of Trayvon Martin was legally justified shows that anti-black racism has persisted unabated in America's post-racial era.

25. His focus is made clear in his book talk. In the discussion period, a question came up regarding black ethnic diversity that Shelby did not seem to appreciate fully. Tommie Shelby, C-SPAN book discussion on *We Who Are Dark*, 13 December 2005. A video clip is available in the C-SPAN Video Library.

26. This courtesy cannot be taken to extend to black ethnic groups or individuals from black ethnic groups who practise anti-black racism.

27. One major factor is perhaps the Latin social policy of "whitening", which is now a deeply embedded cultural value in many Latino groups. This issue is critically examined in George Reid Andrews, *Afro-Latin America, 1800–2000* (Oxford: Oxford University Press, 2004), ch. 4. See also Melissa Nobles, "The Myth of Latin American Multiracialism", *Daedalus* 134, no. 1 (Winter 2005): 82–87.

28. Although Haney-Lopez's proposed remedy reflects dissatisfaction with the census categories, Anthony Appiah has pointed out that government intervention to render social identities more scientific, or logical, will most likely only make matters worse. See Ian Haney-Lopez, *The Ethics of Identity* (Princeton: Princeton University Press, 2005), ch. 5.

29. See Alan Hughes and Milca Esdaille, "The Afro-Latino Connection: Can This Group Be the Bridge to a Broad-Based Black-Hispanic Alliance?", in *The Afro-Latin@ Reader: History and Culture in the United States*, ed. Miriam Jimenez Roman and Juan Flores (Durham: Duke University Press, 2010), 364–72, and

Aida Lambert, "We Are Black Too: Experiences of a Honduran Garifuna", also in *The Afro-Latin@ Reader*, 431–33.

30. Hintzen acknowledges the Nation of Islam as a model minority.

31. Bobby Austin, "African-American or Black: Is There a Difference?", *Tony Brown's Journal*, 5 November 2004. Video clip available at Tony Brown's Online Video Library.

CHAPTER 9

THE PERCEPTION OF MADNESS
Escapes and Flights of Fancies in
Claude McKay's *Banana Bottom*

JARRETT HUGH BROWN

ALL DIASPORIC COMMUNITIES DEVELOP LITERATURES THAT are forged
within the changing circumstances of their particular time and place. Caribbean literature is extraordinarily rich in creative characters who reflect the
variegated social, economic and political realities. Nevertheless, understanding exactly what those characters should be communicating to the reader is
never easy. The literary creation of madness in the Caribbean novel presents
one such problem.

The depiction of madness in Caribbean literature is ambiguous and sometimes paradoxical: Caribbean writers represent mad figures as curiously
strange, different and alienated beings who nevertheless perform conscien-
tiously or imaginatively. Why is madness such a curious matter in Caribbean
literature and culture? And how does the idea of madness in Caribbean
society provide a useful theoretical frame for interrogating the rationality or
irrationality of the Caribbean self, especially when Western epistemologies
usually construct the Caribbean space as a mad bacchanalian place, one
existing outside of the normal bounds of time (i.e. on island time)? Madness, as it is represented by Caribbean authors, goes beyond just "an illness
of the mind" or "a deviation from some norm of thought and feeling".[1] It
is not conceived merely as a "social terror", but also as a form of "literacy
of the imagination", to coin two concepts from Wilson Harris.[2] Thus the

characters we see in some of these texts "are designed to portray the mind as constructing and exposing its own symbolic framework out of fragments that all readers recognize as familiar – customs, attitudes, places, institutions, traits of character, desires and the fears they have encountered in their own lives".[3] The idea of madness, then, must be understood to have a character of literacy that calls us to "alter the criteria which we bring to bear on certain matters".[4] As a "theme of myth and Literature [madness] has always dealt with personal responses to environmental influences, which include political, social, and cultural pressures, or perhaps it would be more correct to say which excludes nothing".[5] By excluding nothing, madness becomes a way to expose and transform an already complex dialogue about vocabulary – this is the way we "dress" or name ourselves and others.[6]

What does it mean to be "mad" anyway when madness in itself can be an emergence into the freedom of speech? Such an emergence into speech-making challenges Foucault's claim that "madness is primarily, a lack of language, an 'absence of production', the silence of a stifled, repressed language".[7] Maybe also as Shoshana Felman suggests, "madness poses in more than one way a question whose significance and meaning have not been fully assessed and whose self-evidence is no longer clear".[8] The question of the significance and meaning of madness is at the heart of this chapter, which examines the paradoxical nature of madness as a discursive idiom within Caribbean literature and culture. Specifically, I am interested in examining the figure of the madwoman/man in Caribbean literature as a "paradox" in the way that Wilson Harris defines the term, that is, as "both a cloak for, and a dialogue with, eclipses of live 'otherness' that seek to break through in a new light and tone expressive of layers of reality".[9] What this break-through reveals is how madness itself is useful for describing the complex and dynamic workings of Caribbean culture, in much the same way that Antonio Benítez Rojo's chaos theory reveals how the Caribbean is defined by a polyrhythmic, repetitive set of actions performed "in a certain kind of way", which I will call "a Caribbean way". This way refers to the "processes, dynamics, and rhythms that show themselves within the marginal, the regional, the incoherent, the heterogeneous . . . [and] the unpredictable that co-exist with us in the everyday world".[10] It is this co-existence with the "everyday us" that I would like to explore further, the ways in which madness works as a meta-narrative for reading itself, for defining itself "in a certain kind of way". The Caribbean space therefore becomes a product of its own cultural systems in which binaries collide, not violently but creatively, to produce and magnify a syncretism in Caribbean societies that mirrors madness itself. Because madness is delineated in Caribbean texts in "a certain kind of way", what escapes from this realism is an imprecise and ambiguous definition of madness. This manifests itself as a difficulty to write or read the character and meaning of madness in Caribbean literary societies, families and spaces, especially when the character of the madman seems to exhibit a "normalized" and "intelligent" capacity that flies in the face of the clinical definition of madness which is built around the aberrant, bizarre or deranged mentality.

Madness in Caribbean literature, except for the instance in Jean Rhys's *Wide Sargasso Sea*, is not represented as psychosis, a mental dissolution and derangement that clinically makes the condition a disease. Caribbean representations of the madman usually eschew the simple clinical diagnosis; instead, madness maintains an intelligent codification, a reasoned prerogative, and an artistic reverence and peculiarity whereby the madman lives in communion with the community while still living outside normal societal bounds. Thus, I find the idea of madness in Caribbean literature to be an elusive concept, one that although ambivalent and amorphous, is also relational.

Madness is especially difficult to define in Caribbean literature also because the nomenclature that is used to describe Caribbean mad figures reflects passive ambiguous or figurative descriptions, such as "gone off his head", "turned crazy" or "had a nervous breakdown". The nomenclature, while suggesting a shift in the nature of the being, does not distinctly reflect the individual's psychological state. Even though the phrases "a nervous breakdown" or "gone off his head" do have an element of the clinical definition of madness, there is still ambiguity resting in the metaphors. This has the effect of silencing the clinical vulgarity and "diseased" subjectivity that the term madness usually carries, so that the persona has some control over the negotiation of his state in the eventualities of the narrative. Thus, the perception of madness in Caribbean literary contexts is particularly fascinating because the character is never codified in the same way each time and a close observation will reveal a creative, rather than a created, self.

Claude McKay presents in his third novel, *Banana Bottom*, characters

whose actions do not fully reflect elements of traditional madness, especially
as he does not locate his madmen outside of the society or in the demented
preoccupation of their minds. It seems that McKay's representations imply
the autonomy and value of the mad character; he creates a figure who, according to Lillian Feder, "is rooted in a mythical and literary tradition in which
distortion is a generally accepted mode of expression [and where] the inherent aesthetic order by which his existence is limited also gives his madness
intrinsic value and meaning".[11] Feder further asserts that this figure "must
be approached on his own terms, through the verbal, dramatic, and narrative
symbols that convey the unconscious processes he portrays and reveals".[12]
The respectability that Feder argues for is part of the paradox inherent in the
existence and performance of the madman in Caribbean literature: such a
figure is intimately implicated in the lives of those around him because "the
madman, like other people, does not exist alone. He both reflects and influences those involved with him. He embodies and symbolically transforms
the values of his family, his tribe, and his society, even if he renounces them
(or if the community renounces him), as well as their delusions, cruelty and
violence, even in his inner flight."[13] What is at stake here is the various ways
in which the mad self "is created . . . and redefined in its relation to [Carib-
bean] society and history".[14] Therefore, even though the madman should
repel, frighten and threaten, he does not, but actually fascinates, confounds
and lives both consciously and unconsciously as a trope of desire, not fear.

Banana Bottom (first published in 1933 and since reprinted) opens with
the female protagonist Bita Plant returning to the "tiny country town of
Jubilee and the mountain village of Banana Bottom" after "seven years of
polite upbringing" and education in England – the mother country, as it was
referred to by the press and official persons.[15] However, as the narrator notes,
"Bita was a girl with a past", and her past, we learn, is intimately bound up
with the "village madman", Crazy Bow Adair. Crazy Bow is the last child of
a "Scotchman who had emigrated to Jamaica in the eighteen twenties . . .
bought the vast mountain estate of Banana Bottom, [and not only] liberated
[his] slaves [but even] married one of the blackest of them". The narrator
describes Crazy Bow's progenitor as "the strange liberator" because he also
allowed many slaves to cultivate lots on the estate, thus giving them economic
and political autonomy. His "strangeness" did not end there, because he

proceeded to cut up his "thousands into small holdings for the blacks who wanted to buy" (p. 3). The audacity of such an act and his public disavowal of slave subjugation are partly why the narrator deems him strange and hints at his actions as evidence of an "other" kind of madness. These defiant actions of this slave owner, which fall outside of the racist norms of the social, economic and political conventions of the time, place the Scotchman at the fringe of a slave-holding Jamaican society and not only mark him as strange but also as totally mad. Furthermore, by calling Crazy Bow's father a "Scotchman" rather than a "Scotsman", McKay makes an ironic pun on the subtle corruption of Crazy Bow's father's creolized subjectivity. McKay's play on the word "Scotchman" also provokes, at the very least, the idea that he is stricken with chronic alcoholism.

The narrator describes Crazy Bow's father as the "rude progenitor", in an indication of another instance of his odd character and radical, out of order prominence. What seems to be suggested here is that Crazy Bow was conceived in a particular kind of sin; he was the product of a disrespectful "mixing of different human strains", which many whites on the island believed the act of emancipation did not sanction. Crazy Bow's madness, then, seems to be inherited, on the one hand, and on the other, a punishment for his father's "insanity". The narrator confirms this idea when she says: "And they [extant species of white humanity] may point out to you the village of Banana Bottom and the descendants of the last owner of the original estate as a picture of decadence and degeneracy." (pp. 3–4).

Crazy Bow is first described as a "precocious child" and "the first of the Adair stock to show signs of an intellectual bent". This intellectual proclivity immediately sets him up for success; the village headmaster believes he will be in an "official job some day" or he will become someone who will "make a mark for himself in the bigger life of the island". Crazy Bow then receives a secondary education at a private institution for boys in Jubilee. However, there is a peculiarity to his presence at the school because, after his first year, which was marked by his brilliance in work and discipline, we are told "he shot right off the straight line and nothing could bring him back" (pp. 4–5). This euphemism is the first revelation of Crazy Bow's dissociative, irrational and bizarre personality. There is no indication as to why he "shot off the straight line", neither is any explanation proffered for his psychosis; but it seems as if the island space, as much as the educative arena in which Crazy Bow resides, is much too limited for his gifts and he cannot be contained within these boundaries. The straight line preserves the imperial idea that the island was only able to support and supply a very basic quality of education for the island's young, and what it did give was itself inferior at best or parochial. Thus, Crazy Bow was never expected to appreciate in intelligence or autonomy because his path was already paved for him and his going to school was just a formality that satisfied the conscience of those around him who regarded him as special. But Crazy Bow's precociousness is proof of the prescient mental acuity and sophistication that made him a candidate for secondary schooling in the first place. It should come as no surprise then that he "shot off the straight line" because he was always possessed with audacity. The euphemism highlights Crazy Bow's genius, and while the literary device does not outright suggest that he went mad, the implication is that he became possessed with something that no one in the community or in school could understand, support or relate to. Crazy Bow was something of a musical oddity, possessed with the genius of a maestro, the likes of which the island had never seen before. His presence clearly confounds those around him; they marvelled that, even as a boy, he could make "flutes out of bamboos and blow new joys into the [old] village tunes". In fact, "he was an imitating wonder", a prodigy who "could play any of the instruments found among the peasants in the hill country: fiddle, banjo, guitar". He was also a genius on the piano. "But what drove him right crazy at the school was a piano that he taught himself to play there. It knocked everything else out of his head: composition, mathematics and the ambition to enter the civil service" (p. 5). When the headmaster failed in his attempts to renew Crazy Bow's interest in his studies, he sent Crazy Bow home.

The attitude towards the young artist calibrates his madness as something far more complex than what the text iterates. Crazy Bow does not show evidence of being in "psychic conflict or confusion",[16] neither does the narrator describe him as a confused subject in time or space; the language and metaphor used to describe his actions deny his madness. At the level of metaphor, Crazy Bow is possessed by music and also he demonstrates a strange language that only he can express in his renditions. His compositions destroy the teleological singularity of the world he inhabits and his passion is interpreted as part of the strangeness of his diversion. When he is eventually sent home, he is relegated to a place of ambivalence because his ambitions outweigh and outlast his physical environment and carries a threat to the colonial law of the land, which prescribes that black artistic expression be muted under the presumptive power of neo-imperialism and post-emancipation paternalism. Crazy Bow is only mad in so far as his artistic expression does not fit the typical racial paradigm of the island's emancipated class and his desire (for music) does not conform to the social narratives within which the practices and intentions of black bodies are constrained in the colonial environment. Crazy Bow represents desire itself, inasmuch as he chooses to live an inventive, experimental and (com)passionate life. Crazy Bow becomes a manifestation of both protest and apathy in the Jamaica of the early 1900s. His musical genius protests the "small place" mentality that colonial language and culture imposes on the island. This musical genius, at the same time, challenges the apathy of black Jamaicans who accepted the "ethos of colonial education [which is that] there was no beauty, no nobility, no history, no culture . . . nothing of any worth – barring the natural resources and markets for the metropolis manufactured goods – in that which existed locally".[17]

Crazy Bow's madness does not preclude his interaction with the community he lives in. He navigates this space with the same passion and desire that he displayed while he was studying. He plays "all the village fiddles" and "the owners were glad to let him" (p. 6), especially because he knew all kinds of music: village tunes, hymns and anthems, jubilee songs. The level of intimacy he maintains with the people of Banana Bottom ironizes Crazy Bow's actions. He becomes, in the eyes of the public, a phenomenon that is unexplainable with the lexicon or vocabulary of their ordinary world. He is an extraordinary musician who brings to light the absence of a clear definition of madness within the colonial Caribbean space. Madness becomes a cliché within the world of the peasants.

This particular rendering of madness prevents any traditional interpretations or expectations that would reduce Crazy Bow's condition to a disease or make him a creature who brings uneasiness to the community. Hence, he does not represent a threat to the community but is an object of their fascination, wonder and speculation. Thus the community's acceptance of his "harmless insanity" (p. 6) captures, ironically enough, not Crazy Bow's madness, but his undefined, unclassified, excessive and paradoxical state which is consonant with their own. Though mad, Crazy Bow is not a threat because he has not performed any acts of violence or irrationality that are believed to be an inherent part of clinical insanity. Yet, the oxymoron creates a narrative that refuses to subordinate Crazy Bow, or give form to "the principle of his irrationality" and leave him irresponsibly in the text as a dissociative, ridiculous or psychotic member of Banana Bottom. This tension between Crazy Bow's representation and the inability to name him as mad highlights the author's ambivalence to the meaning of madness and the subjectivity of the literary madman in Caribbean literary practices. The narrator notes that the nomenclature is not derogatory or used unkindly, but carries a silent or salient reverence for the character's undeniable genius.

Crazy Bow is aware of the ambivalence surrounding his "state" in Banana Bottom and how this ambivalence gives him access, occasionally, to his music. It is the same ambivalence that functions as a "rational" principle governing the nature of the peasant class's reluctance to punish Crazy Bow for the "alleged" rape of the minor, Bita Plant. The reactions of the community further complicate this ambivalence because, it is clear that Bita was raped, by legal standards, by Crazy Bow. Bita is described as a "tomboy" who was remarkably "self-reliant and strong" (p. 7), who climbed mango and star apple trees on her father's property, and could swim and ride a horse bareback. It seems that it is because of this self-reliant trait that, unlike the other village children, she grew attracted to the village fiddler. They were kindred spirits since they were both peculiar – she because she was a tomboy and he because he was a talented musician. Their meetings and subsequent relationship are described thus: "She sometimes met him when she went down by the riverside to get mangoes. And one day they romped together in the soft brown fox grass that grew upon the slope. And after that she grew familiar with him when he came to the house or when she met him down by the riverside, mostly on Saturday when there is no work" (p. 8).

The relationship that developed, and was allowed, unfolded in full sight of the villagers and Bita's guardians. For "neither Jordan or Naomi Plant nor even the wags of Banana Bottom gave the slightest thought to that companionship. Crazy Bow was harmlessly light headed and none could imagine him capable of any natural aberration" (p. 8). Crazy Bow, though a strange being, still occupied a rational place in the imagination of the villagers and they trusted him. Yet, what this also shows is that they ignored his humanity and sexuality; they negated the existence of those instincts in Crazy Bow in the same manner that they suffocated his talent. Crazy Bow's friendship with Bita serves to highlight the rhetorical significance of "harmless insanity" and how this rhetorical moment in the narrative informs our understanding of Crazy Bow's humanity. Especially as the narrator describes Bita's passionate response to Crazy Bow's performance of a sweet tea meeting love song, "and as he played Bita went creeping upon her hands and feet up the slope to him and listened in the attitude of a bewitched being" (p. 10). It is Bita who has "lost her mind", bewitched by the beauty of Crazy Bow's music. Immediately after he completes his rendition, it is she who climbs on top of him, kissing his face. Even as Crazy Bow tries to stop her by pushing her off, "Bita hugged and clung to him passionately. Crazy Bow was blinded by temptation and lost control of himself and the deed was done" (p. 11). It is only at this juncture in the text that some level of aberration is recorded. It is the only time that Crazy Bow "lost control of himself", lost his rationality and, so, comes into conflict with his community. Ironically, he does not lose it voluntarily or violently because of some psychotic behaviour; the loss comes from the power his artistic creativity has upon others to drive them crazy. This is the same creative process that influenced the headmaster's decision to send him from school in the first place.

The Dionysian frenzy that takes hold of Bita led to Crazy Bow's transgression. The loss of control is not a measure of his madness but a measure of the seduction that was carefully orchestrated by the teenager. The incident is later described as a "rape" because Crazy Bow is twenty-five years old and Bita is only twelve or thirteen, clearly underage, and, by law, Crazy Bow can be charged with statutory rape. Crazy Bow is eventually punished for his violation; he is "arrested, tried in the criminal court, and sent to the madhouse" (p. 11). It seems contradictory and "criminal" that he is confined to the madhouse for what, in the final analysis, is considered a criminal act. The legal system, like the education that labels Crazy Bow mad in the first place, reaffirms this madness to support the ambivalence and irony that controls his creativity and artistic genius. Even as the villagers appreciated Crazy Bow's fine skills as a fiddler, they laughed at the idea of greatness in him or in themselves. The stranglehold of colonial cultural debasement convinced them that "greatness could not exist in the backwoods. Nor anywhere in the colony. To them and to all the islanders greatness was a foreign thing" (p. 8). The narrator's revelation of the psychosis of the village society highlights the entrenchment of colonial attitudes about that which is foreign and that which is native – where "foreign" defines things that are good, exemplary, imitable and celebratory, while "native" breeds revulsion, self-deprecation/hate, and disavowal. There is no reason for, or evidence of a possessive mentality that seeks to honour or preserve the local desire as "the force of positive production" or "the action that creates things"[18] or even the action that continues to dramatize the "performance of existential freedom[s]".[19]

Crazy Bow's "madness" emphasizes the unreliability and irony of language because it fails to contain him as a character without intelligible expressive capacity. He speaks overpoweringly with his music and mesmerizes all who come in contact with him. Crazy Bow is silent throughout the text; he only plays music, and it is the very thing that makes him an aberration or which names him "mad" in order to reverse the supremacy of language. What Crazy Bow's strange acts show is that he is actually a mirror of his society and that he speaks as the society, within reason and not outside of it. In essence madness "no longer adheres to its meaning; it stands at a distance from itself, takes a strategic step back from the condemnation it suffers [acting merely as] a social mask, a role to be played".[20] In other words, Crazy Bow's actions imply that his naming is foolish and arbitrary, absent of reason and lacking in perspective.[21] He also draws attention to those around him who only see in his character the hyperbolic, the excessive, the boundless flight away from the straight line.

Herald Newton Day – the heir apparent to the white missionaries, Priscilla and Malcolm Craig, who are Bita's adoptive parents after the rape incident – does not "go off the straight line" in the same artistic fashion as his village compatriot Crazy Bow. He seems to crumble under the psychological pressures of the colonial expectations to be a clergyman and a husband in an arranged marriage with Bita Plant. Herald had won a scholarship to a theological college and the expectation was that "as soon he was graduated[,] there would be a coveted place ready for him as assistant to Malcolm Craig" (p. 95). This was not the only coveted position that was awaiting him after his graduation. Bita was promised to him as well and the two were expected to continue the work of the two missionaries. Bita's betrothed was supposed to "herald a new day", having been trained to "constrain" himself and renounce his ways as a member of the peasant class. Thus, Herald Newton Day takes special care of his speech, his dress and his decorum, refusing to be, in manner or style, like the people he calls "bush villagers" (p. 99).

Herald is an example of what Frantz Fanon describes in *Black Skins, White Masks* as a symbol of "objecthood".[22] Newton Day embodies a bankrupt ontology. His sense of self is built on elements that are poorly conceived in mimicry of white progress, civilization and culture. Thus the self-loathing and disavowal of his blackness make him a "tight arsed" colonial who is also part of the Craigs' "work", part of their ministry to bring "Freedom and Light for the jungle folk" (p. 12). This ministry is also designed to help them reha-bilitate what Priscilla Craig describes as "the lack of restraint among them [the blacks]", especially because "sex was approached too easily" and "they were apparently incapable of comprehending the opprobrium of breeding bastards in a Christian community" (p. 16). Newton Day had become indoc-trinated into believing this version of the black self, and that devaluation of his cultural self leads him to suppress and silence not only his libido but his masculinity. Thus, he returns to Banana Bottom a restrained cleric who renounces the tea meetings of the community, the obeah practices of the peasants, and the music and speech of his fellow men. His ultimate desire is to be like a "pure-minded white lady", just like Mrs Craig, and this is not only his own dream but his dream for Bita as well. When he suggests this to Bita, she tells him that "whatever I was trained like or to be, I know one thing. And that is that I am myself" (p. 100). Herald Newton Day is not "himself" but a caricature of Caribbean colonial identity. He is a passive subject who has appropriated, wholesale, western cultural values, believing that whites "are all ahead . . . more modern and progressive and everything" (p. 169).

It is this desire to appropriate whiteness that results in Newton Day's mis-understanding of what his education means and leads him to defile a goat. There is no previous indication of Newton Day's loss of mental faculty nor is there any moment in the text, prior to the act of bestiality, which foreshadows his strange behaviour. What is ironic is that Herald Newton Day is the only one who is aware of his mental condition. Prior to the deed, he prepares for his sermon and the narrator claims he could be heard practising his sermon taken from Psalm 119, the longest psalm in the Bible. The emphasis Day places on his sermon suggests that he was both the speaker and the listener. The psalm itself is a meditation on the law of God, the need for His "servant" to commit, and follow His rules as a way of life and be obedient to His Word, His power and authority. While the details of Day's sermon are not revealed in the narrative, the portion of the psalm the narrator reveals questions whether he can commit to such a stupendous ritual. And these words are the only indication that Newton Day will in fact herald a new day by his actions:

Wherewithal shall a young man cleanse his ways . . .
By taking heed according to Thy Words . . .
With my whole heart . . .
Oh, let me not wander from Thy commandments

Newton Day seems to find his ascetic lifestyle a challenge and does not feel himself to be "pure in mind" or secure in his Christian ways. The question he asks about cleansing his ways is a rhetorical one; it verbalizes the peril of colonial inscription that the black body is overly sexual, impure and therefore immoral. Herald Newton Day must have been troubled by his previous encounter with Squire Gensir, an atheist and a British transplant who revels in the very practices of the folk that Day's religiosity, benefactors and education prohibit. Something in Day had been challenged to act differently and he was clearly wrestling with the "spirit" of power that had brainwashed him to silence his own ideals, his folk self.

Once again it is necessary to recall the moment prior to his descent "from the dizzy heights of holiness to the very bottom of the beast" (p. 175). Nearing the end of Newton Day and Bita's visit with Squire Gensir, Day confidently recommends the power of God as the source of intelligence that solves problems. The squire had no luck finding a very exotic orchid after searching for several hours and when he decided to look the next day, Newton Day tells him: "By God's help you will succeed in finding it sir." The narrator declares that Bita was "shaking from suppressed laughter" (p. 171) while the squire had a humorous expression on his face, which made Newton Day uncomfortable. Soon after, Bita begins to play on the piano what is only intimated by the narrator as a "popular" tune. The playful and provocative manner in which Bita "touched the keys at random with her left hand" suggests that she intended to play something that was not in harmony with Newton Day's pretentious palate and he would find repulsive, especially because Day had announced that "popular music does not stir me" (p. 172). As the chapter ends, it is evident to the discerning reader that Bita is going to "play" with Day's overwrought persona, if only to make him question and re-evaluate his own ontology.

The author deliberately leaves us wondering about the effect this entire experience has on him, because we are taken to his preparation for his sermon, described by the third person narrator. Newton Day is thus rendered a passive subject in this scene: he does not speak, and his distancing from the narrative heightens his internal conflict as he prepares the sermon. In fact, this technique increases the level of speculation about his act, and makes the perception of madness regarding his act, gossip and hearsay. In the end, he is spirited away by his father out of the country as if this incident had not happened in the first place. This moment creates a flaw in the narrative because his transgression, while it reflects a rebellious tendency, is not sustained because Newton Day is not present in the community to use the act as an instrument of his own relief. By writing Day out of the text, McKay leaves the door open for madness to be used as an explanation for the character's act of bestiality. Thus Day is not clinically mad when he is caught mating with the nanny goat and neither is he amnesiac as Squire Gensir claims, but he is fully conscious when "ministering" a new word to the public, one which – even though it materializes through the most bizarre of circumstances – destroys the racist myth that the colonized Negro is a tabula rasa or has no individual will.

The narrator informs us in chapter 17 that Newton Day was frequently heard during the week rehearsing his sermon, and that the schoolmaster and his wife were both disturbed and annoyed by Newton Day's pacing in his room. His actions speak to the internal conflict he was wrestling and the decision he must have been contemplating as he emphasized the sub-headings of his sermon:

> How youth should go cleansed before the Lord . . .
> Avoiding the pitfalls of youth . . .
> The personal purity of the body . . .

of the soul . . .
of the spirit . . .
of the mind . . .
The attainment of purity
by daily meditation . . .
by constant prayer . . .
by thinking purely . . .
by watchful vigilance against corrupting influences.
by wrestling with God for the Beauty of Holiness. (pp. 173–74)

Herald Newton Day was not only wrestling with God's ways but also with the ways his education had prescribed that he should express his black body. He was inundated with or subsumed by statements that inscribed within him hate for his material and spiritual self. It is through his service to the "ministry", and his own servility and mimicry of whiteness, that he would perpetuate this message of self-hatred by continuing to communicate it to his congregation. It is the perception of the black body as dirty, the mind as impure/corrupt, and the spirit as unholy that makes Day seek this military routine to attain a Hegelian notion of ontology. However, as Fanon argues in *Black Skins*, not only does the colonized body experience his ontology through others but "every ontology is made unattainable in a colonized and civilized society".[23] Fanon's assertion exposes Newton Day's condition and ultimately the reason behind his actions. For the character does not regress by having sex with the goat; rather, he consciously orchestrates the act to reject the racially denigrated self by using one of the very notions that had been imposed on him in the most extreme fashion. It is not that Newton Day proposes a new self as a result of his actions, but it is how he uses unreason to make reason. His "madness", then, is what I call *proposed*, because his actions are internally mobilized by a series of conscious and unconscious stimuli wherein the subject reasons deliberately, but not necessarily in plain sight, to secure access to another way of being.

Day's action suggests madness but it is the method of his action that makes others perceive his madness. Day is at odds with the rules of colonial law and authority which conditioned the people to accept obedience and servitude. The "non-being" that he becomes as a result of this "training" frustrates his ability to act in rhythm or ultimately connect with those around him. So the fact that he chooses a Sunday, the day of worship, to commit his sin, is deliberately meant to shock the community but it also symbolically disrobes him. This emphasizes how Day was fooled only for a time by this law but deceives both reason and colonial law in this moment by refusing to become mad. Thus, when his act is carefully analysed, in this light, it reveals, in fact, that he is rebelling against the madness of colonization.

It is symbolic because, by taking out his sexual and personal frustrations on the goat, he calls attention to the ways in which the Bible is the frontispiece of a repressive colonial ideological tool. His sinful act insults the "Work" of the Craigs and confounds the systems of ontology that govern how the "natives" should live. Ultimately, his "crazy" act provides a back door to a new consciousness that cancels out what the cultural historian Rex Nettleford describes in *Mirror, Mirror* as the "predetermined victory of Europe", and dispels the belief that the colonial subjects are "deprived of individual wills and are seen as exact mirrors of this parlous state of existence".[24] So even though Newton Day's bizarre act defies logic and the villagers spread the rumour that he "had suddenly turned crazy and defiled himself with a nanny goat", he is shipped off to Panama to avoid the "law".[25] The law is, however, turned on its head and that in itself is "crazy", for the natives are supposed to obey both God and His benefactors. Priscilla Craig feels that "she herself has failed", and remarks to her husband Malcolm that "our work here is wasted. All our giving freely of our money and ourselves. Spending, planning, building – all broken down and buried in the mire" (178–79).

Herald Newton Day now exists outside of the law. His act is what makes him "mad" and Squire Gensir, the rebel English transplant, offers a compelling theory about what had happened to the young cleric. "His theory was that the case of Herald Newton Day might be attributed to temporary amnesia, the result of too much exclusive concentration on sacred textbooks and holy communion" (p. 177). The author then quotes the invective that the governor of Judea, Porcius Festus, utters in front of Caesar while St Paul is being tried for preaching the Gospel to the Gentiles: "Paul, too much learning hath made thee mad" (Acts 26:24).[26] McKay leaves out Paul's rebuttal to Festus: "I am not mad, most noble Festus; but speak forth the words of truth and soberness" (Acts 26:25).[27] The comment from Acts 26:24 shows how Festus's perception frames education as a threat to Paul's reason and reputation. His comment to Paul reflects on a long-standing myth floating within the peasantry in Jamaica that one can become crazy from too much "book learning". The hidden script behind such a comment highlights a lingering suspicion that is born from imperial domination and abuse. This kind of suspicion is dramatized in the sparse resources and schools that were provided on the island post-emancipation or the prejudicial and paternalistic process that was engineered to offer higher education to those who were most talented. Furthermore education, like religion, was used to manage the cultural discourse around race, class and place in both colonial and postcolonial Jamaica. By injecting Festus's invective at this point in the text, McKay ironizes Day's sin to highlight the fact that Day is indeed culpable for being so wantonly devoted to a religious identity and a cultural aesthetic that is itself unreliable. Madness in this postcolonial sense is a complex display wherein the performer, in this case Newton Day, exercises freedom from certain archetypes, essentially throwing those stereotypes, concepts and expectations of the colonization into madness.[28]

Claude McKay creates his characters out of a Caribbean cultural realism that highlights a hybrid culture that was, at the time of his novel, wrestling with ways to define its New World Africanity, as much as its individual identity. It seems to be his characters' natures to expose the cultural and personal dilemmas that education, religion and modernity on a grander scale offer up as part of the challenge in the discovery of ontological existence. Madness is a useful mirror for examining some of perceptions of this new world Africanity that is being formed amid the angst of colonial rule and economic depression. McKay shows, through his two characters, Crazy Bow Adair and Herald Newton Day, how colonial education did much to continue the work of slavery and imperialism, and confine its subjects within "immoral" bodies and recalcitrant minds. Whether it is conscious or not, McKay develops these two characters without the embellished philosophical or delusional component that is reminiscent of Shakespeare's mad men (Othello, Macbeth, King Lear) and provides us with ordinary men who look like the people around them. In this manner, he illustrates how the island space refracts the notion of madness, and corrupts and subjects its meaning to ambiguity through arbitrary and dynamic definitions: madness is more than clinical and not at the same time. It can in the context of the Caribbean

space exist in plain sight, as with Crazy Bow, and it can be "borrowed", as in
the case of Herald Newton Day, to communicate a radical or bizarre point.
At the same time, the novel provides a sort of lens through which one can
observe the diasporic community constructing a unique reality conditioned
by time, place and circumstances.

NOTES

1. Lillian Feder, *Madness in Literature* (Princeton: Princeton University Press, 1980), xii.
2. Wilson Harris, *The Womb of Space: The Cross Cultural Imagination* (Westport, CT: Greenwood, 1983).
3. Feder, *Madness*, xiii.
4. Wilson Harris, "Literacy and the Imagination: A Talk", in *Selected Essays of Wilson Harris: The Unfinished Genesis of Imagination*, ed. Andrew Bundy (London: Routledge, 1999), 77.
5. Feder, *Madness*, xi.
6. See Harris, "Literacy and the Imagination".
7. Cited in Shoshana Felman, *Writing and Madness*, tr. Martha Noel Evans and Brian Massumi (Ithaca: Cornell University Press, 1985), 14.
8. Ibid., 12.
9. Harris, *Womb of Space*, xvii.
10. Antonio Benítez Rojo, *The Repeating Island: The Caribbean and the Postmodern Perspective*, trans. James E. Maraniss (Durham: Duke University Press, 1997), 3.
11. Feder, *Writing and Madness*, 9.
12. Ibid., 9.
13. Ibid., 5.
14. Ibid., 8.
15. Claude McKay, *Banana Bottom* (London: Serpent's Tail, 2005), 1. Subsequent references are to this edition and appear parenthetically in the text.
16. Feder, *Madness*, 7.
17. Winston James, *A Fierce Hatred of Injustice: Claude McKay's Jamaica and His Poetry of Rebellion* (London: Verso, 2000), 43.
18. Elizabeth A. Grosz, *Space, Time, and Perversion: Essays on the Politics of Bodies* (London: Routledge, 1995), 179.
19. Claudia Tate, *Psychoanalysis and Black Novels: Desire and the Protocols of Race* (New York: Oxford University Press, 1998), 10.

20.   Felman, *Writing and Madness*, 82.

21.   Felman argues that the generalized and relativized nature of madness makes it "nothing more than an effect of perspective"; ibid., 84. I use the term "perspective" to reflect on the nature of madness but with the implication that it reflects an absence of perspective, not necessarily the loss of perspective; you cannot lose what was never visibly present in the first place.

22.   Frantz Fanon, *Black Skins, White Masks*, tr. Charles Lam Markmann (New York: Grove, 1967), 109.

23.   Ibid.

24.   Rex Nettleford, *Mirror, Mirror: Identity, Race and Protest in Jamaica* (Kingston: LMH Publishing, 2000), 188.

25.   This migration is an act of redemption for Newton Day, and at the same time his migration highlights the kind of transnational movements taking place in the Caribbean at this time. McKay uses Day's flight to Panama to call attention to the waves of post-emancipation and pre–World War I migrations to Latin American (Venezuela and Costa Rica), Cuba, Canada and the American south. These men and women left to help construct railways and work in mines, on banana and sugar plantations, and tobacco fields. This particular movement of labourers from Jamaica and other Caribbean islands to places other than England signifies a cultural shift in colonial attitudes away from Englishness.

26.   It should be noted that McKay took liberties here with the King James version, omitting parts of the verse to satisfy his novelistic representation. The full version in the King James Bible reads as follows: "And as he thus spake for himself, Festus said with a loud voice, Paul thou art beside thyself; much learning doth make thee mad."

27.   Newton Day is silent and is not present to offer a rebuttal, like Paul, for the bestiality he performs in the text and for which he is called crazy.

28.   See Fanon, *Black Skins*, 35.

CHAPTER 10

THE CARIBBEAN DIASPORA AND BLACK INTERNATIONALISM

WINSTON JAMES

GEORGE SHEPPERSON, THE DISTINGUISHED SCOTTISH HISTORIAN of Africa and the African diaspora, noted half a century ago that the "persistence" of what he dubbed "the West Indian factor" in pan-African movements was "remarkable". A few years later, Imanuel Geiss, the German author of the most ambitious history of pan-Africanism, similarly observed that "The West Indies were the breeding ground of such men as E[dward] W[ilmot] Blyden, Sylvester Williams, Marcus Garvey, George Padmore, all of whom played a prominent role in the history of Pan-Africanism." Geiss added, for good measure, that "Du Bois' father came from the West Indies". Shepperson also made the important observation, albeit *en passant*, that the emergence of pan-Africanism has largely been through "English-speaking agencies".[1] Both Shepperson and Geiss agreed that the ideology of pan-Africanism did not take articulate form in the Portuguese language, or in Spanish, Dutch or French, but in English. The ideological formation was, as Geiss put it, "largely an English-speaking affair".[2] Neither Shepperson nor Geiss ventured an explanation; both seemed rather perplexed by the phenomenon they noticed and recorded.[3] How may we account for this striking phenomenon in the story of the African diaspora and its key ideological expression, pan-Africanism? Why the prominence of West Indians and why the dominant medium of English in the pan-Africanist saga?

While the pan-Africanist contribution of individuals from the anglophone Caribbean has long been recognized by scholars, surprisingly, no one has systematically documented, analysed or explained the pattern of this contribution to pan-Africanist projects over time and space. My work over the last decade or so has largely been focused on the Caribbean diaspora and, in particular, the latter's intriguing role in radical political discourses and practices within the wider African diaspora and the Atlantic world. In this chapter I hope to share some findings and reflections on the role of the Caribbean diaspora, and – given the widely acknowledged English-speaking character of the movement – especially that of the anglophone Caribbean in pan-Africanism and pan-Africanist efforts. I want, in particular, to look beyond the experience of Caribbean people in the United States, the subject of my earlier book, *Holding Aloft the Banner of Ethiopia*, and instead register the direct and little-known contribution of the Caribbean diaspora on the African continent itself, from the early nineteenth century to the moment of decolonization in the middle of the twentieth century.[4] I wish to provide evidence of the disproportionate role of African-Caribbean people in pan-Africanist projects on the African continent, and second, to put forward an explanation for this phenomenon. In short, I want to at least begin a discussion of those questions left unasked and therefore unanswered by Shepperson, Geiss and indeed others.

It is a remarkable, and in many ways astonishing, fact that an area as small as the Caribbean, physically as well as demographically, should produce such an outstanding roster of pan-African intellectuals and political activists: John Brown Russwurm, Edward Blyden, John Jacob Thomas, Theophilus Scholes, Henry Sylvester Williams, Hubert Harrison, Marcus Garvey, Amy Ashwood Garvey, Amy Jacques Garvey, C.L.R. James, Ras Makonnen, Claude McKay and George Padmore, to name just a few; this list reveals just the tip of the iceberg, limited, as it is, to only a small sample of some of the most well-known activists from the English-speaking areas of the archipelago up to the mid-twentieth century.

But before documenting and offering an explanation of the phenomenon, we need to be clear about what I mean by pan-Africanism and black internationalism. By pan-Africanism, I mean the basic set of beliefs that (1) people of African descent have a common ancestral home (Africa); (2) they share a history of oppression at the hands of non-Africans, mainly of European descent; (3) they constitute a nation (even one without a state); (4) that it is right to extend solidarity to fellow Africans at home and abroad, thus transcending national, linguistic and juridical boundaries. Aligned with this set of beliefs are practices and ideologies aimed at the realization of black solidarity – "attempts by African peoples to link up their struggles for their mutual benefit", as Tony Martin puts it.[5] It should be added, however, that such attempts need not take collective organizational form. Pan-African efforts can be highly informal and sometimes even operate at the level of individual endeavour. It is noteworthy, too, that the practitioners and advocates of pan-Africanism included many who also regarded themselves as socialists, even Marxists, and not just those who defined themselves as black nationalists. Thus it is perfectly legitimate to include the socialists Claude McKay and C.L.R. James as well as the black nationalists Edward Blyden and Marcus Garvey among the pantheon of pan-Africanists. Pan-Africanism, in this light, may be seen as the highest level of black internationalism, the latter being defined as the ideological manifestation of an "imagined community" of peoples of African descent, one which transcends the boundaries of nation states and empires.[6]

The term "pan-Africanism" is of surprisingly recent vintage. There is no evidence of its usage before Henry Sylvester Williams and his colleagues established the African Association in London in 1897 and soon thereafter began planning the Pan-African Conference of 1900.[7] But if the term is relatively new, the sentiment and practices associated with it go back at least to the beginning of the transatlantic slave trade, and the forced migration of Africans to the New World at the beginning of the sixteenth century.

Pan-Africanism cannot be properly understood without appreciating the responses of different segments of the African diaspora to its appeal and dissemination. Scholars generally speak of the African diaspora in the singular, but for analytical purposes I have become more and more convinced that we ought to speak of diasporas. It might even be preferable to avoid the term, singular and plural, altogether. For, despite the broadly common provenance and experience of slavery, the variation in the transformation and evolution of African peoples in the Americas, let alone Asia, is so profound that it is sensible to be very cautious about generalizations. Unfortunately, there are too many glib and ignorant generalizations on the subject. The experience of one particular national or regional group of the African diaspora, usually that of the United States of America, is often extrapolated to the rest – despite the fact that the black experience in the United States is the most atypical of Africans in the Americas.

It is not insignificant that Africans in the Americas came from widely differing parts of the continent; that the slave trade ended in 1808 in some parts and the 1860s in others; that slavery ended in 1838 in one area and 1888 in another; that some slaves had greater autonomy in the labour process than others – for instance, ranching in Cuba, diamond mining in Brazil and toiling on sugar plantations in Barbados required quite different forms of labour with different work regimens, and thus had different implications for the evolution of those societies, their cultures and the groups involved. Additionally, the character of the post-emancipation settlement varied, and the economic and political transformation that issued from them in the post-emancipation period cannot be ignored. It is with the consciousness of such broad variations that the Caribbean experience should be viewed as a subset.

Few societies in human history, and virtually none since the beginning of the modern period, have been as profoundly shaped and marked by the phenomenon of migration as the Caribbean. Hardly any places on the planet have had its indigenous population so rapidly decimated and replaced by outsiders – by Europeans of various nationalities, by Africans during the slave trade, by indentured labourers from different parts of Asia (India, China, Java), and by Levantines in the post-slavery period, among others. To the present day, the movement in, within and out of the region continues. The flow, however, had been decidedly outward in the twentieth century. Despite, and to a great extent because, of the massive level of inward Asian migration in the immediate post-slavery period, ever since the late nineteenth century the Caribbean, particularly the anglophone region, has generated a disproportionately large, second African diaspora – a diaspora of a diaspora, so to speak.

The Caribbean diaspora began soon after Columbus arrived, with the capture and removal of indigenous people from the Bahamas and other "useless islands" – as the Spanish dubbed them – to work in the gold mines of Hispaniola. But this intra-Caribbean diaspora expanded dramatically in the seventeenth century, when British slaveholders in Barbados took their slaves with them as they populated and colonized more and more islands and the British North American mainland, most notably Virginia and South

Carolina. Even after the British abolished the slave trade in 1807, some twenty thousand slaves were traded between British Caribbean colonies, largely illicitly but often with the connivance of the British colonial authorities.[8] But it was in the aftermath of slavery that this intra-Caribbean diaspora became even more far-flung and, in fact, became a decidedly extra-Caribbean one as well. Within the British Caribbean itself, Trinidad and Guyana, by virtue of their more robust post-emancipation economies, served as magnets for overexploited workers as well as some members of the black intelligentsia of the eastern Caribbean, especially Barbados. Cuba, the Dominican Republic, Puerto Rico, Haiti, North America, Central America, Venezuela, Brazil, and western, central and southern Africa were some of the key points of circulation and settlement. Some, mainly students and seamen, made their way to Europe; others went as far as Australia during the gold rush, as did others to California.[9] And at least one, James Patterson from St Vincent, went as far as Tahiti to serve as a Seventh Day Adventist missionary after previously living for many years in northern California. Patterson then lived in Panama City before returning to St Vincent where he died.[10] Others worked in British India and Ceylon (Sri Lanka), some even ended up in China. Ras Makonnen, a keen observer of the Caribbean diaspora, reported that after the Second World War a number of Barbadians, former seamen, were found living with their Japanese wives in Japan. "Wherever you go in the world", declared Makonnen, "you will find a Bimsha – a Barbadian".[11] There is even island lore, probably apocryphal but no less instructive, of a Bajan (as the Barbadian is commonly called) found running a restaurant in Jerusalem![12] It is therefore apt that it was a Barbadian poet-historian, Edward Kamau Brathwaite, who lamented in wonderment:

> Never seen
> a man
> travel more
> seen more
> lands
> than this poor
> path-
> less harbour-
> less spade.[13]

No other national grouping of Africans in the Americas – not those in the United States, not those in the Spanish Caribbean, not those in Brazil, and not even those in the French territories – has produced such a large and widely scattered diaspora as the British Caribbean. Moreover, it is a centuries-old, secular phenomenon, and it continues to this very day with even greater intensity and no sign of abating. Significantly, although this diaspora included important segments of the Afro-Caribbean intelligentsia, it was overwhelmingly proletarian and comprised a significant component of the skilled artisanry. Its relative size, class composition and wide range of destinations are easily explained.

From its small beginnings in the seventeenth century, and even after the loss of its North American colonies and before Latin American independence, Britain had emerged as the largest and most powerful imperial force. It is sad, but true, that Britannia did rule the waves. At its height, the British empire ruled over a fifth of the world's peoples (almost 460 million in 1922) and exercised dominion over almost a quarter of the planet's total land area. During its heyday, it was the largest empire in history. Though contested by Germany and the United States, especially in the early twentieth century, Britain did not lose its formal world hegemony until the hurricane of post-war anticolonialism blew the Union Jack to shreds. It was their peculiar membership in this far-flung imperial system – one on which the sun never set – that enabled Afro-Caribbeans such easy access and mobility to countries around the globe.

In the Western Hemisphere, especially in the late nineteenth and early twentieth centuries, American capital from the United States – with its preference for an English-speaking, readily available and low-waged proletariat habituated to the rigours of plantation labour – exacerbated the incidence of anglophone black diaspora dispersals to Cuba, the Dominican Republic and Puerto Rico, over which it ruled, *de facto* if not *de jure*. Similarly, American capital – through the agency of the Isthmian Canal Commission in Panama and the United Fruit Company throughout the rest of the isthmus – stimulated the migration, especially of Barbadian and Jamaican workers, to toil on the canal in Panama and the banana plantations of Central America. But even in this emergent US sphere of influence inspired by the Monroe Doctrine, John Bull still had the capacity in the late nineteenth and early twentieth centuries to pull along the Caribbean proletariat with him on his capitalist adventures to Putamayo and northeastern Brazil.[14] In West Africa, Caribbean emigrants – workers, missionaries, colonial civil servants – settled in Lagos, the Gold Coast, Sierra Leone and Liberia among other places. By the end of the nineteenth century, colonies of Jamaicans and Barbadians could be found in the southern African seaports, chiefly Capetown and Luderitz, in today's Namibia.

The dispersal of Caribbean people was facilitated by a remarkably thick network of transportation in the late nineteenth and early twentieth centuries. Bridgetown, Barbados, since the seventeenth century had served as the first port of call for British ships coming across the Atlantic. This advantage of its being the point of first landfall developed over the centuries to make Barbados into the "Clapham Junction of the West Indies" by the end of the nineteenth century, with shipping networks extending to all parts of the Americas and the world.[15] Bridgetown was the busiest port in the British Caribbean, with facilities and connections far better than those in any other island in the eastern Caribbean. It is not surprising, then, that when Ras Makonnen and his friends decided to go to Oriente in Cuba in the 1920s they first left Georgetown, British Guiana, on a small boat to Bridgetown for a ship to Cuba. And it was back in Bridgetown that they caught another boat for New Orleans. Similarly, Hugh Mulzac left Union Island in the Grenadines for Bridgetown in order to serve on a ship that would take him to the United States. During the building of the Panama Canal, Caribbean workers from eastern Caribbean islands, such as St Kitts, typically caught boats to Central America from Bridgetown. It was therefore not just the intolerable conditions which prevailed in Barbados, nor the existence of opportunity for work abroad that accounted for the extraordinary migrant stream from Barbados. An indispensable element that accounts for the large numbers leaving Barbados for far-flung destinations (some settled as far away as Japan and South Africa) was that the working classes of that country had almost unique access to relatively cheap transportation to a bewildering variety of different points on the globe. Barbados also had more than its fair share of black seamen plying the seas, many of whom abandoned the peripatetic life and settled far away from home.[16] Jamaica, in the western Caribbean, had also benefited from an extensive shipping network since its capture by the

British in 1655. At the end of the nineteenth century this was augmented by the development of the banana trade.[17]

Domestically the islands, especially Jamaica and Barbados, adapted institutionally to mass migration during these years; for migration, especially on the scale that it occurred in these small islands, required and induced transformations of family forms and kinship networks, especially as they related to child rearing and child care, during these pivotal decades.[18] Having established, largely inadvertently, these vectors for communicating both people and ideas, the anglophone Caribbean diaspora, not surprisingly, was positioned to play – and did play – a disproportionately large role in the spread of pan-Africanist ideas. The fact that they enjoyed a higher rate of literacy compared to their counterparts in the United States, Brazil and the Spanish- and French-speaking Caribbean, facilitated and enhanced their role in the dissemination of these ideas. Largely unaccustomed, in their native islands, to the naked racism they encountered in various parts of the world – the hostility in Oriente province in Cuba, the Jim Crow crackerdom of the Canal Zone in Panama (most of their supervisors on the canal were unreconstructed white racists from the southern states of the United States), the apartheid in Cape Town before Apartheid, and the sheer brutality of colonial rule in western and central Africa – these Caribbean men and women played a major role in transforming pan-Africanism from a largely inchoate and unarticulated political and cultural sensibility to a modern political ideology, movement and social project.

But the circumstances and forces that I have just outlined – *de facto* membership of the largest empire, economic hardship in the Caribbean islands, extraordinary mobility and willingness to migrate to distant places, the encounter with more brutal forms of racism than that to which they were accustomed at home, high levels of literacy among those who emigrated (even among the proletarians) – all contributed to the prominence of what Shepperson called the "West Indian factor" in the history of pan-Africanism, and to the explanation of why pan-Africanism was, as Geiss put it, "largely an English-speaking affair".[19]

The pan-Africanist efforts were not confined to work in the Americas and Europe; these Caribbean nationals also did excellent work in Africa itself, especially in western and southern Africa.[20] John Brown Russwurm

(1799–1851), born in Port Antonio, Jamaica, made his contribution both in the United States and Liberia; Edward Wilmot Blyden (1832–1912), from St Thomas, Virgin Islands, made his all over West Africa, but especially Liberia and Sierra Leone, where he settled, and also in the diaspora through the sheer power of his intellect and force of his ideas, which were widely disseminated; Robert Campbell (1829–84), another remarkable Jamaican, made his in both the United States and Nigeria, but mainly Nigeria. Campbell had partnered African American black nationalist Martin Delany (1812–85) on the Niger Valley Exploring Party (1859–60), to seek a site of African American settlement in Abeokuta (Nigeria). Both men returned to the United States in 1860 intent on recruiting fellow African Americans to settle in Nigeria. But after the outbreak of the Civil War in 1861, Delany abandoned the idea. Campbell, however, decided to return to his "motherland" with his wife and children. He spent his remaining years in Nigeria.[21]

Russwurm, Campbell and Blyden were pioneers, but they were by no means the only Caribbeans to figure in the annals of pan-African dissent in nineteenth-century Africa. Other distinguished figures appeared in western, central and southern Africa. A number of historians, most notably Christopher Fyfe and Nemata Blyden, have highlighted the extraordinary role that Caribbean immigrants played in the struggle on the continent, especially in Sierra Leone.[22] Thus, a fuller account of the role played by these immigrants (such as William Ferguson, Alexander Fitzjames, William Drape and William Rainy) is now possible. Drape and Rainy in particular made profound contributions to the articulation of pan-Africanism through legal advocacy and the medium of the press.

Drape started the first black newspaper, the *New Era*, in Sierra Leone in 1855. Its outspokenness about government policy in the colony attracted the enmity of the governor, who unsuccessfully sought its suppression.[23] It was Drape's successful struggle against the heavy hand of Governor Hill in Sierra Leone in 1857 that saved Campbell's newspaper, *Anglo-African*, in Nigeria from being strangled at birth in 1863 and helped to launch other dissenting newspapers in British West Africa in subsequent years.[24] Russwurm was the great pioneer in African journalism, effectively founding the *Liberia Herald* in 1830, after having earlier co-founded and edited America's first black newspaper, *Freedom's Journal*, in 1827.[25]

Rainy, born in Dominica and trained as a barrister in London, was by far the most formidable Caribbean opponent of colonial despotism in Sierra Leone in the mid-nineteenth century. In addition, he boldly raised his voice against the rising tide of pseudo-scientific racism in the second half of the century. He was so incensed by Sir Richard Burton's racist diatribe, *Wanderings in West Africa* (1863), which targeted the educated African in particular, that he penned his own riposte in the form of a pamphlet.[26] Rainy could not stand silently by and observe what he called "the wide-spread conspiracy" to "lower the negro in the scale of creation".[27] His eyes were trained not only upon Africa, but, like Campbell's, upon developments in the Americas, especially the events surrounding the Morant Bay Rebellion in Jamaica and its bloody suppression.[28] More explicitly than others in Sierra Leone at the time, he expressed a pan-African vision aimed at creating "a spirit of nationality in Africa", and sought to induce others to follow his example. "We have the cause of Africa at heart", he declared in 1866, "and shall welcome every labourer in the field who honestly strives to establish it and strengthen it".[29] Described by a Sierra Leonean correspondent to the London-based *African Times* as "our indefatigable and warm-hearted advocate and champion", Rainy was also a hero elsewhere in West Africa. In 1871 he fell ill and left for London in July. He never returned to Sierra Leone.[30] His friends at the *African Times* recognized the loss that his departure from Africa meant for Sierra Leone and West Africa in general, and implored Sierra Leoneans to continue the struggle. As the *African Times* editorialized, "It is difficult to obtain the removal of officials however evil their course may be . . . but persistent efforts for their removal, such as Mr. Rainy has made, will at least prevent any perpetuation, in the persons of subsequent officials, of these abominations which they may have practised; and we are sure that in the future African Pantheon the name of 'Rainy' will be prominently inscribed by a grateful people."[31] From London, Rainy immigrated to Australia, where he had spent time in the 1850s, and died near Melbourne in 1878.[32]

Persons of Caribbean origin also played an important part in the anticolonial struggle in the Gold Coast in the latter part of the nineteenth century and the first decades of the twentieth century. Their contribution was remarkable – William Finlason, Francis Grant, George Christian and the Barbadian-born bishop John B. Small made their mark in this part of West Africa.[33]

In Nigeria, too, after Robert Campbell's death in Lagos, other Caribbeans, particularly Edward Ricketts (Jamaica) and John Amblestone (Dominica) kept up the pan-Africanist project there over a period of time stretching from the late nineteenth century to the twentieth century.[34]

The year 1897 is a particularly important one in the history of pan-Africanism, for, in that year, Henry Sylvester Williams (1869–1911), a Trinidadian law student, started the African Association in London, right in the heart of the largest empire. This organization aspired to give formal expression to pan-Africanist sentiment and aspirations. By organizing the historic Pan-African Conference in London in 1900, the first of its kind, Williams opened the new century with a resolute gathering of people of African descent from the diaspora and the continent. The association did not last beyond 1902, but its legacy was rich and enduring. Williams himself continued to agitate on behalf of oppressed black humanity – including a stint in Cape Town, where he practised as its first black barrister – right up to his untimely death in Trinidad at the age of forty-two.[35]

The First World War and its aftermath galvanized new forces in a pan-African effort. In London, another Trinidadian, Felix Hercules, was one of the founders of the Society of Peoples of African Origin, bringing together Africans and others of the diaspora living in Britain. He, in fact, served as the general secretary of that society and as associate secretary of a similar organization, the African Progress Union, before the two merged in 1919. Hercules edited the organization's magazine, the *African Telegraph*, and was uncompromising in championing the cause of African people around the world. To the alarm of the Colonial Office and the governors in the British West Indies, Hercules made a tour of the region and forcefully expressed the pan-Africanist aspirations of the Society of Peoples of African Origin. He was frequently made a scapegoat for the labour unrests in the Caribbean in 1919. The African Telegraph was sued for libel by the colonial authorities and was thus pushed into bankruptcy. Pleased with this victory, the colonialists were further relieved when Hercules migrated to the United States after his Caribbean tour.[36]

Far more enduring was the effort of Marcus Garvey and his Universal Negro Improvement Association (UNIA). Although Garvey was never able to set foot on African soil, his organization had a profound impact on the nationalist struggles on the continent, especially in western and southern Africa. And here, once again, one finds the mobilization of Caribbean immigrants on the continent, this time through the agency of the UNIA.[37] In Lagos, the centre of UNIA activity in West Africa, the president of the organization was Wynter Shackleford, a Jamaican immigrant, and the treasurer was Amblestone, from Dominica.[38] In southern Africa, Arthur McKinley and J.G. Gumbs, two Afro-Caribbeans, were leading members of Garvey's organization. Gumbs was also vice president and later president of the Industrial and Commercial Workers Union, the primary working-class organization in southern Africa at the time. In southwest Africa (now Namibia), Fitz Herbert Headley and John De Clue, both immigrants from the Caribbean, founded and led the UNIA in Lüderitz, the main port city in the territory, and later Windhoek. The list is not exhaustive. One of the remarkable features of this group in southern Africa, unlike that in Lagos, for instance, was that they were deeply involved in the working-class movement, and saw no contradiction between their black nationalism and radical trade unionism.[39]

The crises of the Great Depression and the Italian invasion of Ethiopia in 1935 brought another Trinidadian to the fore one of the most distinguished pan-Africanists of the twentieth century, George Padmore (1902–59), who came from Arouca, the same Trinidadian town in which Henry Sylvester Williams was born. He studied in the United States at Fisk and Howard universities, where his already radical inclinations became more pronounced. After joining the Communist Party he eventually became, in 1929, the head of the Negro Bureau of the Red International of Labour Unions (Profintern), the international trade union affiliate of the Communist International (Comintern), based in Moscow. Disillusioned with Stalin's disinclination to support the anticolonial struggle, he left the Communist movement in 1935 and settled in London. There, he launched the International African Service Bureau with like-minded Caribbeans and Africans, most notably C.L.R. James and Ras Makonnen. The bureau agitated against colonial oppression in Africa and the Caribbean, and was particularly vocal about the devastation of Ethiopia and its people by Mussolini's fascist troops. Padmore also drew attention to the complicity – through inaction – of the other members of the League of Nations, especially Britain and the United States, in the suffering of the Ethiopian people.

Padmore's office and small flat in central London virtually became the ideological workshop of the African anticolonial struggle. Kwame Nkrumah and Jomo Kenyatta were two of the more distinguished African nationalists to pass through their apprenticeship under Padmore's guidance. Padmore later served as Nkrumah's advisor on African affairs in the newly independent Ghana. In 1959 he became ill, travelled to London for treatment and, at the age of fifty-seven, died there under mysterious circumstances.[40] C.L.R. James went so far as to call Padmore, "the father of African Independence".

So, how do we account for the disproportionate (given the size of the British Caribbean population at the time and the relatively small number who went to Africa) contribution of Caribbean people to these pan-Africanist projects? The fact that this question has never been adequately addressed is probably due to the complex nature of the answer. I think the following summary points may help us towards an understanding of this striking phenomenon.

First, the Caribbean diaspora was among the most far-flung and widely travelled peoples since the end of the slave trade. This was especially true of Jamaicans and Barbadians, whose lives in the post-emancipation period became especially difficult, even by Caribbean standards. Second, related to this were the limited economic options in the British Caribbean because of the generally depressed state of its economies in the late nineteenth and early twentieth centuries. Third, the desire to emigrate was facilitated by a vast transportation network linked to Caribbean port cities, especially Bridgetown and Kingston.

A fourth point is that many sought new opportunities in Africa and elsewhere because of the racist attitudes that impeded advancement in the Caribbean. Black professionals, for example, endured severe restrictions in relation to whether or not they were allowed to work in the colonial civil service in the Caribbean, and at what level. But on migration to Panama, Cuba, the Dominican Republic, the United States and even Africa, they also met with racism; perhaps they felt an even greater legitimacy in resisting racist and colonial structures in Africa, their ancestral home, and became determined to wrest a homeland – the "motherland", as Campbell called the continent – from the grip of the imperialists. As the peripatetic Barbadian doctor, J. Albert Thorne put it in 1896, "Africa is the only quarter of the world where we will be permanently respected as a race."[41] Thus the desire to create a liberated oasis in a desert of oppression was a compelling force. A century before Garvey, Russwurm spoke of the need to establish an "asylum" for the diaspora on the continent.

A fifth point is that there was a greater willingness on the part of Caribbean intellectuals and workers to settle in Africa than among many of their American counterparts. It is interesting to note that Martin Delany decided to stay in the United States while his Jamaican partner and friend, Robert Campbell, returned to Nigeria. Blyden made Africa his home; the Afro-American Alexander Crummell, Blyden's close friend and collaborator, decided, after almost twenty years of living in Liberia, to return to the United States.[42] Afro-Americans generally thought that the United States could be a good place to live, if only it could be reformed. Caribbean people had little hope of transforming the Caribbean and even less hope for the United States, so they generally decided to stay in Africa in larger proportions. In addition, Caribbean people arguably had a closer cultural affinity with Africa and Africans than did African Americans. This is in large part due to the fact that towards the end of the eighteenth century, the African American population became self-reproducing; the first country in the New World to achieve that distinction. Thus the transatlantic slave trade was less important for the United States, while in the Caribbean there was a continual infusion of new blood, replenishment, from Africa as the slave population died out. Because of this, the United States had the most creolized black population in the Americas; the societies of the British Caribbean, in contrast, had a higher proportion of African-born people at the end of slavery. This was especially true of Trinidad, Guyana and Jamaica. Moreover, so-called liberated Africans – those taken from Spanish, Portuguese and Brazilian slave ships after 1808 by the British Navy – were resettled in the thousands in the Caribbean right up to the 1860s.[43] This brought another infusion of the African presence, especially in Jamaica and Trinidad where many were resettled – something that is frequently overlooked by scholars of African "retentions" in the New World. The connection with Africa was thus strengthened even after the slave trade had been abolished. The United States did not experience a similar level of reinfusion.

The sixth and final point pertains to the question of "Why the English language agency?" The fact that British Caribbeans belonged to the largest empire, one with the largest holdings on the continent, contributed to their relatively easy settlement there since, thanks to this linguistic and colonial commonality and entrée. It is also true that the French colonial authorities were more adept at co-opting members of the black intelligentsia in Africa, including those from the francophone Caribbean, through their divide and rule policy of assimilation. The French colonial state, especially in West Africa, was exceptionally effective (far more so than its British counterpart) in its surveillance of individuals and organizations perceived as threats to the status quo. Its censorship laws and banning of publications, especially against Garvey's *Negro World*, were draconian (one could be executed if found reading the *Negro World* in Dahomey). And like the other colonial powers in West Africa, its deployment of brutal violence against those opposed to French colonial rule was swift and unrestrained.[44] Unlike the French and Portuguese, however, the British had no assimilationist policies, and this more overt blockage contributed to the discontent among the educated in Britain's African colonies.[45] Nevertheless, France's assimilationist policies did also have the effect of giving a voice to black internationalism, although the language barrier somewhat muted the global audience for such appeals.

These, then, are the fundamental elements that help to explain the extraordinary character of Caribbean involvement in pan-Africanist projects. There is still need for deeper and further research, but what I have attempted here is the presentation, in broad terms, of the line of continuity and logic linking Russwurm's search for social and political freedom in the early nineteenth century, and Padmore's dream for the same, which culminated in the decolonization of the African continent.

NOTES

1. George Shepperson, "Pan-Africanism and 'Pan-Africanism': Some Historical Notes", *Phylon* 23, no. 4 (1962): 355.
2. Ibid., 356; Imanuel Geiss, "Notes on the Development of Pan-Africanism", *Journal of the Historical Society of Nigeria* 3, no. 4 (1967): 722.

3. Shepperson, "Pan-Africanism", 356; Geiss "Notes", 722. This theme is also found in Geiss's monumental study, *The Pan-African Movement*, translated by Ann Keep (London: Methuen, 1974), 8–11.

4. Winston James, *Holding Aloft the Banner of Ethiopia: Caribbean Radicalism in Early Twentieth-Century America* (London: Verso, 1998).

5. Tony Martin, *The Pan-African Connection: From Slavery to Garvey and Beyond* (Cambridge MA: Schenkman, 1983), vii.

6. I have, of course, borrowed the term "imagined community" from Benedict Anderson's celebrated analysis of modern nationalism. The nation, he suggests, "is imagined because the members of even the smallest nation will never know most of their fellow-members, meet them, or even hear of them, yet in the minds of each lives the image of their communion". Benedict Anderson, *Imagined Communities: Reflections on the Origin and Spread of Nationalism* (London: Verso, 1983), 15.

7. Owen Mathurin, *Henry Sylvester Williams and the Origins of the Pan-African Movement, 1869–1911* (Westport, CT: Greenwood, 1976), 52, gives 11 November 1899 as the date for the first documented usage of the term.

8. For analyses of this largely forgotten episode in British Caribbean history, see Eric Williams, "The British West Indian Slave Trade After its Abolition in 1807", *Journal of Negro History* 27, no. 2 (1942): 175–91. See also D. Eltis, "The Traffic in Slaves between the British West Indian Colonies, 1807–1833", *Economic History Review* 25, no.1 (1972): 55–64.

9. See James, *Holding Aloft the Banner*, 9–49, and the references therein. The literature on the subject is vast and growing. See, in particular: Bonham Richardson, "Caribbean Migrations, 1838–1985", in *The Modern Caribbean*, ed. Franklin Knight and Colin Palmer (Chapel Hill: University of North Carolina Press, 1989), 203–28; Peter Fryer, *Staying Power: The History of Black People in Britain* (London: Pluto, 1984); Peter Fraser, "British West Indians in Haiti in the Late Nineteenth and Early Twentieth Centuries", *Immigrants and Minorities* 7, no. 1 (1988): 79–94; Paul Rich, "The Black Diaspora in Britain: Afro-Caribbean Students and the Struggle for a Political Identity, 1900–1950", *Immigrants and Minorities* 6, no. 2 (1987): 151–73; Jeffrey Green, *Black Edwardians: Black People in Britain, 1901–1914* (London: Frank Cass, 1998); Rudolph Lapp, *Blacks in Gold Rush California* (New Haven, CT: Yale University Press, 1977), especially 266–68; Barry Higman, "Jamaicans in the Australian Gold Rushes", *Jamaica Journal* 10, nos. 2–4 (December 1976): 38–45.

10. William Patterson, *The Man Who Cried Genocide: An Autobiography* (New York: International, 1971), 18–20, 22–23, 46–47.

11. Ras Makonnen, *Pan-Africanism from Within*, rec. and ed. Kenneth King (Nairobi: Oxford University Press, 1973), 57–58.

12. I have analysed elsewhere the forces behind the creation of this massive Barbadian diaspora. See James, *Holding Aloft the Banner*, 30–49.

13. Edward Brathwaite, *The Arrivants: A New World Trilogy* (Oxford: Oxford University Press, 1973), 40.

14. Sidney Greenfield, "Barbadians in the Brazilian Amazon", *Luso-Brazilian Review* 20 (1983): 44–64a; Howard Johnson, "Barbadian Migrants in the Putamayo District of the Amazon, 1909–11", in *Caribbean Migration: Globalised Identities*, ed. Mary Chamberlain (London: Routledge, 1998), 177–87.

15. Anthony De V. Phillips, *Modernizing Barbados, 1880–1914* (Bridgetown: Ancestor, 1996), 13; Cecilia A. Karch, "The Transport and Communications Revolution in the West Indies: Imperial Policy and Barbadian Response, 1870–1917", *Journal of Caribbean History* 18, no. 2 (1983): 22–42. For an excellent history of the development of Bridgetown, see Pedro L.V. Welch, *Slave Society in the City: Bridgetown, Barbados 1680–1834* (Kingston: Ian Randle, 2003). Clapham Junction, located in London, was, and is, one of the busiest and most densely networked railway intersections in Britain.

16. Makonnen, *Pan-Africanism from Within*; Hugh Mulzac, *A Star to Steer By* (New York: International, 1963); Bonham C. Richardson, *Panama Money in Barbados, 1900–1920* (Knoxville: University of Tennessee Press, 1985); Alan Cobley, " 'Far From Home': The Origins and Significance of the Afro-Caribbean Community in South Africa to 1930", *Journal of Southern African Studies* 18, no. 2 (1992): 349–70.

17. B.W. Higman, "Jamaican Port Towns in the Early Nineteenth Century", in *Atlantic Port Cities: Economy, Culture, and Society in the Atlantic World, 1650–1850*, ed. Franklin W. Knight and Peggy K. Liss (Knoxville: University of Tennessee Press, 1991), 117–48; Gisela Eisner, *Jamaica, 1830–1930: A Study in Economic Growth* (Manchester: Manchester University Press, 1961); Thomas C. Holt, *The Problem of Freedom: Race, Labor, and Politics in Jamaica and Britain, 1832–1938* (Baltimore: Johns Hopkins University Press, 1992), ch. 10; James, *Holding Aloft the Banner*, ch. 1.

18. There is a growing body of literature on this subject, but see in particular Raymond T. Smith, *Kinship and Class in the West Indies: A Genealogical Study of Jamaica and Guyana* (Cambridge: Cambridge University Press 1988); Elizabeth Thomas-Hope, *Explanation in Caribbean Migration: Perception and the Image, Jamaica, Barbados, St Vincent* (London: Macmillan, 1992).

19. Shepperson, "Pan-Africanism", 356; Geiss, "Notes", 722.

20. These ideas are expanded in my article, "The Wings of Ethiopia: The Caribbean

Diaspora and Pan-African Projects from John Brown Russwurm to George Padmore", in *African Diasporas in the Old and New World: Consciousness and Imagination*, ed. Geneviève Fabre and Klaus Benesch (Amsterdam: Rodopi, 2003), 133–70.

21. For more on Russwurm, see Winston James, *The Struggles of John Brown Russwurm: The Life and Writings of a Pan-Africanist Pioneer, 1799–1851* (New York: New York University Press, 2010), and for Blyden, see Hollis Lynch, *Edward Wilmot Blyden: Pan-Negro Patriot, 1832–1912* (London: Oxford University Press, 1967). There is no biography of Campbell. Richard Blackett is the only scholar to have provided a biographical portrait. Blackett's is a pioneering and splendid effort, but there is still much work to be done to fully unveil Campbell's remarkable life. See Richard Blackett, "Return to the Motherland: Robert Campbell, A Jamaican in Early Colonial Lagos", *Journal of the Historical Society of Nigeria* 8, no. 1 (1975): 133–43; Richard Blackett, "Martin R. Delany and Robert Campbell: Black Americans in Search of an African Colony", *Journal of Negro History* 62, no. 1 (1977): 1–25; Richard Blackett, "Robert Campbell and the Triangle of the Black Experience", in Blackett's collective biographical portrait, *Beating against the Barriers: The Lives of Six Nineteenth-Century Afro-Americans* (Ithaca: Cornell University Press, 1989), 139–82.

22. Christopher Fyfe, *A History of Sierra Leone* (Oxford: Oxford University Press, 1962); Nemata Blyden, *West Indians in West Africa, 1808–1880: The African Diaspora in Reverse* (Rochester: University of Rochester Press, 2000).

23. See Fred Omu, "The New Era and the Abortive Press Law of 1857", *Sierra Leone Studies* 23 (1968): 2–14; Blyden, *West Indians in West Africa*, 96–100.

24. Omu, "The New Era", 13–14; and Fred Omu "The Dilemma of Press Freedom in Colonial Africa: The West African Example", *Journal of African History* 9, no. 2 (1968): 279–98.

25. James, *Struggles of John Brown Russwurm*.

26. Richard Burton, *Wanderings in West Africa: From Liverpool to Fernando Po*, 2 vols (London: Tinsley Brothers, 1863), see especially vol. 1, 193–281; William Rainy, *The Censor Censured, or the Calumnies of Captain Burton on the Africans of Sierra Leone* (London: Geo. Chalfont, 1865).

27. Quoted in Blyden, *West Indians in West Africa*, 151.

28. Ibid., 151–52.

29. Quoted ibid., 142.

30. Fyfe, *History of Sierra Leone*, 386–87.

31. Editorial, *African Times*, 23 December 1868 and 22 July 1871, quoted in Blyden, *West Indians in West Africa*, 154 and 156.

32. Fyfe, *History of Sierra Leone*, 263 and 387.

33. There are good vignettes of these figures in David Kimble's remarkable and unsurpassed study, *A Political History of Ghana: The Rise of Gold Coast Nationalism, 1850–1928* (Oxford: Clarendon, 1963). Small is also discussed in Geiss, *Pan-African Movement.*

34. See especially Rina Okonkwo, *Heroes of West African Nationalism* (Enugu: Delta, 1985), ch. 4, and Rina Okonkwo, "The Garvey Movement in British West Africa", *Journal of African History* 21, no. 1 (1980): 105–17, and Ade Adefuye, John Gershion and Joshua Ricketts, "Jamaican Contribution to the Socio-Economic Development of the Colony Provinces of Nigeria", in *Studies in Yoruba History and Culture: Essays in Honour of Professor S.O. Biobaku*, ed. G.O. Olusanya (Ibadan: University Press, 1983), 135–52.

35. For more on Williams, see Mathurin, *Henry Sylvester Williams*; J.R. Hooker, *Henry Sylvester Williams: Imperial Pan-Africanist* (London: Rex Collings, 1975); and the excellent recent study by Marika Sherwood, *Origins of Pan-Africanism: Henry Sylvester Williams, Africa, and the African Diaspora* (New York: Routledge, 2011). See also Jonathan Schneer, *London 1900: The Imperial Metropolis* (New Haven: Yale University Press, 1999), especially ch. 9.

36. W.F. Elkins, "Hercules and the Society of Peoples of African Origin", *Caribbean Studies* 11, no. 4 (1972): 47–59; Winston James, "The Black Experience in Twentieth-Century Britain", in *Black Experience and the Empire*, ed. Philip D. Morgan and Sean Hawkins (Oxford: Oxford University Press, 2004), 358–60.

37. See Tony Martin, *Race First: The Ideological and Organizational Struggles of Marcus Garvey and the Universal Negro Improvement Association* (Dover, MA: Majority Press, 1986); Okonkwo, "Garvey Movement"; Rupert Lewis, *Marcus Garvey: Anti-Colonial Champion* (London: Karia, 1987); G.O. Olusanya, "Garvey and Nigeria", in *Garvey: Africa, Europe, the Americas*, ed. Rupert Lewis and Maureen Warner-Lewis (Trenton, NJ: Africa World Press, 1994), 121–34; and the pioneering volumes on Africa among the Garvey Papers, Robert Hill, ed., *The Marcus Garvey and Universal Negro Improvement Association Papers* (Berkeley: University of California Press, 1995), especially vol. 9.

38. Okonkwo, *Heroes of West Africa*, ch. 4.

39. Hill, *Marcus Garvey Papers*, 9:204–5, 211–12, 267–69, 566; Cobley, "Far From Home"; Tony Martin, "Marcus Garvey and Southern Africa", in his book *The Pan-African Connection*, 133–53; and Robert Hill and Gregory Pirio, " 'Africa for the Africans': The Garvey Movement in South Africa, 1920–1940", in *The Politics of Race, Class and Nationalism in Twentieth-Century South Africa*, ed. Shula Marks and Stanley Trapido (London: Longman, 1987), 209–53; Robert Trent Vinson, *The Americans are Coming! Dreams of African American Liberation in Segregationist South Africa* (Athens: Ohio University Press, 2012). A thorough

account of the evolution and practices of both the Industrial and Commerical Workers Union and the UNIA in Namibia during the period is given in Tony Emmett, *Popular Resistance and the Roots of Nationalism in Namibia, 1915–1966* (Basel: Schlettwein, 1999), 125–54.

40. Hooker's *Black Revolutionary* is the only biography of Padmore. See also Penny von Eschen, *Race Against Empire: Black Americans and Anticolonialism, 1937–1957* (Ithaca, NY: Cornell University Press, 1997); Philippe Dewitte, *Les Mouvements Nègres en France, 1919–1939* (Paris: L'Harmattan, 1985); Brent Hayes Edwards, *The Practice of Diaspora: Literature, Translation, and the Rise of Black Internationalism* (Cambridge, MA: Harvard University Press, 2003), ch. 5; Fitzroy Baptiste and Rupert Lewis, eds., *George Padmore: Pan-African Revolutionary* (Kingston: Ian Randle, 2009); Minkah Makalani, *In the Cause of Freedom: Radical Black Internationalism from Harlem to London, 1917–1939* (Chapel Hill: University of North Carolina Press, 2011), ch. 6 and 7; and the memoirs of some Padmore's associates and comrades: Makonnen, *Pan-Africanism from Within*; C.L.R. James, "George Padmore: Black Marxist Revolutionary – A Memoir", in his *At the Rendezvous of Victory: Selected Writings* (London: Allison and Busby, 1984), 251–63; Dudley Thompson, *From Kingston to Kenya: The Making of a Pan-Africanist Lawyer* (Dover, MA: Majority Press, 1993); Peter Abrahams, *The Black Experience in the Twentieth Century: An Autobiography* (Bloomington: Indiana University Press, 2000).

41. Quoted in George Shepperson, "Notes on Negro American Influences on the Emergence of African Nationalism", *Journal of African History* 1, no. 2 (1960), 300.

42. For an excellent biography of Crummell, see Wilson J. Moses, *Alexander Crummell: A Study of Civilization and Discontent* (New York: Oxford University Press, 1989).

43. The best overview of the slave experience in the United States is found in Peter Kolchin, *American Slavery, 1619–1877* (New York: Hill and Wang, 1993). For the slave experience in the British Caribbean in the nineteenth century, see B.W. Higman, *Slave Populations of the British Caribbean, 1807–1834* (Baltimore: Johns Hopkins University Press, 1984). For an excellent case study of the impact of indentured Africans in the post-emancipation period, see Monica Schuler, *"Alas, Alas, Kongo": A Social History of Indentured African Immigration into Jamaica, 1841–1865* (Baltimore: Johns Hopkins University Press, 1980). See also Mervyn Alleyne, *Roots of Jamaican Culture* (London: Pluto, 1988).

44. See, in particular, G. Wesley Johnson, *The Emergence of Black Politics in Senegal: The Struggle for Power in the Four Communes, 1900–1920* (Palo Alto, CA: Stanford University Press, 1971); J. Ayodele Langley, *Pan-Africanism and Nationalism*

in West Africa, 1900–1945 (Oxford: Clarendon, 1973); Richard D.E. Burton and Fred Reno, eds., *French and West Indian: Martinique, Guadeloupe and French Guiana Today* (London: Macmillan, 1995); Hill, *Marcus Garvey Papers*, vol. 10; Gary Wilder, *The French Imperial Nation-State: Negritude and Colonial Humanism between the Two World Wars* (Chicago: University of Chicago Press, 2005), esp. parts 1 and 2; and Véronique Hélénon, *French Caribbeans in Africa: Diasporic Connections and Colonial Administration, 1880–1939* (New York: Palgrave Macmillan, 2011), esp. ch. 2. In a pioneering essay, François Manchaunelle has shown that many of those exiled by the French from the Caribbean played important roles in the nationalist struggles on the continent, including North Africa. See François Manchaunelle, "Le rôle des Antillais dans l'apparition du nationalisme culturel en Afrique noire francophone", *Cahiers d'Études Africaines* 32, no. 3 (1992): 375–408. It is interesting to note, however, that the French-speaking black intellectuals who actively supported and sympathized with the pan-Africanist projects before the birth of negritude in the 1930s were mainly Haitians rather than French Caribbeans proper. See Shepperson, "Pan-Africanism", 355–56; Geiss, *Pan-African Movement*; Martin Steins, "Black Immigrants in Paris", in *European-Language Writing on Sub-Saharan Africa*, ed. Albert S. Gérard (Budapest: Akadémiai Kiadó, 1986), 1:354–78; and Oruno Lara, *La Naissance du Panafricanisme: Les racines caraïbes, américaines et africaines du mouvement au XIXe siècle* (Paris: Maisonneuve and Larose, 2000).

45.   It is noteworthy that this corporatist element within French colonial policy led even an astute an observer as Henry Sylvester Williams to compare French colonialism favourably to the British version. See H. Sylvester Williams, *The British Negro: A Factor in the Empire, and The Ethiopian Eunuch: Two Lectures* (London: n.p., 1902), 15–16 and 21.

CHAPTER 11

BLACK POWER IN THE AFRICAN DIASPORA

QUITO SWAN

FROM BERMUDA IN THE CARIBBEAN TO Vanuatu (formerly known as New Hebrides) in the South Pacific, Afrodiasporic intellectuals from the Caribbean and the Americas have, in significant ways, shaped global struggles for justice and equality in the twentieth century. This chapter focuses on the modern odyssey of Roosevelt Osiris Nelson Browne, alias Pauluu Kamarakafego, who epitomized the global dynamics of diasporic intellectuals in the era of decolonization. Tracing Kamarakafego's travels from Bermuda to Cuba, the United States, Fiji and Papua New Guinea enables us to construct a bridge between the conventional analysis of nationalist narratives centring on Black Power and the transnational linkages between members of the Atlantic African, Mediterranean and Asian diasporas, and other oppressed polities in the Pacific. This retelling of the contributions of Kamarakafego's sojourn in places near and distant from his birthplace of Bermuda seeks to widen the scope of the conventional discussions of Black Power movements. It aims to do so by moving away from discussions that are centred on particular nation states and engaging in an examination of its global aspects, interweaving the different strands of pan-African activism that have been separated by time, circumstances and specific geographical location.

Kamarakafego, whose global activities elicited unprecedented responses from the empires of the day – Britain and France, and their Australian allies – gained fame or notoriety for successfully confronting imperial and hegemonic powers ruling over the Atlantic and Pacific communities. His odyssey

mirrors those of many diasporic personalities – who through their intellectual prowess, and their passionate political activism against racial segregation
and oppression – embraced not only their African heritage but also a mantle
of global leadership to construct a better world, free from the legacies of
enslavement and the confining yoke of colonial rule. In this process, some
like Kamarakafego broke through the barriers of the hierarchies that had
marginalized the global activities of African diasporic intellectuals whose
cosmopolitan experiences greatly inform the narratives of black nationalism
and pan-Africanism. This chapter represents a first step towards acknowledging the dynamism of the African diasporic contributions to freedom and
equality of all peoples in the twentieth century.

On 30 June 1975 Kamarakafego, a Black Power advocate and ecological
engineer who had been invited by the New Hebrides Nationalist Party to
conduct "political education" among the "rural indigenous masses", was
arrested by the British Police commissioner.[1] British and French colonial
administrators accused him of "propagating Black Power doctrines" and a
"bitter anti-white racialistic outlook which galvanized colonial subjects to
engage in detrimental activities".[2] His "crime" was that he had developed
projects that enabled rural residents to make key commodities such as locally
made soaps, oil from coconuts, salt from the sea, sweeteners from sugar cane,
and cement from calcium carbonate deposits and clay. Using science and
innovative technical expertise to economically empower communities led
to the disengagement of the colonized from the predations of British multinational companies.[3] Faced with such pacifist yet effective defiance, British
officials sought to "extract" Kamarakafego from this South Pacific outpost.
They feared that this resistance could spread to other subaltern communities
of the empire, and so considered flying in British troops from Singapore and
Fiji, or the Gurkhas from Hong Kong to prevent this.[4]

Kamarakafego's arrest and deportation was far from a quiet affair.
Twenty-six protestors tried to prevent the police from placing him aboard
an aircraft. They then drove onto the runway, parked and locked their cars
in front of the taxiing aircraft, and threw away their keys. Clashes broke
out, arrests were conveniently made at nightfall, charges filed, fines levied,
and Kamarakafego was sent on his way back to Bermuda.[5] However, while
in transit in Los Angeles, with the help of two African American women,

Kamarakafego evaded his escort from the Federal Bureau of Investigation. As soon as one of his contacts at an African embassy obtained a new passport for him, he headed back to the Pacific, this time to Fiji and then to newly independent Papua New Guinea as a rural development consultant.[6] Fusing his political advocacy with self-determination to empower rural communities, he built bridges between the colonized peoples of the Atlantic and the Pacific.

Kamarakafego's role in the struggles for decolonization in Australasia reflects the similar experiences of other black men and women who have traversed the diaspora and beyond as political agents of change, conduits of information, artists and international organizers.[7] These histories, which have been marginalized in the postcolonial era, need to be placed in the context not only of those who joined the anticolonial struggles of the African continent but also of those who globalized the struggle against imperial domination.

Kamarakafego's sojourn through the diaspora reads like a proverbial pan-African epic. In 1951 he was shot in the leg during an anti-Batista and United Fruit Company demonstration in Cuba. Between 1951 and 1954 he was a student athlete at New York University. In the mid-1950s he joined the African American freedom struggle while a student at South Carolina State College; this was marked by a few altercations with the Ku Klux Klan. After obtaining a doctorate in ecological engineering from the California Institute of Technology, Pasadena, in 1959, he taught science in Liberia, Sierra Leone, Kenya and Tanzania throughout much of the 1960s. Between the 1970s and 1980s he worked with Pacific Islander indigenous communities as a consultant, as noted earlier. In Bermuda, Kamarakafego was involved with the Committee for Universal Adult Suffrage (CUAS), served as a parliamentarian, and pushed for the island's decolonization at the meeting of the United Nations' Special Committee on Decolonization (the Committee of 24). He played key roles in coordinating the First International Black Power Conference (BPC, Bermuda 1969), the Congress of African Peoples (CAP, Atlanta 1970) and the Sixth Pan-African Congress (PAC, Tanzania 1974). As a scientist, he was world-renowned for his pioneering contributions to environmental studies and the sustainable development movement.

Kamarakafego's global activism offers a narrative of Black Power that spans the Americas, Africa and Australasia. It demonstrates that Black

Power globally was more than just a sidebar to the US-based movement.[8] It calls for "New Black Power Studies" to seriously look at Black Power from a global perspective, rather than to attempt to pack this wider experience into a US-centric narrative.[9] Kamarakafego's experiences add fundamentally to US-centric appraisals of Black Power, which often exclude the moments, personalities, interpretations, significance and lessons of Black Power in the wider diaspora.

BERMUDA, CUBA AND THE UNITED STATES

Born in Bermuda in 1932, Kamarakafego grew up during the island's staunch system of racial segregation, black political disenfranchisement and British colonialism.[10] His mother, Henrietta Brown, had migrated to Bermuda from St Kitts in 1917. She taught all of her children how to knit, a skill that Kamarakafego retained and utilized his entire life. His maternal grandfather, Joel Brown, was an agricultural worker, but worked as a machine mechanic on Bermuda's tugboats. His maternal grandmother, Ruth-Ann Nesbitt, was a dark-skinned "African looking", quiet woman from Nevis. Kamarakafego spent a lot of time in her kitchen in Middletown (Back-a-Town), drinking traditional bush tea and eating spicy West Indian foods made from yams, taro, ado, dumplings, salt pork, salt beef and Johnny bread.[11]

His father, also from St Kitts, had lived in the Dominican Republic and Brazil before coming to Bermuda as a mason and later working as a building contractor.[12] Kamarakafego was grounded in African West Indian culture: his father danced Gombeys, practised traditional medicine, spoke Spanish and Portuguese and had travelled to visit relatives in Liberia and Nigeria. Because of his familial links to Liberia and Nigeria, he was one of the few twentieth-century pan-African intellectuals who understood African languages, such as Kpelle and Ibo. It was from his father that Kamarakafego learned how to "wield" profanity like a weapon, and also how to fight white men and injustice. Kamarakafego's cosmopolitanism was influenced by his father's multiculturalism, which combined African and West Indian traditions with knowledge of Spanish and Portuguese and a strong sense of social justice. He would follow in his father's footsteps throughout his life.

For example, once while working as a hotel dishwasher, he was kicked in the back by his white manager. In reply he hit the manager across the back of his head with a shovel, as hard as he could. Upon being told what happened, his father responded, "That's good."[13] The future scientist and engineer's world-view was one that acknowledged and celebrated the shared history of Africa's diasporic peoples in the Caribbean, the Americas and Asia – an expansive view that later led him to embrace the struggles for self-determination among the communities of the Pacific islands. Small in stature, Kamarakafego was physically fit. Built like a miniature juggernaut, he lifted weights, played football, ran track and was a Boy Scout. While on school holidays he worked in construction with his father, where he learnt masonry, carpentry and how to cut limestone. In addition he could read house plans, landscape, and create house profiles, engineering concepts and architectural designs. He did all this while developing an awareness of colonial exploitation.[14]

He was raised in a politically conscious environment, and was familiar with Marcus Garvey's Universal Negro Improvement Association and the activists of the Black Star Line. In 1945, C.L.R. James stayed at his home during a visit to Bermuda. James was a friend of the union leader Dr E.F. Gordon (who hailed from Trinidad), who arranged for him to stay with Kamarakafego's family as he could not find lodgings in Bermuda's then exclusively white-owned, segregated hotels.[15] This opened up new relation-ships with renowned Caribbean scholars from an early age.

Kamarakafego spent the summers of 1951 and 1952 in Cuba, visiting his great uncle who worked on the sugar cane plantations.[16] He lived in Central Chaparra in Cuba's Oriente, where a number of British West Indians resided. While there he learned to fly a small seaplane, obtained a pilot's licence, and developed his Spanish language and dancing skills. In 1952, while in Havana, he witnessed a demonstration against the US-backed dictator, Fulgencio Batista, and the United Fruit Company. He recalls, "They [the protesters] blamed Batista, the US Mafia and the United Fruit Company for the poverty in Cuba. At an early age, I had learned from my father and my mother's uncle that all people have rights and that I should not just stand by while other people were denied their rights. I had to make the wrong right . . . I joined in the demonstration."[17] Batista's soldiers fired on the crowd, and he was shot in the leg. An elderly Afro-Cuban woman hid him in her home, and patched up his wound with some "traditional medicine".[18] This appears to have been his first involvement in an organized protest against discrimination, but it would not be the last time he suffered gunshot wounds for doing so.

In the fall of 1951, Kamarakafego had enrolled in New York University to study science. He was on a swimming and track scholarship, and represented the school at the 1954 Penn Relays. In Harlem he encountered and embraced "African America". He became a weekend regular at nightspots such as the Savoy Ballroom and the Apollo Theatre, exploring the world of Duke Ellington and Count Basie, and dancing the mambo, meringue, cha-cha-cha and pachanga. In 1952, he again met C.L.R. James at one of the latter's lectures given at Adam Clayton Powell's Abyssinian Baptist Church. He was also introduced by a friend to the Progressive Labor Party (United States), where he met William Patterson, chairman of the US Communist Party and author of *The Man Who Cried Genocide*.[19]

His stay in New York was cut short when his scholarship was revoked after he challenged a white sociology professor's racist views on segregation and southern black culture. Forced to leave New York University, he accepted an invitation by Mattie Pegsie, head of South Carolina State College's Department of Home Economics, to attend the school. The experience of riding the segregated train from New York to Orangeburg reminded him of Bermuda; once the train stopped in Washington, DC, he had to sit in the coloured section. He noted that the oppression of African Americans, although not as overtly colonial, shared common themes with the oppression of blacks in the Caribbean: "hard times, money problems, racism, segregation and not having the opportunity for justice and equality. As the train moved, I could see the landscape and my mind went back to slavery times and how the slaves worked in the cotton fields."[20]

When he arrived at South Carolina State College in 1954 to study biological sciences, Kamarakafego entered a historically black college at a tumultuous political moment, just months after the historic *Brown vs Board of Education* Supreme Court decision that declared that state laws establishing separate public schools for black and white students were unconstitutional. Around this time, also, fifty-seven black residents of Orangeburg presented a petition calling for the elimination of segregation in public schools. Drawn up and circulated by local NAACP leaders, it represented a cross-section of the black community. In response, local whites formed a white Citizen's Council, which devised a campaign of "economic coercion" against the petitioners. The NAACP retaliated by organizing a "selective buying campaign" against a number of white businesses.[21]

Kamarakafego became involved in Orangeburg's black freedom struggle. He joined the college's Student Government Association, which supported the NAACP's boycott of Coca-Cola and Sunbeam Bread, both businesses that had contracts with South Carolina State College. Led by student president Fred H. Moore, the students organized hunger strikes in the school's dining halls, mass meetings and freedom marches in solidarity with the wider black community. Moore was eventually expelled and Kamarakafego suspended from the school for protesting, though this did not prevent his organizing defensive militias against the intrusive visits to the campus of the Ku Klux Klan.[22] Kamarakafego and other male students gained access to rifles from the armoury of the campus' Reserve Officers' Training Corps and surprised the Klan by firing warning shots over their heads. The Klan returned later, accompanied by National Guard troops. They conducted searches for firearms and maintained a military presence on the campus for approximately two weeks. Major civil rights leaders such as Thurgood Marshall, Adam Clayton Powell Jr, Martin Luther King Jr and Bayard Rustin visited the campus, heightening tensions between the political antagonists in Orangeburg, and providing some notoriety and short-lived protection for student activists. When the Klan returned a week after the guard had dispersed, Kamarakafego was seriously injured and had to be hospitalized. His protest activities led to his second expulsion from an academic institution in the United States.[23]

Kamarakafego was briefly enrolled at North Carolina College, where he joined the football team as a kicker. However, in 1956, after an altercation at a football game with a white police officer in Raleigh, his subsequent arrest and a high-profile court case, he was once again asked to leave. He did not give up his education but continued on to the California Institute of Technology where he enrolled in graduate studies and gained a doctorate in ecological engineering in 1959.[24] He continued his civil rights activities, attending campus lectures by radical leaders such as Malcolm X, and went on a road trip to Atlanta to hear W.E.B. Du Bois speak. When not engaged in his studies he knitted sweaters to support himself, and he played percussion in a highlife band with Kenyan, Nigerian, Congolese and Gambian musicians. During his last year at the California Institute of Technology, he decided that he wanted to go to visit his family in Liberia. His girlfriend was an Afro-indigenous Cayugan woman from Canada, who also had family in Liberia. They got married in a traditional ceremony and left for Africa.[25]

DISCOVERING AFRICAN ROOTS: BECOMING PAUULU IN LIBERIA AND EAST AFRICA

In 1959, Kamarakafego and his wife, Betty Brown, arrived in Monrovia, Liberia, by ship. He noted the class divisions in Liberian society between Americo-Liberians and indigenous Liberians. They obtained jobs at Cuttington College in Suakoko, Bong County. According to Kamarakafego, he served as a biological science teacher, athletics director, football coach, student council advisor and overseer of the college's physical development, and she as the administrator of the college's clinic. In addition he also taught science at Fourah Bay College in Freetown, Sierra Leone. Due to a shortage of pilots, he had to air taxi himself and other passengers back and forth between Monrovia and Freetown.

It was during his first Christmas in Africa that "Roosevelt" became "Pauulu". He knew from his Aunt Mae that his family was Kpelle, a historically rice-cultivating, Mande-speaking ethnic group. He travelled to a village in the Kpelle district, Sanayea, where he was reunited with members of his family. Amid a ten-day period of celebrations, which included the slaughtering of a cow, daily drumming, drinking palm wine, and eating monkey and rice, the elder of the village, Chief Kamara welcomed him as a son. He was ceremoniously given the name Pauulu Kamarakafego, which means "brown-skinned son of Chief Kamara". During his time there he used local materials to design and build a water tank, a village school and a health aid post. He also witnessed how young men from Sanayea were routinely rounded up at night by armed soldiers, taken to plantations and forced to tap rubber. The village elders asked him to assist, but before he could do so, his wife contracted malaria and they returned to Canada, where she remained.[26] Upon his return to Liberia in October 1961, along with a small group of Liberians,

Ghanaians and Nigerians, he organized a general strike among the rubber tappers; this eventually included longshoremen and civil servants. President Tubman of Liberia ordered the arrest of the Liberians involved. Grazed by bullets fired by Liberian soldiers and narrowly avoiding capture, Kamarakafego and the others fled the country primarily by foot into neighbouring Ivory Coast and then to Ghana, where he was welcomed and sheltered while he recuperated from the injuries he sustained during the firefight and the gruelling journey.[27] In Ghana he was hosted by President Kwame Nkrumah whom Kamarakafego had met before in 1953 at C.L.R. James's residence in London. While in Ghana, he met such political luminaries as W.E.B. Du Bois, Shirley Graham Du Bois and Nelson Mandela. He also briefly lectured at the University of Ghana in Kumasi.[28] On Nkrumah's advice, in 1962 he continued on to Kenya. While there he taught biological science, ecology and environmental studies at the University of East Africa in Nairobi. As usual, Kamarakafego found himself in the midst of political upheaval in this new place; Jomo Kenyatta had only been released from prison the year before. Amid calls for national elections, he attended political demonstrations, some of which were comprised of up to 150,000 persons.[29]

Kamarakafego here, too, noted striking similarities between racism in Kenya and racism in Bermuda; for example, although whites consisted of less than 1 per cent of the population, there were over eight secondary schools that they could attend exclusively. In comparison, for the 99 per cent black population, there were only three schools.[30] After Kenyatta won the 1963 elections, Kamarakafego was asked to assist with the implementation of policy changes in the education system. He wrote: "I recall that I was not always compensated for the post, but seeing the changes coming in the country and the regaining of African rights fueled me to work as hard and as long as I possibly could. I needed no greater motivation. No amount of money could have equaled the satisfaction I received."[31] As Nkrumah had predicted he would, Kamarakafego embarked on a number of projects beneficial to Kenya. This included establishing a science teacher's college, which could allow Kenya to produce its own scientists as opposed to inviting colonial technicians back to run the county. He served as a curriculum developer and worked with a team of science teachers writing culturally relevant O-level and A-level science exams for East Africa. While there, he wrote his first book, a manual on how to build water tanks using natural bamboo and cement; this was published in several different languages and aimed at rural audiences. He also helped to organize the Kenya Secondary School Sports Association; in 1966 he organized the Inter-Provincial Secondary Schools Athletics Championship. In 1962 he was asked to be a United Nations consultant, and in 1972 he helped to establish a UN environment headquarters in Nairobi.[32] In 1964, he met Malcolm X for the second time during the latter's second trip to Africa; this would prove to be an historic meeting.

BLACK POWER IN THE WEST INDIES AND BEYOND

The various political and racial struggles occurring around the world largely inspired the youth in the Caribbean to do something about the unfulfilled socio-economic and cultural promises made by the (neocolonial) black political leadership after independence.[33] Black Power advocates often emerged out of the labour and independence struggles for decolonization and West Indian federation.[34] According to Walter Rodney, Black Power in the West Indies represented a "break from imperialism" which had been "historically White racist"; the "assumptions of power by the Black masses"; and "the cultural reconstruction of the islands in the image of the Blacks".[35]

A decade of intense political activism directly preceded Black Power's emergence in Bermuda in the late 1960s, with Kamarakafego returning continually to participate in various activities. These included an island-wide theatre boycott (led by the anonymous Progressive Group) against segregation and a dockworkers' strike (1959); the formation of the local black Muslim (Nation of Islam) political group; and a violent clash between predominantly black strikers of the Bermuda Electric Light Company and the British police force (1965). Collectively, these struggles challenged segregation (which the white government deemed necessary to draw white elite North American tourists to Bermuda), colonialism, sexism, racism, job discrimination, police brutality, poverty, the increased cost of living, housing shortages, and the persistence of a white oligarchy colloquially known as the "Forty Thieves". In Bermuda, Black Power was an anticolonial, revolutionary youth movement that aimed to dismantle British colonialism and the latter's support of the island's white oligarchy. British, US and Canadian security forces saw Black Power as a threat to their geopolitical interests in the Americas. They beleaguered the movement via collaborative, international networks of intelligence and repression. Black Power was attacked via legal perse- cution, police brutality, infiltration, surveillance, an extensive propaganda campaign and military suppression. Kamarakafego was often a target of such tactics. Although he spent many years away from the island, Kamarakafego remained committed to the political struggle in Bermuda. In the summer of 1960 he had returned to Bermuda from Liberia, after learning that his father was seriously ill. By then, the most visible sign of racism was perhaps the disenfranchisement of Bermuda's majority black population; Bermuda's white oligarchy was buttressed by a fraudulent electoral system and Bermu- da's constitutional boundaries boosted the white vote. Furthermore, until 1963, only those persons owning land assessed at a certain value could vote. In 1963 a parliamentary act allowed all those above the age of twenty-five to vote, but those meeting the property requirements were given an extra vote.[36] In response, Kamarakafego helped to launch a committee for univer- sal adult suffrage, CUAS, which was a grassroots effort to politically educate and mobilize the public around the issue of the right to vote through commu- nity meetings held across the island. The CUAS also circulated a document, "An Analysis of Bermuda's Social Problems", which was created and covertly distributed by the Progressive Group, and which outlined a number of the aforementioned issues affecting blacks.[37]

Kamarakafego also publicly asserted that the CUAS was the first of seven steps aimed at achieving true democracy in Bermuda. He was summoned to a meeting with Bermuda's governor, Sir Julian Gascoigne, who told Kamarakafego that he had broken the law by distributing the "Analysis of Bermuda's Social Problems". He also demanded to know what the other six steps were. When Kamarakafego refused to respond to Gascoigne, the gover- nor became increasingly irate. Unsurprisingly, the governor rejected a CUAS petition calling for a national referendum on the franchise issue.[38] After years of agitation, however, Bermuda's first election held after the adoption of universal adult suffrage took place in 1968.

Kamarakafego was harassed, threatened and placed under close surveil- lance by the government for his political activities; despite his qualifications, he was denied a teaching job in the country.[39] Undaunted, in 1966 he joined

Bermuda's Progressive Labour Party (PLP), which had been founded in 1963 as the party of the black working class; Kamarakafego eventually became a member of the colonial parliament. The PLP consistently advocated national independence and the revision of voting acts and districts. It directly challenged Bermuda's 1966 constitution which stipulated that a British-appointed governor would have jurisdiction over Bermuda's external affairs, defence, internal security, the Bermuda regiment and the police force.[40] In response to the PLP, Bermuda's white oligarchy formed the United Bermuda Party (UBP) in 1964 to protect its interests.[41] According to the PLP, the "pirate-ancestored aristocrats" of the UBP formed a "present power structure" that maintained a "vile attitude of segregation" while advancing the "selfish interests of their outrageous oligarchy".[42]

In 1967, the PLP promised to use social legislation to give "economic power to the people of Bermuda". The provision of full employment and effective training programmes for Bermudian workers, the ending of "the present retrogressive system of taxation", the implementation of a low-cost housing programme allowing all Bermudians to have decent homes and the establishment of a fully integrated education system were part of the platform. In addition it demanded economic equality for businesses through the creation of anti-monopoly laws, the formation of government boards that reflected Bermuda's racial demographics, the granting of full political independence, the establishment of an arts council and fund to help develop local creative talent, and the establishment of a system of socialized medicine as well as a free medical health scheme.[43]

In April 1968, after being racially discriminated against and denied entry into a fair, youths from the "Back-a-Town" area of Hamilton city spontaneously clashed with the British police force. This swiftly transformed into a weekend-long organized uprising. In response, the British government sent a company from the Royal Inniskilling Fusiliers to suppress the rebellion, marking the first of four occasions between 1968 and 1977 when the British sent troops to suppress local protests. Many involved in the disturbances supported Black Power; some identified themselves as Black Nationalists, affirming that Black Power had officially arrived in the colony.[44]

During these clashes, Kamarakafego created the PLP Youth Wing to help organize and further politicize these "Back-a-Town" youth. Along with other

PLP members, he also attended the Black Power conferences in New Jersey (1967) and Philadelphia (1968).[45] Malcolm X had previously informed members of the Black Power Steering Committee (such as Benjamin Wright, Nathan Wright and Chuck Stone) of Kamarakafego's work in Africa, and he was asked to address the Philadelphia audience on that basis. Kamarakafego suggested that as Black Power had relevance for the entire black world, then perhaps a conference should be held outside of the United States. It was eventually decided that one would be held in Bermuda in 1969, with the aim of formally launching the movement in the West Indies.[46] Kamarakafego coordinated this conference, and the PLP Youth Wing was its official sponsor.

The conference aimed to "establish a variety of techniques, workable methods and alternate strategies to help black people achieve political, economic, educational and cultural Black Power in their respective communities". Kamarakafego urged participants not to engage in:

(a) "I'm Blacker than you" speech. All of us are in the same psychological Black bag regardless of colour.
(b) Passionate "Let's get guns and undo our castration" speech. The biggest struggle we have right now is getting ourselves together.
(c) "Black is Beautiful" speech. All of us are committed to the task of strengthening our identity.
(d) "If you're over thirty, then forget it" speech. For we know if it were not for the dedicated troops over thirty who fought to desegregate our communities, saying we wanted to be separate in any way would never have had any validity.[47]

Bermuda's black youth as well as older individuals such as African American reverend John Brandon, a local African Methodist Episcopal Minister, strongly supported the conference. The *Bermuda Recorder*, a newspaper formed by Garveyites, gave the conference positive coverage.[48] In contrast, the *Royal Gazette*, reflecting the views of the local white elite, supported a ban on the conference. It argued that the meeting would bring "animosity" to the races and threaten law and order in Bermuda. Both its editorials and letters pages reflected the view that Black Power was a form of "reverse racism" synonymous with Hitler's ideals, a poisonous, evil, horrific and "imminent danger" to the colony. Black Power, they argued, would force whites to leave

Bermuda thereby destroying tourism and transforming the island into an impoverished territory.[49]

In response, Kamarakafego declared that even "God couldn't come down" to stop the conference.[50] Yet, behind closed doors, Henry Tucker's UBP government planned to attempt to do just that. However, the British government intervened, arguing that a ban would help to legitimize Black Power, increase support for the PLP and create further security threats by driving Black Power underground. British prime minister Harold Wilson supported this position, which he articulated within the Foreign and Commonwealth Office (FCO). Aiming to implement countermeasures to thwart the conference, the FCO's Information and Research Department (IRD) requested information from the British Security Service (MI5), Secret Intelligence Service (MI6) and US officials about the "operation and . . . finances of Black Power organizations, advocates and activities in the Caribbean and US", and on potential conference attendees.[51]

FCO officials placed Kamarakafego under intense surveillance as he canvassed for the conference, travelling to countries such as Anguilla, Antigua, Cuba, Guyana, St Kitts, Guadeloupe, Barbados, Grenada, Venezuela, Curaçao, Martinique, St Vincent, Mexico, Jamaica, Trinidad and Tobago, Bahamas, Canada and the United States. They documented when he was denied entry into countries such as St Vincent and they were aware that he had contacted several African American nationalists and assumed US-based "subversive" elements.[52] Officials also noted that while in Guyana he met with Janet Jagan, a self-styled communist and prominent member of the leftist People's Progressive Party, and Eusi Kwayana, head of the Black Power–oriented African Society for Cultural Relations with Independent Africa (ASCRIA).[53]

Charles Manning, US consul to Bermuda, reported that Kamarakafego had a large following among Bermuda's black youth. Furthermore, he had been "actively recruiting potential Conference participants in the United States, many of them known militants . . The G.O.B [Government of Bermuda] has forty-odd names contacted by Brown in the District of Columbia area . . . Brown is supposedly trying to arrange a chartered air flight to bring delegates from the Los Angeles area, including Watts."[54] In the months leading up to the conference, Bermuda tightened immigration controls with the explicit intention of obstructing the entry of North American and West

Indian Black Power activists. At the behest of the British, the UBP imple-
mented a Race Relations Act that criminalized verbal and in-print racial
slurs and incitements of "race hatred"; British troops were stationed on the
island, and Canada placed two warships in Bermuda's waters. Interestingly,
Lord Shepherd, British minister of state for Foreign and Commonwealth
Affairs, informed British governor to Bermuda, Lord Martonmere, that the
British Defence Department would happily "arrange" for a vessel to have
"engine trouble" off Bermuda during the conference.[55] The Federal Bureau
of Investigation and British officials collectively created an immigration stop
list, and several would-be conference participants were denied entry into
Bermuda. The Central Intelligence Agency noted that about eleven hundred
persons attended the conference, but only about one hundred were from
outside Bermuda, including some forty from the United States. It felt that
these numbers would have been higher without the imposed immigration
controls.[56]

   However, several critical activists did manage to attend, among them
C.L.R. James, Queen Mother Moore, Flo Kennedy, Yosef Ben-Jochannan and
Acklyn Lynch. Local participants were able to have extended discussions with
these political stalwarts. Moore and Kennedy led workshops on women and
youth, and Ben-Jochannan on religion and history.[57] James led a workshop on
politics, and gave the opening night-time address at a packed Pembroke Hamilton Club football stadium. Aiming his message directly at the black youth,
James contextualized Black Power within a global, revolutionary framework
of a "mighty struggle against the forces of American imperialism", the world
of "Vietnam, Cuba and Tanzania", and continued colonialism in the Caribbean. For James, it was not neocolonialism, but the same old colonialism
that had increased in strength after political independence in the Caribbean.
He challenged the black youth not to "play with revolution", arguing that
mobilization of the masses was the only way to successfully resist imperial
intervention after a revolution.[58]

   Key themes emanating from the conference included pan-Africanism,
anticolonialism and Black Power's relationship to African and Asian liberation struggles. Conference workshops included economics, politics, religion
and history, culture, technology and communications. It dealt with local,
regional and international issues related to African people. On a regional

level, it addressed how West Indian leaders were beholden to foreign eco-political interests while their countries had yet to move beyond their plan-tation structures.[59] On this last note, the US Central Intelligence Agency confirmed this, as it reported:

> Neither political independence in Guyana, Trinidad-Tobago, Jamaica and Bar-bados nor progressively increasing internal autonomy in most of the other territories has significantly altered their socioeconomic structures. In many ways, the social patterns that developed in the plantation economies during the days of colonialism persist today . . . Blacks still make up the bulk of the lower classes . . . The relatively small middle classes are composed largely of "coloured" (i.e. mulatto) people with an admixture of East Indians (especially in Guyana and Trinidad), Chinese and whites. The apex of the social and economic pyramid is occupied by a small white or near-white elite, accounting for less than one percent to about four percent of the populations. A highly disproportionate share of the agricultural estates, businesses, commerce, banking and industry is controlled by the white minorities – and by foreign-based companies.[60]

At the conference, resolutions were passed regarding black nationhood, sol-idarity with Black Power globally, African liberation struggles and the West Indian student–led Black Power protests at Montreal's Sir George Williams University, the creation of independent black schools and global commu-nication networks, for public education systems across the West Indies to increase access to literature related to the global black experience, and for Bermuda's government to retract its ban on progressive black materials. A boycott of the daily *Royal Gazette* was also proposed, along with the creation of an alternative Black Power publication, *Umoja: The Bermuda Voice of the Black Power Conference.*[61]

The conference received messages of solidarity from numerous organi-zations and individuals across the globe.[62] From his exile Kwame Nkrumah extended "revolutionary greetings" to the "historic Black Power meeting" as part of "the world rebellion of the oppressed against the oppressor". For Nkrumah, this was a fight – against colonialism, neocolonialism and racism – in which blacks should unify in armed struggle "against the common enemy".[63] Stokely Carmichael, who was then Nkrumah's political student, also submitted a statement, proclaiming that "Black Power is the struggle for the possession of economic, cultural, social and political power which [black people] in common with the oppressed of the earth must have in order to ... overthrow the oppressor".[64]

Regarding the effect of the conference, on a regional level, FCO officials suggested that the conference had been a catalyst for the increase in overt Black Power activity in the Caribbean in the following year.[65] US president Richard Nixon called for an investigation into the relationship between Black Power in the United States and the Caribbean. A subsequent Central Intelligence Agency report, "Black Radicalism in the Caribbean", described Caribbean Black Power as a "home-grown phenomenon" with developing ties to militant US-based groups. The report contended that concrete contacts across the Americas had been established during the organization of the Bermuda Black Power conference, and that there had been serious efforts to establish a regional grouping of West Indian radicals.[66] Kamarakafego's name is littered across these documents.

The conference also had a significant impact on the political education of blacks in Bermuda.[67] The PLP Youth Wing embraced and attempted to implement many of the resolutions of the conference. *Umoja* became its official newspaper. In the aftermath of the conference, Youth Wingers formed the Black Beret Cadre, which aimed for a total revolution in the island.[68] The Black Beret Cadre quickly emerged as the vanguard of Bermuda's Black Power Movement. Led by John Hilton Bassett Jr, it formed relationships with the US Black Panther Party. Kamarakafego remained an advisor to the Black Beret Cadre, often reminding them of the need to establish a wider political base among Bermuda's masses as opposed to direct military action against the state. Through political education, liberation schools, survival programmes, publications, rallies and low-scale urban guerrilla warfare, the Black Beret Cadre clashed with the island's security forces. In 1977, Beret associate Erskine "Buck" Burrows was hanged for the 1972–73 assassinations of Bermuda's British police commissioner and governor.[69]

AUSTRALASIA

The Bermuda Black Power conference had global repercussions. During the meeting, an Australian radio station conducted a phone interview with

Kamarakafego. In the interview, he stated that blacks in the Americas were concerned that whites were abusing the land and human rights of their indigenous black "brothers and sisters" in the Pacific region. Shortly afterwards, he received a telegram from Koori activists Bob Maza and Bruce McGuinness – chairman and director, respectively, of the Aborigines Advancement League (AAL). They had heard the broadcast and invited him to come and support their own Black Power struggle in Australia, which consisted of indigenous Australians' fight for land rights, self-reliance, aboriginal-controlled communities, and economic and political independence.

According to Gary Foley, the "Australian version of Black Power, like its American counterpart, was essentially about the necessity for black people to define the world in their own terms, and to seek self-determination without white interference".[70] Roberta Sykes, member of the Australian Black Panther Party and delegate to Jamaica's 1973 Sixth PAC regional meeting, remarked that Australia had been a "Black man's country" for over "thirty thousand years," but in the past two hundred years it had been dominated by "white-western Europeans" who "murdered, poisoned, rounded up, and confined on Reserves" the original inhabitants. Indigenous persons were still placed on reserves, faced dual and discriminatory legislation, malnutrition, and high infant mortality rates. There was a virtual absence of blacks in the fields of medicine, law, engineering, economy, or any positions of power.[71]

Kamarakafego's arrival in Fitzroy, a suburb of Melbourne, in August 1969 "catapulted" the term Black Power into "the Australian imagination".[72] At the request of Maza, whom he had met previously as a petitioner to the UN Committee of 24, he addressed a press conference at the AAL's headquarters. Maza felt that the broadcast could further inspire blacks across the Pacific who were engaged in their own respective struggles against French, British, Dutch, Portuguese and American colonialism.[73] Announced as the "president of the Black Power Movement in the Caribbean and Latin America", Kamarakafego's presence was denounced by the Australian media. During the meeting, elder aboriginal activist Pastor Doug Nichols told Kamarakafego that he was "hurting their cause".[74] The media fuelled the debate, and portrayed it as a warning about the "violent nature" of Black Power.[75] Indeed, Kamarakafego's visit revealed tensions within the AAL itself, which was also comprised of paternalistic white Australians. Writing in 1970, Patsy Kruger (who became president of the Victoria branch of the AAL) stated that the AAL had "existed for thirteen years on money given from people from all walks of life, but it is a charitable organization and we don't want charity we want justice".[76] In October 1969, Nichols resigned from the AAL, as McGuinness (the AAL's first Koori director) and Maza sought to remove all non-Koori members of the organization from positions of power.[77]

Meanwhile, the Koori youth of Sydney's inner suburbs of Redfern were developing their own political movement. With the streets as their "only true meeting place", activists such as Gary Foley, Paul Coe and Roberta Sykes were inspired by a legacy of resistance to indigenous exploitation, such as the 1965 "Freedom Rides". Though they saw themselves as "inheritors of a long tradition of political struggle", after "government inaction" dashed high expectations of a 1967 referendum that was supposed to address core questions about aboriginal citizenship, these activists "felt a strong sense of betrayal and cynicism at the more non-confrontationist methods and tactics of the older generation". According to the Minjerribah indigenous poet and political activist, Kath Walker (Oodgeroo Noonuccal), the referendum "did not benefit the black Australians though it eased the guilty conscience of white Australians in this country and overseas". Hence, she felt it could be regarded as a victory for white Australians who formed a coalition with black Australians.[78]

This reflected the youth's criticism of the presence of white liberals in positions of leadership in organizations formed to address aboriginal concerns. According to Coe, "there were too many white liberals running black affairs", and he felt that nothing would get done "until young blacks [took] the initiative".[79] Having met with veteran activists and been aware of liberation struggles across the world, they saw the Koori situation in the context of decolonization. They studied African American political struggle and leaders, such as Malcolm X, Huey P. Newton, Bobby Seale, George Jackson, Eldridge Cleaver and Angela Davis, as well as Vine Deloria Jr, and the American Indian movement. *Bury My Heart at Wounded Knee*, a history of the plight of native Americans, was as widely read as Cleaver's *Soul on Ice*. In addition, the presence of African American Vietnam veterans on leave in Sydney exposed them to the latest developments in American racial politics, African American political literature and music.

In 1971, Dennis Walker (the son of Kathy Walker) and Sam Watson formed the Australian Black Panther Party in Brisbane. Walker, who supported armed struggle (a position his mother disagreed with), allegedly once told reporters, "If you haven't got a gun, you have nothing. We're not going to get what we want by standing here and talking."[80] Along with activists such as Foley, Coe and Sykes, they focused on issues such as police brutality, the frequent rape of indigenous women and children by whites, legal injustices and the reclamation of ancestral lands. They also created a number of survival programmes, police patrols, medical services and free legal consultations such as the Redfern Aboriginal Legal Service formed in 1970 by aboriginal activists and lawyers.[81] Critical moments of Black Power in Australia occurred at a 1971 Springbok rugby tour; the 1972 opening of the Black Theatre (inspired by Barbara Ann Teer's theatre in Harlem) and incidents surrounding the Aboriginal Embassy in 1972.[82]

Before returning to the Americas, Kamarakafego travelled to Fiji, the Ocean Islands, the Solomon Islands and Hawaii. While making contacts with indigenous leaders in the region, he was able to observe the political and social conditions of indigenous peoples across Australasia. This marked a decade-long relationship between Kamarakafego and the black communities in the region.

FROM BLACK POWER TO PAN-AFRICANISM

According to Nkrumah, Black Power was the "daughter of Pan-Africanism" and "the vanguard in a global revolt against capitalism, neocolonialism and imperialism, which aimed to liberate Black people across the diaspora".[83] Events surrounding Bermuda's Black Power conference clearly demonstrated this syncretic relationship between the Black Power and pan-African movements. According to James Garrett, the "genesis" of the Sixth Pan-African Congress was during the Bermuda conference, after a letter from Nkrumah that called for a similar conference to be held in Africa had been read.[84] Sylvia Hill, one of the key organizers of the PAC, asserts that Kamarakafego initially raised the idea for the Sixth PAC with the encouragement of Nkrumah and C.L.R. James.[85]

Kamarakafego, like other pan-African activists of his generation, was involved in both the Black Power and Pan-African movements. In the aftermath of the Bermuda conference, C.L.R. James remained in the island for about a week. He and Kamarakafego had extensive discussions about the need for a Sixth PAC. They also discussed the need to include black people who had historically not been represented at such meetings, such as those from the Pacific Islands and from South and Central America. This launched a five-year process of organizing and collaboration with organizers around the world.[86]

Kamarakafego set about organizing a subsequent Black Power conference in Barbados in July 1970. He had secured the support of Nkrumah, who, writing from Conakry, Guinea, stated, "Thank you for your letter of March 3, 1970. I have noted with interest that there will be a meeting of Black people from Africa, Asia, the Americas, the Caribbean, Australia and other parts of the world . . . I shall be glad to be an official patron."[87] However, in April 1970, Barbados's prime minister, Errol Barrow, rescinded his initial support due to "international pressures". After discussions with the Black Power Steering Committee, the title of the conference was changed to the Congress of African People (CAP), and held in Atlanta.[88] According to Garrett, it was at this moment that Amiri Baraka was invited to take on a leadership role because he had the organizational apparatus that could allow such a conference to be held at short notice.[89]

CAP represented an impressive collage of black political thinkers from across ideological spectrums and backgrounds. However, many international delegates felt that it lacked the presupposed global pan-African focus and instead focused primarily on African American issues. According to Kamarakafego, the international black and Asian participants informed him that they were disappointed with the conference, particularly the "Politics workshop" which exclusively focused on the problems of "Newark and New Jersey".[90] This seemed to be the sentiment expressed by Dominica's Roosevelt Douglas, student leader of the Black Power movement at Sir George Williams University. He felt that the contributions of Caribbean pan-Africanists such as Garvey and Henry Sylvester Williams, "an African born in Trinidad", had been dismissed. However, he felt it important to understand this experience because "Africans in the Caribbean [had] played a very significant role not only to the development of Pan-Africanist thought but to the liberation of African people wherever they [lived.]" He continued,

> Today there are 130 million African people in the Americas. Let us understand that there are only 35 million Africans in America. Therefore, we have to move to unite 130 million African people in the United States, in Latin America, and the Caribbean and this can only be done if we are serious about realizing that we can only depend on ourselves; we cannot depend on liberals . . . we cannot depend on Marxists.[91]

Douglas also felt it important to state that while blacks were not only fighting against the United States, but also Europe, NATO and, "when the time comes", the Soviet Union. This was similar to what Acklyn Lynch had called for at the Bermuda BPC: that the black community needed to look at itself from a pan-African perspective "of 600 million Black people who occupy the continent of Latin America, the Caribbean and parts of the US".[92]

At Kamarakafego's invitation, five Koori activists, including Maza, Kruger and McGuinness, were able to attend the CAP, but only at great economic expense. According to Australia's newspaper, the *Sun*, they were going to the United States to study self-help programmes for "negroes" there in order to try to introduce those programmes to Australia.[93] While there, they found that conference delegates knew very little about their experiences and raised questions about their African identity. According to Kamarakafego, CAP organizers had agreed to reimburse the group for their expenses in travelling to the United States, but this did not happen. Such issues tremendously bothered him. In addition, a serious rift developed between himself, Baraka and what he would call the "Newark, New Jersey group". This was part of the reason that he resigned from CAP later that year.[94] Kamarakafego hoped that in organizing the Sixth PAC he could avoid such issues. The complications of CAP were a prelude to the major challenges that he and other organizers would face. In 1971, Kamarakafego covertly called the first organizing meeting which was held in Bermuda and included individuals such as Abas Sykes (Tanzanian ambassador to the United States), C.L.R. James (who arrived but was denied entry into Bermuda), Courtland Cox, Jimmy Garrett, Calvin Hicks, Sonia Sanchez, Frankie Cox, Fay Garrett, Ansel Remy (Haiti), Joann Darrell (Bermuda) and Suzanne Cann (Bermuda). The organizers divided the world up into ten regions, including Africa, North America, Central and South America, the Caribbean, Europe, Asia and the Pacific. Kamarakafego stressed that the congress should focus on technology and science as opposed to only politics.[95]

The call for the Sixth PAC, drafted and written by James, Fletcher Robinson and Geri Augusto,[96] stated:

> The 20th century is the century of Black Power. It has already been marked by two dynamics. First, a unified conception of all peoples who have been colonized. They are known by friends and enemies as members of the Third World. And the most significant members of the Third World are those who strive for power to the people and Black Power to the Black people . . . The colonial peoples have begun one of the greatest movements toward human freedom that the world has ever known. The Sixth Pan-African Conference, to be held in the Republic of Tanzania . . . is part of that Movement.[97]

The call also outlined plans to establish in Africa a pan-African Science and Technology Centre. The centre was to serve the vast array of needs of African people in the scientific and technology fields. The overarching theme was to use human, technological and scientific resources to develop a self-supporting agricultural system in Africa. Finances were to come from Africans across the world, and it was to be staffed on a rotating basis based on current projects. In addition, the centre was "to be seen as a living concept among all African people", relevant to Africans "at home and abroad" and was a move towards pan-African self-reliance.[98]

Kamarakafego was responsible for coordinating South and Central America, Asia, the Pacific and Europe. He had many difficulties in doing so. For example, while he was able to bring Brazil's Abdias do Nascimento into the fold, he had less success with Cuba's Carlos Moore, who was adamant that not all blacks were African and who did not support the term "pan-African". Along with Sonia Sanchez he was placed under house arrest in Trinidad and Tobago. Nevertheless, he was still able to meet with Geddis Granger, Black Power leader of the National Joint Action Committee. In London, Garrett and Kamarakafego had trouble in garnering the support of various Black Power groups who were bent on using the term Black Power as opposed to pan-Africanism. They also raised questions about the value of science to revolution, and wondered whether that approach reflected a bourgeois capitalist agenda. Eventually, due to myriad personal and ideological issues Kamarakafego resigned from the organizing committee, much to the chagrin of James. However, finding himself in Tanzania when the congress was set to occur, he sorted out a number of logistic issues on the ground.[99]

As has been well documented elsewhere, the Sixth PAC began as a grassroots effort with government support but eventually became a government-dominated affair – including neocolonial conservative inputs. This led to the exclusion of Caribbean non-governmental organizations and activists such as Rodney from the congress. C.L.R. James did not attend based upon this issue. US officials heavily monitored Sixth PAC and this dynamic warrants further investigation. The major ideological battles surrounding the conference were also flanked by other divisive matters, such as egotism, pettiness and sexism. The interpersonal fallout that emerged from the Sixth PAC endured for a very long time.[100] This cast a cloud over the PAC and gave the impression that it was a largely unsuccessful affair. However, Kamarakafego asserted that despite these issues the Sixth PAC did garner a few positive results – though a Pan-African Centre of Technology was not of them. One of its successes was the distribution of medical supplies, organized by Sylvia Hill, to the revolutionary groups of Mozambique, Angola, South Africa and Namibia. In addition, indigenous groups, organizers and political leaders from Australasia and the Indian Ocean who were present benefited from meeting other black leaders from other hemispheres. They continued to organize and to push successfully for political independence in their respective localities in the aftermath of the PAC, similar to what African leaders such as Nkrumah did following the Fifth PAC in Manchester, England.[101]

BACK TO THE PACIFIC

Between 1970 and 1971 young, black and indigenous New Hebrideans formed the New Hebrides National Party in an effort to achieve political independence from British and French colonial rule. After travelling to the UN Committee of 24, its chairman, Father Walter Lini, passed through Tanzania and was introduced to the grassroots organizational structure of its Tanzania

National Union (TANU). The party endorsed this concept and organized itself via village party cells.[102] Kamarakafego was already well known to the party. He had met a number of Pacific Islanders from the United Nations.[103] His first visit to New Hebrides was in 1974 while organizing the Sixth PAC. In 1975, the party invited him to the island to be their "Party Adult Education Officer", with the specific task of conducting "political education" among "New Hebrideans from the rural indigenous masses".[104] Hosted by party chairman Lini, he arrived in New Hebrides in May 1975. He was to stay for an initial four months, and then possibly extend his time to a year. Under the guise that he would be training urban school dropouts, he used resources provided by the government to develop projects wherein rural residents could make key commodities from natural ingredients. The economic self-sufficiency of these communities posed a threat to multinational companies, such as the Australia-based Barnes Philips.[105]

At a public speech in Leleppa, Vila, Kamarakafego informed about two hundred persons that he was from Africa and had come to set up a youth centre for athletics, discussions and technical classes. He also said that students such as Peter Salemalo and Daniel Nato who were studying in the United States at the Center for Black Education (based at the Drum and Spear Bookstore in Washington, DC) would, at the request of Garrett (who had also been in New Hebrides), teach at the school. British authorities claimed that he delivered "a long diatribe against whites on familiar lines tailored to the history and condition of New Hebrides".[106] During the speech Kamarakafego attacked white "missionaries for not telling the people that religion began in Africa and that Jesus Christ was black". He also told the audience that the population of the area had once been more than forty-five million before the missionaries arrived, but that it was now less than one hundred thousand due to the introduction of diseases by Europeans and the nefarious practice of "blackbirding", which involved New Hebrideans being forced aboard ships and taken to Australia to work in its sugar cane fields.[107] Kamarakafego also stressed the need for the island's blacks to retain their local customs as well as to produce and consume local food as opposed to inferior European-based diets. He advised locals not to sell any more land to white men; that land was being sold without their knowledge; that family planning would decimate their population; and that whites should be chased out. Ironically, the acting head of the Special Branch of Vanuatu's police force found his discussion of "blackbirding" and the European spreading of diseases to be mostly correct.[108] He also felt that Kamarakafego "had made quite an impact on the people" and "was regarded as being very well educated and intelligent".[109]

While British officials had not underrated the possible "insidiousness" of his speech, they "had pinned some hopes on" Kamarakafego's "approach being so novel and sophisticated as to be somewhat above the heads of rural audiences here". However, it seemed clear to them that he had "been well briefed" and was "adept at matching his style to the occasion". This had led to a "difficult and potentially dangerous problem".[110] French authorities echoed this sentiment. Paris regarded "all Black Power propagandists as a threat to security", and knowledge of Kamarakafego's presence alarmed French expatriates and National Party opponents.[111] The British and French resident commissioners had "considered long and carefully" – for at least a year and half – about preventing both Kamarakafego and Garrett, "two agents of the Black Power Movement, from entering New Hebrides". They were concerned about the "perniciousness of the doctrines expressed but also the damage which" they could do in the political condominium, discussing how to best "contain the spread of such doctrines, and limit or counteract their effects".[112]

British resident commissioner R.W.H. du Boulay summoned Lini to "warn" him of what "[Kamarakafego] was doing to his own and [his] Party's prospects" and told him that he "would need to be convinced that [Kamarakafego] would really behave himself and cause no trouble" before he would extend his stay. Lini had told him that he would be personally responsible for ensuring that Kamarakafego ceased "propagating Black Power doctrines". Du Boulay was also concerned whether others of the National Party might "constitute a Black Power cell". However, he felt that without intimidation, the mass of New Hebrideans would "recoil from these repugnant Black Power doctrines (whilst never forgetting the injuries they believed to have been done to them by the first white settlers and traders)".[113] The French were less optimistic. They felt that if the "intense propaganda" of these "agents of Black Power" was directed towards the upcoming national elections, it would "encourage racial hatred", "public order disturbances" and lead to "violence" and "fatal actions". They called for a quick end, and as Kamarakafego was a British subject, left the task in the hands of the British.[114] However, Kamarakafego had the support of party "extremists" and some villagers, and it was felt that he would resist deportation by force. British officials recommended using a joint Anglo-French force to "extract" Kamarakafego via a "clean and effective" operation. While strong French apathy to the National Party could have led to violent clashes with French forces and prejudiced present constitutional reforms,[115] the British hoped that French gendarmeries from Noumea could be placed on standby. They preferred to fly in British troops from the region, as they wanted to avoid sending troops from the United Kingdom for political and logistical reasons.[116]

While the National Party decried the deportation proceedings on the grounds that Kamarakafego's services were severely needed by the rural community, they did not resist his initial arrest by force. However, the protestors were tried and found guilty of violating airport laws by driving their cars onto the runway. Godfrey Toa, Barrack Sope, Juan Nopa and Peter Kalpau Taurakoto were fined above the others.[117] The National Party responded by asking that a number of Australian nationals residing in New Hebrides be deported. In an interesting letter to du Boulay, Lini stated:

> We have been accused [of being] Communists and Black Power [activists] . . . We have not in any way taken anybody's land and divided it all up for sale to other people. This to us is White Power so for all accusations if it is judged internationally we are not Black Power and [Pauulu Kamarakafego] is not Black Power either because he does not advocate taking other peoples custom and tearing it down to suit their own ends. We believe we are not Black Power nor communists as you think we are.[118]

To this, du Boulay responded, "The Movement of which Dr. [Kamarakafego] is a prominent member of . . . believes that changes can only be brought about through violence directed by members of one race against those of another."[119] Both responses are perplexing, for perhaps Kamarakafego did not call for violence in New Hebrides, but he *was* most certainly Black Power.

CONCLUSION

The case study of the political career of Pauulu Kamarakafego illustrates the importance of time, family connections, place and circumstances in transforming an individual. Kamarakafego's Bermudian family and background predisposed him to global political activity. He would fight for black people wherever he found himself. Africa had always been present through his Aunt Mae, but he chose to go to Liberia to experience Africa first-hand. While there, he found not only his family but workers being exploited by rubber plantations. His fight against neocolonialism in Liberia drove him to the beacon of pan-Africanism in West Africa, Nkrumah's Ghana. Finding himself amid the repatriated African diasporic world of Ghana, he then travelled to Kenya on the eve of its independence. It was in East Africa where he blossomed as an ecological engineer and his horizons broadened to include international political activity.

Like a political alchemist, these experiences abroad transformed his political action back in Bermuda as a member of parliament, as a grassroots activist for universal adult suffrage, as an advocate of decolonization at the United Nations, and as an organizer of the important 1969 Black Power Conference. In Australia, he immersed himself in the budding Black Power movement of the indigenous Koori. The support of pan-African elders such as C.L.R. James and Nkrumah led him to begin organizing the CAP and the Sixth PAC. Faced with challenges and opportunities, amid ideological tensions, government shenanigans and interpersonal frustrations, he continued his life's work in their aftermath. Along the way he made friends and enemies, and made useful contributions.

Despite the political harassment by state powers, Kamarakafego never capitulated. He spent many years observing how the labour of black people was exploited to produce raw materials. In Bermuda it was stone; in Cuba, sugarcane; in the American South, cotton; and in Liberia, rubber. Ironically, he would encourage people to use their hands to transform natural materials into tools of liberation, as opposed to commodities by which they could be exploited. Kamarakafego knew that he was a global citizen, a son of the African diaspora long before he travelled afar. In this sense, for him, Black Power and pan-Africanism were both banners for his politics and driven by a deep-rooted desire to serve his wider global black and disfranchised community as an intellectual and activist. Nevertheless, Kamarakafego's narrative highlights the quagmire of studying Black Power from a global perspective. The challenges are self-evident. An analysis of Kamarakafego's striking autobiography, *Me One*, takes one down the proverbial "rabbit hole" in terms of political networks, time and space, the need to cross-reference dates, memories, names and moments, and a need to give agency to those communities in which he worked. It also suggests that definitions of Black Power include questions of political, economic and technological self-sufficiency. Furthermore, it calls for diaspora studies to incorporate the black indigenous experience in Australasia and elsewhere.

The rewards are well worth the work, however. His political life illuminates the deep-rooted relationship between Black Power and pan-Africanism, revealing a rich tapestry of connections that extend well before and beyond the 1960s. In teasing out the centrality of Bermuda as a logistic hub of global pan-African activity between 1969 and 1974, this chapter hints at the possibilities of other black metropoles that may have functioned similarly at different moments. In the case of New Hebrides (today, Vanuatu), there are glaring connections between colonialism, neocolonialism, "trans-whiteness" and the collaborative suppression of Black Power and black political movements by European states. That the French and British governments considered jointly "extracting" Kamarakafego, with the support of troops flown in from neighbouring colonies, further strengthens the need to "internationalize our discussions of J. Edgar Hoover and the FBI's Counter Intelligence Program (COINTELPRO)". His deportation calls for explorations on the use of immigration control as an instrument of political control. Kamarakafego's experiences have contemporary significance, as a lot of the issues he encountered and tried to rectify still obtain today. His ability to blend his politics with technical expertise, for example, would be useful for today's would-be agents of change. But this cannot happen as long as Kamarakafego and other important contributors to the history of the African diaspora remain obscure.

NOTES

1. "Roosevelt Osiris Nelson Brown", Foreign Commonwealth Office (hereafter FCO) 32/1231.
2. R.W.H. du Boulay to Monsieur Gauger, FCO 32/1231, 22 May 1975; "Roosevelt Osiris Nelson Brown", FCO 32/1231.

3. Pauulu Kamarakafego, *Me One: The Autobiography of Pauulu Kamarakefego* (Canada: PK Publishing, 2001), 241.
4. Callaghan to Flash Vila, FCO 32/1231, 27 June 1975.
5. R.W.H du Boulay to A.E.W. Bullock, FCO 32/1231, 1 July 1975.
6. Kamarakafego, *Me One*, 245–46.
7. C.L.R. James to Roosevelt Brown, 5 October 1976 (Copy of letter in possession of the author). See Penny Von Eschen, *Race Against Empire: Black Americans and Anticolonialism, 1937–1957* (New York: Cornell University Press, 1997); Jonathan Fenderson, "Journey Toward a Black Aesthetic? Hoyt Fuller, the Black Arts Movement and the Black Intellectual Community" (PhD diss., University of Massachusetts, 2011); Marika Sherwood, *Claudia Jones: A Life in Exile* (London: Lawrence and Wishart, 2000); Carol Boyce Davies, *Left of Karl Marx: The Political Life of Black Communist Claudia Jones* (Durham: Duke University Press, 2007); Timothy Tyson, *Radio Free Dixie: Robert F. Williams and the Roots of Black Power* (Chapel Hill: University of North Carolina Press, 2001); Rupert Charles Lewis, *Walter Rodney's Intellectual and Political Thought* (Detroit: Wayne State University Press, 1998); Stokely Carmichael and Michael Ekwueme Thelwell, *Ready for Revolution: The Life and Struggles of Stokely Carmichael (Kwame Ture)* (New York: Scribner, 2003); La TaSha Levy, "Remembering Sixth-PAC: Interviews with Sylvia Hill and Judy Claude, Organizers of the Sixth Pan-African Congress", *Black Scholar* 37, no. 4 (Winter 2007): 39–47.
8. See Cynthia Young, *Soul Power: Culture, Radicalism and the Making of the U.S. Third World Left* (Durham: Duke University Press, 2006); Michael West and William Martin, eds., *From Toussaint to Tupac: The Black International in the Age of Revolution* (Chapel Hill: University of North Carolina Press, 2009); Michael Clemons and Charles Jones, "Global Solidarity: The Black Panther Party in the International Arena", in *Liberation, Imagination, and the Black Panther Party*, ed. Kathleen Cleaver and George Katsiaficas (New York: Routledge, 2001), 20–40; Ronald Walters, *Pan Africanism in the African Diaspora: An Analysis of Modern Afrocentric Political Movements* (Detroit: Wayne State University Press, 1993); Sohail Daulatzai, *Black Star, Crescent Moon: The Muslim International and Black Freedom Beyond America* (Minneapolis: University of Minnesota Press, 2012); Peniel Joseph, *Waiting 'til the Midnight Hour: A Narrative History of Black Power in America* (New York: Holt Paperbacks, 2007); William Lux, "Black Power in the Caribbean", *Journal of Black Studies* 3, no. 2 (1972): 207–25; Walter Rodney, *Groundings with My Brothers* (London: Bogle-L'Ouverture, 1971); Quito Swan, *Black Power in Bermuda: The Struggle for Decolonization* (New York: Palgrave Macmillan, 2010); Victoria Pasley, "The Black Power Movement in Trinidad: An Exploration of Gender", *Journal of International Women's Studies* 3, no. 1 (2001):

24–40; Winston N. Trew, *Black for a Cause, Not Just Because* (Derbyshire: Derwent, 2010); R. Bunce and Paul Field, "Obi B. Egbuna, CLR James and the Birth of Black Power in Britain: Black Radicalism in Britain 1967–72", *Twentieth Century British History* 22, no. 3 (2011): 391–414; Anne-Marie Angelo, "The Black Panthers in London, 1967–1972", *Radical History Review*, no. 103 (2009): 17–35; Harry Goulbourne, "Africa and the Caribbean in Caribbean Consciousness and Action in Britain", David Nicholls Memorial Lecture, no. 2 (2000), http://www.dnmt.org.uk/dnmt/images/docs/dnmlecture_2000.pdf; Colin Palmer, "Identity, Race and Black Power in Independent Jamaica", in *The Modern Caribbean*, ed. Franklin Knight and Colin Palmer (Chapel Hill: University of North Carolina Press, 1989), 111–29; Herman Bennett, "The Black Power February (1970) Revolution in Trinidad", Modern Caribbean, 130–47; Bert Thomas, "Caribbean Black Power", *Journal of Black Studies* 22, no. 3 (1992): 392–410; Lewis, *Walter Rodney*; Horace Campbell, *Rasta and Resistance* (Trenton, NJ: African World Press, 1987); Michael West, "Seeing Darkly: Guyana, Black Power, and Walter Rodney's Expulsion From Jamaica", *Small Axe*, no. 25 (February 2008): 93–104; David Austin, *Fear of a Black Nation: Race, Sex, and Security in Sixties Montreal* (Toronto: Between the Lines, 2013); "Kathy Lothian, "Seizing the Time: Australian Aborigines and the Influence of the Black Panther Party, 1969–1972", *Journal of Black Studies* 35, no. 4 (March 2005): 179–200; Gary Foley, "Black Power in Redfern, 1968–1972", http://www.kooriweb.org/foley/essays/essay_1.html; Roosevelt Browne, "An Interview with Roosevelt Browne", by Gayleatha Cobb, *Black World Digest* (March 1976): 32–43; Eddie Glaude, ed., *Is It Nation Time? Contemporary Essays on Black Power and Black Nationalism* (Chicago: University of Chicago Press, 2001); Fanon Che Wilkins, "The Making of Black Internationalists: SNCC and Africa before the Launching of Black Power, 1960–1965", *Journal of African American History* 92, no. 4 (Fall 2007): Anthony Bogues, "Black Power, Decolonization, and Caribbean Politics: Walter Rodney and the Politics of *The Groundings with My Brothers*", *Boundary 2* 36, no. 1 (2009): 127–47; Brian Meeks, *Narratives of Resistance: Jamaica, Trinidad, and the Caribbean* (Kingston: University of the West Indies Press, 2000); and Johanna Fernández, "Denise Oliver and the Young Lords Party", in *Want to Start a Revolution? Radical Women in the Black Freedom Struggle*, ed. Komozi Woodard et al. (New York: New York University Press, 2009), 271–94.

9. See V.P. Franklin, "Introduction: New Black Power Studies – National, International, and Transnational Perspectives", *Journal of African American History* 92, no. 4 (Fall 2007): 463–66.

10. Quito Swan, "Bermuda Looks to the East: Marcus Garvey, the UNIA and

Bermuda", *Wadabegei: A Journal of the Caribbean and Its Diaspora* 13, no. 1 (2010): 30–33.

11. Kamarakafego, *Me One*, 25–31.

12. The story of the modern Caribbean is very much one of migration. See for example, Knight and Palmer, *Modern Caribbean*; Winston James, *Holding Aloft the Banner of Ethiopia: Caribbean Radicalism in Early Twentieth-Century America* (New York: Verso, 1999); Glenn Chambers, *Race, Nation, and West Indian Immigration to Honduras, 1890–1940* (Baton Rouge: Louisiana State University Press, 2010); and Lara Putnam, "Nothing Matters but Color: Transnational Circuits, the Interwar Caribbean, and the Black International", in *From Toussaint to Tupac: The Black International in the Age of Revolution* (Chapel Hill: University of North Carolina Press, 2009), 107–30.

13. Kamarakafego, *Me One*, 25–31, 36.

14. Ibid., 38.

15. Ibid., 25–26, 84. For further information on Gordon, see Ira Philip, *Freedom Fighters: From Monk to Mazumbo* (London: Akira, 1987).

16. For discussions on race and diaspora in Cuba, see Ada Ferrer, *Insurgent Cuba: Race, Nation and Revolution, 1868–1898* (Chapel Hill: University of North Carolina Press, 1999); Frank Guridy, *Forging Diaspora: Afro-Cubans and African Americans in a World of Empire and Jim Crow* (Chapel Hill, University of North Carolina Press, 2010); and Carlos Moore, *Pichon. A Memoir: Race and Revolution in Castro's Cuba* (New York: Lawrence Hill , 2008).

17. Kamarakafego, *Me One*, 76.

18. Ibid.

19. Ibid., 85.

20. Ibid., 87.

21. William C. Hine, "Civil Rights and Campus Wrongs: South Carolina State College Students Protest, 1955–1968", *South Carolina Historical Magazine* 97, no. 4 (October 1996): 310–31.

22. Kamarakafego, *Me One*, 88.

23. Ibid., 88.

24. Ibid.

25. Ibid., 101–3.

26. Ibid., 103.

27. Ibid., 106.

28. Ibid., 106–7. For more on black American expatriates in Ghana during this time, see Kevin Gaines, *American Africans in Ghana: Black Expatriates and the Civil Rights Era* (Chapel Hill: University of North Carolina Press, 2008).

29. Kamarakafego, *Me One*, 129. For the importance of political developments in

Kenya to the wider black world, see Gerald Horne, *Mau-Mau in Harlem? The U.S. and the Liberation of Kenya* (New York: Palgrave Macmillan, 2009).

30. Kamarakafego, *Me One*, 129.
31. Ibid., 131.
32. Ibid., 132–33.
33. See Meeks, *Narratives of Resistance*; Lux, "Black Power in the Caribbean"; Rodney, *Groundings*; Swan, *Black Power in Bermuda*; Palmer, Black Power in Jamaica; Bennett, *Black Power February*; Thomas, *Caribbean Black Power*; Lewis, *Walter Rodney*; Campbell, *Rasta and Resistance*; West and Martin, *Toussaint to Tupac*; Austin, *Fear of a Nation*; and Bogues, "Walter Rodney".
34. See Gerald Horne, *Cold War in a Hot Zone: The United States Confronts Labor and Independence Struggles in the British West Indies* (Philadelphia: Temple University, 2007).
35. Rodney, *Groundings*, 28.
36. British Government, *Report of the Bermuda Constitutional Conference* (London: Her Majesty's Stationery Office, 1967), 20–23.
37. The document, "An Analysis of Bermuda's Social Problems" was reprinted in Kamarakafego, *Me One*, 391.
38. Ibid., 119.
39. Ibid., 102.
40. British Government, *Report of the Bermuda Conference*, 2.
41. J. Randolph Williams, *Lois: Bermuda's Grand Dame of Politics* (Bermuda: Camden Editions, 2001), 56, 97, 331.
42. "PLP Hurls Trenchant Criticism of UBP", *Bermuda Recorder*, 27 January 1967.
43. Ibid.
44. See Wooding Commission, *Bermuda Civil Disorders, 1968: Report of Commission and Statement by the Government of Bermuda* (London: Her Majesty's Stationery Office, 1969).
45. "Visitors of Black Power to Bermuda", FCO 44/195, 11 August 1967.
46. Kamarakafego, *Me One*, 157; *Black Power Conference Reports, Philadelphia, August 30–September 1, 1968; Bermuda, July 13, 1969* (New York: Action Library, 1971), 3–4; "Programme: 1st Regional Black Power Conference" (copy in author's possession).
47. *Royal Gazette*, 5 April 1969; "More Data on Black Power Conference", *Bermuda Recorder*, 5 April 1969.
48. "Roosevelt Brown Says", *Bermuda Recorder* (January–July 1969).
49. Letter to the editor, *Royal Gazette*, 14 January, 11 February, 13 April and 12, 23, 25 June 1969.
50. *Royal Gazette*, 5 April 1969.

51. Price to Sir Edward Peck, FCO 44/203, 14 March 1969.
52. "West Indies and Caribbean Area, Monthly Intelligence Summary", FCO 44/202, July 1969.
53. "Bermuda, Black Power Activities in Bermuda", FCO 44/196, 14 March 1969.
54. Charles Manning to US Department of State, file A-29, CFPF 1967–69; POL 23 BER, 9 May 1969.
55. "Bermuda: Black Power Conference", FCO 44/199, 16 May 1969.
56. Central Intelligence Agency, CIA memorandum, "Black Radicalism in the Caribbean", 6 July 1970.
67. Swan, *Black Power in Bermuda*, 77–95.
58. C.L.R. James, "Open Statement to Black Power Conference", C.L.R. James Papers, 1933–2001, Columbia University Archival Collection, New York.
59. "West Indies and Caribbean Area: Monthly Intelligence Summary", FCO 44/202, 15 August 1969.
60. CIA, "Black Radicalism", 2.
61. "West Indies and Caribbean Area: Monthly Intelligence Summary", FCO 44/202, 15 August 1969.
62. Kamarakafego, *Me One*, 160, 189.
63. Kwame Nkrumah to Black Power Conference, West Indies, 11 July 1969, reprinted in Kamarakafego, *Me One*, 190.
64. Stokely Carmichael to Black Power Conference, West Indies, 11 July 1969, reprinted in Kamarakafego, *Me One*, 191.
65. Swan, *Black Power in Bermuda*, 90.
66. CIA, "Black Radicalism", 1, 14.
67. Kamarakafego, interview with author, 12 October 2004.
68. Michelle Khaldun, interview with author, Bermuda, 10 October 2004; Swan, *Black Power in Bermuda*, 102–4.
69. See Swan, *Black Power in Bermuda*, 1, 8, 10.
70. Foley, "Black Power".
71. Roberta Sykes, "Word from Down Under", *Negro Digest* (June 1973): 46–47.
72. Foley, "Black Power".
73. Australian aborigines have had a long interest in the fate of their overseas fellow men, and that was reflected in the long association with Marcus Garvey from the 1920s. See Franklin W. Knight, "Marcus Garvey and Australian Aborigines", *Jamaica Observer*, 2 March 2011.
74. Kamarakafego, interview; Kamarakafego, *Me One*, 163.
75. Foley, "Black Power"; "Happy to Forget that Visit", *Herald*, 30 August 1969.
76. "Patsy Wants to Learn How to Start a Thought Revolution", *Australian*, 2 September 1970.

77. Foley, "Black Power".

78. Ibid.

79. Ibid.

80. "In White Australia Aborigines Seeking Black Power: Black Power Has Hit White Australia", *Boca Raton News*, 16 January 1972. 81. See Browne, "Interview", 32–43; Lothian, "Seizing the Time"; Foley, "Black Power".

82. See Kathy Lothian, "Moving Blackwards: Black Power and the Aboriginal Embassy", in *Transgressions: Critical Australian Indigenous Histories*, ed. Ingereth Macfarlane and Mark Hannah (Canberra: ANU E Press and Aboriginal History Incorporated, 2007), 19–34.

83. Kwame Nkrumah, "The Spectre of Black Power", in *The Struggle Continues* (London: Panaf, 1973), 40.

84. James Garrett, "A Historical Sketch: The Sixth Pan-African Congress", *Black World/Negro Digest* (March 1975): 4.

85. Sylvia Hill, interview, "From the Sixth Pan-African Congress to the Free South Africa Movement", in *No Easy Victories: African Liberation and American Activists over a Half Century, 1950–2000*, ed. William Minter, Gail Hovey and Charles Cobb Jr (Trenton, NJ: Africa World Press, 2007), 165–66.

86. Kamarakafego, *Me One*, 194.

87. Kwame Nkrumah to Roosevelt Browne, 30 March 1970, reprinted in Kamarakafego, *Me One*, 225.

88. Kamarakafego, interview. For more on the general history of the CAP, see Michael Simanga, " 'The Congress of African People': History and Memory of an Ideological Journey (1970–1980)" (PhD diss., Union Institute and University, 2008); Woodard, *A Nation within a Nation: Amiri Baraka (LeRoi Jones) and Black Power Politics* (Chapel Hill: University of North Carolina Press, 1999); Joseph, *Waiting*.

89. Garrett, "Historical Sketch", 6.

90. Kamarakafego, *Me One*, 169.

91. Roosevelt Douglas, "Speech", in *African Congress: A Documentary of the First Modern Pan-African Congress*, ed. Imamu Amiri Baraka (New York: William Morrow, 1972), 83.

92. "Delegates to Black Power Conference Give Their Views", *Bermuda Recorder*, 11 July 1969.

93. "Aborigines to Study in USA", *NorthCote Leader*, 2 September 1970.

94. Kamarakafego, *Me One*, 169.

95. Ibid., 194.

96. Geri Augusto, "No Easy Victories Interview: Geri Augusto", by Charles Cobb, 26 January 2005.

97.   Kamarakafego, *Me One*, 196.

98.   Ibid., 199.

99.   See Brenda Plummer, *In Search of Power: African Americans in the Era of Decolonization, 1956–1974* (Cambridge: Cambridge University Press, 2012); The "clashes" with Baraka and the "New Jersey group" continued; Kamarakafego felt they constantly asked divisive questions, such as about who made the calls for the conference; ibid., 195–96, 200.

100. See Levy, "Remembering Sixth-PAC"; Hill, "From the Sixth Pan-African Congress"; Augusto, "No Easy Victories", *Resolutions and Selected Speeches from the Sixth Pan African Congress* (Dar es Salaam: Tanzania Publishing House, 1976).

101. Kamarakafego, *Me One*, 203–4.

102. Browne, "Interview".

103. Kamarakafego, *Me One*, 241.

104. "Roosevelt Oris Nelson Brown", FCO 32/1231.

105. Kamarakafego, *Me One*, 241.

106. R.W.H. du Boulay to Priority FCO, FCO 32/1231, 29 May 1975.

107. C.M. Dumper to R.W.H. du Boulay, FCO 32/1231, 13 May 1975.

108. Ibid.

109. "Black Power: Roosevelt Brown", C.M. Dumper to R.W.H. du Boulay, FCO 32/1231, 29 May 1975.

110. J.A. Burgess to R.A. Eilbeck, Pacific Dependent Territories Department, FCO 32/1231, 29 May 1975.

111. R.W.H. du Boulay to Priority FCO, FCO 32/1231, 29 May 1975.

112. "Mr. Roosevelt Brown", R.W.H. du Boulay to Monsieur Gauger, FCO 32/1231, 20 May 1975.

113. Ibid.

114. "Activitiés d'un agent du 'Black Power' ", Monsieur Gauger to R.W.H. du Boulay, FCO 32/1231, 5 May 1975.

115. R.W.H. du Boulay to Immediate FCO, FCO 32/1231, 26 June 1975.

116. Callaghan to Flash Vila, FCO 32/1231, 27 June 1975.

117. "Verdict", R.M. Hampson, FCO 32/1231, 18 August 1975.

118. W. Hadye Lini to De Boulay, FCO 32/1231, 19 June 1975.

119. R.W.H. du Boulay to Reverend W. Hadye Lini, FCO 32/1231, 24 June 1975.

INDEX

CONTRIBUTORS

FRANKLIN W. KNIGHT is Leonard and Helen R. Stulman Professor of History and Director of the Center for Africana Studies, Johns Hopkins University, Maryland. His publications include *Slave Society in Cuba During the Nineteenth Century*; *The African Dimension of Latin American Societies*; *UNESCO General History of the Caribbean*, volume 3: *The Slave Societies of the Caribbean*; *The Caribbean: The Genesis of a Fragmented Nationalism*; and, with Teresita Martínez Vergne, *Contemporary Caribbean Cultures and Societies in a Global Context*.

RUTH IYOB is Professor of Political Science, University of Missouri–St Louis. Her publications include *The Eritrean Struggle for Independence: Domination, Resistance, and Nationalism, 1941–1993*; with Gilbert Khadiagala, *Sudan: The Elusive Quest for Peace*; and the co-edited volume, with Edmond J. Keller, *Religious Ideas and Institutions: Transitions to Democracy in Africa*.

JARRETT HUGH BROWN is Assistant Professor of English, Howard University, Washington, DC.

CHRISTIAN CWIK is Lecturer in European and Atlantic History, University of the West Indies, St Augustine, Trinidad and Tobago.

YVONNE DANIEL is Professor Emerita of Dance and Afro-American Studies, Smith College, Massachusetts. Her publications include *Rumba*; *Dancing Wisdom: Embodied Knowledge in Haitian Vodou, Cuban Yoruba and Bahian Candomblé*; and *Caribbean and Atlantic Diaspora Dance: Igniting Citizenship*.

TAMARA GANJALYAN is a PhD student at the University of Leipzig and researcher at the Leipzig Centre for the History and Culture of East Central Europe.

EVELYN HU-DeHART is Professor of History and American Studies, Brown University, Rhode Island. Her publications include *Missionaries, Miners, and Indians: History of Spanish Contact with the Yaqui Indians of Northwestern New*

Spain, 1533–1830; Yaqui Resistance and Survival: Struggle for Land and Autonomy, 1821–1910; and *Across the Pacific: Asian Americans and Globalization.*

WINSTON JAMES is Professor of History, University of California, Irvine. His publications include *Inside Babylon: The Caribbean Diaspora in Britain; Holding Aloft the Banner of Ethiopia: Caribbean Radicalism in Early Twentieth-century America; A Fierce Hatred of Injustice: Claude McKay's Jamaica and His Poetry of Rebellion;* and *The Struggles of John Brown Russwurm: The Life and Writings of a Pan-Africanist Pioneer, 1799–1851.*

MICHELE A. JOHNSON is Associate Professor, Department of History, York University, Canada. Her publications include a number of articles and book chapters as well as (with Brian L. Moore) *Land We Live In: Jamaica in 1890; "Squalid Kingston", 1890–1920: How the Poor Lived, Moved and Had Their Being; Neither Led nor Driven: Contesting British Cultural Imperialism in Jamaica, 1856–1920;* and *"They Do as They Please": The Jamaican Struggle for Cultural Freedom after Morant Bay.*

JANE LANDERS is Gertrude Conaway Vanderbilt Professor of History, College of Arts and Science, Vanderbilt University, Tennessee. Her publications include *Atlantic Creoles in the Age of Revolutions; Black Society in Spanish Florida; Colonial Plantations and Economy in Florida; Against the Odds: Free Blacks in the Slave Societies of the Americas;* and (co-edited with Barry M. Robinson) *Slaves, Subjects, and Subversives: Blacks in Colonial Latin America.*

TOMMY L. LOTT is Professor of Philosophy, San Jose State University, California. His publications include *The Invention of Race: Black Culture and the Politics of Representation; Subjugation and Bondage: Critical Essays on Slavery and Social Philosophy; African-American Philosophy: Selected Readings;* and the co-edited volumes *The Idea of Race* (with Robert Bernasconi); *Philosophers on Race: Critical Essays* (with Julie K. Ward); and *A Companion to African-American Philosophy* (with John Pittman).

QUITO SWAN is Associate Professor of History, Department of History, Howard University, Washington, DC. He is the author of *Black Power in Bermuda and the Struggle for Decolonization.*